PRAISE FOR
THE CRAFT AND BUSINESS OF SONGWRITING

"Braheny's book makes use of plenty of current examples of good songwriting and gives you a logical and surprisingly practical path toward improving your own. Although it concentrates on the basics, there are enough important tips to make it a valuable reference for even an industry pro."
—Dan Fredman, *Music Connection Magazine*

"There is such a broad spectrum of usable information in this book that even the most experienced pros can learn something, if it's only to learn how to explain something they already intuitively know."
—Society of Composers & Lyricists—Score

"In college, I wrote a thesis entitled *A Songwriters Guide to Troubleshooting Songs*. I have read hundreds of books, journals, and articles. Two books stand out firmly in my mind: John Braheny's *The Craft and Business of Songwriting* and Sheila Davis's *Successful Lyric Writing*. Both books are absolutely essential to the diet of a starving artist hoping to develop into a serious songwriter."
—Lou Heffernan, *American Songwriter Magazine*

"I'm awed by the comprehensiveness of the book! What a service you've performed for songwriters—so much information in one place!"
—Sheila Davis, author of *Successful Lyric Writing*, *The Craft of Lyric Writing*, and *The Songwriters Idea Book*

"I wish this book was available when I started writing songs. It covers every aspect of songwriting. You won't just read it once and put it away. You'll refer to it constantly."
—Jay Graydon, Grammy Award-winning songwriter and producer

"A veritable songwriter's bible. This is a definitive work on the subject of songwriting for both hobbyists and career-minded hopefuls. . . . [It] delivers the goods with clarity and style."
—Kevin Odegard, National Academy of Songwriters' *SongTalk*

The Craft and Business of Songwriting

second edition

The Craft
and Business
of Songwriting

JOHN BRAHENY

WRITER'S DIGEST BOOKS
CINCINNATI, OHIO

www.writersdigestbooks.com

The Craft and Business of Songwriting. Copyright © 2002 by John Braheny. Manufactured in the United States of America. All rights reserved. No part of this book may be reproduced in any form or by any electronic or mechanical means including information storage and retrieval systems without permission in writing from the publisher, except by a reviewer, who may quote brief passages in a review. Published by Writer's Digest Books, an imprint of F&W Publications, Inc., 4700 East Galbraith Road, Cincinnati, Ohio 45236. (800) 289-0963. Second edition.

Other fine Writer's Digest Books are available from your local bookstore or direct from the publisher.

Visit our Web site at www.writersdigest.com for information on more resources for writers.

To receive a free weekly e-mail newsletter delivering tips and updates about writing and about Writer's Digest products, register directly at our Web site at newsletters.fwpublications.com.

06   05   6   5   4

Library of Congress Cataloging-in-Publication Data

Braheny, John
  The craft and business of songwriting / by John Braheny.—2nd ed.
    p.   cm.
  Includes bibliographical references (p.) and index.
  ISBN 1-58297-085-8 (alk. paper)
    1. Popular music—Writing and publishing. I. Title.

MT67.B65   2001
782.42164'13—dc21   2001045428
                                                                              CIP

Editors: Jack Heffron, Kim Agricola, and Brad Crawford
Designer: Sandy Conopeotis Kent
Cover photography: David Muir/Masterfile
Production coordinator: Mark Griffin

Pages 365-366 constitute an extension of this copyright page.

John Braheny is a music industry consultant and mentor/coach for songwriters and performers. His clients are individuals as well as companies and include TAXI (the independent A&R service), songwriter organizations, and Web site services.

John has been a musician, songwriter/performer, recording artist, film composer, commercial jingles producer, and music publisher.

He and Len Chandler cofounded and directed the legendary BMI-sponsored Los Angeles Songwriters Showcase (LASS), a national non-profit service organization for songwriters, from 1971 until joining forces with the Songwriters Guild of America in 1999. He coproduced twenty-two annual Songwriters Expo international education and discovery conferences.

John contributes articles to national songwriting publications and Web sites, including a regular column in *Music Biz* magazine. He has taught classes on songwriting and the music business at UCLA, Musicians Institute, and Grove School of Music and is a guest speaker and teacher at universities and songwriter organization seminars around the country.

He is past president of the California Copyright Conference, an organization for entertainment attorneys and music publishers, and has served several terms on the board of the Recording Academy (the GRAMMY organization).

He currently cohosts "Samm Brown's For the Record," a weekly music industry talk show on KPFK (Pacifica Radio Network) in Los Angeles.

If you fly United Airlines, you will hear John conducting in-flight audio interviews with hit songwriter/performers on the Salute to Songwriters channel. His Web site is www.johnbraheny.com.

acknowledgments

There are many people who, both directly and indirectly, helped to write this book. It's impossible to put them in any order of rank, so I'll do it in a roughly chronological order.

My parents, William and Cecilia, who always encouraged me to do my best at whatever I did. My brothers, Dan and Kevin, and my sister, Mary, who did the same.

My friend and partner in the Los Angeles Songwriters Showcase (LASS), Len Chandler, who generously gave his support and took on an extra workload while I worked on the original book. The LASS office staff, and Joy Wildin in particular, who shared that extra load with great patience.

The LASS sponsor, BMI, and in particular the late Ron Anton, Ed Cramer, Thea Zavin, and Frances Preston, whose support for 18 years allowed us to continue to create new ways to help songwriters.

Music Connection magazine publishers Michael Dolan and Eric Bettelli, who asked me to write a column for their new magazine in 1977 and who continue to offer their support and expertise. Mandi Martin, who convinced me I could do it.

My wife and soulmate, JoAnn, for her good ideas and countless hours of typing and editing that also helped shape this book. Her experience in the entertainment industry and her expertise in the creative process not only contributed immeasurably to my own education but also made her my best critic. She continues to enrich my life with her love and wisdom. I'm a lucky guy.

My friend and agent for this book, Ronny Schiff, who persistently pursued getting it published and contributed her expertise on the print music business.

David "Cat" Cohen, whose "Theoretically Speaking" column I admired so much when he was a fellow *Music Connection* writer that I asked him to contribute chapter six, "Writing Music." He continues to grow as a teacher. And Chris Blake, whose "The Imagination of the Listener" in chapter three provides such valuable information on how lyrics are effectively communicated.

Many friends have read various parts of this book and contributed information and critiques. They include hit songwriter Alan O'Day, publisher Dude McLean, A&R exec Neil Portnow, music business consultant Thomas A. White, and attorneys Michael Fletcher, Jeffrey Graubart, Kent Klavens, Al Schlesinger, Jack Whitley, and Gary Wishik. Literally hundreds of other music industry pros have contributed to my understanding of the craft and business of songwriting and the ability to teach it.

Judging from the comments of so many readers, they've found this book inspiring and enlightening. It helped them pursue their dreams, armed with the information they needed. Hit writers like Jason Blume (who has written a wonderful songwriting book of his own) have told me how much they appreciated the book. It has put me in the company of great songwriting teachers too numerous to mention (and besides, whom do I leave out?) from whom I've learned so much about both the topic itself and teaching it. They're all in this new edition in many ways.

Special thanks for their expertise in this revised edition go to: David "Cat" Cohen; *Music Connection* magazine and its publishers, Michael Dolan and Eric Bettelli; *Music Biz* magazine editor Kenny Kerner; Michael Laskow and the great staff at TAXI; marketing consultant Tim Sweeney; songwriter/producer Hank Linderman; attorneys Steve Winogradsky, Jeffrey Graubart and Ken Helmer; tax accountant Mark Rothstein; songwriters and teachers K.A. Parker, Pat Pattison, and Patty Silversher; Kevin Kauffman and Libbe S. HaLevy of Broadway on Sunset; Ron Simpson and his songwriting class at Brigham Young University for their diligent research; to the many other songwriting teachers, including Michael Aczon, who use this book as a text; Mary Vandenberg of Hal Leonard Publications; and Ronny Schiff and Disc Marketing, who make it possible for me to continue to interview legendary songwriters for United Airlines Inflight Entertainment's Salute to Songwriters channel.

With gratitude to my son, Michael Toth, who teaches me in many ways and with whom I share the joys of music and technology.

Much has happened because of this book since the first edition was released. It brought me new friends all over the world. It presented me with opportunities to pursue my love of teaching at Grove School of Music in L.A., the Musicians Institute in Hollywood, and the National Guitar Summer Workshops in Nashville and L.A., and to be a guest speaker at Berklee College of Music in Boston, among others. It let me hang out with, interview, learn from, and share many a panel at events with my songwriting heroes. It introduced me to some amazingly talented new writers who found me because they read the book.

Thanks to the leaders and members of all the songwriter organizations around the country who have hosted JoAnn and me at their seminars, showcases, and events. And thanks to those who host Web sites for songwriters for spreading the good word about this book and for keeping the community vital and growing.

I also want to thank the thousands of hopeful and successful songwriters whose songs continue to enrich my life. This is a kind of payback and, I hope, an investment in encouraging you to give us all more great songs.

The Gender Question

Since both men and women work in all facets of the industry, and since I didn't want to have to write "him/her, he/she" throughout the book, I arbitrarily used either pronoun.

table of contents

Introduction

Welcome to my book. Before I start showing you around the place, I think it's only right that I tell you why I brought you here. The reason is that I know you're out there slaving over a cold piece of paper and a hot guitar, keyboard, or computer. You have dreams of writing hit songs, becoming a recording artist, a producer, or anything that will bring you recognition and/or money (or at least buy you a tuna fish sandwich) for doing what you love to do. You care enough about doing it well that you're willing to invest some time in research and development to make sure you're not missing any tricks that helped others be successful. And you also want to make sure you don't make some dumb business move that could blow all your progress.

So I thought that, instead of giving you that information one-on-one for the next few years (which I wouldn't mind, really), it would be much smarter for me to bring you all here at once. It will also help me buy my own tuna fish sandwich.

How did I know you were out there? Easy. You've been calling and e-mailing me with your problems, fears, and dreams for years, and I think I've returned most of your calls and e-mails by now.

HOW DID I LEARN WHAT I KNOW?

How do you know I'm giving you good information? Trust me! (This is the last time you should accept that answer.) This question deserves a serious answer, so if you'll come with me for about two minutes I'll give you some background on how this "music information junkie" has fed his habit and can help feed yours.

The Los Angeles Songwriters Showcase (LASS), which Len Chandler and I founded in 1971, filled a need by providing a focus for songwriting activities and information. Sponsored by Broadcast Music, Inc. (BMI) for eighteen years, the Showcase drew song-hungry music industry pros to a weekly gathering of the best new songwriting and writer/performer talent around. Stevie Nicks and Lindsey Buckingham, Stephen Bishop, Karla Bonoff, Wendy Waldman, Warren Zevon, R.C. Bannon, Kieren Kane, Chick Rains, Oingo Boingo, Alan O'Day, Jules Shear, Janis Ian, Robbie Nevil, and the world's most successful songwriter, Diane Warren, are among the thousands of writers and writer/performers showcased since then.

We found that many of the writers we auditioned exhibited raw talent but little understanding of songwriting craft that could make their songs more commercially viable. Those writers whose songs we rejected wanted to know why. To offer them some constructive help, we looked for ways to explain those basic principles that seem to be the common denominators of artistically and commercially successful songs. We also needed information about the music business so we could counsel the writers who were on the brink of making major career decisions. Several circumstances helped us to develop the information we needed.

In 1972, the LASS (then called the Alternative Chorus Songwriters Showcase) began a weekly music industry interview session. It gave us an ongoing opportunity to question hundreds of industry pros including hit songwriters and producers, attorneys, publishers, record company executives, recording artists, managers, record promoters, radio personalities, program directors, club owners and others. Largely because of this experience, publishers Michael Dolan and Eric Bettelli asked me to write a songwriting column for their new biweekly, *Music Connection* magazine, in 1977. The magazine has subsequently developed into one of the country's best music publications.

During the next six years, I wrote more than 150 "Songmine" columns on all aspects of the art, craft, and business of songwriting. It was a golden opportunity to consolidate and focus the information derived from this unique vantage point.

In 1979, we created "Cassette Roulette" at the Showcase, in which a different guest publisher was invited to critique songs each week. "Pitch-A-Thon," an extension of that idea, brought in a different producer or record company A&R (artist and repertoire) representative each week to screen songs for specific recording projects. These weekly events gave us and our audiences the opportunity to observe the critical processes of hundreds of publishers, producers, artists, and record company representatives. In addition, our friends in the industry, who believe there is no such thing as a dumb question, generously shared their information with us whenever we asked.

After LASS joined forces with the National Academy of Songwriters (NAS) in 1996, (which, in turn, joined forces with the Songwriters Guild of America) I ran the West Coast office of Wynnward Music, a publishing and production company, for two years. It gave me the opportunity to get valuable experience from "the other side of the desk."

Since then, I've been a consultant for hundreds of writers and writer/artists on their songs and careers. I have interviewed scores of my songwriting heroes for United Airlines Entertainment Network (in-flight audio) as a consultant for Disc Marketing's in-flight division and continue to interview music industry pros as co-host of the talk show *Samm Brown's For the Record* at KPFK (90.7FM) in L.A. I've also been a consultant for TAXI, JPFolks.com and several new publishing companies. All these situations keep me connected to and fascinated by this ever-changing industry.

So there's my background. As you might imagine, for an information glutton it's an endless banquet. Because this industry continues to evolve, so does the information. That's why you and I will never stop learning about it. But at least this book will give you a good start.

SONGWRITING PRINCIPLES

There are no absolute rules or formulas for songwriting. For every "rule" you'll find a song that broke that rule and succeeded. The music industry has many "right" ways to do anything, including writing hit songs.

If you want to write successful songs, instead of learning "rules" you need to be aware of principles, the freedoms and restrictions of the medium for which you want to write, and have at your command a wide range of options with which to solve each creative problem.

This book will provide you with these options. In most cases you'll find that you already know them instinctively but haven't ever seen them in writing. In recognizing them you'll commit them more strongly to memory and use them more often and more effectively.

Writing a great song is only part of being a successful songwriter. Unsung thousands possess the talent and craft to write great songs, but without understanding the business and knowing how to protect your creations and get them heard by those who can make them successful, those songs are like orphans.

This book explains in plain language how the music industry works relative to you, the songwriter, or writer/performer. It will demystify and humanize what can often feel to a newcomer like a cold, monolithic, and impersonal industry.

Success in the music/entertainment industry requires a combination of talent, love for the art and craft, hard work, a tremendous amount of persistence, and a good dose of dumb luck. To capitalize on dumb luck, you need to be ready when opportunity drops out of the sky. To be ready for your big break, you have to pull your craft and business together. By reading this book (and others recommended in this book), by listening to and analyzing all forms of popular music, especially the music you love, and by meeting as many people in the business as your circumstances will allow, you'll maximize your chances for success.

CAN SONGWRITING BE TAUGHT?

Can you learn to write songs from a book? Are songwriting classes a waste of time? Critics of songwriter education say it's a waste, that "You're born with knowing how and, if you're not, there's nothing you can do to get it." Since classes in the craft of songwriting are usually accompanied by some business information, there may be a few among the critics who fear education because they can no longer take advantage of a writer's ignorance. But for the most part, music industry pros recognize that they actually benefit from informed writers who understand the business and how to approach it in a professional manner.

In terms of craft, I do believe that, though you may have been born with a predisposition to music and language skills, it's more important to have been raised in an environment where you were encouraged to explore, read, and express yourself verbally and musically and were given positive strokes for it. Some people with natural talent and drive will pick up what they need to know about the craft by trial and error as they go. Many others with as much talent need, by way of classes, books, and workshops, to be in a supportive environment and be provided with a base of information to help their creativity bloom.

Though the "trial and error" method is a great teacher and will never be replaced by classes and books, the time you can waste in the "school of hard knocks" may also be devastating to your ego and your will to persevere. "If I knew then what I know now" has been a sad commentary on too many wasted careers. Getting as much information as early as possible about both craft and business can save you years. Assuming that you're starting with some talent, imagination, and a love for music and/or language, there are basic principles involved in being a good and commercially successful songwriter that *can* be taught. Primarily, you'll be organizing material that you already instinctively know and putting it in a context that helps you remember it when you need it. All types of artists need a knowledge of the media in which they work, their limitations, freedoms, and properties. Painters need to know about the properties of acrylics, oil paints, and watercolors, the types of brushes and canvas, the mechanics of visual perspective. They need to train their eyes.

As songwriters, you need to train your ears. For you, it's important to know, for instance, that Top 40 radio, musical theater, and film all have different requirements for the way songs are written. It's important to have the choice of many different ways to achieve dynamics in a song, and to know why an artistic choice would work in one situation and not in another. Awareness is a tool that can save time and get you what you want much faster. Knowledge serves your inspiration.

Great songs are a combination of substance and form. Substance is what you're saying and form is the way you communicate it.

You can't be taught inspiration or imagination. You *can* be taught ways to get in touch with what you have to say and how to communicate it effectively. It's sad to hear songs on the radio with great form and zero substance. It's sadder for me to know that you're out there with something to say that could make me laugh, cry, think about something in a new way and otherwise enrich my life, but don't know how to do it. This book's for you!

WHAT'S NEW IN THIS EDITION?

Though very little changes in the craft of songwriting—the same song structures and basic principles still work—the industry has changed considerably. Primarily driven by technology, the ability of writers and artists to produce demos at home and gain more control over their careers has increased. And in the process, it's influenced the types of deals available because it has considerably leveled the playing field. These changes are reflected here as well as new information on:

new income from digital sources

contemporary radio formats

song casting

expanded information on single-song contracts, including sample reversion clauses

independent song pluggers

why a major-label deal may not be best for you

online record deals

production music libraries

online song-pitching services and marketing strategies

Web sites for a range of services, from online rhyming dictionaries to the Copyright Office and pitching services

FIND ONGOING UPDATES TO THIS BOOK AT WWW.JOHNBRAHENY.COM

Because the industry changes quickly, some of the information you get here may be dated by the time you read it. That's a big problem with music industry books. However, because my Mac and I are avid Web surfers and information-collecting partners and because my fellow information junkies are always sharing new discoveries with me, I can update you via my Web site, www.johnbraheny.com, where you'll be able to locate the new information you need. You'll also find:

- updated examples of songs that demonstrate principles, forms, etc. where they're used in the book
- links to current articles of interest on craft and current copyright challenges
- links to organizations and services
- interviews with hit songwriters, film composers and industry professionals
- my own articles, experiences and opinions
- a way for you to ask specific questions and get answers

It's funny how, not that long ago, books and direct contact were the only ways we could keep up-to-date and connected. Now we have the advantage of access to an almost infinite amount of information on the Internet whenever we need it. Who knows how we'll get our information ten years from now? There's one thing we can be sure of, though. Regardless of the medium that conveys it, we'll always look to music to make a powerful human connection. That's where you come in!

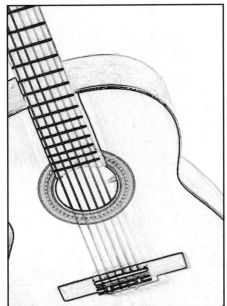

part one

The Craft

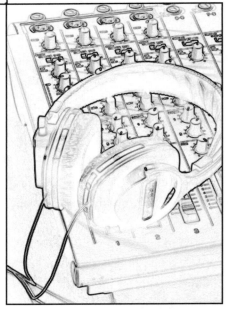

chapter one

Creativity and Inspiration

Creativity: What Is It and Do You Have It?

The subject of creativity has always been a fascinating one because we, as songwriters, are so dependent on the muse, that it becomes very important that we understand and make some attempt to control it. Stimulating creativity and keeping it flowing past the dreaded spectre of "writer's block" are very real battles, particularly for those whose livelihoods depend on constant creative output. Hence, there have been many studies and theories put forth on how creativity works, who's "creative," and who's not.

Psychologists who study creativity have found there are several qualities that are shared by most creative people. It may be useful for you to see how many of these qualities apply to you. Don't be discouraged if you don't possess all of them. This is a broad generalization.

1. You're a risk-taker. You don't play it safe. You take intellectual and emotional risks (like submitting your songs for criticism).

2. You have a talent in a particular area, and since you're reading this book, we'll assume it's in language or in music.

3. You tend to think for yourself and make up your own mind about things. You feel that *you*—and not fate, luck, or society—are in control of your life.

4. You're a nonconformist and you may often find yourself going against the grain.

5. You're playful. You like to try new things or new ways of looking at or doing things just for fun.

6. You have a sense of humor. You tend to see the humor in novel or incongruous situations that others may not see.

7. You find it easy to entertain yourself and seldom get bored.

8. You're a daydreamer with a rich fantasy life. You can get totally lost in a fantasy and be oblivious to everything else.

9. You can function in a state of confusion. You can tolerate ambiguity. This quality can help you look at more than one side of a problem. You find yourself saying, "It could be this way, but on the other hand . . ." You can be comfortable in either structured or unstructured situations in which there are no clear directions or guidelines.

10. You enjoy complexity. It's intriguing and challenging. You have an ability to see complex relationships between seemingly unrelated situations or ideas.

11. You're flexible. You can usually figure out a variety of novel solutions for any problem.

12. You're self-motivated, persevering, and passionate about what you do. You work at something until you finish it.

Creative people also have the ability to absorb, digest, and organize external stimuli; reshape them into something novel; and recommunicate them in an art form. To a noncreative person, telephone touch tones are just sounds they hear when they make a call. To a creative person, they may become the basis of a melody that can eventually become a full-blown composition. To a creative person, a combination of words overheard on an elevator unlocks the memory of an old love affair. The writer's lover stepped into an elevator after a last traumatic good-bye. The conversation not only produced a memory but a song title, "Going Down for the Last Time." The songwriting process gave the writer a therapeutic way to deal with that experience. For an uncreative person, it was just another conversation.

Dr. Roland Jefferson, a psychiatrist, novelist, and screenwriter, believes that there are three categories of creativity. These are:

1. Some people have genetic predispositions to visual creativity including painting, photography, sculpture, and architecture.

2. Others have inherited abilities to use words. Lyricists, poets, novelists, and journalists fall into that category.

3. Some have an ability to internalize and manipulate auditory stimuli. This would include musicians, composers, and sound engineers.

He says it's not uncommon for creative people to possess combinations of these talents, such as the composer/lyricist or the composer with the ability to visualize his music. Obviously novelists and screenwriters, actors, and filmmakers use a visual/auditory and verbal combination.

There is also a broadly held belief that creativity is an essential part of being human, and it is not necessary to produce a product to prove it. Choosing a gift for a friend, what you'll wear to a party, or what to eat at a restaurant are fundamentally creative acts that all of us do regularly.

Studies of the characteristics of creative people are done with those who have contributed visibly to the arts and sciences and who we all would agree are creative. There is certainly a value in noting those characteristics. However, buying into the "us and them" syndrome of "those people are creative and I'm not" is a self-fulfilling statement that has inhibited more potential than anything else.

Buying into the "us and them" syndrome of "those people are creative and I'm not" is a self-fulfilling statement that has inhibited more potential than anything else.

Developing Your Creativity

Since you're reading this book, you're searching for ways to make the most of the talent and creativity you already have. Psychologists have been working for eons to gather all the information you need.

Dr. George Gamez is a psychologist, songwriter, and author of *Creativity: How to Catch Lightning in a Bottle* who specializes in helping people develop their creativity through self-hypnosis and visualization techniques.

Self-hypnosis or **autosuggestion** emphasizes achieving a "state of receptivity" to suggestions you give yourself.

Visualization involves picturing yourself being who you want to be and/or doing what you want to do the way you want to do it.

Both techniques have been used successfully to help develop a positive self-concept, which is, in turn, related to our self-expectations and consequent behavior. Statements like "I'm not a very good songwriter," "I'll never be that good," or "I just don't think commercial," become self-fulfilling because they both reflect and reinforce a negative and limiting self-image. Developing a positive self-image can help you not only in writing songs, but in being effective in dealing with the industry, something that involves perseverance and overcoming the fear of rejection.

Stages in the Creative Process

Psychologists who specialize in creativity generally agree that the creative process goes through four stages. These stages—as they relate to songwriting—are:

1. **Preparation:** the gathering of the physical tools and the establishment of form, theme, and style. In a broader sense, it involves your music education, life experiences, and the development of your unique viewpoint and style.

2. **Incubation:** the unconscious process leading to creation in which, given the theme or problem, the subconscious works on a solution.

3. **Illumination:** the outward stage at which words and music are initially created, written down, or taped. This is also described as the "Aha!" or "Eureka!" phase. During this phase we should suspend the inner critic, be spontaneous, and allow a free flow of ideas. Too often we stop the flow by being too self-critical, by working on a detail of rhyme or meter. Ideas flow from each other, and a tangent idea may be better than the original if we don't stop ourselves before we can get to that tangent.

4. **Verification:** the stage at which we *need* to be critical, looking at the song as a product—in an objective and detached way—rewriting, polishing, and looking for the right meter and rhyme. Separation of the illumination and verification stages is crucial, though occasionally in this phase you'll get another "Aha!"

People in the music business always seem to be telling you to listen to the radio. But how do you listen and what do you listen to? The following listening exercises help unite your whole body in the process of songwriting. Every time you perform an exercise, you create a sensory memory that goes along with the song you're hearing. Eventually, when you're writing, you can use these memories to help trigger your creative process. You can start a "groove" going by dancing or by "conducting" the band or imagining the chords

The following are some exercises that will help you listen to the radio in ways that will improve your writing.

Pick one instrument and listen to it all the way through a song. Become aware of the sound of the instrument, its tone, timbre, or character. Is it soft, mellow, hard-edged, piercing? Can you vocally reproduce it as a vowel or consonant sound? *Oooo, uuuu, rrrrr, ssss, mmmm,* or percussive *f, p* or *k* sounds (called *plosives*) are all quite different. Noting a sound's likeness to one of these will help you recall it for later reference.

Also think about the *function* of the instrument in the overall arrangement. Is it a sustain function like a string section, providing a chordal or single note "pod" that "grounds" and contrasts with all the other parts? Background vocals, strings, horns, and sustained guitar chords often provide that function.

Does it provide a *rhythm* function? All percussion certainly does. Bass, guitar, and keyboards can provide a combination of *rhythmic, chordal,* or *melodic* functions in the arrangement. Listen to how those functions change within each song.

If you've got some rhythm in your bones and love to dance, pick out an instrument and "assign" it to your right arm and another instrument to your left. Assign the bass to one or both feet, and "conduct" the song by dancing it out. Play some air guitar, drums, bass, or keyboards.

Pretending you're playing the instrument may seem silly if you tend to be inhibited. But as a creator, it's your job to stretch yourself. Listen to the melody line and try to visualize it as an actual line. Is it jagged and angular or smooth and flowing? Are there significant differences between the melodies in the verses and those in the choruses and bridges? Sing along whenever you can. Sing or—in some other way—vocalize the instrumental parts as well as the lead vocals.

your "air guitar" is playing. Imagery is a powerful tool to creativity, and the more of our senses we integrate into the process, the more easily we create.

So what good does all this do? It gives you a valuable perspective on the various functions of instrumental parts in an arrangement. A songwriter is more effective if he or she can also wear arranger and producer hats. And it's valuable to have a sense of what to put in and what to leave out of a demo and have a ready repertoire of dynamic musical "tricks."

If you're a lyricist who doesn't play an instrument or sing, it's essential to get a "feel" for vocal phrasing against a rhythm track. What helps you grow as a songwriter is to be aware of how your words can be stretched and bent in performance in ways that you seldom see when they're on paper. You become more aware of the variations of forms available, of which words do and don't "sing," and where and when to use them.

Motivation—Overcoming the Barriers

To become more creative, it's important not only to know how to enhance creativity but to be aware of what can kill it. Psychologist Teresa Amabile, Ph.D., author of *Creativity in Context: Update to the Social Psychology of Creativity and Growing Up Creative*, has conducted many tests to find out the following, which I've adapted to songwriting situations.

Dr. Amabile tested the "intrinsic motivation principle" of creativity and found that people will be most creative when they feel motivated primarily by the interest, enjoyment, satisfaction, and challenge of the work itself, not by external pressures.

Among the creativity killers she discovered are:

1. **Evaluation:** Concern with what someone else will think of your work. We all need love and approval, and it's easy to allow that need to become your motivation. You can learn about your craft in a classroom situation, from a music publisher (or from a book), and do exercises to develop skills. These skills may be evaluated by your teachers as part of your learning process. But you need to shut out that concern for outside approval *while you're creating*.

2. **Surveillance:** Like the above, if someone is literally watching you work, it can kill creativity. You tend, again, to want to please them instead of yourself. Even imagining someone is listening or watching can be inhibiting. But surveillance can enhance your performance of previously learned motor skills. When you're performing live, the audience can inspire you. That's obviously different, though, than someone standing over you while you're working something out.

3. **Reward:** When you focus entirely on the goal or reward—the gold record, the recording deal, the hit single, or the money—something dangerous can happen. Once you get it, you could be robbed of your internal motivation. You'll also tend to write in a way that takes the path of least resistance and minimal exploration to get to the next reward. On the other hand, giving yourself a treat for work that you feel good about is positive because the motivation and reward remain internal.

4. **Competition:** People will be more creative when they're less conscious of competing *during* the process. Again, if you're focused on competition, you'll tend to let someone else's reaction determine whether you should be satisfied with your own work.

5. **Restricted choice:** The more restricted you are in your choice of ways to achieve your goal, the less creative you'll be. You'll tend to internalize the *restrictions* rather than the *freedoms* you have in achieving the goal. In songwriting, you'll focus on the parameters rather than on the many options within the parameters.

When you get to a point where you can no longer enjoy the process and you're overwhelmed by the externals (thinking, for example, "This song needs to be a hit," or "If I don't get this recorded, I'm worthless"), you're entering "creative burnout." You're no longer writing for yourself and you're doing it for all the wrong reasons. If you're a

People will be most creative when they feel motivated primarily by the interest, enjoyment, satisfaction, and challenge of the work itself, not by external pressures.

professional writer, you're probably in a situation in which you need to please someone else as well as yourself. Even at that, there will be times when your publisher will say, "That's good, but could you change this verse?" and you may have to say, "No, this is for me and I don't care if it doesn't get recorded." Sometimes, when you're writing with that kind of freedom, writing from your heart and your emotional core, that's the very thing that *will* make your song appealing to another artist and an audience.

So the operating principle in all this is: To operate at peak performance during the creative process, you should be motivated internally by the spirit of play and exploration and forget about what others might think. You'll have plenty of time to think about that later.

Craft and Inspiration Writers: Philosophies

I've asked many hit songwriters whether they write from craft or inspiration. Some view writing as a profession, a job, pure craft. They're very disciplined about it and never refer to the cosmos as a source of inspiration. They actively look for song ideas in everything they read, watch, listen to, and experience. They give little credit to inspiration and approach songwriting as they would a nine-to-five job that they enjoy. The craft of song-writing is described as a game of organizing ideas, a kind of word engineering and problem-solving experience. It's like a big puzzle in which the "pieces" come from rhyming diction-aries, thesauruses, and real life and in which there are several right ways to construct the "picture." Their knowledge of the most effective construction principles gives them a goal and methods that help them put this picture together clearly.

Most amateur writers and many writer/artists fall into another general category. I'll call them "inspiration" writers, which, I should add, doesn't mean that those in the first category never get inspired. In this category, they *rely* on inspiration rather than craft. My profile of hard-core inspiration writers is that they won't rewrite, feeling that the magic moment they got from the Creator and put on paper is sacred, and they will only write when inspired. It's that attitude that stands in the way of success for these writers, regardless of how wonderful their inspirations are.

It's risky for industry pros to work with this type of writer. Many "inspiration" writer/artists have had short careers because their first album contained the best of their songs to date. They had ten years to write them. When they need to turn out ten more songs for their second album, they face the dreaded "sophomore slump." They discover that they're too tired to be inspired when they're on the road for six months; and when it comes time to get back in the studio, they no longer have the luxury of waiting for the inspiration. If they don't have discipline and command of their craft at that point, they're in trouble.

People who sit down and write a hit song in ten minutes are usually those who have the craft down so well that they don't think about it. It's automatic. They get the idea, focus on exactly what they want to say, and the rest of it comes easily. "If you think of a great title, the song writes itself" is a typical statement for that phenomenon. On the other hand, pro writers (even ones who *have* written a hit in ten minutes) will more typically write pages to get one great line or will write several mediocre-to-good songs for every song they'd consider great. There are also writers who find it difficult to discuss their creative processes and downplay the craft involved in their work. They deny making conscious craft decisions. The songs, nonetheless, show organized thought processes and good command of the craft.

I believe that many successful writers have unconsciously acquired their craftsmanship by osmosis. They've been emotionally affected by so many great songs for so long that they instinctively know, for instance, when there "needs" to be a chorus or bridge, when a lyric line could be stronger, etc. They go by "feel," but behind it there's been a subconscious analytical process developing. When a writer plays me a nine-line song with twelve verses, a "chorus" that occurs only once, and no rhymes at all, I know I'm not listening to a natural writer who has unconsciously learned the craft. I'm prompted to ask whether the writer has ever listened to the radio.

There are dangers inherent in both extremes. I've heard writers who are trying so hard to write a well-crafted, formula "hit" that they forget about imagination and originality and end up with songs that remind me of science fiction cyborgs who look great on the outside but have nothing inside but machinery. On the other hand, I've heard writers with great ideas but no discipline or knowledge of how to communicate them. All that good inspiration goes to waste.

In contrasting "craft" and "inspiration" writers, I'm depicting two extremes. Ideally, the inspiration is recognized as only the beginning of the songwriting process. Your craft is at the service of your inspiration and gives you the confidence and a dependable vehicle to communicate those inspirations in a way that an audience can easily understand and enjoy.

Developing a "Songwriter's Consciousness"

Regardless of which songwriting philosophy you subscribe to, it's helpful to learn how craft and inspiration work together when we create.

There's a popular theory with which I agree: The human mind is a complex computer that responds only according to the way it's been programmed. The problems occur when we give the computer conflicting messages like "I'd love to write a hit song!" and "I'm not a good enough musician to be a songwriter" or "I don't know how." Your mind just sits there and says, "Let me know when you decide." Giving yourself a positive "I am a songwriter" program is very important to what I call "songwriter consciousness." Once you grasp some of the basic principles of what makes songs "work," the world can become an endless supplier of ideas that you can then use. "Songwriter consciousness" filters everything through this network of "idea inspectors" who sit there on duty watching for a big juicy idea to come down the road. They've already been trained to see it coming,

When I asked Dwayne Blackwell about writing the Garth Brooks hit "Friends in Low Places," he said he was having a drink one night with his friend Earl "Bud" Lee. "That wasn't my title. That was Bud Lee, my co-writer on that. When I heard him say, 'Who's going to pay for these drinks if I have friends in low places?' I said, 'Is that a title?! Is that a song?' And he said, 'Not yet!' "

so they start getting excited when they see one. Sometimes an idea is low key and subtle and they don't see it right away. Sometimes it's one they're already familiar with and it doesn't seem exciting anymore. Some ideas have worn out their welcome and, because he's bored with those, an inspector may miss a part of them that's still worthwhile. But to those juicy ones that are fresh and original, the inspector will say, "Wait a minute, Juicy, I'm not letting you by 'til we can play awhile and check out your potential. You may be just the one we're looking for!" In short, "songwriter consciousness" is the readiness to recognize what could be a good song idea. If you have it, you'll start to find ideas everywhere.

Being Ready

You're lying in bed, half asleep in that twilight zone where ideas just seem to pop into your head. You've got one! It rolls out like a movie in your mind, a great concept, exciting lines, you see it all. You've had a hard day at work and your body doesn't want to move to get a pen and paper. "It's such a good idea," you say to yourself. "No way I'll forget this one."

The next sound you hear is the alarm clock. You're up, showered, breakfasted, and on the job. About noontime you remember that you had an idea for a song last night, but you can't quite recall what it was. Another great idea down the tubes. That could have been the hit that paid the rent for the rest of your life! Do you think it would have been worthwhile to keep a pencil and paper by your bed? Or easier yet, a cassette or portable digital recorder? (The obvious advantage of the recorder is that you can also capture melody and phrasing.) Always have one or the other with you. Have an extra pad and pencil in your car for those freeway daydreams, too. Driving time and those times between being asleep and awake seem to be when the brain allows the best communication between the conscious and subconscious. That's fertile, creative territory. Protect it!

Every writer I know has some kind of book or other place to store those little pieces of paper they collect with lines or fragments of ideas. You should have one, too. When you get a chance to write, you've got lots of ideas in front of you. It's a good idea to periodically transfer them from those scraps of paper into a notebook or computer. In the process, you reinforce your memory of them and make it easier to link them with other ideas or phrases with which they'll fit.

There will be times you'll get an idea in a situation where it won't be socially acceptable

The Tubes' Fee Waybill showed me his notebook once. It was thick with very meticulously laid out individual lines as well as pages of finished songs, and the lines were all numbered with some crossed out. He said he did that because he came up with a lot of interesting one-liners, and whenever he got stuck for a line for a song he was working on, he'd go back through the book, find a line he could use, and then put a line through it so he wouldn't accidentally use it on another song. He's probably got them all in his computer now.

to whip out your pen and start writing. In those situations, such as formal social gatherings or in midconversation, use what Len Chandler calls "The Weak Bladder Syndrome" and head for the rest room to work in private.

You may also want to write about someone you're with at the time. That's when it's beneficial to have a personal brand of shorthand. I know one writer who developed a whole code of geometric symbols that only he could understand. Many writers are very candid in writing about their personal relationships and have difficulty expressing negative feelings a lover is not yet aware of. You can say, "This isn't really about us, it's just something I'm creating from the memory of another relationship," or "It's about a friend's romance," or "Don't get paranoid. I'm a songwriter and I make this stuff up! I don't want to have to worry that every time I write something, you're going to think it's about us." Of course, depending on the circumstances and what you wrote, any of those approaches could sound utterly ridiculous, so don't quote me.

Since you never know where or when a great idea is going to appear, the only thing you can control for sure is your readiness to catch it when it falls on you. Be prepared!

Finding Your Own Creative Process

Every writer eventually finds his or her own process (or more than one) for creating. Though it's a good idea to explore many, your own unique personality will determine an approach that's comfortable and productive for you.

It's important not to put yourself down for having a creative style that's different from someone else's. Don't worry about which style works for someone else unless you want to collaborate with that person, in which case your styles should be compatible. The following are some of the more typical styles of writers.

"Deadline" writer: You're part of a very large breed. You've got a lot going on in your life and need an external force to make you put this song on the front burner. Someone says, "I need this by tomorrow morning. The music supervisor needs it at 10 A.M." Your adrenaline starts pumping and every synapse in your brain is working full out. The ability to write and rewrite well under deadline pressure is extremely valuable, since those opportunities happen constantly in the music business. If you get a reputation for being able to

Every writer eventually finds his or her own process (or more than one) for creating.

deliver, you get the jobs. If you're the type of person who needs deadlines to get things done, but don't happen to have any external deadlines, find a way to trick yourself into one. Making an appointment to show a publisher or producer a new song or booking studio time to record a demo are great ways to create your own deadlines.

"Total focus" writer: You like to sit down with a project and devote your total attention to it until it's finished. No other projects. No diversions or distractions. Straight-ahead concentration from start to finish, no matter how long it takes. You polish each line as you go.

"Scattered" writer: You may have several songs going at once, get bored or burnt out with one and work on another, then go back to the first later, maybe with fresh ideas generated by working on the others. You're the kind of writer who has difficulty sustaining interest. You'll work for a while, look for inspiration in the refrigerator, make a sandwich, watch TV, go back to work, stop, make some phone calls, take out the garbage, back to work, stop, read a magazine, back to work again. You may feel guilty for not keeping at it, but, in fact, the song is getting written in your subconscious as you do all those other things.

"Project" writer: You work best in some kind of framework with an established goal or motivation ("I'll pay you a thousand dollars to write a theme for a play in two weeks."). You have a direction, a framework, and a motive. You may be very creative within that type of situation, but otherwise you're not very productive. Recognizing that, you need to search for projects or create them. People with your approach frequently write for TV series, films, and commercials.

Some writers can only write when they're alone. Some can write in a roomful of people with the radio and TV going at the same time. Some need silence. Some, though they might be equally adept at writing words and music, are more productive in a collaboration.

Individual Preferences

Sheila Davis, in her *Songwriters Idea Book*, relates creative styles with your personality type as shown by the Myers-Briggs Temperament Sorter based on the work of psychologist Carl Jung. Sheila has developed her own version of the profile, and I feel it's a valuable tool not only for getting better acquainted with your own individual process, but understanding those of collaborators.

My wife, JoAnn, covers this in her "Goosing Your Muse" creative process seminars on how to stimulate and maintain your productivity. One area she has found particularly helpful is how we process information. Conflicts can be alleviated by understanding that each of us, based on our individual preferences, values a different aspect of the project. She refers to our different approaches or modes as being more auditory, visual, or kinesthetic. Some people simply respond to the creative process with an attitude of "I don't know *how* I know, but I know." We usually refer to that as *intuition*. Going beyond that, these modes help us to clarify the "Aha!" when an idea surfaces. Most of us experience a combination of modes but favor one. What shape does the experience of getting an idea

RITUALS

Getting ready to "commit" to writing may involve a common process that Len Chandler calls "sharpening pencils." You seem to be doing everything but writing. You're cleaning the house, preparing the writing space, and actually sharpening pencils. You make sure you have your "surefire hit" songwriting pencil and paper and maybe your "great idea" hat. This is a kind of ritual that is very valuable because it gets you ready and primes your creative pump. While you're doing it, you're probably actually working on the song without realizing it.

You may think you must be the only writer in the world who goes through this craziness or that if you're a real pro, you won't have to. Wrong! Yours may be a unique ritual, but most writers have one or more. Your approach may incorporate elements of more than one of those listed here, and it may also change with time and experience, but it's important for you to realize that whatever works for you is right.

take for you? Our preference is usually revealed in the way we express ourselves. When someone says, "I can *see* how . . ." or "It *looks* to me like . . . ," they are revealing a *visual* preference. Those who are more *auditory* will say, "It *sounds* to me as if . . ." or "I *hear* what you mean . . ." and those who are more *kinesthetic* might respond with "It *feels* to me as if . . ." or "I *get* what you mean. . . ."

It's helpful to realize which preferences we have so that we can recognize the difference between ourselves and our collaborators, we can work less judgmentally and more amicably with our collaborators, and we can use this information as a powerful tool to move past our creative blocks. (JoAnn defines a collaborator as anyone who is involved in our project, e.g., a co-writer, a singer on a demo, a producer, anyone who is a "partner" in our project.) How we "look" (clothes/hair/image of the band, for example), how we "sound" (production, performance), or the overall "feel" of the project is valued differently by different members of the group.

To Break Through a Block, Do Something You're Not

Find out which modality is yours. Then, when you experience a creative block, try to switch to a mode that is unusual for you. Do what does *not* come naturally to you, even if it's just for an hour.

If you're an auditory type of person and you have reached a lull in your songwriting, spend the afternoon painting or coloring (visual) or take a long walk (kinesthetic). New ideas will appear more quickly than if you simply stay in your rut, hammering at your piano or guitar, trying to force them out.

If you are blocked and you are more visual, then listen to music while sitting in a dark room. Indulge in a massage or listen to a good novel on tape. Pictures will form in your "mind's eye."

For a quick way to find which "modality" may apply to you, notice which of these seem more natural to you. (Remember, we tend to combine some of our preferences, like auditory/kinesthetic or visual/kinesthetic.)

1. Videotape a TV program that has plenty of action, like car chases. When you play it back, turn the volume off. Try to create a musical or rhythm track that fits the action segment. If you can watch something and respond to it easily with your own soundtrack, then you may be more "auditory." Or go to an art gallery and after you've viewed the various art works, notice if you have a melody or lyrics developing in your head. You are responding to what you see by *hearing* something in your head.

2. Listen to some recordings of symphonic, "new age," or other instrumental music. Notice if you tend to "see pictures" in your mind. Sometimes you may only "see" colors or patterns, but this could indicate that you are predominantly more "visual" in how you receive information.

3. Think about your favorite places, your favorite experiences, and notice, as you describe them, how you *feel*. People who are more "kinesthetic" seem to be more affected by atmosphere, mood, ambiance, or rhythm/movement/dance and can be repulsed by or enamored of a combination of sensory input. These people might avoid a restaurant because it just doesn't "feel right" to them.

If you are blocked and you are more kinesthetic, sit in a lecture or class and concentrate on the presenter and the material. Most kinesthetic people want to move when they know they can't. In fact, they reveal their preference by pacing when they think or talk, and they tend to gesture with their hands or their whole body. Keep a journal (written or on tape) of experiences that "move" you. Describe the various elements of the events in as much detail as you can, for example, "When I squatted down to meet the puppy, his warm, wet tongue on my face tickled me." Lyric ideas can develop from feelings such as these.

Breaking Writer's Block

You're sitting in front of a blank piece of paper or computer screen, just knowing that you've come up with all the ideas you'll ever come up with and that anything you do think of has already been written. You try your brand-new pen with the easy glide point but can't convince it to write anything. You go through all your customary rituals, but still nothing happens.

At this point, you've landed where nearly every other writer has been at one time or another: the Planet of the Dry. It is comforting, in a way, to know you're not the only writer in the world who has ever felt totally stupid and useless.

Though there are those who deny there's anything such as writer's block, to deny it is to acknowledge that it exists. For some people, denial is the best way to deal with it. Whatever works! Here are some of the other ways writers have dealt with this problem.

1. **Just start writing anything:** a grocery list, a letter to the editor, anything to jumpstart your creative engine and get something on the blank page. Julia Cameron (author of *The Artist's Way*) prescribes doing "morning pages" in which you write three pages of anything and everything that comes into your head without stopping, censoring, editing. Pat Pattison (author of *Writing Better Lyrics*) has a related morning exercise he calls "object writing" in which you select an object in the room to jumpstart the process, free-associating whatever memories come up but using a maximum of sensory images to describe the sights, sounds, taste, and feelings. Limit yourself to ten minutes so you'll always know you can have time to do it. The beauty of these exercises is that you create something every day and don't get hung up on needing it to be a "work of art."

2. **Psych yourself out of the pressure** to produce a hit or great work of art. Focus on having fun. Remind yourself that nobody else will ever see your bad work. I frequently hear successful writers say things like, "If I get one in ten to twenty songs that I think is viable, I figure I'm doing great." "I had to write a hundred bad songs before I started getting to the good stuff." And these are people with multiple hits! I used to think, naively, that once a writer figured out how to write a hit, she could pretty much nail it every time. Wrong! So stop beating yourself up!

3. **Create an atmosphere.** Listen to your favorite artist's records. Listen to music that puts you in a mood, and savor it.

4. **Find other places to write:** the beach, the woods, on a mountain, in a car, in a bus station, a noisy restaurant, a dance club. Try writing at a different time of day.

5. **Just forget about writing altogether.** Relax, have some fun, go to a movie, go bowling, bicycling, whatever.

6. **Try the stream-of-consciousness or problem-solving techniques** explained in this chapter.

7. **If you're a musician, play scales you don't usually play**, play a CD you don't normally listen to, and learn solos from other instruments. If you're a guitarist, for instance, learn a Bach violin solo and maybe try playing it back at half-speed or learn a jazz sax solo.

8. **Write with someone you haven't written with before.**

It's possible that none of the above will work. At that point it may be useful to dig a little deeper.

Writer/psychotherapist Lynne Bernfield says, "Being blocked doesn't mean that you don't want to produce, are self-destructive or lazy, have dried up or been deserted by the muse. It is a coded message from your unconscious telling you that something must be attended to and, as such, is a blessing in disguise." She believes that one of the things to be attended to is "unfinished business" in other areas of our lives. We won't allow ourselves

In an interview by Theresa Ann Nixon, Paul McCartney discussed a prose piece he'd been working on: "So when my hand didn't know what to put on the paper, my head just said to my hand, 'Write! Put it down. It doesn't matter what you say, just put it down. Even if it's all mistakes. Just put it down.' I got this method of just forcing my hand to write, no matter what it was. And later I talked with Quincy Jones about this when we were doing 'The Girl Is Mine' with Michael Jackson. He said he had gotten this book twenty years ago that had changed his life, where the fellow explained that there were two aspects to a creative act. One was just to create it, just do it. The other was judicial, checking everything. He said the biggest mistake everyone makes is to try to do the two at once. And suddenly—ding!—that's exactly what my problem is. In all those years with essays in school, you know, I was trying to get that wonderful opening. . . . When you try to do everything at once, there's just no time. Your brain can't cope. You'll kill all your enthusiasm and creative spirit by checking your spelling and going to see 'Is this the right word, is it clever enough? Will the *LA Times* critic like it if I say "hobgoblin"? Yes, there is a better word. Or shall I just say, "demon"? No. Hobgoblin. No, demon.' And you've just spent half a bloody hour."

to start new business until we've finished that old business. Try to identify it and deal with it. You *will* get through this!

Two other effective methods merit more of an in-depth explanation. Even if you don't feel you're blocked, they're great ways to get started.

Stream of Consciousness

One approach is the *stream-of-consciousness* technique. It's used in what was described earlier as the "illumination phase" of the creative process in which spontaneity is encouraged and the "inner critic" is ignored. It's a great way to generate ideas. This is a technique used by many successful writers.

Now you're into the "verification phase" of the process. Be critical. Pull out all the good lines and ideas. Write them down, leaving plenty of room to rewrite and add other lines that you think of. Now is the time to pay more attention to form, continuity, rhyme schemes, meter. You may find that most of those were established during that free-form session, and now they just need to be rethought and looked at a little more closely. You may discover that what you thought was the chorus works better as a verse or vice versa. Perhaps what you thought was the first verse should be the last. Maybe the first phrase you wrote down that triggered this whole process is no longer nearly as good as other ideas the process produced.

What happens during the "stream-of-consciousness" process is that you pull out a lot of ideas and make a lot of creative hookups and links that you might not ordinarily make

You hear a friend use an interesting phrase and you write it on a notepad, napkin, your hand (or you memorize it). Later on, you're noodling with your piano, guitar, or whatever is handy, turn on your cassette recorder, and forget it's there. Next, you grab some chords, maybe just play a bass line, get a nice groove going with your feet, get an attitude going—sad, bittersweet, mad, haughty, playful, loving, romantic— picture yourself with that attitude talking to someone, and just say out loud everything you can think of that relates to the situation that you're remembering or creating.

It's strange to hear yourself talking out loud when you're alone, but the more you do it, the less strange it becomes. You want to rhyme this line? If it doesn't just appear, forget it. Keep going. Don't stop the flow; you'll fix it up later, but get all the ideas out there for now. Babble on awhile. None of it has to make much sense or have any continuity at this stage. You can influence the direction of the flow by describing a scene, a setting, or a feeling. If there is another person in this setting, consider your relationship to him. What motivates that person and dictates your attitude toward him? What does he/she say? What do you say? What happened before and what happened after? If you get off on a tangent, that's OK because the tangent may take you to a better place. Don't worry, just keep it going.

All talked out? Rewind the tape and listen. Yes, you'll think some of it is total nonsense, but did you really think everything you said would be profound? Some of the stupid stuff may be a bridge to something better. This line could have smoother meter, a better flow, if you changed a couple of words.

when you're trying too hard. You also avoid getting hung up trying to make something rhyme or make your meter tight at the expense of flow and focus. Once you've filled a few pages, you'll have a better concept of how to structure the idea and you'll also have come up with some great lines, some rhythms that those lines may suggest, and some good rhymes that will feel natural because you'll be writing closer to the way you think and speak. At that point you can start a new page with the best lines you've created. The stream-of-consciousness exercise in this chapter is a sample scenario of that process, using a tape recorder.

Keep in mind that while you're in the critical phase, nothing is sacred. Don't get married to a line that's great by itself but doesn't seem to fit the rest. Put it away in your collection of great lines and use it to trigger another session. As a matter of fact, don't throw anything away. If you're working on paper, don't erase. Draw a single line through the reject. If you work with a word processor, cut or copy sections you don't want to another area or "save as" new version and save your old drafts. If you're working on tape, always save your tapes. Not only can you return to them for musical ideas, but if you're ever involved in an infringement case, they may be helpful to show the process by which you arrived at your finished song.

Keep in mind that while you're in the critical phase, nothing is sacred. Don't get married to a line that's great by itself but doesn't seem to fit the rest.

Problem Solving

Another creative springboard is the *problem-solving* technique in which you make up arbitrary "problems" to solve creatively.

In a way, writing a good title before you write the song is an exercise in problem solving. This is a pretty typical approach for country writers, since the success of a country song depends (much more than other styles) on finding a strong *concept* embodied by the title. The problem is to find a great way to set up the title and pay it off. Maybe the title suggests a mood and the "problem" is to maintain and heighten the mood. Maybe the title suggests a story to develop.

The fact is that a substantial amount of the creative process involves problem solving anyway. Like putting together a crossword puzzle, it's word and music architecture and design.

The following problem-solving exercise will give you some ideas on which to build. If you ever run into trouble getting started, just pick one of your premises at random and link it with a lyric idea from your collection. Remember that trying to make the puzzle work is a great exercise of your creativity and will force you into solutions you may not have otherwise discovered. At the same time, remember that creativity is a fluid process; and if the exercise only serves to get you started, it has done its job.

Remember, too, that many musical and lyrical innovations have resulted from creative accidents in which the artist had the presence of mind to recognize a good idea that she accidentally stumbled across on her way to something else. Taking advantage of those situations requires that you maintain an open mind and that you stay flexible.

The fact is that a substantial amount of the creative process involves problem solving anyway. Like putting together a crossword puzzle, it's word and music architecture and design.

Developing Good Work Habits

Not everyone can form consistent writing habits. Many of the most successful writers have schedules that allow for very little consistency. Developing a regular pattern or schedule for your writing, however, can have valuable advantages. Say you make a commitment to yourself or, even better, to a collaborator, that you're going to meet every Saturday from nine till noon to write. First, you'll feel better that you're no longer procrastinating; second, getting something accomplished every week will do a lot for your self-confidence; and third, it activates a psychological phenomenon that's very productive.

When your subconscious knows that next Saturday morning at nine it has to have some new ideas or to solve a creative problem from last week, it works on it while you do other things. The same phenomenon is at work when you can't remember someone's name. You finally give up until an hour later, when the name seems to pop into your mind from nowhere. It actually just "downloaded" from storage in the "back" of your mind to the front because you had assigned the "search" function to your subconscious.

Hit songwriter/composer Tom Snow ("He's So Shy," "You Should Hear How She

In the absence of a "real world" creative problem, simulate one or come up with an arbitrary premise or set of parameters. Here are some samples:

- An eight-bar verse with a nine-bar chorus. A 120 tempo. The bass with a maximum of four notes every two bars. Rapid fire sixteenth-note lyric in the verse, half-note lyric in the chorus.

- A ten-bar verse (two five-bar sections), eight-bar chorus. A maximum of five chords.

A 28 ½-second jingle for a teddy bear, conveying warmth, playfulness. (You'll have to name the bear.) A ten-second "donut" (a hole in the lyric for dialogue) fifteen seconds from the start. Write the jingle for a female vocalist.

Create several of these "puzzles" to solve. Mix and match information on:

1. Form (number and length of sections, bars per section)
2. Tempo
3. Time signature(s)
4. Key
5. Melodic mode
6. Number of chords per section or song
7. Number of instrumental tracks
8. Density of instrumental parts
9. Mood
10. Rhyme scheme
11. Lyric density

Talks About You") likes to get an idea started at the end of a writing session but saves developing the idea till the next session. He says it keeps him excited about working on the idea, and by the time he gets into it, his brain is already cooking. The technique is one of Snow's personal methods of manipulating his creative juices.

Learn to develop techniques that suit your own personality.

chapter two

Subject Matter

Finding Ideas

Your subject, of course, is the raw material of songwriting. Coming up with that fresh sounding "hook" phrase or an idea that hasn't been stated in quite the same way before is important if you want to be viewed as a creative writer. You'll need to develop your ability to recognize and generate lyric ideas from a variety of everyday sources. This chapter will explore some specific places to look for ideas and a few general subject areas with hints on how to approach them effectively.

Sources for song ideas are everywhere. Here are a few that are endlessly productive:

• **News and human interest programs on radio and TV.** Talk shows on radio and TV are extremely popular and elicit an incredible array of emotional problems and conflicts from their callers and in-studio audiences. Each day's topic usually deals with current news events or ethical problems. These shows involve the general public in passionate interchanges that reflect human conflicts. See if there are any shows in your area hosted by psychologists discussing personal problems. These are particularly juicy, especially on radio, where the callers are anonymous. They're a tremendous education in human behavior as well. As you listen, remember it's not just the subjects you're listening for, but the language with which people express themselves.

The networks present special, in-depth programs on a variety of informative and controversial topics. You'll find yourself agreeing or disagreeing and, in the process, solidifying your own point of view. So again, it's not just the topic of the program you're watching but a distillation of your personal viewpoint, which will work its way into your songs.

• **TV soap operas and prime-time dramas.** The writers of these shows are also listening to the talk shows for ideas.

• **Listening to music on the radio** is really stimulating, especially on the freeway, where your left brain is driving and leaves your right brain to daydream. I've half-heard lines of songs on the radio and said to myself, "What a great line!" only to discover to my pleasure that, when hearing it again, it wasn't really the line I thought I'd heard after all. By some strange approximation of vowel sounds, it had triggered a new line that I could use.

Give yourself the challenge of finding one good line, idea, or title in a five-minute slice of conversation from any source. It's a great way to demonstrate to yourself what a wealth of material is available almost anywhere.

- **Examine your own life experiences.** Think about your feelings toward your lover or romantic situations, positive or negative, past or present, and turn those feelings into actual dialogue or a story. Some writers only write from personal experience. Don't forget that, like a novelist, you're a creator; and if you hear someone else's story and it moves you, chances are it'll move others, too. You can also change, embellish, or totally fabricate a story that will move or entertain people just as much. It's called "poetic license," not dishonesty.

Once you "program" your subconscious to look for ideas, it'll automatically do it. But you have to help by getting ideas down on paper, computer, or recorder as soon as possible or your subconscious won't believe you're serious. The "idea inspectors" will say, "We pick up on these great ideas, but the turkey never does anything with them. Why should we bother?"

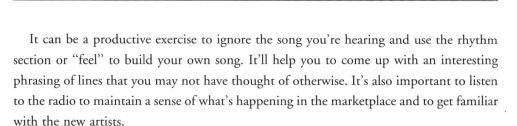

It can be a productive exercise to ignore the song you're hearing and use the rhythm section or "feel" to build your own song. It'll help you to come up with an interesting phrasing of lines that you may not have thought of otherwise. It's also important to listen to the radio to maintain a sense of what's happening in the marketplace and to get familiar with the new artists.

- **Poetry and books with great colloquial dialogue** are inspirations and "triggers" for new ideas. Also check these reference books, which contain a wealth of ideas: *A Dictionary of Contemporary and Colloquial Usage*, *The Dictionary of American Slang*, and *NTC's American Idioms Dictionary*.

- **Conversations with friends or discussions you overhear** will provide some great titles, especially if the language is particularly distinctive or colorful. Most of the great lyricists I've interviewed tell me they're "conversation voyeurs."

The Commerciality of Subject Matter—Mass Appeal

At some point before, during, or after a song is written, it behooves a writer to decide whether the song idea itself is "commercial." Now don't get defensive! I'm not saying that every song you write must appeal to a massive audience. At the risk of repeating this message too many times, I'll say again that you should write everything and anything your creative impulses trigger. At some point, though, if you want to make a living at songwriting, you've got to develop some perspective on your songs. The one you wrote about your second cousin's appendicitis may be important to you personally, but everybody else will

You should write everything and anything your creative impulses trigger. At some point, though, if you want to make a living at songwriting, you've got to develop some perspective on your songs.

say, "So what?" Decide which songs are going to be meaningful in some way to a mass audience before shopping them to publishers or producers. Lots of different kinds of songs can work.

Relatable Themes

Occasionally a monster will emerge with far more than the basic ingredients. One of the classics was "I Will Survive," the number 1 hit that Freddie Perren and Dino Fekaris wrote for Gloria Gaynor in 1979. Along with the great groove and production, the song had a lyric idea that made its popularity continue long after that groove and production would have burnt out by repetition. The lyric was an anthem for women, something positive from someone who sounded like she knew what she was talking about, with a story that sounded familiar. The message was positive: No matter how her lover had treated her before, she didn't have to take it anymore because she had found a new self-respect. The song is still popular more than twenty years later.

One of the most important functions of a song is to give people a vehicle to express hopes, dreams, and inner conflicts that they might otherwise keep inside.

One of the most important functions of a song is to give people a vehicle to express hopes, dreams, and inner conflicts that they might otherwise keep inside.

Songs have a way of uniting us by defining those common strings that bind us together. Dan Hill's "Sometimes When We Touch" expresses the apparent contradictions, the love/hate aspects of an intense relationship. Those of us who've been there may have felt like we were a little crazy for having those kinds of feelings and were relieved to hear someone else express them. We were even more relieved that hundreds of thousands of other people love the song.

The Madonna hit "Papa Don't Preach" explored one of the sad choices of a pregnant teenager.

Often the more "commercial" songs are the ones that not only express more personal situations and feelings, but do it in a way that everyone else can easily understand and identify with.

Being Believable

Hopefully, the values and experiences reflected in your songs are either ones you feel comfortable with or that reflect your own situation. If you're a writer/artist, a major part of your appeal will be that people will identify with your point of view. Don't take a different point of view on every record—people will never really learn who you are. Also, as an artist, be leery of recording a song with which you're not completely comfortable. You may be doomed to playing it for years. If you're a nonperforming writer, you're not so restricted; you can write "for the market" or from the point of view of the artist.

Cleverness

Beyond the considerations just discussed, there are some stylistic considerations that affect the commerciality of a song. One of those is *cleverness*. Country music has always been the home of clever wordplay, the new twist on an old cliché, and the lyrical "turnaround." Some examples are "Lying Time Again," "Yippi Cry Yi," "Nothin' Sure Looked Good on You," and "Wishful Drinkin.' " The old pop tune, "I Had Too Much to Dream Last Night," is another example of the kind of cleverness designed to stick in the listener's mind. The lyrical "turnaround" with the surprise ending has wide appeal. The John Michael Montgomery hit, "The Little Girl" (H. Allen), and the Clay Walker hit, "Chain of Love" (Jonnie Barnett/Rory Lee Feek), are great examples.

To pure "heart" writers, songs built around cleverness may seem trite and contrived. "Punch line" songs run the risk of wearing out their welcome quickly, like a joke you've heard too many times. The only thing that makes a song like these worth hearing again is a great storyteller and an interesting story leading up to the punch line.

The more conversational and natural the lyric feels and the more vivid the visual imagery, the less contrived they seem. In other words, the trip should be as rewarding as the destination. The classic "The Gambler," by Don Schlitz, is a very cleverly contrived story; and even though the use of a deck of cards as an analogy for life isn't a new idea, the song's natural, rhymed, colloquial language and movielike imagery make it a wonderful piece of work.

Crossover Records

If you're concerned about selling records, you must appeal to a large section of the record-buying population. Consistently at the top of the "best-seller" and "most played" lists are "crossovers," which you'll hear a lot about in the recording industry.

A crossover record is one that can be played on more than one radio format. Crossover artists include Mariah Carey, Babyface, Toni Braxton, Madonna, and Whitney Houston (whose records regularly get played on R&B/hip-hop, Top 40, and adult contemporary radio stations). Country artists LeAnn Rimes, Trisha Yearwood, Faith Hill, and Lonestar cross over to adult contemporary (AC) and Top 40 charts.

Modern rock artists like Limp Bizkit and mainstream rock artists like the Offspring and Metallica seldom cross over; though artists such as Aerosmith, Creed, and 3 Doors Down will, with certain singles, cross to pop and AC formats. Crossover potential, in fact, is based more on the record than the artist. Record companies frequently promote different songs on an album in different radio formats. The principle of crossover is that the more radio stations that air the record, the more people will hear it and be motivated to buy it. Video and film exposure are still other avenues that can further contribute to the power of a crossover song, record, and artist. Savvy Internet marketing via artist's and record company Web sites and Web radio can also introduce their music to potential fans who may not, as a habit, listen to or have available to them certain radio formats.

Themes of Love

A quick survey of the top singles in any category of the trade charts will show that over 75 percent of their subject matter pertains to love or lust.

Of all possible song themes, love is the most popular. No other subject is as universal, no other human need so emotionally rich, provocative, and potentially traumatic. A quick survey of the top singles in any category of the trade charts will show that over 75 percent of their subject matter pertains to love or lust. We spend most of our lives looking for it, exulting in it, or losing it.

To illustrate, I've broken the subject down into several categories based on the span of a relationship, with a variety of samples for each:

- **Feeling the need:** The longing to love and be loved has inspired some classics: "Lookin' for Love," "When Will I Be Loved?," "Dream Lover," "Looking for Another Pure Love," "You Can't Hurry Love," "I Would Do Anything for Love," and "Again."

- **I think I've just found her (or him):** This is the part where you've just seen someone, you think you might be in love already, and you're scoping out the situation: "I'm Into Something Good," "I Saw Her Standing There," "Like to Get to Know You," "I've Just Seen a Face," "Pretty Woman," "Sharing the Night Together," "Must Be Somebody's Baby," and "Love, or Something Like It."

- **The big come-on:** A formidable category, since so many love and lust games are played out to a background of popular music. It encompasses both the bold and tender: "Let's Spend the Night Together," "Kiss You All Over," "I'm in the Mood for Love," "Feel Like Makin' Love," "Lay Lady Lay," "Sexual Healing," "Make Yourself Comfortable," "I'm Ready," "Tonight's the Night," "Temptation," "Come on Over," and thousands more.

- **This is it, I'm in love:** For better or worse, you've passed the point of no return: "Fooled Around and Fell in Love," "Can't Help Falling in Love," "It's So Easy," "Truly," "Baby I Love You," "Your Song," "My Girl," "My Own True Love," "True Blue," "Nothing's Gonna Stop Us Now," "Thank You," "The Way You Love Me," and "Head Over Feet." This may possibly be the biggest category of love songs.

- **The honeymoon is over:** Or "The Thrill is Gone," "Don't Be Cruel," "Cold as Ice," "Suspicious Minds," "We Can Work It Out," "This Masquerade," "You've Lost That Lovin' Feeling," "You Don't Bring Me Flowers," "Love on the Rocks," "You Keep Me Hanging On," "Say My Name," and "Smoke Rings in the Dark."

- **Cheating:** Songs of infidelity, guilt, suspicion, and jealousy are popular, despite their negativity, because they're great drama and everyone can identify with those feelings and experiences: "Lying Eyes," "If Loving You Is Wrong," "Me and Mrs. Jones," "Your Cheatin' Heart," "You Belong to Me," "Who's Cheatin' Who," "What She Don't Know Won't Hurt Her," "The Thunder Rolls," and "Whose Bed Have Your Boots Been Under?"

- **Leaving:** Along with cheating, the trauma of good-bye is an emotional minefield, with heavy pathos: "I'd Rather Leave While I'm in Love," "For the Good Times," "By the Time I Get to Phoenix," "Bye Bye Love," "Don't Think Twice, It's All Right,"

"Breaking Up Is Hard to Do," "If You Leave Me Now," "I've Been Loving You Too Long," "I Will Survive," "Fifty Ways to Leave Your Lover," "My Lover's Gone," and "If You're Gone."

- **Remembering how it used to be:** After the breakup and the passage of time, the more positive among us tend to fondly remember the good times and forget the bad. If we've been on the losing end, there's a profound sense of loss and longing that has created some classics: "I Can't Stop Loving You," "As Tears Go By," "Tears on My Pillow," "Hello Walls," "Funny How Time Slips Away," "San Francisco Bay Blues," "I'm Sorry," "She's Gone," "Same Auld Lang Syne," "Yesterday," and "I'll Be Over You."

- **Philosophy:** It's also human nature to aid the recovery process by trying to provide a rationale and perspective for it all. "All in Love Is Fair," "Only Love Can Break Your Heart," "The Things We Do for Love," "It's All in the Game," "The Rose," and "Please Remember Me."

Sex sells just about everything. It is an international preoccupation, particularly for those in the prime record-buying age groups. A look at any week's *Billboard* Hot 100 singles chart shows that outright sex themes are still prime song lyric topics.

Radio wasn't always as tolerant as it is now. If writers wanted to get that powerful, money-making airplay they had to avoid the subject or be very clever about it. In the early fifties, even songs like "Teach Me Tonight," as tame as it sounds today, were considered risqué. See how jaded we've become?

Throughout history there's been a wealth of bawdy balladry. During the sixties' folk revival, Oscar Brand ("Bawdy Songs and Backroom Ballads"), Ed McCurdy ("When Dalliance Was in Flower"), and others resurrected volumes of it to record that never got airplay but enjoyed underground success. A heavy division has always existed between what can be sold on record and what's considered fit fare for the air, but in the past few years, that division seems to have all but disappeared. If a song isn't getting airplay, it's more likely because it doesn't sound like a hit than because it's offensive. There are rock stations that fifteen years ago would have been shut down for playing songs that seem commonplace today. Record companies release both "dirty" and clean versions of singles complete with "bleeps" where the words have been censored.

Public attitudes are always in a state of change, though, and a songwriter must always be aware of those changes. If you're going to write about sex, the next big question is "How?" Songwriters will always reflect their own personal attitudes about the subject, no matter how self-indulgent, sexist, debauched, or immature they may be.

The important thing is that those of you who have more positive attitudes about sex should get your songs to the marketplace as well. Unless songwriters want to invite censorship, we must make sure there are alternative philosophies and values offered to impressionable minds. Today, female artists in all genres seem to be the ones who counter male artists who disrespect women in their songs. In doing so, they're gaining legions of young fans in the process.

The treatment of sex in a song may be subtle or explicit. Explicitness gets old fast and

Public attitudes are always in a state of change, and a songwriter must always be aware of those changes.

ultimately is not as stimulating as a song that is more clever, subtle, sensuous, perhaps using *double entendre*. It's been said that the mind is the most sensitive erogenous zone. Use your imagination and creativity to stimulate it.

The Censorship Issue

Sex-oriented lyrics of varying degrees of explicitness can be found in all styles of music. Those in rock and R&B/hip-hop and rap are increasingly under fire by self-appointed guardians of our national morality. These elements have raised the specter of music censorship, which, if it materializes, would constitute a major barrier to self-expression. It's apparent that warning stickers on CDs have helped those artists sell albums at least as much as it's hurt their sales.

Perhaps the focus has also made us aware of the power lyricists wield. Songwriters, who spend a substantial part of their careers attempting to gain some acceptance by the industry, are unaccustomed to imagining a ten-year-old kid singing their lyrics. That reality (after the song is a hit) has caused many writers to reassess their responsibility to the listener. I wish more writers would think about it while they're writing the songs. Whether or not you allow this pressure to influence your creative choices, the responsibility should not be taken lightly.

There will always be critics who will only listen to part of what you say and misinterpret based on that incomplete knowledge. Some have been known to condemn a song about drugs without realizing it's an antidrug song. In a situation like that, you should at least have the satisfaction of knowing that you did write the song you intended to write.

Sex is not only a powerful human drive but a major topic on TV, in novels, and in our own conversations. It can't be ignored and won't ever go away. To censor sex as a song topic would be like asking songwriters not to write about love. Having said that, I *am* concerned about the effect of explicitly sexual, misogynist, and violent lyrics coming from talented and successful artists who kids look up to and are heavily promoted by record companies whose primary concern is their bottom line. Maybe the best we can hope for is parents who care enough to discuss these songs and the attitudes they convey with their kids and model the attitudes they want their kids to learn.

Message Songs

Most songwriters, particularly in the early stages of their development, seem motivated primarily by the need to express some kind of emotional turmoil. Most often it's "my baby left me," or "I'm so lonely," or "he/she's cheatin' on me"—all negative scenarios. We may think our experience is unique, that we're the only ones able to feel such pain. But intellectually, we know how common this situation really is. In times of heavy stress, our ability to think rationally is temporarily on vacation.

Consequently, when the professional songwriter in us looks back on those songs after we've cooled out, we're amazed at how trite and unimaginative those "agony" songs are. Not that agony or other strong emotion doesn't occasionally spawn something profound; but most often, it just spawns self-indulgence. There's nothing wrong with writing songs during these periods as therapy. Just don't get the idea that because you wrote something in a heavy emotional state, it's automatically going to produce a fantastic song.

Another song genre that grows out of a strong emotional state, though often a more positive one, is the message song. Even though it's positive, it may have similar results as the "agony" song unless you're careful. Here's an example: You've just had a religious experience and must tell the world about your revelation. The spirits have laid a great truth on you and as a musician and songwriter, you're uniquely qualified to spread the word.

So you dash off a song. After all, this is a very important message, and you don't want to bother with all those crass commercial techniques like rhyme and meter. They seem so unimportant next to the innate power of the message. You just know that when you sing it, everyone within earshot will automatically share your feelings.

Wrong! Suddenly, as you play the song for a publisher or even for someone on the street, reality becomes a new revelation. You realize this person (a) doesn't care, (b) has heard it all before and it doesn't make anymore sense now than it ever did, or (c) he already shares your belief and is bored by the way you stated it. You've told it the way you felt it, but failed to *communicate* it to someone who needs the message or failed to move someone who already knows it by not presenting it in a fresh, new way.

Very few "message" songs actually communicate their message. If the lyric is weak, the music has to be doubly strong to make up for it. The Beatles' "All You Need Is Love" is one of the most trite lyrics on paper, but it works, thanks to the Beatles' fame, an interesting melody, a 7/4 time signature, and strong production. Without a powerful musical vehicle, the words have to stand on their own.

Len Chandler and I have a phrase, "man on the mountain," for a particularly preachy kind of stance. It translates to "I, at my tender age, have gone to the mountaintop and learned the secret of the universe. And now, from this lofty perch, I'm going to tell all you unfortunate, unenlightened people how to live your lives."

As a listener, I have one demand: Don't preach to me! If I want to be preached at, I'll go to church. If I need guidance, I'll look for someone with credentials.

I'm not anti-message songs. On the contrary, I don't think there are enough effective ones around. I'd just like writers to take their messages seriously enough to devote some time and craft to ensuring I receive them.

Now that I've told you what doesn't work, what does? Some people might respond to the sledgehammer, preachy "You've got to," "You'd better," "Don't ever" school of thought, but more of us would probably rather be led gently than driven to enlightenment with a whip.

Not that agony or other strong emotion doesn't occasionally spawn something profound; but most often, it just spawns self-indulgence.

The most effective songs are the ones that involve me in a scene I'm a part of or one I feel is cut so realistically from the fabric of life that I *could be* a part of it. Jesus, Buddha, and all the great religious leaders used parables to get their messages to masses of people, to relate those messages to people's everyday lives. The Good Samaritan was one of Jesus' greatest hits. Wouldn't you feel great if you wrote a song that two thousand years later still taught the same message as strongly as it did when it was written?

One of the classic examples of this type of song comes from the late Harry Chapin and his wife, Sandy. The message, that we should all try to spend more time with our parents and children, is important in a time when all of us have so many activities that keep us away from each other. The Chapins could have written a song that said, "You'd better spend time with your families or the family unit will be destroyed." Sledgehammer! No poetry, too general, impersonal, and pompous. Instead, they wrote "Cat's in the Cradle."

"Cat's In The Cradle"
WORDS AND MUSIC BY HARRY CHAPIN AND SANDY CHAPIN

My child arrived just the other day
He came to the world in the usual way
But there were planes to catch and bills to pay
He learned to walk while I was away
And he was talkin' 'fore I knew it,
and as he grew he'd say
"I'm gonna be like you, Dad
You know I'm gonna be like you."

And the cat's in the cradle and the silver spoon,
Little boy blue and the man in the moon.
"When you comin' home, Dad?" "I don't know when,
But we'll get together then,—you know we'll have a good time then."

My son turned ten just the other day
He said, "Thanks for the ball, Dad, come on let's play.
Can you teach me to throw?" I said, "Not today,
I got a lot to do." He said, "That's okay."
And he walked away but his smile never dimmed, it said,
"I'm gonna be like him, yeah,
you know I'm gonna be like him."

And the cat's in the cradle and the silver spoon,
Little boy blue and the man in the moon.
"When you comin' home, Dad?" "I don't know when,
But we'll get together then,—you know we'll have a good time then."

Well he came from college just the other day
so much like a man I just had to say,
"Son I'm proud of you, can you sit for a while?"
He shook his head and he said with a smile,
"What I'd really like, Dad, is to borrow the car keys
see you later, can I have them please?"

And the cat's in the cradle and the silver spoon,
Little boy blue and the man in the moon.
"When you comin' home, Son?" "I don't know when,
But we'll get together then; you know we'll have a good time then."

I've long since retired, my son's moved away
I called him up just the other day.
I said, "I'd like to see you if you don't mind."
He said, "I'd love to, Dad, if I can find the time.
You see, my new job's a hassle and the kids have the flu,
but it's sure nice talkin' to you, Dad, it's sure nice talkin' to you."
And as I hung up the phone, it occurred to me,
he'd grown up just like me. My boy was just like me.

And the cat's in the cradle and the silver spoon,
Little boy blue and the man in the moon.
"When you comin' home, Son?" "I don't know when,
But we'll get together then,—you know we'll have a good time then."

The Chapins didn't give us any "shoulds" here. They didn't have to. They held a mirror up to life that made listeners think about their relationships with their parents and did it with real-life dialogue and situations we've all experienced. They also did it from a first-person point of view.

The point of view is very important in message songs. It's effective to describe a situation in terms of your own personal involvement. If you're offering a message, you're really being a kind of salesman. Testimonials are always very effective sales devices. A good approach is to let people in on your own discovery—what got you so excited that you wanted to tell us about it. Your enthusiasm will motivate us without your having to preach to us. The first-person (I, we) approach, assuming you put the song together in a way that makes people want to sing along with you, lets your audience internalize the message by saying "I" or "we" along with you.

Another effective point of view is that of the seemingly uninvolved storyteller. This type of song doesn't moralize because, if the story is told well, there's no need for it. One of the most powerful examples is Bob Dylan's "Ballad of Hollis Brown," about a man who kills his family and himself rather than see them starve to death because he can't find a job. Dylan wrote many other powerful songs in this way. Stevie Wonder's "Living for the City," "The Way It Is" by Bruce Hornsby, and Eminem's "Stan" are other good examples.

I don't mean to imply that there are only a few approaches to writing effective message songs. What I'm focusing on here are ways to write for mass audiences who don't necessarily share your point of view. You can use a sledgehammer approach as a rallying song for people who are already on your side. You can use humor, satire, anything that works. And don't forget that the music *is* also important in helping people to hear the message *and* remember it.

If you can write a powerful lyric but are a little shaky in the music department, look for someone who composes well in a contemporary style.

Message writers generally choose not to collaborate, perhaps for fear their message will somehow become compromised. In fact, they may be compromising their ability to get that song to a wide audience. If you can write a powerful lyric but are a little shaky in the music department, look for someone who composes well in a contemporary style. The music is such a powerful vehicle for delivering the message that it shouldn't be taken lightly. Social and political message songs occasionally become hits. A controversial message may help a song gain notoriety, but it's still the power of the performance, the music, and the record that makes a radio station play it. Your message deserves the best of all ingredients.

Novelty Songs

Every writer seems to have at least one crazy, off-the-wall novelty song written just for fun. The spirit can be as infectious and as much fun for an audience to hear as it is for the writer to write.

Novelty songs, however, are extremely difficult to place with an artist. Aside from a very few artists such as Ray Stevens ("The Streak," "People's Court"), Jim Stafford ("Spiders and Snakes"), Ross Bagdassarian (The Chipmunks), Weird Al Yankovic ("Eat It"), and Pinkard and Bowden, who built careers on novelty records, most artists, their producers, and record companies view novelty records, particularly for new artists, as career killers. If an artist gets a hit on a novelty record, it's next to impossible to get radio to accept any kind of serious music from the artist after that. If you feel you've got a terrific novelty song, forget pitching it to publishers. Instead, pitch it directly to the few artists who do them, their managers, or producers. It's a long shot, but one that might work.

The Dr. Demento show is a nationally syndicated radio program featuring novelty material from unknown writers. "Weird Al" got his start there. Contact the show at:

Dr. Demento, c/o The Demento Society

P.O. Box 884

Culver City, CA 90232

www.drdemento.com

Another approach is to pitch your song to a non-novelty artist who might use it in a live performance. Most artists like to lighten up their stage act by inserting a funny song. They'll often hire writers to create such "special material" for the act based on the personality of the artist and the function the material needs to fulfill in the act. Contact the artist's manager. If they like it, chances are (even if they use it in the act), they won't record it, so charge them a fee for using it.

Be careful, though, if you write parodies of well-known songs. Though it may be considered a "fair use" area, you could still be subject to a lawsuit. The safest approach is to get permission from the publisher first. (See "Copyright Infringement/Plagiarism," chapter eight.)

Christmas Songs

Every year I receive a few Christmas songs to critique by mail. A lot of them are on lead sheets (lyrics with musical notation), which tells me these people are novices because lead sheets went out of style years ago for pitching songs. Maybe they figure that if they could just write one good Christmas song, like "White Christmas," they'd be set for life. It's rare to find one that manages to avoid clichés. But let's assume they did manage to skate past the frosty snowman in the silent night, past the chipmunks and the reindeer, to roast chestnuts and sit by the cozy fireside as their kids ask when Santa's coming and ponder why it can't be this way all year round . . . and decided to write a song about it.

What does the Christmas song market look like?

I spoke with publishers and other industry folks and the consensus is that it's an even bigger long shot than trying to get a hit record. Obviously, the first barrier is that the song is seasonal, not the kind people will buy year-round. The real barrier, though, is that a record needs airplay to become a hit, and few radio stations allot that much time for Christmas music.

Veteran publisher and industry consultant Jay Lowy explains that right after Thanksgiving, the radio rotation of Christmas songs begins and escalates until most stations have a couple days' worth of solid Christmas fare at Christmas Eve and Day. The airplay of these songs is encouraged by the stations' ad salespeople to stimulate Christmas shopping activity for their accounts.

Now, with few exceptions, stations keep playing their regular hits with only an occasional holiday song thrown in. They figure their audience isn't tuning in to hear Christmas music. Unless major artists like Christina Aguilera or 'N Sync record a Christmas CD, it's seldom worth it for a record company to ship records for a short period of time, then pay to have the leftovers shipped back. The retailers would rather use their stockroom space for records that sell all year. In the 2000 holiday season, however, more than twenty-five major artists released Christmas CDs, and though many of them were re-releases (Nat King Cole, The Carpenters, etc.), others were debut albums that undoubtedly will be released again in the future. If the song fits a contemporary rock or other mass-appeal radio format, it's more likely to get played on those stations than something like "White Christmas," but it would still help if you had a contemporary superstar to perform it.

One of the publishers who specializes in holiday songs is Justin Wilde. His company, Songcastle Music, can be contacted via his Web site: *http://www.christmassongs.com*.

Print:

Ronny Schiff, an expert in the field of print music, says that she knows of several Christmas songs that have become successful in the educational market by virtue of having great choral arrangements. These were popularized mainly by word of mouth among choral directors and presented in annual school and church pageants. One of the best examples is Albert Burt's "Do You Hear What I Hear?" Another is the Ukrainian folk song "The Carol of the Bells," which was popular as a choral piece for generations before someone recorded a pop Christmas arrangement.

The "backdoor" method, says Schiff, is the best for this type of song. When she was working for publishers in New York a few years ago, she saw many people plugging Christmas songs to recording artists, but not one she knew of was successful. "We Need a Little Christmas" still gets performed frequently on TV shows, but since it was from *Auntie Mame*, not only a popular play but a movie, it got widespread exposure automatically. Schiff adds that Christmas songs sell best in books and not in individual sheet music. This, I suspect, reflects the fact that people will buy a book of standards first, and it takes continued popularity of an individual song before it starts being included in the books.

TV:

Every year major artists perform on Christmas TV specials. Your song may have a shot at one with some ingenuity, good timing, and contacts, or a good publisher. Otherwise that new song that's needed by the special is written "for hire" by musical directors who work for the show.

Contemporary Christian and Gospel:

This part of the industry is very popular and may be more receptive than pop radio to Christmas songs with a religious message. Look at *Billboard* magazine's The Contemporary Christian Chart for artists and labels that specialize in this area. There is a wide range of traditional to contemporary musical styles within this category and a plethora of Christian radio stations. (See "Radio Formats," chapter three.)

If you're a long-shot player and an excellent writer, if you're willing to start pitching your songs in July and to work for years to develop a standard, you may be one of the few who gets a big royalty check for Christmas. My friend Nadine McKinnor had her Christmas song "This Christmas" recorded many years ago by the great Donny Hathaway, and in 2000 it was included on three different Christmas CDs, including Christina Aguilera's. It *can* happen!

chapter three

The Media and the Listeners

The Media

Let's assume you're a songwriter who ultimately wants your songs to reach the public. As much as you'd like to just wave that magic wand and have everyone automatically hear them, the reality is that, before that happens, your song must pass judgment by a whole series of people. Publishers, producers, record company A&R representatives, record promoters, radio program directors, and club owners all, in their own ways, decide in which medium your music belongs or whether your music is appropriate for their particular medium.

When we attend a classical music concert, we expect to hear long compositions with several different movements. In a film, we expect to hear music that creates a mood that enhances and heightens the action and drama.

When we turn on a pop, country, R&B, rock, or other contemporary music station, we know we'll hear songs that will hold our attention with excellent production and arrangements; that have frequent and regularly recurring changes in lyrical, musical, and rhythmic texture; and have a fairly predictable form.

In musical theater, the songs reveal the characters' personalities and help tell the story. When a character sings a song, the lyrics and music must feel natural to that character. However, they don't *need* to be structured like radio songs unless they're also intended for airplay. Since theater is a *visual* medium, it already holds our attention and isn't as dependent on the type of "reach out and grab you" dynamics that radio needs.

The point is that every medium has both restrictions and freedoms that are created by the function of that medium, the needs of the industry, and the expectations of the audience. The more we understand the medium in which we want to work, with its principles and forms, the better we can manipulate it.

A Poem Is Not a Lyric

In the print medium, we have an exceptional legacy of poetry in all languages. Much of that poetry also lends itself to recitation and, in fact, may be written specifically to be

The more we understand the medium in which we want to work, with its principles and forms, the better we can manipulate it.

recited. It is one of a poet's creative options, and if she chooses it, she knows that there are certain words or syllables that won't flow comfortably in speech but will work fine on paper. Other words that can conjure pictures when spoken passionately don't have nearly as much impact on paper. Dylan Thomas's poetry, though it does work on paper, was clearly written to be recited, and recordings of him or Brendan Behan reciting it can bring tears to the eyes. The point is that poetry lives in the media of print and speech. Lyrics, on the other hand, live elsewhere.

A common misconception is that songs are poetry put to music. An immense number of treasured lyrics do work as well on the printed page as in a musical context. Writer/artists such as Jackson Browne, Joni Mitchell, Bob Dylan, Paul Simon, Leonard Cohen, and others possess vocal and writing styles so integrated that an unusually poetic phrase feels right at home in their styles, but would not work comfortably in another artist's style. How many Joni Mitchell songs can you imagine other artists performing without imitating her style?

Performers such as these are considered "album artists." In other words, we buy their albums not because they have a hit single, but because we like their style and like who we perceive them to be. We're likely to read their lyrics on the CD inserts and allow them a little more "poetic license," a little more abstraction and a few more obscure references that we're challenged to figure out. We don't mind because we're already fans.

The point, though some lyrics work as poetry, is that a good poem does not necessarily make a good lyric. The obvious difference is that a lyric must function with music. It must be sung. A poem written for the printed page alone can use graphic style and unusual placement of words on a page to emphasize subtleties in meaning. It's not expected to rhyme. It can use sight rhyme *(board, bored)*. It can indulge in abstractions, because if the words aren't readily understood, our eyes and minds can stop for as long as we need to let them sink in and bounce around in the brain.

Much of what is referred to as "poetry" is actually verse. The difference is that between substance and form, imagination and craft. Verse is really anything that conforms to accepted metrical rules and structure. Anyone can write good verse that rhymes and has accurate meter, but if it's devoid of substance and imagination, it's still not poetry.

Good lyrics need to have all those attributes and more and less. In an interview with Oscar-winning lyricist Dean Pitchford ("Footloose"), I asked what he felt was the difference between poetry and lyric since he had been a poet prior to becoming a lyricist:

I think poetry, in its final form, is on the page. Maybe when it's read, it achieves something else, but poetry is on the page. Lyric is only 50 percent of the work of a song, and it's spare. It can't be very full or fleshed out. Otherwise you don't leave much room for the music to do anything or for the interpretation of the singer, which is why I learned very early on that you don't read lyrics to people who aren't in the music industry. It doesn't read, it doesn't speak, and a musician could maybe hear it like the song it could become, but a lyric is not a finished thing. You also have to resist the temptation to fill all the corners, to expand to fill your space. People hand me these typewritten sheets saying, "What do you think?" and it looks like the Gettysburg Address—long extended lines and they're very erudite and smart and there's lots of thought and inner rhymes and alliteration, but there's no space for the music.

The lyric, like a poem, seeks to express an idea or emotion imaginatively in a condensed, yet powerful way. Music helps it do that. Film composer/teacher Eddy Lawrence, in his classes, asks a student to walk across the room the same way several times. Each time, he plays different music expressing different moods behind the walk. Each time the music expresses a different idea about what that person is feeling, where he or she is going. You can do that to a lyrical phrase with different music, too. The right (or wrong) music can give that spare and lean phrase exactly the right or wrong meaning. New lyricists have a tendency to minimize the importance of music as a vehicle to deliver their message.

Unlike poetry, the words in a lyric must be able to be sung well. Words like "orange" are not only impossible to rhyme, but difficult to sing. A lyricist must be able to imagine someone singing the words.

In writing lyrics for radio songs, we need to remember that, in a quick three to four minutes, the listener doesn't have time, as in poetry, to wonder what the words really mean.

A lyricist must be able to imagine someone singing the words.

A Song Is Not a Record

Making a record is a craft in its own right. Today, the craft of making a recording involves the combined skills of singers, musicians, arrangers, producers, and recording engineers. Their creativity and command of the technology involved can transform a mediocre song into a wonderful sonic experience. But they'll never make it a great song. A great song has a life of its own. It will move you even if it's sung *a cappella.* It can be sung by different artists in different eras with the same results.

Many writers voice the complaint, "My song is better than a lot of stuff I hear on the radio, so why doesn't anyone want it?" They're usually right, but what they've failed to recognize is the difference between a "hit record" and a "hit song."

The appeal of the *record* may be based primarily on any of the combination of ingredients aside from words and melody; a powerful vocal performance, an artist or group with a unique identity or sound, a great arrangement, or business considerations such as timing or promotion. There are a lot of hit *records* that we can't remember the melody to or the lyrics; perhaps we just remember the hook line. We may even find ourselves humming the bass line. Those aren't songs—they're records.

You can't write a *record* unless you're in control of that recording situation as a producer or artist (though you can put together a demo that suggests the ingredients that give the producer a blueprint from which to work).

I've bought CDs solely on my love of their sound, even though I couldn't hum the melodies or had no understanding of the lyrics, but I enjoyed them as a listening experience. If there had been great lyrics to go with that experience, I would have had a much greater level of enjoyment.

Those of you who record your own material will, I hope, remember that the more you approach your art and craft with a desire to communicate and a commitment to excellence, the more powerfully an audience will experience it.

Some producers and artists strive for the best product possible by seeking out the best songs available, whether they write them themselves or go for "outside" (other writers') songs. Others, more concerned about collecting royalties than turning out a quality product, would rather record a mediocre song of their own than go for a great song by someone else. It's up to the record buyers whether they'll continue to subsidize mediocrity.

Writing for Radio

Radio isn't in the music business. It's in the *advertising* business. It'll play or do whatever will attract the largest possible listening audience. The bigger the audience, the more money advertisers will pay to sell everything from zit cream to retirement homes. The approaches vary widely, from high-energy Top 40 (or 20) stations, with hard sell styles, to instrumental Muzak-type stations, where the commercials register almost subliminally. Some stations seek to reach a wide variety of listeners and age groups with music that's interesting and not too high energy. This used to be called MOR (middle of the road) or "easy listening," but is now classified as AC (adult contemporary). Others attempt to pinpoint a specific market with a specific style of music. (See "Radio Formats" on page 42.)

The competition is fierce among radio stations, particularly among those with similar formats. They're obsessed with preventing "dial outs." Once they have you tuned in, they don't want you to go away. Consequently, one of the most important requirements for music on the radio is that it holds the listener's attention. While it's true that holding someone's attention on the radio is accomplished by a combination of song, artist, and production, you need to start with a song that lends itself well to radio. The following chapters will help you create that type of song.

One of the most important requirements for music on the radio is that it holds the listener's attention.

| Song Length

The greatest percentage of hit radio songs used to be approximately three minutes long. Today they average more than four minutes. You rarely hear them much longer than five minutes because radio wants to play more songs yet keep more space for commercials. Knowing this, few publishers, producers, and record companies want to buck those kinds of odds by signing/producing/recording a longer song. They also know that exceptionally long songs won't get maximum "rotation," that is, the number of times per hour or day a song gets played. They'd rather a short song got played once an hour than a long one every three hours. With a higher frequency of airplay, you, as a writer, will make more money

A great story is told about country music legend Buck Owens ("Act Naturally"), who had a radio background before his career as a recording artist. Knowing that DJs frequently had less than three minutes to go before a newsbreak or commercial, too short to play a three-minute record and maybe too long to fill with idle chatter, he fashioned his first hits to two minutes or under and let the DJs know it. Consequently, he got lots of airplay in those awkward time slots.

from BMI, ASCAP or SESAC, the performing rights organizations. (See "Where Your Money Comes From," chapter nine.) It's interesting to note that, when radio was much tougher about keeping songs down to three minutes, record companies were known to put 2:59 on the label of a single that may have actually run 3:04, just for that extra edge!

Mainstream radio personnel will play a longer song if there is such an incredible public demand for it that they might lose listeners to another station. However, that song had better be able to hold an audience's attention from beginning to end and make them want to hear it again.

Major artists can get away with long songs on hit radio because everyone wants to hear these artists. A common practice is to edit a record for different functions: a short version for the radio single and longer versions and special mixes for "specialty" radio shows and the dance club market.

Something else to be considered in the length of the song is the *introduction*. "Intro" lengths vary, but it's generally considered that for a slow song, approximately ten seconds of introduction is optimum. For an upbeat dance tune, twenty seconds or more can work because, if it grabs your body, you'll keep listening.

Even though these general time guidelines are important, it's more important that the intro be easily identifiable and *musically interesting*. It should involve changing textures, adding instruments, or other arrangement devices to keep it developing. Nothing induces boredom faster than an intro that goes nowhere.

A unique, identifiable introduction will make a radio station's program director pay attention. If he pays attention, he feels his audience will, too. DJs love to talk over intros. Many people find it irritating, but it gets back to radio trying to save more time for commercials. Some DJs just get excited about having sound tracks behind their intros. It's a good idea to include the time of the intro on the DJs' promotional copies, so they'll know how long to talk, though it's easy these days for DJs and programmers to quickly get those timings on the CD player. (See "Intros," chapter twelve.)

Singles, Albums, Live Performances, and Video

The ability to distinguish between the requirements of these four different media and art forms can eliminate a lot of confusion for a writer or writer/performer.

RADIO FORMATS

Here's a list of the major new music (as opposed to "oldies") radio formats in the United States and Canada courtesy of independent radio airplay promoter Bryan Farrish (*www.radio-media.com*) with his comments on each. Obviously, the number of stations in these categories is subject to change.

Country

2,300 stations. Country is the real "Top 40" of the United States because of its popularity. "Young country" and "hot country" appeal to the younger listeners, using newer artists, younger DJs, and a more energetic approach. The "new" approach really took hold about the time Garth Brooks began gaining popularity. More traditional country stations (sometimes known as "Heritage" stations) are sort of the "oldies" of country radio . . . but they also are specific in which new artists they play.

One special subcategory of country is the "Americana" format. It is a cross between rock and country, and it has about one hundred stations, most of which are small. Americana is an interesting new format, with some really eclectic artists and new labels.

Religious

1,900 stations. Includes Christian in several music styles, gospel, and many stations with a large amount of teaching content. Although a big format, hundreds of stations in the religious format offer less chance for new music because of the large amounts of talk, satellite programming, and older songs that they play.

There is no absolute number of religious stations that play new music. Instead, it is a variable, and a particular station can play anywhere from one hour to twenty-four hours of new music.

Adult Contemporary

1,500 stations. Also called "AC." Includes "mainstream" AC, "modern" AC, "hot" AC, and "soft" AC. AC is similar to religious in that hundreds of stations have limited capacity for new music because of the talk, satellite, or sports programming they carry.

Nevertheless, AC still remains as one of the melting pots for new artists on small labels. By this I mean that there are enough small AC stations (that play new music) for a new artist to stand a chance . . . if promoted correctly.

Rock

800 stations. Includes "modern" rock, "alternative," and straight rock. Most people know of these stations. Problem is, they are tougher for independent artists to get airplay. One thing saves the day, however . . . their specialty* shows.

Spanish

600 stations. All variations included.

Top 40

400 stations. Includes "rhythmic crossover" stations, i.e., Top 40 with a beat. A very difficult format for indie artists. But again, specialty shows (and mixshows*) save the day.

Urban

300 stations. Includes urban, R&B, hip-hop, and urban AC. Also very difficult for new artists, but thankfully it also offers mixshow support.

Classical

150 stations.

Jazz

150 stations. Includes "straight" jazz (i.e., traditional) and "smooth" jazz. Straight jazz is a viable format for an indie artist. Smooth, however, will be very difficult.

Kids

50 stations. These mostly are the Radio Disney stations, and they are all programmed from the home office.

*A specialty show or a mixshow is a one- or two-hour show on a commercial station, usually late at night, and many times on the weekends, and it plays music the station normally does not play.

| Live Performance

It's not unusual to have a writer/performer play a mediocre-to-fair song for me (in a critique session) and be shocked when my response is less than enthusiastic. He'll say, "The *people* love these songs when I play them in the clubs and, after all, aren't *they* my audience?" Yes, they *are* your audience and they'll almost always respond to a high-energy, enthusiastic *performance*, a heartfelt delivery, and to a performer with conviction and personal charisma. The positive response a writer/artist gets from a club performance can be very misleading when he doesn't separate the performance from the song.

The writer/artist often takes his performing ability for granted. He may be relatively new to songwriting and writing songs in which he's invested a lot of himself. The songs, in his mind, take the focus, so he assumes that people are applauding the songs rather than the performance.

When we go to a club with a date and drop twenty dollars in cover charges and possibly forty more on drinks and food, we're willing to go more than halfway to be entertained. Give us a performer with the qualities mentioned above, and we can be ecstatic. Take the same songs on a demo to a hard-nosed publisher or a record company A&R rep who's separating the performance from the song and looking for a hit, and it's a whole new situation. Since they can't *see* the performance, be moved by the charisma, and aren't communicated to via facial expressions and body language, the song has to stand on its own. This is particularly true for publishers, who have to convince another artist to record the song.

| Singles

A lot of music works in clubs that wouldn't work as a hit single. A ten-minute vamp will work for a dancing crowd and a ten-minute guitar or drum solo can bring a club or concert crowd to a frenzy; but put it on the radio, and even the same person who loved it in concert may change the station. Performance groups like Phish, the Dave Matthews Band, and Widespread Panic sell records to those concert-goers who relive the concert experience through the recording, not because the group has a hit single.

You'll be learning more about the qualities of hit singles in the following chapters. Let's just say here that the dynamics needed for a hit single can certainly work in a club, though the reverse is not necessarily true.

| Albums

I'll forgive an artist for being adventurous on an album, even if it falls short of my expectations, but not for copping out by giving me empty "filler" just to have an album to sell.

Albums are another medium altogether. Generally speaking, albums allow more creative latitude, particularly for self-contained bands and writer/artists. An artist's hit singles can be a completely different listening experience from their concerts or albums. Both of the latter can be much more spontaneous and unpredictable. They can stretch the forms and create tremendous tension with long repetitive vamps that could never work in the limited time frame of a hit single. Longer, more dramatic songs are possible, often coming closer, in fact, to musical theater. Most great performing artists and bands present an audience with quite a different experience in concert than on record.

Sound and style are also among the selling points for album artists. Sting and Radiohead are good examples. New age artists like Jim Brickman, George Winston, and Yanni are bought because they create a *mood* that's comforting. The appeal of other album artists like Tom Waits, Joni Mitchell, Dar Williams, and a rapidly expanding list of independent artists is their personal point of view. We get to know them and relate to them in a more intimate way and come to feel like they and their songs are old friends.

We'll read the liner notes, follow the lyrics, and generally pay attention in a way not far removed from the attention we pay at a concert. The songs don't have to *demand* our attention like a hit single. They already have us.

Given that, the album has an obligation not to betray the buyer's trust. We're all tired of having been seduced by a hit single and profoundly disappointed by a mediocre album with mundane and unmemorable songs and performances. Personally, I'll forgive an artist for being adventurous on an album, even if it falls short of my expectations, but not for copping out by giving me empty "filler" just to have an album to sell.

| Video

Somewhere in between is video, which can deliver some of the excitement of a live show and allow artists tremendous exposure over established outlets like MTV, BET, and CMT as well as individual specialty shows. With a growing number of broadband Internet connections, more fans will be watching videos on their computers. I don't believe video has much relevance to your songwriting craft. No matter what kind of song you write, creative video producers will find ways to make it visually exciting, often creating scenarios that bear little, if any, relationship to what the song is about. Record companies make videos primarily based on what they feel works best on radio. Because video has so much power as a marketing tool however, it has influenced record companies to sign artists who are visually exciting and great looking and, in the mix of ingredients they look for, it can be a determining factor despite what they say about its being "all about the songs." Video, on an artistic level, gives an artist an opportunity to create images for their music that can stay in a listener/viewer's mind. Another factor at work, particularly in performance videos, where you can actually see the artist sing (as opposed to "concept" videos that almost show everything but . . .) is that it's possible for the viewers to "get" the lyric faster. Either way, your craftsmanship is still extremely important.

The Listener: Know Your Audience

Most new writers give little conscious thought to whom they're writing for. They may write primarily for themselves and automatically reach an audience of their peers who share their emotional problems, social scene, political concerns, colloquial language, and musical styles. They're a reflection of what is happening around them, and they're popular because of it. They aren't deliberately writing for a target demographic group. They *are* that group. Self-contained writer/artists and groups like the Rolling Stones may not only keep an audience who grew up with them, but also continue to appeal to an audience maybe thirty years younger who can still identify with their attitudes. On the other hand, the Stones still write about the same things they wrote about thirty years ago.

If you want the creative challenge of writing songs for artists in different styles of music than the one(s) you've been most at home with, you need to do some stretching. The challenge is to analyze the appeal of an artist and the characteristics of his or her audience (see "Casting," chapter eleven). Then write a song in that artist's style. Immerse yourself in the artist's work. Listen to the radio stations that play her records. Buy some of them yourself, especially recent successful ones.

Be careful not to make quick, stereotyped judgments or harbor any negative attitudes about the style. I counseled a writer, for instance, who expressed interest in writing country songs. I asked who his favorite country artists were, and he said, "I don't know. I never listen to country. In fact, I don't even like it! It just seems like it would be easier to write than pop and more artists record songs they don't write." I told him to forget it. The motivation was all wrong.

It's difficult enough to come up with something worthwhile even when you know and love a style. Having the wrong attitudes about a kind of music you haven't really lived with or made a thorough study of can easily get you way off track. You have to know, for instance, that complex melodies and chord changes, while jazz fans may love them, don't work in country songs. Abstract lyrics that might spark a pop or rock piece would turn off a country audience.

One of the most common problems in targeting listeners comes from inappropriate combinations of music and subject matter. For instance, heavy metal appeals to primarily young, white males age twelve to eighteen. A romantic lyric like "I Will Always Love You" doesn't make it in heavy metal; rebellious lyrics do. Attitude is very important in rock and roll. A hard, frantic edge in the music needs attitudes that aren't soft, mushy, or tender. Artists like Creed and 3 Doors Down appeal to both young men and women because there's room in their image and repertoire to do romantic ballads as well as rockers. The point is that you need to understand who an artist's audience is to write effective material.

Visualize the audience for whom you're writing the song. A writer once played me a song involving a man propositioning his wife's best friend. He reminds her he's still in love with his wife, so she shouldn't think about getting too involved. Musically, it was a mellow pop ballad, a style that appeals primarily to women, and the song was obviously directed to a woman. But the song had a few obvious flaws. The audience is being asked to identify with the best friend. Even if we assume she liked the guy and was flattered by the come-on, she would not feel great about hearing him say he was still in love with his wife! The other category of potential record buyers—wives—is not going to enjoy a song in which the husband propositions her best friend. So the song effectively negated the very audience that would be most drawn to the musical style. If he had thought about how his audience would feel hearing the song, he would not have considered it a pitchable song.

Whether you're writing a song for yourself or for someone else, if you want it to sell to an audience, it's important to have an idea who they are and how they will respond.

I interviewed Chris Blake around the time I started writing this book and discussed with him what makes songs "work" for an audience. I found him to be even more obsessed with the subject than I was, to the degree that he had spent a lot of time in research. I was even more pleased to see how well he articulated that research and decided that the material was important enough to be included here. Though Chris's experience is mostly in country, where lyric is king, I feel this information is extremely valuable no matter what style of music you're involved in.

THE IMAGINATION OF THE LISTENER
by Chris Blake

Imagination plays a large part in our perception of a song. The imagination converts words into experiences, turning songs into old friends that we want to hear again and again. The hit song lyric is one which, one way or another, gives the imagination what it needs to do that job, simply, easily, and completely.

The theater of the imagination performs twenty-four hours a day. It literally cannot *not* function, but as a mechanism it has certain characteristics—certain ways of acting and reacting—that we, as writers, need to know about.

Much remains to be learned about the human imagination and how it works, but a review of some of what has been found so far could make a difference to your work as a lyricist. I'm going to spare you the specific references and "technical" talk that is in much of the scientific literature. For those of you who enjoy that sort of thing, see the bibliography. But I do want to point out some specific characteristics of the imagination that have been confirmed by scientific research and are totally relevant to the job of the song lyricist.

The imagination is a stimulus-response mechanism. That is, it will not act unless acted upon, at which point it will act (or more properly, react) totally automatically.

What stimulates the imagination is just about any "cue" it perceives. To keep it simple, we can talk about "cues" as *internal* and *external.*

Internal cues are those that originate from within—from thoughts, associations, and memories. Fantasies and daydreams are good examples of the imagination responding to internal cues. While it's important to notice that the imagination itself cannot originate a stimulus, it can and does respond to its own images all the time. All of us who have ever been guilty of daydreaming (while that half-finished lyric sits unattended in front of us) have been caught up in what the people in the lab jackets call an "associative response chain"—really, an instance of the imagination taking off on its own material and going on and on.

This ability of the imagination to entertain itself is one of your major concerns as a lyricist. For now, just know that it is a relatively weak phenomenon. It is easily interrupted by external stimuli that, because they exist in present time, appear to hold a much stronger demand for the attention of the imagination. That ringing phone, with all its potential for who might be calling, will stop a daydream every time. Sometimes, that's a shame.

External cues are just what they sound like—the sights, sounds, smells, and touch sensations—the whole world we perceive outside us. We take them in and interpret them in our own experience, giving them meaning and order in our own "reality." We then attempt to communicate our realities to one another using a set of mutually agreed upon sounds we call "words." These words, when spoken and heard, become powerful external cues to the imagination—the cues we, as lyricists, are primarily concerned with right now.

Nowhere is the stimulus-response characteristic of the imagination clearer than in the domain of words. The imagination can't resist them. Indeed, it's a good thing! Were it not for the ability of our imaginations to convert words into images, we simply could not communicate with each other. (Nor could we communicate with ourselves, for it is in our imaginations that we put the world together.) But, let's keep it simple.

The theater of the imagination performs twenty-four hours a day. It literally cannot *not* function, but as a mechanism it has certain characteristics— certain ways of acting and reacting—that we, as writers, need to know about.

It's 6:30 A.M., and Larry, fanatic that he is, is going out jogging. This morning he's trying a new running route and, as he heads out the door, his roommate, Max (who has run the new route before), yells after him to "watch out for the dog." As Larry goes down the steps he wonders, as he always does, why he's doing this crazy thing. But not as hard as he's wondering what Max was talking about. Dog? What dog? Watch out? Why? Larry has been hooked. And his imagination is off and running (faster than Larry, probably).

Before we find out what happened, let's take a look at what went on inside Larry's head after the dog warning. It may seem a dry exercise, but as a lyricist, this had best become a well-practiced way of thinking for you.

Larry's mind now launches into an enormous amount of activity, but let's just touch on the highlights. *"Watch out for the dog."* What does that mean? It's not just automatic—he's got to remember—what, exactly, does "watch out" mean, and what is a "dog"?

Well, Larry's no dummy. He is now somewhere in the "watch out for the dog" ballpark in his mind, with a vague kind of picture of what those words mean to him. And there he would remain if he didn't have an imagination. But he does have one, and because it's an automatic response mechanism, it reacts automatically to the words.

Now, the imagination is not a selective machine; that is, it doesn't make choices for us. It is programmed to retrieve from the files and project on our "screens" exactly what it's told to—no less. And what is in our files—our memory—on any given subject? *Only every experience, thought, fantasy, emotion, and impulse we've ever had that we associate, however loosely, with that subject.*

Poor Larry! All he ever did was decide to take a new running route. Let's listen in while his imagination does what it is built to do:

Dog. Yessir, coming right up. Hmm, let's see, "dog" . . . ah, here it is—Lassie, Rin-Tin-Tin (excitement)—German police dogs, big, teeth (fear)—memory of being bitten by Mrs. Smith's Doberman (fear, pain, anger)—old Fido and me playing on the front lawn (happy)—Fido grew old and had to be put to sleep (sad)—your parents bought you a new puppy, but he had to be housebroken (disgust)—and so on . . .

As much as all this information is, it's just a fraction of what Larry has filed away with the word "dog." But, his roommate wasn't just talking about any "dog." He was talking about a "watch out" kind of dog:

Hmm, let's see, "Watch Out"—oh, yeah, it's right here (pain, anger)—what Mom said just before I burned my hand on the stove (fear, pain)—it's what you're supposed to do because Santa Claus is coming to town (confused)—what that kid shouted at me just before the baseball hit me in the head (pain)—what a roommate would say if I were about to go running past a man-eating dog (fear, anger) . . .

So now, Larry's imagination has "watch out" and "dog" files on tap. It puts them together and begins to feed Larry the following kinds of images:

Rabid wolves chasing starving children through the Russian woods (terror)—Mrs. Smith's Doberman resurrected from the past and waiting for me just around the corner (fear)—Cujo crouched behind the next bush, waiting—The Big Bad Wolf—packs of wild dogs, led by an evil-minded little mutt who looks suspiciously like Fido. . . .

All this sounds a little silly but, to Larry, these kinds of images don't seem silly at the time. The point is to notice the enormity and the complex variety of the information that becomes available to Larry's imagination from just a few words.

And he can't help himself. Notice that nothing about Larry's wild imagining was voluntary. Unless he particularly enjoys being afraid, we have to think that Larry probably wished he could think of something else while running. What I hoped to demonstrate is that the imagination (given appropriate cues) will do its thing, no matter what. It is a stimulus-response mechanism.

But please notice that the imagination is literally "wild" and has no discipline to it. You, the writer, must realize that you set off this same crazy process in the listener's head with every word you write; and it is you who must bring discipline to the listener's imagination. You need to impose controls on it in order to keep it somewhere in the domain in which you intend it to be.

Your tool for this job of channeling imagery is the *specificity* in your words. It's why God invented nouns and verbs and modifiers—adjectives and adverbs—tools to specify *exactly* who, what, where, when, how, and why.

As we saw with Larry, the imagination will come up with the whole crazy "file" unless it gets further directions. The quality of the image will be generalized and nonsensical. The tendency of the imagination is to quit the job under these conditions—for reasons we shall see—or to re-create only one particular image for arbitrary reasons, and *it may or may not be the image you want the listener to experience.*

Experiment for yourself. How intensely can you become involved with the following words?

Car

Book

Musical instrument

Not very, huh? You may have chosen to focus on one image that had personal meaning in your experience. The problem is that I *meant you to see:*

My great 1982 Porsche 928 with the broken right tail light

My paperback book with a blue cover and the words "Gifts of God" printed in gold on the front

My old white Telecaster guitar with the broken B-string and the missing volume knob

While the examples may seem arbitrary, the implications for your work are direct. You want the listener's imagination to re-create what *you* want it to; and for that,

You, the writer, must realize that you set off this same crazy process in the listener's head with every word you write; and it is you who must bring discipline to the listener's imagination.

You want the listener's imagination to re-create what *you* want it to; and for that, you need to be specific, or the imagination will abandon you, your words, and your song and wander off down God-knows-what corridors of its own.

you need to be specific, or the imagination will abandon you, your words, and your song and wander off down God-knows-what corridors of its own. It may pay more attention to other more specific and immediate information—the car ahead, the fight he had with his wife last night, or whatever. It's called "getting bored," and it is astonishing how often we simply bore listeners away from our songs by refusing to give them specific items to imagine. The imagination is a restless and highly distractable child, full of all good intentions and no self-control. If you want its attention, you'd better keep it busy with specific tasks.

But what tasks? Read on.

The imagination is an "analog information" mechanism—that is, it can only create pictures out of the information already stored in the mind's experience. Larry's "dog" emerged as a composite of many past real and imagined events, feelings and pictures. Nothing really new was a part of that image, save possibly some new combinations of old information.

The phrase "floating in space" can only be imagined by memories of experiences we've already had—none of which, of course, include really floating in space. The feeling of semiweightlessness we've had floating in water—various remembered scenes from sci-fi movies—perhaps the sensation of room and freedom around us (because we've heard space is empty, vast, and infinite). All sorts of images, feelings, and sensations occur, but all of them are taken from experiences real and imagined that we've already had. Nothing new. The imagination literally cannot deliver to us the experience of floating in space, but it tries hard (as it's designed to do) to re-create the experience out of old bits and pieces of information available to it. Our experience of the words can only be "imaginary" because we cannot come up with the real thing.

This is the primary reason why songs must be built on universal themes. As a songwriter, you simply cannot write about things that are outside of most people's experience and expect them to be able to relate to—to become involved in—the song through their imaginations. If they cannot relate *at the level of their imaginations*, the song becomes meaningless simply because they don't have the machinery to deal with it. Their reaction, of course, is one of instant frustration and turnoff. And your song doesn't get listened to.

It's amazing how often songwriters seem to believe they can get around this one. I wish I had a dime for every song I've heard from people who want to crash into the commercial market and yet who write about such obscure items as working on the floor of the stock market, the intricacies of shifting through ten different truck gears, and the tactics employed in nineteenth-century sea battles.

It's one matter to use specific detail to contribute to a universal emotion (plot). It's another to write your song exclusively about something with which you're familiar but about which a large block of listeners would have no experience or little knowledge.

Just remember to be very careful about the ideas, metaphors, and images you use in your song, and keep a ruthless eye out for the possibility that you are excluding large blocks of people from participating in your song. One of the chief villains here are songs that are totally about marriage or totally about divorce. You have to remember that lots of people have neither been married nor divorced.

Mental images are complete neurophysiological events, meaning that they occur in the brain and throughout the body simultaneously.

"Unreal" as imagined experiences are, they actually can produce the *experience* of reality. It's a testimony to how powerful the imagination truly is that we don't just "imagine" the sensation of weightlessness; we feel it. Indeed we react emotionally and physically to images in our mind. Our bodies produce what scientists call "secondary sympathetic responses" to mental imagery. The word *red* causes "red" activity in the parts of our eyes that react to color; the word *ouch* causes muscle contraction. And nerve endings truly react to the phrase "the touch of your hand."

Notice for yourself the number of song titles and lyrics that use images that suggest or involve physical action:

"With Arms Wide Open"

"Jumpin' Jumpin' "

"We Danced"

The list would be nearly endless. The usefulness of such physical action imagery is obvious when you consider the fact that we react to mental images with actual physical sensation and action. In short, lyrics that involve such demands in their imagery hook the listener not just from the standpoint of their beauty or cleverness but from a physical standpoint as well. Remember that the imagination responds automatically to words. You literally tell it what to do and it is helpless not to respond. If you give clear, simple, precise directions to it, you can produce powerful *emotional* and *physical* events in the listener.

Are you beginning to understand just how totally listeners are "hooked" by a good lyric? We don't *have* images; we *do* them. We imagine with our whole selves.

We can produce audio "images," feeling and sensation "images," and so forth. We can, in fact, "image" just about any experience we've ever had, think we've had, or imagine we've had; and you as the songwriter can direct us to do that if only you are clear in your directions and keep in mind the response characteristics of the imagination.

But you must realize some of the imagination's limits. Chief among these is its inability to re-create conceptual abstractions. An abstraction, for our purposes, is a subjective, usually very general, piece of information.

An abstraction just floats there. It's not grounded in *specificity* (who, what, where, when, or why). It is nonspecific, and the imagination, because it works the way it does, doesn't know what to do with it and isn't interested. Try to imagine such external cues as "decency," "belief," "transcendent," "wonderful," "beautiful" and so forth. Abstractions lack focus.

On the face of it, this creates an alarming problem for songwriters. For the worst abstractions of them all are the body of words that refer to the emotions, one of which is "love."

So how do you write a song about an emotional state such as love? Your goal is to involve the listener as deeply as possible by writing words that are usable by his imagination so that he can re-create the words of the song. The very words you would think the listener wants to hear—all about "love," "sad," "sorrow," "you hurt me," "I need you"—are abstractions the imagination cannot process.

The key to resolving this dilemma is simple enough. First, remember that listeners want "the real thing," information accessible to their imagination as they listen. Second, notice that abstractions are convenient for organizing and labeling our life experiences, but they are most definitely not life itself.

For the fun of it, let's look at the abstract phrase "falling in love." At the risk of offending the romantic poet in all of us, those words don't really refer to anything at all. They are only a kind of organizing label system, a file into which we put what for each of us have been unique and very real experiences. When I remember "falling in love" (the last time it happened to me), what I remember is:

- being able to think of nothing else except Betsy
- feeling lightheaded and slightly dizzy when I was around her
- losing my appetite
- daydreaming about us together
- making plans for our future
- wishing time would go faster so that I could be with her
- having my phone bill quadruple
- loving the smell of her perfume on my sweater

And on and on. Even that list is not too specific, but I *know* it brought you into a more real contact with my experience of "falling in love" than the phrase itself ever could. Are you beginning to get the drift?

Life is not an abstraction. It is moment to moment—real, specific, and concrete. And so it is that when the imagination re-creates life, it can only do so with specific and concrete images. So, when you write lyrics, you must give the mind the kind of cues and information it needs to do its job or it won't bother with the information.

Abstractions simply do not work in the imagination. They, in fact, serve to turn it away.

And yet it is true that songs are about abstractions. It's been said that there are seven possible "plots" to a commercial song: love, hate, loneliness, happiness, sadness, jealousy, and revenge. Every one of those words is an abstraction—every one of them is basically unusable by the imagination—and every one of them refers to what is at the heart of universal commerciality.

Nonetheless, it does present an apparent contradiction. How does the writer write about abstract emotions in a way that engages and involves the listener so he can participate in the song? How do you give the imagination the concrete specifics it needs to kick into gear? The answer lies in those questions. *The successful lyricist writes about abstractions through the use of detailed, concrete, specific (nonabstract) information.*

Two classic and fine examples of what I'm talking about are in the songs "Miss Emily's Picture" and the country classic "The Gambler."

"Miss Emily's Picture," recorded by John Conlee, is about a man who's lonely, blue, and missing "Miss Emily" terribly. But notice how dry that description is. The vehicle—the medium—through which the writer, Hollis R. De Laughter, communicates those feelings are simple, repeated descriptions of the act of looking at Miss Emily's picture. Notice that that is a physical act in which you can imagine and participate. Remember the number of times you've looked at pictures of someone very special to you. The idea is easy to re-create in your imagination. Absolutely nowhere in the song does the singer talk about missing Emily, or how he loved her, or anything else like that; and yet the impact of those emotions is profound and lasting. It is a very emotional song in which not one emotion is ever mentioned by word.

"The Gambler" outlines a whole philosophy of living. And if Don Schlitz, the writer, had gone at it directly, it could have been one of that year's ten worst songs. If, instead of telling us about when to "hold 'em" and when to "fold 'em," he'd said something like:

It's important to know when to persist in trying to achieve your goals and when to give up.

You have to know when to decide to give up what you're doing gradually and to know when to give up quickly.

You should never make a judgment about how your life is going while it's going on. There'll be plenty of time to look back to see how it all went after your life is over.

Those statements are an attempt at a straight, conceptual description of "The Gambler's" philosophy. It's what we all know he meant. But, obviously, the words are simply *poison* in terms of retaining our interest and involving us in the song. As ludicrous as the examples seem, many songwriters actually write their lyrics at this level of abstraction. The lyrics are accurate. They say what the songwriter wants to say. They have meter and rhyme. But they are extraordinarily uninvolving and boring.

Examine your songs rigorously to be sure you're not falling into the trap of settling for abstractions when you could express your abstractions in a way that would be alive and imaginable—preferably in the form of some kind of action—for the listener. Notice that "The Gambler" got its job done by delivering the abstraction but doing so using the action metaphor of a poker game. Also note that the song is one of the very few that went three verses before it got to the chorus, a tribute to the fact that *action* held our attention anyway.

The imagination is addicted to action. Notice in your imagination the difference between "the red brick" and "the brick flew toward the store window." It's not that the imagination cannot handle the idea of "the red brick." It's OK as images go. It has a color. It has a form with which we're all familiar. It's concrete (so to speak). You can feel it. You can see it. You might turn it around in your imagination and examine it and (with some encouragement) spend enough time to really get into its "brickness." But chances are, you'd get bored fast and lose interest.

That is because mental images have a rapid decay rate. Research shows that images last less than a second and, visually speaking, are not too clear in the first place. The picture in your "mind's eye" is somewhat granular (something like a snowy television picture) with best definition and clarity in the center of the picture and degeneration of that image away from the center. So we "see" our images for only a very short time and they are not too clear to start with. This is true for one image, for that one instant in time.

So to stay with that brick long enough to produce any involvement, one must re-create the image a number of times in succession. Re-creating the same image is not something the imagination does too eagerly. Try it and you'll see. The imagination quickly gets bored with the same item over and over again. And when the imagination gets bored, it wanders (away from your song).

What keeps the imagination on target and involved is action. The reason is that action demands change in an image—usually movement—and that allows the imagination to re-create a new image each time. This keeps the quality of imagery fresh and our involvement more complete. The image of the brick headed toward that store window is a cue for a whole series of images the imagination cannot resist.

Here's another experiment. Try to remember the last blue-eyed person you saw. Notice whether or not your imagination is re-creating that person in one image or in action. Are you not remembering your blue-eyed person *doing something?* Try the image in "freeze-frame" (no action) and notice how fast it fades away.

The only way the imagination can sustain an image is if that image involves some sort of action. Among other things, this is the problem the imagination has with abstractions: There's no action. They may suggest action, cause a desire for action, or even describe a whole series of actions, but an abstract word does not refer to action itself nor does it describe a specific action.

"Sorrow," for example, is a fairly specific abstraction, but it is not truly useful for producing an image. If the image of sorrow—the imagined *experience* of sorrow—is what you want to deliver, try "falling teardrops . . . aching feeling," "breaking

Mental images have a rapid decay rate. Research shows that images last less than a second and, visually speaking, are not too clear in the first place.

heart," and so forth. Such action words will produce the *experience* of "sorrow" and make your lyrics come alive—seem lifelike—in the listener's imagination. In a sense, because of the mental and physical effects of images, the good writer will allow the listener to *do* sorrow.

Hit writers understand this double need for action and abstraction and strive to combine the two:

"Take Your Memory With You When You Go"

"Stand Inside Your Love"

"Falling Away From Me"

Each title mentions the abstraction itself but gives it action metaphorically. Memory doesn't do anything, obviously; but in "Take Your Memory With You When You Go," Vince Gill said something that the imagination can do something with and thereby hooked the listener. Notice how much more alive that line is than "I Don't Want to Have to Think About You Anymore" or "When You Go, I'm Gonna Miss You." It's the action that hooks us.

The imagination functions at its best with simple images. This is implicit in the examples we've already seen. An image lasts in the mind for only a short time. The "field of image"—the vision of the "mind's eye"—resembles our true field of vision, with objects being clear toward the center and increasingly indistinct toward the edges. For these two reasons—its short "memory" and limited field of clear vision—the imagination engages best with *simple images*. It does its job best when requested to produce one, single object or action that it can place right in the center of its field of vision. Notice the ease with which you can produce the image: "Lipstick on Your Collar" vs. "The Marks of Cheating Are All Over You."

While some would-be hit writer might try her hand at that second line, as an image it is overly complex. The tendency of the imagination is to abandon the task if the image is too complex and varied. One "broken white feather" stays in your imagination far longer than "a flock of many colored seabirds." Specific, simple images get more mileage out of the imagination than groups of things do. It's why songs that deal with "I" or "you" (meaning a specific person) work better than "people" songs—"everybody" songs. Such message songs run the risk of providing too much for the imagination to handle. ("The Gambler" got away with it mostly because of the specific setting of a conversation between the old man and the singer and because of the specific imagery of a poker game.)

When imagery becomes too complex and varied, the imaging process is no longer free and experiential but rather becomes more like mental work. And mental work is not what the listener has in mind when she turns on the radio.

Look through your songs to find those places where you could narrow your images to one single item—one specific instance—one emotion—one moment in time. I know you're trying to sum up all of life and capture it in a three-minute pearl of wisdom. But, believe me, your goal will elude you if you try to do it in one song. A song that tells the truth about one simple moment in time can deliver the experience of living more vividly than all the writings of philosophers over the ages.

With all due deference to you poets out there, *life—moment to moment—is* outrageously simple. The imagination knows it. The listener knows it. Everybody knows it. So keep it simple. Cut narrow and cut deep.

The risk to the writer (and one of the reasons many writers avoid simplicity) is that simplicity and specificity render one vulnerable. Your simple song could be—and may be—simply awful (especially when you're trying out an unusual story, theme, plot, etc.). It's far safer to stick with tried-and-true banalities and abstractions that "sound like" other great songs you've heard.

The problem is that, while there is much to be learned from other songs, there is really no safe harbor for a songwriter. If he/she hides, so will the song.

So, say what you've got to say directly and take your lumps. You'll be surprised at how few lumps there are when you write "straight." It's part of growing professionally.

But don't write in code. Write "user-friendly" songs and remember that the users listen with their imaginations. Let them.

Enjoy.

Chris Blake has been a professional songwriter with many credits, a songwriting teacher, and has served as manager of Nashcal Music, the West Coast subsidiary of the Nashville-based Fischer Music Group. His songs have been recorded by Moe Bandy, Joe Stampley, John Conlee, Johnny Carver, Billy "Crash" Craddock, and others. Since the first edition of this book, he has immersed himself in university research in the study of the mind and the imagination.

chapter four

Writing Lyrics

When we think in terms of the world's population, there are very few people who have the opportunity and talent to communicate their feelings and opinions to anyone beyond their immediate family, friends, or co-workers. Politicians use the electronic media. Actors do, too, but they're usually speaking someone else's thoughts. Novelists and journalists, when they're allowed to speak freely, may reach a large audience, but its numbers are still fairly limited.

Radio, TV, and films have become the vehicle by which most people receive information from the rest of the world. These media share a form of communication that reaches and influences people all over the planet: music. As a skilled songwriter, you wield a tremendous power to communicate to millions of people. That realization (along with your desire to prove to your relatives that you can make a living at this) should make you want to do your best.

In this chapter I'll discuss various techniques and principles that will help you express your lyrics as effectively as possible so that when you get that opportunity to talk to the world, they'll love listening.

Simplicity

I asked hit producer John Ryan what he felt was one of the most important common denominators of successful songs. It was a question I had asked many others, and the reply is almost always the same:

> Simplicity—in saying something that everyone experiences in his or her life, but doesn't know quite how to say. You're taking a song out of your head and giving it to an artist or performing it yourself. Then you have to try to get someone else to receive your communication. You're not doing it just for yourself. *You want someone else to feel what you feel about life, maybe challenge them.*

When hit songwriter/producer/publisher Jack Keller was critiquing songs one night, he remarked to songwriters several times, "You've got too many ideas here. Focus on one idea, and build your song around it."

We've all read how-to manuals that say things like "insert the strand in the elliptical aperture," when they could say "put the thread through the hole in the needle" or "thread the needle." Applying that example to lyric writing, two common problems are saying more than you need and not saying clearly what you mean. Have you ever had a friend with whom you communicated so well that you could convey a whole idea in two words that would mean absolutely nothing to anyone else who heard them? Made you feel clever, didn't it? Sorry, but you can't bring that friend with you into the songwriting game. Instead of setting up a very private communication that excludes everyone else, the big game is to make yourself understood by as many listeners as possible.

A songwriter once played me five songs, none of which made any sense. She wanted to know why the songs didn't work for me. I read her back a few lines and asked what they meant. Some of her explanations were worth whole songs in themselves, but nowhere in what she had written could I make the connection until she told me the background. She had a song called "Geraldine" that made no sense until she told me that Geraldine was the name of a truck. I told her I thought it was a lesbian love song. The writer was intelligent and talented, but she was playing an intellectual game with her lyrics. She seemed to be saying, "How obtuse and clever and abstract can I make this so it's challenging to listen to?" The songs were so challenging, they weren't worth bothering to figure out.

Ironically, the most accessible lyric of the five was her first song, which she said was "too simple" for her and she didn't like much anymore. Those abstract lyrics in her other songs might work as poetry, since we could look at the words for as long as we needed to decipher the message. But when we also have music to focus on and the song is presented on a dance floor, a jukebox, or a car radio, tricky lyrics only make us feel as though we're missing something. She asked, "What about art? Do you think I should write commercial crap?" I said, "No thanks, we seem to have an overstock in that department. Think about the art of songwriting as the ability to communicate an idea or a feeling in a unique, interesting, enjoyable way."

If your lyric doesn't attempt to communicate, you're operating in a vacuum, which is fine if you just want to write for yourself. You can derive some benefits from keeping a personal diary, but if you want to make a living writing, your songs have to communicate their messages easily to others.

Focus

Another critical aspect of effective lyric writing is *focus. You should be able, in one word, to describe the emotion or mental state that a song expresses.* Happiness, sadness, love, hate, jealousy, and resentment are just some of the emotions we've all felt. Any of these could

You should be able, in one word, to describe the emotion or mental state that a song expresses.

Several basic questions will help you brainstorm an idea or bring the idea into focus after that initial inspiration:

Who is singing the song? Male? Female? You? Someone else?

What is the point of view? Someone who's been left? Someone who's leaving? Someone who's sad? Angry? Lonely? Happy?

Who is the song being sung to? A lover? Someone you'd like to meet? The general public? A friend? God?

What does the singer want to accomplish? To express love or other emotion? Give people a philosophy? Teach something? Criticize? Arouse?

As a purely commercial consideration, you should also ask: Is this a subject or attitude an artist, other than myself, would be interested in expressing? For example, if you write a song with the message "I'm a thoroughly despicable person," you have to ask yourself how many recording artists would want to record a song like that even if they believe it about themselves. Generally speaking, artists will stay away from songs that are depressing, express negative attitudes, or make them appear unlikable. Having said that, it can work to say, "I've done something terrible. Won't you please forgive me?" It's a staple of country writing, since both men and women, it seems, never get tired of hearing someone sing about how they made the biggest mistake of their lives when they did him/her wrong.

Listen to a few songs on the radio and write down one line for each that expresses what the song is about. Then do it with your own songs. If you have trouble condensing them, they're not focused.

be, in a broad sense, the subject of your song, provided you focus on specifics. Beginning songwriters tend to want to settle on the first thing that comes out of their heads whether it's focused or not. While it's a good idea to write all your thoughts down, you need to eventually zero in on a single idea. You may want to express that idea as a story or just explore different aspects of it. Many successful songs don't follow a linear "story line" or plot. But if you do write about a feeling, make it just one.

You should also be able, in a short phrase, to describe what the song is about. In chapter two, "Themes of Love," I listed several subject areas as they related to love relationships. "I think I've just found her (him)," "Remembering how it used to be," and "Cheating" all describe what a song is about.

Attitude, which in a songwriting context means an aggressively stated point of view, is another factor that requires consistency and focus. Though we most commonly find rock,

Generally speaking, artists will stay away from songs that are depressing, express negative attitudes, or make them appear unlikable.

rap, and hip-hop songs that express an attitude, it's very important in first-person songs (I, me, my) of any style. Alanis Morissette's songs have attitude. Listen to the attitude of Bonnie Raitt's "Something to Talk About," Toby Keith's "How Do You Like Me Now?," Destiny's Child's "Independent Women," Mary Chapin Carpenter's "He Thinks He'll Keep Her," and one of my favorites, Deana Carter's "Did I Shave My Legs for This?" If attitude is an important ingredient of your song, it needs to be consistently maintained by the lyrics and supported by the music.

Titles

A strong title can go a long way toward ensuring that industry people and the general public will remember your song.

Of course, you don't have to have a great title to have a hit song. Look at any list of Top 10 songs and you'll see titles that are dull and ordinary, as well as titles that are imaginative and intriguing. Some very intriguing titles have failed to live up to their promise in the body of the song musically or lyrically.

For the most part, if you're searching (as you should be) for a way to say something in a fresh and unusual way, you're likely to arrive at an imaginative title in the process. Concept and title are so wedded that, particularly in country music, many writers don't even begin to write a song until they have a great title/concept. It's a very common and practical way to start. Sometimes, if you have the right title, the song practically writes itself.

Pretend you're a publisher, producer, or artist with two demos in front of you, one called "I Love You" and another called "Silent Partners." Which one do you think you'd be most interested in hearing? You've already heard "I Love You" twenty times this month. You've never heard "Silent Partners," but it's an interesting concept that makes you start guessing right away what the song's about. If it's interesting to you, it might also interest a radio program director.

If you can come up with a short title phrase that embodies a concept, it's easier to focus your lyric from the beginning. Here are some hit titles that are intriguing in themselves: "She Talks to Angels," "Tears in Heaven," "Cleopatra's Cat," "Standing Outside the Fire," "Kryptonite." Some titles stick in the mind because of unusual word combinations: "Mandolin Rain" and "Silent Lucidity."

Not only is the *concept of* the title important, but you'll increase its memorability if it sounds "catchy." A "catchy" title has a combination of a pleasing meter and some poetic device like alliteration (a repetition of consonants)—"We Can Work It Out," "I Need to Know"—or assonance (repetition of vowel sounds)—"Achy Breaky Heart," "Boot Scootin' Boogie," "Show Me the Meaning of Being Lonely" (both)—or rhyme—"Okie From Muskogee."

Common phrases from everyday language also become more memorable in songs: "It's Always Somethin'," "Knock on Wood," "I Heard It Through the Grapevine," "She's All

That." Twists of common phrases also work: "Stop! In the Name of Love," "You Ain't Hurt Nothin Yet."

Aside from the benefits derived from a phrase that's catchy, clever, and conceptual, in most successful songs the real magic of the title comes from the way it fits with the music and is supported by the rest of the lyric. That combination can make an otherwise mundane title seem profound. City and state name titles are a good case in point. Randy Newman's "I Love L.A." and Billy Joel's "New York State Of Mind" could make someone feel nostalgic whether they'd been there or not. Hoagy Carmichael and Stewart Gorrell's classic "Georgia on My Mind" does the same.

Sometimes a musical figure or the emotional intensity of the music itself suggests a title. This is a spontaneous process that resembles a sort of musical Rorschach test: "What does this chord, riff, or melody make you think of?" It's a process in which the musician shuts down that very practiced intellectual approach and gets very close to his emotional core. A good groove can be hypnotic, put you in a mood, and trigger ideas and phrases that you might never come up with while you're staring at a piece of paper.

Place that good title in the strategic first or last line of your chorus (or verse, depending on the form), ensuring that it will be repeated several times during the song. You can then practically guarantee it will be remembered. If it's easy to remember, a potential record buyer knows what to ask for at the record store or on the radio request line. This is an important commercial consideration. Many potential hits may have been lost for lack of an obvious title in the right place.

Another commercial reason to craft a unique title is that, occasionally, a common one like "I Love You" gets mixed up with another song called "I Love You" and someone else gets your royalties through computer or human error. That's a fate neither you nor the other writer deserves.

First Lines

The first words from a singer's mouth are critical, particularly if they're the first words you've ever heard from that artist. It all goes into that evaluation you make as a listener about whether or not you like the record. So with your writer's hat on, think about how strongly you can interest the listener with that first line or lines. When a publisher or producer hears that first line, she's deciding whether to keep listening or turn it off, too. If it doesn't sell her, she's not optimistic about selling it to an artist. Don't fall prey to the temptation to start with "I'm just sittin' here (a) writing this song, (b) thinking about you, or (c) looking at the . . . " or "Woke up this mornin' . . . " (didn't we all?) or other equally uninteresting clichés. Though these might be penciled in to get your motor running, when you get down to a rewrite, they should be the first things that get penciled out.

Your first line should set the tone for the whole song and make us want to hear what comes next. You can set your first scene by asking several questions. Their answers will contribute to what you want your lyric to accomplish.

1. Where is it taking place? Is it important to the song? What kind of a place is it? Are there evocative features? If you allude to a particular country or city, the mountains, beach, etc., be careful of passive picture postcard openers that don't carry with them action, flavor, attitude, or emotional charge. "Ten miles west of Houston," "In a dirty downtown doorway," "At home in your love," "Halfway into Heaven" are all about places, either geographical or emotional.

2. Can the hour, day, season, or year offer a flavor that enhances the emotional impact of your song? Think of the number of songs that use "morning" or "night" to evoke a mood.

3. If the song is addressed to someone, is there something arresting you can say?

4. If the song is *about* someone, can you say something that immediately gives a picture or a quick personality sketch?

5. Is there an *active image* you can use? (See "The Imagination of the Listener," chapter three.)

6. If you're expressing an emotion, can you do it in a *poetic* or *dramatic* way? "I feel so out of place," for instance, just kind of lays there. Contrast that with George Gobel's old line, "The world's a tuxedo and I'm just a pair of brown shoes." Of course, that type of cleverness isn't always the answer—it depends on the tone you want to establish.

A listener should have the answers to the "who, what, when, and where" by the end of the first verse, as well as know the song's attitude and mood. But most importantly, the listener should be persuaded to keep listening, no matter how you accomplish it, with your lyric, your music, or better, by both.

Rhyme

I'd guess more than 99 percent of all commercially successful songs use rhyme. Why is it so important? What is it that makes rhymes work?

There's a reason why people still remember the nursery rhymes of childhood. The rhymes are strong and predictable and the meter is solid and consistent. Rhyme and meter, together, serve as a powerful memory trigger. How many lyrics do you think you'd remember if nothing rhymed? Rhyme has other values as well. It can create a sense of symmetry and completion, and it offers an opportunity to enhance the power of a line by giving it an established "stage" to deliver a payoff. Rhyme is a tool you can't afford to ignore. To drop it deliberately just to be different or to assume it's not

THE CRAFT AND BUSINESS OF SONGWRITING

important isn't a sensible attitude for someone who's trying to be a successful songwriter. Not that there aren't exceptions to the rule, but when you want the odds in your favor, you use every tool you have.

In musical theater, the rhymes are expected to be perfect (unless the character wouldn't rhyme perfectly). It's not so much a question of whether the rhymes work, but of how they're judged by critics who hold the power of life and death over a production. Musical theater boasts a long history of exceptional craftsmanship, and they aim to keep it that way. Whenever you start to think it's too hard or impossible to come up with perfect rhymes in a context that makes them feel perfectly natural, study the masters. For instance, listen to the songs in the Barbra Streisand film, "Yentl," for the work of lyricists Alan and Marilyn Bergman. We need such standards to remind us that it's still possible to put in the extra effort and come up with perfect rhymes without sacrificing naturalness.

Whenever you start to think it's too hard or impossible to come up with perfect rhymes in a context that makes them feel perfectly natural, study the masters.

ǀ Types Of Rhyme

Perfect: Stressed sound that ends the line is identical, preceding consonant is different: god/quad, action/fraction, variety/society. This is without question the most powerful rhyme you can use. There is an ongoing debate among writers about whether it is the only form of rhyme to be used. My feeling is that you should make every effort to find a perfect rhyme without having to alter the meaning of the line. If you can't find one, then opt for the next best.

Imperfect, near, false, slant, oblique, or **half-rhyme:** Common and quite acceptable in pop music. It approximates rhyme, and some would argue strongly that it shouldn't be called rhyme at all, but assonance. Anyway, let the nitpickers argue. Sometimes you just can't find a perfect rhyme to fit your meaning and you do find the imperfect "near" rhyme as in port/fourth, loss/wash, around/down, shaky/aching.

Masculine or **"one rhyme":** Single-syllable rhyme, as in pack/rack or a multisyllable word in which the last syllable rhymes, as in compromise/idolize.

Feminine or **"two rhyme":** Two-syllable rhymes, with the stress on the first. The vowels and inner consonants must match, as in maker/shaker, masquerading/ degrading.

Three rhyme: The last three syllables rhyme and the consonants that precede them differ, as in medium/tedium, facilitate/rehabilitate.

Open rhyme: Rhymes that don't end in hard consonants. Use them wherever possible on notes that are to be held, as in glow/snow, fly/try.

Closed or **stopped rhyme:** Rhymes that end in a consonant *(b, p, d, t, q,* and *k)* that makes us close our mouths and that can't be sustained when sung. *M, n, l,* and *r* can be sustained. *V, f, z,* and *s* can be sustained but don't sound very pleasant. *S*'s (sibilants) drive recording engineers crazy. Pay close attention to these "singability" factors as you write your lyrics.

Internal, **inner**, or **inside rhyme:** End rhyme, of course, occurs at the end of the line. Internal rhyme occurs within the line, as in "The *fate* of the *great state.*"

| Rhyme Schemes

To make rhyme work as a memory tool, you must be consistent. Once you establish a rhyme scheme for your verses, it's best to use the same pattern in all the verses. That same verse pattern in the choruses and bridge, however, could get monotonous, so it's better to establish one rhyme scheme for the verse, one for the chorus, and yet another for the bridge. You can introduce a subtle element of surprise this way without affecting the predictability of the song. Another way to surprise the listener is to either precipitate or delay the rhyme. It can be used with any rhyme scheme and the rhyme can occur at any of the underlined positions in the last line:

Ta TUM Ta TUM Ta TUM Ta

Ta TUM Ta TUM <u>Ta TUM</u>

Ta TUM Ta TUM Ta TUM Ta

<u>Ta TUM Ta TUM</u> Ta TUM <u>Ta TUM Ta TUM</u>

Here are the most common rhyme schemes:

1. a *more*   (Rhyming all four lines.) Usually too pre-
   a *score*   dictable. This gets old fast.
   a *floor*
   a *door*

2. a trust   (Rhyming second and fourth line.) Has
   b *guess*   flexibility and the element of predictability
   c hurt   (b) without the boredom.
   b *mess*

3. a luck   (Rhyming first and second lines, third and
   a stuck   fourth lines)
   b *brave*
   b *save*

4. a *able*   (Rhyming first, third, and fourth lines)
   b still
   a *cable*
   a *stable*

5. a *making*   (Rhyming first and third, second and
   b *good*   fourth lines)
   a *taking*
   b *could*

6. a *friend of mine* (Rhyming first and second lines)
   a *send a sign*
   b try

The following is an excerpt from Pat Pattison's *Writing Better Lyrics*, which offers alternatives to perfect rhyme. (For a complete and detailed exploration of rhyme types, read Pat Pattison's *Songwriting Essential Guide to Rhyming*. See Bibliography.)

Remember, lyrics are sung, not read or spoken. When you sing, you exaggerate vowels. And since rhyme is a vowel connection, lyricists can make sonic connections in ways other than perfect rhyme. Here are the most useful:

Family Rhyme

1. The syllables' vowel sounds are the same.
2. The consonant sounds after the vowels belong to the same phonetic families.
3. The sounds before the vowels are different.

Table of Family Rhymes

Here's a chart of the three important consonant families:

	PLOSIVES	FRICATIVES	NASALS
Voiced:	b d g	v TH z zh j	rn n ng
Unvoiced:	p t k	f th S sh ch	

Each of the three boxes—plosives, fricatives, and nasals—forms a phonetic family. When a word ends in a consonant in one of the boxes, you can use the other members of the family to find perfect rhyme substitutes.

Rub/up/thud/putt/bug/stuck are members of the same family plosives, so they are family rhymes.

Love/buzz/judge/fluff/fuss/hush/touch are members of the fricative family, so they rhyme. *Strum/run/sung* rhyme as members of the nasal family.

Say you want to rhyme line two, below:

Tire tracks across my face
I'm stuck in a rut

First, look up perfect rhymes for *rut, cut, glut, gut, hut, shut.*

The trick to saying something you mean is to expand your alternatives. Look at the Table of Family Rhymes and introduce yourself to t's relatives:

Ud	uk	ub	up	Ug
blood	buck	club	hard up	bug
flood	duck	hub	makeup	jug
mud	luck	pub	cup	unplug
stud	muck	scrub		plug
thud	stuck	tub		shrug
	truck			snug
				tug

Continued on page 66

Continued from page 65

Much better. That's a lot of interesting stuff to say no to. Now, how about this:

Tire tracks across my back
There's nowhere I feel safe

First, look up perfect rhymes for *safe* in your rhyming dictionary. All we get is *waif*. Not much. Now look for family rhymes under *f*'s family, the *fricatives*. We add these possibilities:

as	av	az	aj
case	behave	blaze	age
ace	brave	craze	cage
breathing-	cave	daze	page
space	grave	haze	rage
chase	shave	phrase	stage
face	slave	paraphrase	
disgrace	wave	praise	**aTH**
embrace			bathe
grace	**ath**		
lace	faith		
resting-place			
space			

Finally, nasals. The word "nasals" means what you think it means. All the sound comes out of your nose.

Tire tracks across my head
Pounding like a drum

Look up perfect rhymes for *drum:* hum, pendulum, numb, slum, strum.

Go to the Table of Family Rhymes and introduce yourself to *m*'s relatives:

un	ung
fun	hung
gun	flung
overrun	wrung
won	sung
jettison	
skeleton	

Finding family rhyme isn't hard, and its rewards are amazing. So there's no reason to tie yourself in knots using only perfect rhyme when family rhyme sounds so close. When sung, the ear won't know the difference.

7. a *when*   (Rhyming first, second, and third lines)
    a *then*   or
    a *men*
    c *know*   (First, second, and third PLUS last lines
    b *stand*   adjoining verses)
    b *band*
    b *land*
    c *show*

There are other variations. These forms are often doubled, for instance. Given that one of their functions is to help us remember, rhymes in any consistent position in the line may work. In the English language, though, there is an expectation that the *primary* rhymes come at the ends of the lines. Because they're in a powerful position, it becomes more important that they enhance or at least don't distract the listener from the mood and meaning of the song.

Some Common Problems With Rhyme

A common failing among songwriters is to say what you want to say in the first two lines and, instead of finding an equally strong statement to finish the verse, settling for a weaker line for the sake of the rhyme. Sure, you save some work, but you've also effectively weakened your song. Better to have written several versions of the first two lines to come up with an end word that offered more rhyming possibilities. Don't reach for the easy rhyme if it dilutes your efforts, and beware of these possible rhyming pitfalls:

INVERSIONS

Inversions involve twisting the order of words to use a rhyme that wouldn't naturally occur at that point. It almost always feels awkward. Here's an example:

I never knew how much I'd missed
Until your candy lips I kissed

In this situation, I'd go for "lips" as the end rhyme, even though it lacks the perfection of "missed/kissed." "Till I kissed your candy lips" just feels more natural.

IDENTITIES

Identities are not rhymes. Identities are: the same words, words with the same consonant preceding the same final sound (buy/good-bye), words that sound identical even though spelled differently (homonyms) like "bear" and "bare," "no" and "know." You won't get arrested for doing this; it's just lazy writing. Common exceptions include building of parallel constructions like "Gonna talk about it/Gonna shout about it/Gonna sing about it/There's no doubt about it," which uses the "shout/doubt" rhyme before the last word.

Also acceptable is the repetition of a variation of a line for emphasis: "Goin' downtown, goin' way downtown."

SLANG

Slang is a great source of new rhymes, and many hits are based on slang words and expressions. The only drawback is if you're trying to write a song people will record twenty years from now. By then, the slang we use today may sound really dumb. Would anybody record a song today with the thirties' "the cat's meow" or "twenty-three skidoo" in it? "Groovy" puts it squarely in the sixties.

COLLOQUIAL PRONUNCIATION

Colloquial pronunciation has a problem similar to slang. Here the drawback is not change in fashion, but the reduced ability of other artists to record the song. It's good to be able to tailor a song to a particular musical style, like country or R&B, and use the pronunciations common in that style (e.g., to rhyme *thang* (thing) with *hang*, or *pain* and *again*). But bear in mind, you're limiting the coverage of those songs to artists who are comfortable with those styles and pronunciations.

| The Exceptions

We hear more songs these days that don't rhyme. In most cases, they're from self-contained bands. They write their own material and aren't that interested in having other artists record the songs. Because they aren't exposed to the same industry scrutiny, they have a more wide-ranging creative palette from which to paint their songs. More power to them. If you can get your message across to your audience without the use of rhyme, there's no rule that says you have to use it. Be aware, though, that laziness is not a good enough reason to ignore a powerful tool.

Even in pop music there are examples of songs that don't use rhyme. The standard "Moonlight in Vermont" is a good example; Lionel Richie's "Lady," a major hit for both him and Kenny Rogers in the eighties doesn't rhyme. So, why do they work? There are several possibilities:

1. They're both exceptional melodies;

2. one of rhyme's functions is to help us remember the lyric, and both of those lyrics, especially "Moonlight in Vermont," are simple enough to remember without it;

3. in the case of "Lady," the melody's construction is such that it doesn't, through rhythm and meter, set up a *rhyme expectation*, so we don't ever miss it.

The constant creative challenge is to find the best rhymes possible and still retain the flow of natural speech patterns, while at the same time not compromising content and mood. If you read the lines aloud, they should feel as natural as conversation. Every line presents a new challenge and it may be that, after exploring the possibilities, you'll need to choose a less-than-perfect rhyme. It's more important that you opt for naturalness, mood, or clarity of content over convenience or cleverness for its own sake.

| Rhyming Dictionaries and Thesauruses

Some writers look at rhyming dictionaries as a crutch, as though it were cheating to use one. If you've been writing for any time at all, you probably know the most natural possibilities for rhyme. But when you're really stuck, it's always good to know that there's somewhere you can go quickly to make sure you have the best rhyme possible for the line. I've also run across rhymes in these sources that instigated a whole new thought pattern. The human mind has such wonderful facility for "connecting the dots" between seemingly unrelated images and words that anything you feed it can become an ingredient for something new.

A friend of mine once put a few hundred descriptive adjectives in his computer and just ran them through to fill in the blank in a line. The results were often comical, occasionally profound, and usually words that he would have had difficulty coming up with "off the top of his head." This is one of the things a good rhyming dictionary can do for you. And the more you use it, the more you develop a storehouse of rhyme possibilities in your mind.

All rhyming dictionaries contain thousands of words that you'd never use in a song. You'll also be able to come up with colloquialisms that aren't in the dictionaries and make up your own words, so don't let yourself get too attached. *The Modern Rhyming Dictionary* by pro lyricist Gene Lees and Clement Wood's *The Complete Rhyming Dictionary* are both good sources.

If you use a computer, there are very fast and efficient software rhyming dictionaries available. Among the best are:

RhymeWizard

www.rhymewizard.com

A Zillion Kajillion Rhymes & Clichés

www.eccentricsoftware.com

Find others by searching the Internet under "songwriters rhyming dictionary."

When you're looking for a particular word and can only come up with a word that's somewhere in the neighborhood, you need a thesaurus. It will give you words or phrases that mean the same or almost the same thing (synonyms) or the opposite (antonyms) as well as words and phrases that are only remotely related. It incorporates slang and lists words by part of speech. Using a thesaurus is like a treasure hunt in which each new discovery can send you on yet another exciting journey. It's an indispensable tool. *Roget's International* is my favorite. Microsoft Word and other word processing programs also contain thesauruses.

Using a thesaurus is like a treasure hunt in which each new discovery can send you on yet another exciting journey. It's an indispensable tool.

Poetic Devices

The great poets have used many devices throughout history that are regularly put to work by songwriters in the service of a great lyric. At their best, these devices go consciously unnoticed, like the subtle spices in a gourmet dish. Though you might not identify them right away, you know that without them the dish wouldn't taste nearly as good. Only when the chef tells you what the spices are, do you start to separate and recognize them in the overall taste. That's ideally what poetic devices should do. Our attention should not be pulled from the overall meaning and flow of the lyric to these devices. If they're overused or too obvious, our attention goes to them. They say, "Look here, see how I did this! Clever, eh?"

The skill of contemporary writers is in achieving the naturalness of common speech and using the devices in a subtle way. Here are some of the most common ones:

Alliteration is the repetition of accented consonants. This is a device that can get ridiculous if carried to extremes, but if used with taste, can be subtly effective. Dan Fogelberg in "Same Old Lang Syne" writes "She would have liked to say she loved the man, but she didn't like to lie."

Assonance is when the stressed vowels in a word agree, but the preceding consonants do not, as in "You won't be going home."

Similes are comparisons using the word "as" or "like." "Straight *as* an arrow," "hard *as* a rock," and "sleeping *like* a log." Don't settle for these commonplace clichés, though. If something comes to your mind that you've heard before, try a new one.

Metaphors are also comparisons that don't depend on "like" or "as." Paul Simon's "I Am a Rock" is an example. It would have been a simile if it had been written "I'm Like a Rock," but it would not have been nearly as effective.

Allegory is a device that allows the writer to treat an abstract idea with concrete imagery. In other words, you can tell a story on both material and symbolic levels. Paul McCartney's "Ebony and Ivory" used the image of black and white piano keys working together as an allegory for racial harmony.

Personification is attributing human characteristics to inanimate objects: "When the ground started rolling, I heard the buildings scream."

Hyperbole is an obvious exaggeration to drive home a point. The Beatles' "Eight Days a Week" is an example. "You're a hurricane" is both hyperbole and a metaphor.

Irony is saying the opposite of what you mean or pointing up the incongruities of a situation. Paul Simon used irony in "7 O'clock News/Silent Night" by juxtaposing the Christmas classic over news reports of war atrocities.

Antithesis sets two opposing ideas against each other for contrast. Michael Hazelwood and Albert Hammond's "It Never Rains in Southern California" ("it pours") worked effectively this way.

Characterization is the creation and representation of convincing characters. Always look for a line of dialogue or an image that says a lot more about the character or situation.

In Lennon and McCartney's "Eleanor Rigby," we see three beautifully concise character studies. Jerry Jeff Walker's "Mr. Bojangles" is a beautiful example of characterization. Janis Ian's "At Seventeen" was a masterful character study. Even though it contained very personal details, the way Ian wrote it allowed us to experience once again the often agonizing process of growing up. Eminem's "Stan" creates a believable interaction between his character, Slim Shady, and a fan.

Problems With Pronouns

One of the most common problem areas in lyric writing is the use of pronouns. Pronouns take the place of both proper nouns (Paul Simon, Los Angeles, Laurel Canyon) and common nouns (songwriter, city, canyon). The words pronouns replace are referred to as "principals." Here are five rules for the use of pronouns, all established in the interest of clarity:

1. Make it clear what the pronoun you're using is a substitute *for*.

2. The principal must be close by so the listener doesn't get confused about what the pronoun stands for.

3. Avoid putting two principals close by, or the listener won't know which one the pronoun represents. "When John talked to Joe, he realized that he was getting old but not wise." Was it John or Joe who was getting old?

4. Avoid having one pronoun represent two principals at once. "He was rich, but he was poor." Was principal no.1 rich and principal no. 2 poor, or is there only one principal involved?

5. If possible, avoid placing the pronoun before its principal. "She heard the message he delivered but didn't believe the messenger." It takes the listener a few seconds to make the connection that "he" is the messenger.

Be very careful about the number of pronouns you use in a song. Without realizing it, you can create a maze in which only you know who's saying what and to whom. "She said she thought he loved her more than she loved him, and she wouldn't recommend that he move in." There are at least three different ways that line could be interpreted. If you can read the line at your leisure, you can probably figure them out; but when the line goes by in seven seconds in a song, you're in trouble.

On the other hand, pronouns serve a valuable function when they're used properly. They can help to guide the listener away from vagueness by letting them know exactly who is saying or doing what.

| Point of View

Pronouns are important in establishing point of view. Certain creative decisions need to be made by the songwriter. The options are:

1. Relating the song in the first person (I, me, we).

   "I was on my way to nowhere."

Be very careful about the number of pronouns you use in a song. Without realizing it, you can create a maze in which only you know who's saying what and to whom.

2. Having the singer address the song to the second person (you).

"*You Are So Beautiful.*"

3. Third person is relating a song about something or someone else (he, him, she, her, it, they, them).

"*He was a high school hero in a one horse town.*"

The choices you make are based on clarity and impact. For instance, it's usually very effective to deliver a heavy philosophical message in the first person ("Here's what happened to me") or in the third person, in which you tell a story about someone else and we understand the message in our own way. Second-person messages ("You should . . .") can alienate the singer from the listener by implying that "I don't need this message but *you* do"; but second-person positive sentiments ("you're wonderful," "you deserve the best") are very powerful.

Some writers use "you" as a substitute for "I" in a rhetorical sort of way. "What do you do when you fall in love with someone you can't have?" We read this as "What do I do . . . ?" The approach puts distance between the singer and a hurtful problem by using "you" instead of "I." There's no wrong or right here. The impact of the pronoun you choose can vary with each song. It's always a good idea to check out all the possibilities to create the most powerful emotional statement. "I can't pretend that I don't hurt" may be better than "You can't pretend that you don't hurt" because, when the listener sings along, he is singing about himself rather than an anonymous "you."

The most commonsense rule to follow in all of this is to try to put yourself in the listener's place, no matter how emotionally involved you may be in expressing your personal feelings. It's a difficult thing to do in the heat of passionate inspiration, so it's best to put a song away for a few days to allow yourself to look at it more objectively. To study this more closely, try the point-of-view exercise on page 76.

For an in-depth look at the psychological principles in the effectiveness of visual imagery and figurative language, see "The Imagination of the Listener," chapter three.

When the listener sings along, he is singing about himself rather than an anonymous "you."

Prosody and Meter

Prosody is the agreement of lyric and music. If the lyric has an "up," positive message, it would generally be unwise to use a melody in a minor key. Minor chords are used better in songs of pain, longing, despair, loss, and sadness.

Ideally, you want the emotional tone of the music to enhance the message of the lyric. It's possible, however, that your message might be enhanced by doing just the opposite of what feels natural, for effect, as with Bertolt Brecht and Kurt Weill's "Mack the Knife." But that should be a conscious choice, not an accident.

If Jim Webb had written the melody to the line "Up, Up and Away" or Curtis Mayfield to the line "Move On Up" as a series of *descending* notes, the result would have sounded ludicrous. That's the extreme, but it's a graphic example of the importance of prosody.

Other factors also contribute to good prosody. Watch for combinations of words that could be *heard* as other words. "What do I know?" "What a wino?" "Let the winds take hold," "Let the wind stay cold," " 'Scuse me while I kiss the sky," " 'Scuse me while I kiss this guy" (which became the title of a very funny book, *'Scuse Me . . . While I Kiss This Guy: And Other Misheard Lyrics* by Gavin Edwards).

A similar problem exists with adjoining words that end and begin with the same sound. The phrases "teach children" and "strange journey" will give a good singer an anxiety attack unless there's plenty of space in between to allow the tongue to recover. Anyway, I'm sure you get my point. Make certain that what a listener hears is what you *want* them to hear and that the singer can easily sing what you write.

The best way to make sure your lyrics will sing well is to sing them as you write them. Sing your lyrics at the tempo they'll be performed. Words may look fine on paper or sing easily at a slow tempo but will tie a singer's tongue in knots when you increase the tempo even a little. If the words feel at all awkward in your mouth or don't sing smoothly, change them.

Some words like "long" and "cool" carry their own emotional meanings that feel wrong when sung over short, choppy notes. Action words like "jump," "run," "crash," and "flash" may feel out of place in a slow ballad but right at home in a high-intensity rocker.

One of the most important tools in the service of prosody is lyric meter. Its skilled use allows you to *emphasize natural speech patterns and tie them effectively to the musical pulse and melody*. It helps make the words fit comfortably with the music without putting the accents on the wrong syllables or squeezing too many words into too little musical space.

If you were paying attention in English class instead of daydreaming about being a rock star, you would probably already know about what follows. You just didn't think you'd ever need to use it, right?

Why do you need to know about meter? You may not need to remember the names of the patterns, but you should know that they are options to be considered and that they can be used for emotional effect and for variety. Few things are more deadly than an entire lyric in perfect iambic pentameter, and the melodies to those lyrics don't usually save them. When was the last time, by the way, that you heard someone use iambic pentameter in a conversation? So let's go back to English class again.

The groupings of stressed and unstressed syllables and words are called "metric feet." We usually hear them in groups of two or three. Those most commonly used in poetry and lyric are:

Make certain that what a listener hears is what you *want* them to hear and that the singer can easily sing what you write.

Name of Foot	Scansion	Examples	Accent
iamb	⏑ ´	ĭn-sáne, gŏod-bý, tŏ-níght, fŏr góod	ta TUM
trochee	´ ⏑	héal-thў, lóv-ĕr, ḿo-nĕy	TUM ta
anapest	⏑ ⏑ ´	gŏ-ĭng óut, ḿa-kĭng sénse, ŭn-dĕr-stánd	ta ta TUM
dactyl	´ ⏑ ⏑	ṕo-ĕ-trў, úl-tĭ-măte, Í'm ŏ-kăy, yóu're ŏ-kăy	TUM ta ta
spondee	´ ´	dówn-tówn, stár-shíp, héad-lóng	TUM TUM
amphibrach	⏑ ´ ⏑	bĕ-líev-ĭng, cŏn-cérn-ĭng, Ĭ lóve ĭt	ta TUM ta

The emotional impact of a song can be greatly influenced by your choice of meter. Spondees (TUM TUM) have a very deliberate feeling. Iambic pentameter (Ta TUM/ta TUM/ta TUM/ta TUM/ta TUM) is the most commonly used meter and has a long history in English poetry, probably because it's closest to human speech. It's good for seriousness. So are dactyls (TUM ta ta). Three-foot meters, particularly anapests, have a lightness about them that doesn't suit them for particularly heavy subject matter (Ta ta TUM/ta ta TUM/ta ta TUM).

Though overuse of the same meter can be monotonous, just enough repetition can create tension to set a listener up for a dynamic change of meter.

In songwriting, you need to repeat the metric feet in a way that not only makes them fit comfortably with the musical pulse, but *emphasizes the intended meaning of the lyric.* As an illustration, let's take a line that could have several meanings and "work it" to find its best setting:

I **need**/you **in**/my **life**/ (Iambic)	A duple meter (two syllables per foot) emphasizing "need," "in," and "life." "In" doesn't take the emphasis particularly well because it's a weaker word.
or **I** need/**you** in/**my** life/ (Trochee)	Another duple meter emphasizing "I," "you," "my." Feels more natural.
I need **you**/in my **life**/ (Anapest)	A triple meter (three syllables per foot) emphasizing "you" and "life."
or I **need** you/in **my** life/ (Amphibrach)	Emphasizing "need" and "my."

Depending on the length of notes and rests, these versions could be done in either 4/4 or 3/4 time.

Try your own melodies with these variations. Sing them out loud. You'll find your melodies changing with each variation to *accommodate the meaning of the line and the musical meter.* This is a process that should happen regardless of whether you're writing a melody to lyric, lyric to melody, or lyric alone. Once you get used to it, the process goes very quickly.

Let's try a straight 4/4 with equal emphasis on each note.

| ```
     1  2  3  4     1  2  3  4
4/4  /  /  /  /     /  /  /  /
     I need you in    my life
``` | It feels a little stiff this way and "life" held this long is a little strained. Better to make "life" a beat shorter and end in a rest. |
```

How about emphasizing 1 and 3?

	1	2	3	4		1	2	3	4
4/4	/	-	/	-		/	-	/	-
	I	*need* you	*in*	my	*life*

Not bad, but it would again be awkward to hold "life." You can also add to the emphasis of "you" by raising the melody on that word.

Still emphasizing 1 and 3, you can use a "pickup," starting the lyric before the downbeat.

	1	2	3	4		1	2	3	4
4/4	/	-	/	-		/	-	/	-
I	need	*you*	in	*my*	life

This gives you the chance to use the accents *and* maintain your choice of emphasis.

	1	and	2	and		3	and	4	and
2/4	/	-	/	-		-	-
I	need	*you*	*in*	*my*	life

By using eighth notes, you can emphasize "need" and "life." It also gives the line more urgency.

Let's try leaning on the backbeat, 2 and 4:

	1	2	3	4		1	2	3	4
4/4	-	/	-	/		-	/	-	/
	I	need	*you*	in		*my*	life

We're still accenting the "in" here, but can de-emphasize it by raising the melody on both "need" and "life."

Still accenting the backbeat, you can delay the line and try an eighth note feel again.

	1	and	2	and	3	and	4	and
4/4	-	-	/	-	-	-	/	-
	I	need	*you*	*in*	*my*	life

This one feels good too.

Now let's switch to 3/4 waltz time:

	1	2	3		1	2	3
3/4	-	-	/		-	-	/
	I	*need* you		*in*	*my*	life

A little stiff—too predictable

	1	2	3	1	2	3	1	2	3
3/4	-	/	-	-	/	-	-	/	-
	I	need	*you*	in	*my*	life

A little smoother with more room for a singer to play with the words.

```
     1   2   3   1   2   3   1   2   3      More interesting, less predictable
3/4  /   /   -   /   /   -   /   -   -
     I  need you  in  my        life
```

or with a pickup . . .

```
     1   2   3   1   2   3   1   2   3      Again, more interesting with room for a
3/4  /   -   -   /   /   -   /   -   -      singer to move.
     I  need      you  in  my      life
```

In this chapter, I've explored the major areas that concern you as a lyric writer. There's a lot more to learn. If you're serious about being a songwriter, you'll read everything you can on the subject (see the Bibliography for some suggestions), but there's no better and faster way to improve than to write constantly. When you do, you'll create your own examples and encounter problems that will give a practical context to what you read.

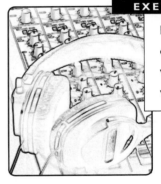

EXERCISE

Look at the lyrics for your favorite songs. If it's in first person, change it to second or third person. If it's in third person, change it to first or second, etc. Think about which one seems to have the most impact for you. You'll usually discover why the writer chose to do it that way. Now do the same for your own lyrics.

chapter five

Constructing a Song:

Words and Music Together

No matter how creative and powerful lyrics or melodies may be by themselves, they take on a whole new life and a whole new power and magic when they're together. The song is greater than the sum of its parts. Whether you're a specialist at one or the other or a genius at both, an essential aspect of your craft is understanding how to make the parts fit together to create that magic. In this chapter I'll cover the elements of songwriting that relate most to words and music as a whole.

Form

The form, also called the "format" or "structure," is a song's basic shape or organization. In this section, I'll examine and explain:

1. how a song's basic components—verses, choruses, bridges, and pre-choruses—work together to keep a listener's interest;
2. a song's basic forms and variations and their best uses;
3. how to analyze form so you can keep up with contemporary trends.

In the fifties and early sixties, there were hardly more than three different chord progressions (formulas) for any kind of popular music. If a song didn't conform to one of them, the odds were heavily against its becoming a hit, so the chord progression formulas perpetuated themselves. The 1-6m-4-5 (e.g., C Am F G) progression spawned hundreds of hits like "26 Miles," "Silhouettes," and "Earth Angel." The twelve-bar blues format was also popular as it laid the foundations for rock and roll (e.g., E (4 bars) A (2 bars) E (2 bars) B7 (1 bar) A (1 bar) E (2 bars)).

Those old progressions are familiar enough to make us feel at home with new songs and new artists. They're predictable: The chords, the words, and the tunes are different, but the basic shape of the songs is the same, so we can learn them quickly. Some basic forms and variations will continue as they have for many, many years for a simple reason: They work.

People have an unconscious desire for symmetry, and the repetition of rhyme, melody, and form satisfies that need. The repetition of form also sets up a degree of predictability that's reassuring and comfortable to a listener. It sets up a solid base on which we can create surprises without taking our audience too far into uncharted territory.

The manipulation of form is a very important game to know. Classical musicians learn form as a basic part of their training; and for you, as a popular songwriter, to be able to make conscious choices about form is to be in control of your art. Once you understand the elements of form, what they do and why, you'll be able to challenge yourself to go beyond the familiar as you write your own songs.

The Components of Form

VERSE

The verse is the major vehicle for conveying the information of the song. Its other major function, both lyrically and musically, is to "set up" (or lead to) the chorus, the bridge, another verse, or a title/hook line. If it doesn't do one of those things well, it's not working. Verses have certain basic characteristics:

1. The lyric, from verse to verse, is different or contains substantial new information each time. It may contain elements of previous verses (such as the title line if the song has no chorus).

2. The melody is essentially the same each time we hear it, although there is room for variation and some flexibility to accommodate the lyric. The reason for keeping the melody the same is because that familiarity makes it easier for the listener to focus on the changing lyric.

CHORUS

In contemporary songwriting, the chorus (sometimes incorrectly referred to as a "refrain") focuses the essence, emotion, and meaning of the song into a simple and easily remembered statement, like "I Can Love You Like That," "Mo Money Mo Problems," or "You Were Meant for Me." The chorus is also usually the segment of the song often referred to as the "hook" (i.e., the catchiest, most memorable part of the song). While verses usually concentrate on detail, the chorus can make a broader statement that bears more repetition. The basic characteristics of the chorus are:

1. The melody is the same each time we hear it.

2. The song's title usually appears in the first and/or last line, and possibly more.

3. The lyric is usually the same each time, although you may want to use some new lyric information in subsequent choruses to develop the story. A good example of that would be a "turnaround": a tactic commonly used in country music, where the "twist" is not revealed until the last chorus.

An example of a song with a chorus that changes every time but still works well is Blessed Union of Souls' "I Wanna Be There." It has an eight-line chorus that repeats the title at the beginning of lines 1, 2, 4, 5, and 8, with the rest of the chorus lyric changing in every verse. A title repeated that many times guarantees that a listener has something to sing along with and can easily learn. It also allows the writers to change other information in the chorus without worrying about losing their listeners.

Even though there may be reasons for you to change the lyric, there is a very practical reason for you to keep at least a substantial part of it the same: You want listeners to learn your song quickly and easily. If they hear the same chorus three times during the song, they can go away singing it. If you change all or even some of the lyric and music on each chorus, you make it harder for the listener to remember. If you have information in the verses that you want people to think about, the chorus should let a listener relax with its simplicity to allow the verse information to sink in. Be aware that, in a song, the listener's attention is divided between the lyric and the music, making it extra important to retain simplicity. So even when you feel you need to change the chorus lyric, a substantial amount of it—particularly the title line—should remain the same and be repeated every time.

You want listeners to learn your song quickly and easily. If they hear the same chorus three times during the song, they can go away singing it.

BRIDGE

Also called a "release," "break," or "middle eight," the bridge provides a variety of important functions in a song. Musically, it helps to relieve the "boredom factor," and for that reason, it's usually placed about two-thirds of the way into the song (after the second chorus in a verse/chorus form), which is normally when people may begin to tire of melodic repetition. The bridge zaps the listener back to attention, helps her to refocus on the song, and can add drama in many other ways. Musically, you can employ any device used to achieve contrast described in the "Song Dynamics" segment that we'll get to later.

The bridge can also be purely instrumental. The melody should sound as different as possible without sounding like it belongs in a different song. Lyrically, it offers you the opportunity to change gears. You can reiterate the philosophy of the song in a whole new way by changing the "person" (going from "they" or "you" to "I," for example), going from specific imagery to something more abstract (or vice versa), or using it as an "aside" or for outside commentary. The basic characteristics of a bridge are:

1. Its melody is different from the verse and the chorus, although occasionally a portion of the verse or chorus melody may be used in the bridge.

2. It usually doesn't contain the title and/or hook, but that's certainly not the law. That decision may depend on how many times you have repeated the title/hook in the song. If you haven't done it much, it might be wise to use it again.

3. It usually occurs only once in the song, but it can be repeated in an extended verse/chorus form. Two things prevent that kind of bridge from sounding like a chorus:

   a. it usually doesn't contain the title and/or hook, and

   b. if it is constructed correctly, its melody leads back into the verse or chorus.

4. It is rarely over eight bars long. After all, it's supposed to be a diversion, not a whole piece in itself. It may be two bars, two lines, or whatever is needed to fulfill the function of breaking up the song.

5. It is entirely optional.

You're most likely to want a bridge if you have a lot of melodic repetition in your verses and choruses. The more repetition, the more you risk inducing boredom, and bridges are great "boredom busters."

PRE-CHORUS

Pre-choruses are melodic segments that are different from the verses, chorus, or bridge. They are known by many other names (climb, lift, channel, B-section, pre-hook, setup), all of which give you clues to their function. They're used extensively in contemporary music—primarily in pop and R&B/hip-hop—although they've been gaining popularity in country/pop. Producers seem to favor pre-choruses to help create an additional level of interest to keep a song exciting, particularly in up-tempo or dance songs where extra length and faster tempo make a straight verse/chorus form feel too repetitive.

When you first hear a pre-chorus, it almost sounds as if it is going to be the chorus, until you hear the chorus that follows. It should increase the tension to the point where there is a great sense of release going into the chorus. Some examples of hits that use a pre-chorus are: "End of the Road," Boyz II Men (written by Kenneth "Babyface" Edmonds, Antonio Reid, Daryl Simmons); "Any Man of Mine," Shania Twain (Robert John Lange, Shania Twain); "I Can Love You Like That," All-4-One, John Michael Montgomery (Steve Diamond, Jennifer Kimball, Maribeth Derry); "Every Day Is a Winding Road" Sheryl Crow (Sheryl Crow, Jeff Trott, Brian Macleod).

The basic characteristics of pre-choruses are:

1. They directly precede the chorus.

2. They usually precede *each* chorus, but may be dropped after the first couple of times if you can find a way (musically) to get back to the chorus without it.

3. Lyrics can be the same each time or different. Melodies are the same each time.

4. The length varies, like the bridge, from one line to four. Pre-choruses usually last no longer than eight bars.

5. Musically, they build tension to increase the feeling of release in the chorus.

Here's a classic example of a country/pop crossover hit by Faith Hill that uses a pre-chorus.

"This Kiss"

BETH NIELSEN CHAPMAN/ROBIN LERNER/ANNIE ROBOFF

Verse   *I don't want another heartbreak*

I don't need another turn to cry

I don't want to learn the hard way

Baby Hello, oh no, goodbye

But you got me like a rocket

Shooting straight across the sky . . .

Pre-chorus	*It's the way you love me*
	It's a feeling like this—
	It's centrifugal motion
	It's perpetual bliss.
	It's that pivotal moment
	It's, ahhh, impossible
Chorus	*This Kiss, This Kiss*
	Unstoppable
	This Kiss, This Kiss
Verse	*Cinderella said to Snow White*
	How does love get so off course?
	All I wanted was a white knight
	With a good heart, soft touch, fast horse.
	Ride me off into the sunset
	Baby, I'm forever yours
Pre-chorus	*It's the way you love me*
	It's a feeling like this—
	It's centrifugal motion
	It's perpetual bliss.
	It's that pivotal moment
	It's, ahhh, unthinkable
Chorus	*This Kiss, This Kiss*
	Unsinkable
	This Kiss, This Kiss
Verse	*You can kiss me in the moonlight*
	On the rooftop under the sky
	You can kiss me with the windows open
	While the rain comes pouring inside
	Kiss me in sweet slow motion
	Let's let every thing slide
	You got me floating, You got me flying.
Pre-chorus	*It's the way you love me*
	It's a feeling like this—
	It's centrifugal motion
	It's perpetual bliss.

It's that pivotal moment
It's, ahhh, subliminal

Chorus   *This Kiss, This Kiss*
                   It's criminal
                   This Kiss, This Kiss

Several different factors make this work:

1. Each section of the song's three sections has a separate melody. This fact diminishes the need for a bridge because there's already a variety of melodic changes to hold the listener's interest.

2. Each section has a totally different lyric meter (see "Dynamics"). Again, this gets the audience attention with each change.

3. The pre-chorus is made up of a series of short lines. The repetition of those lines sets up a tension that begins to release in the last line of the pre-chorus where the lyric meter changes, "setting up" the chorus, signaling for us to join in. Notice that there are three repetitions of the two-line melody in the pre-chorus. Groups of three are a particularly powerful setup to make the last line of the third repeat pay off strongly.

| Analyzing Form

Before getting into the forms themselves, I'll explain how you can analyze the song forms you hear.

To start, consider the first melodic segment you hear (not including the intro) as "A." The next complete melodic section that has a melody different from "A" is designated "B," the third "C," etc. Repeats of any melodic segment get the same letter they got the first time.

Count bars or measures starting at the downbeat as follows:

For 4/4 time: **1**-2-3-4, **2**-2-3-4, **3**-2-3-4, **4**-2-3-4, etc.

For 3/4 waltz time: **1**-2-3, **2**-2-3, **3**-2-3, **4**-2-3, etc.

When the next melodic segment starts, begin counting at bar one again. Enter the total number of bars in each segment. Be sure to include any instrumental breaks, using "inst." or a dash or some other shorthand to designate them, along with the number of bars they run. You'll end up with a diagram that looks like this:

A-8, A-8, B-8, A-8

or

A A B A   or   A B C   ins   A B C
8 8 8 8   8 8 8   2   8 8 8

Here's a more graphic way to lay it out quickly so you can easily add extra bars and make notes. Each of the slash notes represents a beat (in 4/4 time).

```
INTRO   1 / / / 2 / / / 3 / / / 4 / / /
A       1 / / / 2 / / / 3 / / / 4 / / / 5 / / / 6 / / / 7 / / / 8 / / /
B       1 / / / 2 / / / 3 / / / 4 / / /
C       1 / / / 2 / / / 3 / / / 4 / / / 5 / / / 6 / / / 7 / / / 8 / / /
INS     1 / / / 2 / / /
```

Try this exercise with songs on the radio. It will give you a repertoire of basic forms and, more importantly, it will show you a wide range of variations that work, such as extra bars of music between sections. Even though you'll find the forms falling into predictable patterns, the variations often give the song the sense of surprise that makes it special and exciting.

Note how the form contributes to how memorable a song is by helping it achieve a balance between *predictability* and *surprise,* repetition and new information, all within a commercially acceptable time limit.

| The Basic Forms

AAA

A   Title/hook in first or last line unless there is a repeated chorus with the same melody

A   "

A   "

This is an old form, used commonly in traditional folk music but rarely with good results in contemporary songs, because there is no chorus or bridge to help sustain melodic interest. The title line usually appears in the first or the last line, but occasionally there are two repeated lyric phrases, one in the first and one in the last line. The form can have any number of verses. You might use this form if you had a lot of important lyrical content, but wanted to eliminate the time spent repeating choruses. In the absence of a chorus that "sums up" the song, you'll want the verses to end with a dramatic kind of "payoff" line. Often they'll end in a refrain, a line that repeats a couple of times. Some examples are:

Johnny Cash, "I'll Walk the Line"

Bette Midler, "The Rose" (Amanda McBroom)

"By the Time I Get to Phoenix" (Jimmy Webb)

Bob Dylan's "The Times They Are a Changin' "

The following examples are AAA form melodically, although they contain a chorus lyric that repeats:

Bruce Springsteen's "Born in the USA"

Billy Ray Cyrus's "Achy Breaky Heart" (Don Von Tress)

Goo Goo Dolls' "Iris" (John Rzeznik)

The form contributes to how memorable a song is by helping it achieve a balance between *predictability* and *surprise*, repetition and new information, all within a commercially acceptable time limit.

Variations: There are variations of this form, like Don Henley's "Dirty Laundry," which uses a short refrain between every couple of verses. It's not a standard AAA because the refrain isn't a part of the basic melodic structure of the verse, and the refrain isn't a chorus because it's very short and does not contain the hook line (which *is* contained in the verse).

Musically, Bruce Springsteen's "Born in the USA" is an AAA: Although it has a chorus, its melody is the same as the verses. That's very unusual, and if you had written this song instead of "The Boss" and you weren't already a successful artist, your publisher probably would have demanded a rewrite. Without a powerful performance, the song would be musically uninteresting.

Another variation of the AAA form is an extension created by repeating part or all of the last line. This special focus on that line, however, makes it important that it be the title line. A short instrumental section or melodic instrumental hook can be used to break up the potential monotony.

Caution: You need to be very careful to make the melody as interesting as possible (like "The Rose") without making it too complex to be remembered easily. This is generally accomplished with a melodic variation in the last two melodic lines of each verse. Hum any of the examples mentioned to see what I mean.

A A B A

A Title/hook in first or last line—Four 8-bar sections

A Title/hook in first or last line

B New melody and lyric (referred to as the "bridge" or "middle 8")

A Title/hook in first or last line

Variations

A As above

A

B New melody and lyric

A

B Repeat B section with or without new lyric or make up a totally new bridge as Sting did in "Every Breath You Take" (which would make it a "C" section).

A Repeat first A or part of first and part of second A or part of first A and new lyric.

A Repeat second A

AABA is a classic song form with a long and popular history. At one time, it was considered the ultimate song form: It's short, concise, melodically seamless and easy to remember. It is used in all styles of music and all tempos, but most frequently in slow or mid-tempo ballads, because its 32 bars (four 8-bar sections) make for a very short song at fast tempos. Variations have developed that can accommodate faster tempos and the need for more room to tell the story. You'll find your own as the need arises. Hook/title placement is usually in either the first or last line of the verse, but it can occur in both (like "Yesterday"). You'll hear songs in which the title will also be recapped in the "B" section, although the objective is to go to a totally new place in that section both musically and lyrically.

Note that despite it's illustrious history, the AABA form is not usually considered the most commercially viable. Most of the ones you'll hear are written by the artists who perform them. When given a choice, most producers will choose to record a song with a repeating chorus. Examples are:

The Beatles' "Yesterday" (Lennon/McCartney)

Billy Joel's "Just the Way You Are"

Bruce Springsteen's "Fire" and "Streets of Philadelphia"

Shania Twain's "From This Moment On"

VERSE/CHORUS FORMS

The varieties of this most popular form provide a maximum of chorus repetition and two or more verses to tell your story.

# 1	# 2	# 3	# 4	# 5
A Verse	**A** Verse	**A** Chorus	**A** Verse	**A** Verse
B Chorus	**B** Chorus	**B** Verse	**A** Verse	**B** Pre-chorus
A Verse	**A** Verse	**A** Chorus	**B** Chorus	**C** Chorus
B Chorus	**B** Chorus	**B** Verse	**A** Verse	**A** Verse
A Verse	**C** Bridge	**A** Chorus	**B** Chorus	**B** Pre-chorus
B Chorus	**B** Chorus		**B** Chorus	**C** Chorus

Version #1 gives you a maximum verse and chorus repetition. A potential problem is that, if you have a lot of melodic repetition within each verse or chorus, such as an 8-bar section made up of three 2-bar melodies with a slight variation in the fourth 2-bar melody line, you may have too much repetition. In that case, *Version #2* with the substitution of a bridge for the third verse helps to break it up. *Version #3* with the chorus first can give you more repetition of the chorus in a shorter time. The choice of whether to start with a chorus depends on the lyric development of the song. If it's important to generate a dynamic opening to the song, try the chorus first unless you want the verses to build interest and suspense and "set up" the chorus as a "payoff." Many sixties' Motown hits used variations of this form. It's always a good idea to give it a test by switching the verse and chorus positions to see which works best.

Version #4 with two verses in front is also a much-used form. Its workability depends on a very strong lyric continuity between the first and second verses to offset the delay in getting to the chorus. This is a much greater problem in a slow ballad than an up-tempo song because of the additional time it takes to get to the chorus. Every word has to propel the story forward. Repetition of information is deadly. If both verses cover the same information in a different way and don't depend on each other, this may not be the best form to use since you should have a very important reason to delay the chorus. If you do need to use two verses, you may want to look for some arrangement devices or write a variation of the first verse melody to help sustain musical interest in the second verse. You could also consider using your title in the first line of the chorus to avoid even further delay in reaching the hook line.

Variations of this form opening with three verses (AAABAB or AAABAAB) are rare. Two examples that come to mind are The Eagles' "Lyin' Eyes" (Don Henley/Glenn Frey) and Kenny Rogers's "The Gambler" (Don Schlitz). Both have such exceptional lyric continuity that a chorus any earlier would be an unwelcome intrusion.

You'll also occasionally hear an AABAABB variation, particularly on up-tempo songs. Again, those choices will be different for each song, but the guiding principle is that you don't delay the chorus unless you have another good way to sustain the listener's interest. An interesting variation is the beautiful message story song "Chain of Love" recorded by Clay Walker. It has such strong lyric continuity that it was a hit as an AABAABA with only two chorus repeats.

Don't delay the chorus unless you have another good way to sustain the listener's interest.

Version #5 offers the excitement of three different melodic segments. The pre-chorus is the segment that makes the difference here. This form works best in up-tempo songs where the three segments go by quickly. Many variations are possible with this form including repeated instrumental versions of any of the segments and instrumental breaks between segments. Here are some examples:

- AABC ABC BC BC   or
- ABC ABCD BC   or
- ABC ABCD ABCD, the "D" being a bridge with a new melody, with or without lyrics.

| Dance Music

With the increase in the number of dance songs in the four-minute range on the pop and R&B/hip-hop charts, we see much more experimentation with these extended forms. Dance records are developed for pop, rock, and urban radio and singles for the dance club market. The records are usually formatted in a way that allows the record to be re-edited or remixed. This means that, originally, a longer version is recorded with more segments that can be removed to make a shorter version for radio or left in for the dance club market or for radio stations that like to play the long versions.

Records earmarked specifically for the dance club and "rave" market, and not for radio, can break more rules. Since there's a captive audience and you don't need to get their attention and since records well over four minutes are the norm, there can be long, slow-building intros, additional sections, and long instrumental breaks that would be too monotonous on radio. The record's major appeal is based on having a relentlessly exciting dance groove. Beyond that, there are no rules. Aside from a few conventional arrangement tricks like dropping out and bringing in instruments or repeating "loops," there is a lot of room for creativity in vocal and instrumental textures particularly for songwriters with arranging and producing skills. Dance music is usually "written" with the groove first; then other instruments, loops, vocals, etc., are added later. DJ/producers have become the new stars of the dance scene by virtue of their use of new digital "turntable" technology that allows them to seamlessly keep the music going by segueing between songs with different tempos, their choice of recordings, and the creation of their own digital loops to provide transitional grooves.

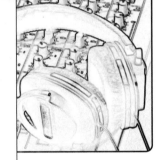

EXERCISES IN FORM

1. Write a song adhering strictly to each of the standard forms mentioned.
2. Pick one of your favorite hits and write a new lyric to its melody. This is called the "dummy melody" exercise and it's commonly used by lyricists who don't have a new melody to write to. Try to write the lyric with the same emotional feeling as the original. You may even try to use the same rhyme scheme.
   a. Have a collaborator create a new melody without letting him/her know the melody you used.
3. Analyze the forms of ten current hits. Do this exercise about once a month with ten new songs. It's a great way to stay current, explore new form variations, and discover why you think they work. There are also weekly countdowns on radio for country and R&B music.
4. Write songs in the standard forms using new variations of those forms.

Choosing a Form

Even when your songs come spontaneously, there is a point at which you need to decide which form to use. Usually writers will come up with a single verse or chorus idea first. After that first flash of inspiration and an exploration of what you want the song to say, you'll need to have an idea of the type of form you'll want to use to help you say it more effectively. You may do that unconsciously, as a natural result of having listened to the radio all your life—you just feel where there ought to be a change without really making a conscious evaluation of the reasons. That approach often works just fine, but sometimes it doesn't, like a beginning guitar player who writes monotonous two-chord songs because he only knows two chords instead of learning a few more chords. You have to remember that what you already know or feel about form could be limiting.

Another problem in choosing form by "feel" is the songwriting equivalent of "painting yourself into a corner." You might lock into a form that, by the time you've said what you wanted to say, has resulted in a five-minute song that you really wanted to be three minutes. You're now faced with a rewrite that might include a restructuring of the whole song. It's much harder to get out of a corner like that than it is to set it up better in the beginning. Even if you do have to restructure the song because the form you chose didn't quite work—or you had another idea halfway through the song—make those decisions on the basis of knowing your options.

So what do you consider in your choice of form? If you're starting with the music, tempo is a major factor in dictating the form. If it's an up-tempo song, you may need a form with many sections (like an ABCABCDC or AABABCB) to help you sustain musical interest. If it's a slow or mid-tempo ballad, you can use either the longer or shorter forms.

If you're starting from a lyric, the mood and subject matter will dictate the tempo of the music. In other words, "Genie in a Bottle" wouldn't work very well as a slow ballad, and the lyric to the *Titanic* theme, "My Heart Will Go On," wouldn't be as effective in a fast dance song.

Tempo is also determined by the ease with which the lyrics can be sung. The problem usually arises when there are lots of words. If the tempo's too fast, you may tie knots in your tongue trying to get them all in. If you want a rapid-fire one-syllable-per-eighth or -sixteenth note lyric, be extra careful that the words are easy to pronounce and sing together. Experiment with a metronome by singing the lyric against various tempo settings. Fewer words generally pose fewer problems, but the challenge is to phrase them in an interesting way against the rhythm. There are other tempo variables available, due to the fact that you can have a slow-moving lyric and melody over a double-time groove.

Whichever way you choose, once you've set the tempo and determined how many lyric lines will be in each segment, you've begun to lock yourself into the form. If it takes one minute to get through a verse and chorus and you're looking for a three-minute song, your options have already shrunk.

Also consider the amount of lyric needed to tell the story. Though it's always a good idea to condense, the AAA form gives you the most room to stretch lyrically, even though, as I mentioned earlier, it's not a good form from a commercial standpoint. Any up-tempo three- or four-section form can give you plenty of lyric space with strong musical interest, particularly if you use pre-choruses for new lyric information each time. One-section (AAA) and two-section (ABABAB) forms at fast tempos, though they allow for a maximum of lyric information, can be melodically boring because the melodies repeat so often.

With a spare, condensed lyric, you have many options. You can lay them over either an up-tempo track or a slow ballad and, in either case, have plenty of room to accommodate the individual phrasing styles of different singers. You can use any form and insure a maximum amount of both repetition and musical interest. However, a spare lyric at a slower tempo has more of an obligation to be interesting. You're making the listener wait for that lyric to unfold, and it had better be worth the wait. The same is true of the music.

Eventually, like anything else, once you've worked with these forms, they'll become second nature to you. You'll also find that you will get yourself into problematic situations for which you will find creative solutions. A substantial amount of innovation in music is initiated by a need to find a graceful way out of a jam. If you already have a repertoire of solutions, you're ahead of the game.

Hooks

"Hook" is the term you'll hear most often in the business and craft of commercial songwriting. (Well, maybe not as much as "Sorry, we can't use your song," but it's possible that the more you hear about hooks now, the less you'll hear "we can't use it" later.)

The hook has been described as "the part(s) you remember after the song is over," "the part that reaches out and grabs you," "the part you can't stop singing (even when you hate it)," and "the catchy repeated chorus." Some of the world's greatest hook crafters are commercial jingle writers. How many times have you had a jingle stick in your mind? Here are several categories of hooks.

The Structural Hook

In this category, part of the structure of the song functions as the hook. The most common is the "hook chorus." It repeats several times during the song, and it should contain the title or "hook line," usually the first or last line (See "Chorus Construction"). We may also consider memorable "B" sections, particularly in an AABA form, to be hooks; but the chorus is almost universally referred to as "the hook."

Instrumental Hooks

There are melodic phrases in songs that may not be part of the vocal melody, yet stick in our minds as though they were. In the last line of the chorus of The Beatles' "Something" after "Don't want to leave her now, you know I believe and how . . ." is a melodic guitar figure that we think of whenever we think of the melody, though there's no lyric over it. If we heard that figure by itself, we'd be able to "name that tune." The repeated riffs or loops that introduce and run beneath Stevie Wonder's "Superstition," Michael Jackson's "Beat It," and Jay-Z's "Can I Get a . . ." are as memorable as any other parts of the songs.

Too often, I think, songwriters tend to believe that creating those instrumental hooks is the job of the arranger, producer, or studio musicians. It should be kept in mind that if those are the hooks that sell the song to the public, they'll sell the song to the producer and artist if *you* create them first.

A substantial amount of innovation in music is initiated by a need to find a graceful way out of a jam.

Some of the world's greatest hook crafters are commercial jingle writers. How many times have you had a jingle stick in your mind?

Story Line Hooks

Have you ever heard a song and afterward couldn't quite remember the melody or the exact words, but you could remember the story? Sometimes the story itself is so powerful and evocative that it's the thing that stays in your mind longer than the exact words or melody. One great example is the Dixie Chicks' "Goodbye Earl."

Production Hooks

Production hooks aren't always possible for a songwriter, but today more writers than ever before have access to sophisticated instrumental and recording technology. The sounds on both demos and master recordings have become very important. Experiment with the way various instruments sound in combination. Experiment with electronic keyboard synth "pre-sets" combined with acoustic instruments or natural sounds. You can digitally sample sound sources or buy them on disks, tapes, or ROM cartridges and modify them yourself. MIDI (Musical Instrument Digital Interface) technology has made possible an almost infinite variety of sonic combinations.

Early recording techniques such as "phasing" and "flanging" were later incorporated into electronic boxes that you could use at the tap of a button and today virtually any sound modification device used in the studio has been converted to some portable digital form that you can use at home or on stage. Certain sounds will evoke certain emotional responses. Use them as artistic tools along with lyric and melody to create mood and emotion. One of the most effective hooks is a sound no one has ever heard before. Remember, however, that once you get into the technology of creating sounds, it can be so much fun that you can easily forget that the song is still the most important thing. No matter how exciting those sounds are, they won't make up for a weak song.

Hooks are essential in commercial music. They are points of reference that keep us interested and focused on the song. They're devices that help us remember and an entertainment in themselves. Part of your job as a commercial writer is to be able to use as many different types of hooks as possible.

Chorus Construction

The part of the song people remember best, after the first couple of listens, is the chorus. Effective choruses are a magic mix of lyric, melody, and phrasing.

The majority of choruses adhere to certain guidelines. I say "majority" because there are songs that ignore some of the guidelines and still win by the strength of their performance, arrangement, and/or production.

1. The title should appear in the chorus in a way that, by virtue of its placement in the chorus and/or its degree of repetition, we know it's the title. If words or phrases other than the title repeat in the chorus or in strong positions, the listener won't know the title when they call the radio station to request it or ask for it at the record store. This is why you sometimes see songs with two titles, like "Untitled (How Does It

Feel)," "Blue (Ba Da Dee)," or "C'mon 'N Ride It (The Train)"—that usually means that someone felt the song's title was not its strongest hook or even that the song has two hooks and they're covering their bets by putting both in the title. Since you can't buy or request a song if you can't remember its name, these are very important commercial considerations.

2. Keep the information simple enough for people to remember easily. If you're a literary genius, you may tend to think most choruses are too simple. Don't worry about it. They need to be simple!

3. They need to distill and focus the song.

4. They need to stand repetition.

5. The words of the chorus need to be easily remembered. It also helps if the melody is fun and easy to sing.

6. The action of the verses should not pass the action of the chorus chronologically. Choruses can run from two to eight lines (depending on your definition of a line).

Here are some common lyric constructions:

1. **Repeat the same line two or more times.** This can get monotonous unless that line is fun to sing or shout (like "Take this job and shove it"), it's sung with a style that makes it interesting (like "Whoomp! There it is"), and/or it's musically exciting.

2. **First and third line the same, second and fourth lines different.** This offers the possibility of having a strong "payoff" line to end the chorus. The last line in the chorus is a power position, and there are high expectations for it to be strong and satisfying. Examples: Bruce Hornsby's "The Way It Is"; Brian McKnight "Anytime" (McKnight/Brandon Barnes); Paula Cole "I Don't Want to Wait."

3. **First and third lines the same, second and fourth lines the same.** Provides maximum repetition of both lines and makes the chorus very easy to remember. Example: Eagle Eye Cherry's "Save Tonight."

4. **First three lines are the same, fourth line different.** This has some of the potential monotony of no. 1 and the payoff advantage of no. 2. The repetition of the first three lines makes for a powerful setup, so the payoff needs to be strong. Example: Steve Winwood's "Higher Love."

5. **All four lines different.** Doesn't risk monotony and doesn't set up as much of an expectation for a powerful last line as no. 2 and no. 3 (but give them one anyway). Examples: Larry Henley and Jeff Silbar's classic "The Wind Beneath My Wings"; Dixie Chicks' "Wide Open Spaces" (Susan Gibson); Mariah Carey's "Dream Lover" (Carey/Dave Hall, David Porter); Natalie Imbruglia's "Torn" (Thornalley/Cutler/Preven).

6. **The first or last part of each line is repeated** (and is almost always the title). This is one of the oldest and most common structures. It goes back to "call and response" songs in tribal music and Gregorian chants. Examples: The Irene Cara hit "Fame" (Dean Pitchford/Michael Gore); Ace of Base's "All That She Wants"; Shedaisy's "Little Good-byes"; "Still the One" (Shania Twain, Robert John "Mutt" Lange).

7. **The first and last line the same, the second and third are each different.** This gives you a chance to repeat the hook line at both the beginning and the end. Examples: Huey Lewis's "The Heart of Rock and Roll."

These are just a few common structures. There are many more. Chorus structures are far less standardized than song forms. Pick up a contemporary songbook at your local music store or listen to a Top 40 countdown and what you'll find is an incredible degree of diversity. In fact, a good share of hits are successful *because* their choruses are unusual—like Macy Gray's "I Try."

Melodic construction of choruses roughly follows the lyric structures; however, there is a tremendous variety of rhythmic and phrasing options available. A lyricist should always keep in mind that there is great flexibility in pop music in the ways lyrics can be stretched, spaced, and positioned relative to the music. Looking at a lyric on paper only gives us part of the story.

Repetition

Repetition is a key part of learning almost anything; so if you want someone to learn your song quickly, you can't afford not to use it.

One of the most important ingredients of successful songs is repetition. Repetition is a key part of learning almost anything; so if you want someone to learn your song quickly, you can't afford not to use it.

Several studies have been made showing that most listeners have some resistance to hearing something unfamiliar. They'd rather hear a song they already know. It may be a little disappointing to learn that most people are so unadventurous, but it's really not surprising: As writers and musicians, we are always looking for something fresh and new and tend to forget that the public, generally speaking, doesn't share that need for change. They feel comfortable with the familiar and uncomfortable with the unfamiliar.

This poses obvious problems for radio stations who'd like to add a new record by a new artist, but whose audience polls tell them they should keep playing established hits instead. The more they repeat those old songs, the more comfortable people feel with them and the more personal nostalgia they generate. Since radio stations are relying more heavily on listener polls and feedback to program their music and since listeners can't request what they haven't heard, new writer/artists are between a rock and a hard place.

If you can write songs for established artists with already familiar and easily identifiable voices and styles, you have an edge, because a new and unfamiliar song by Madonna or Whitney Houston or Garth Brooks is going to get played before an unfamiliar song by an unfamiliar artist.

Whether you're writing for yourself or someone else, you need to minimize the odds against you. Since your problem with a new song is to break through that resistance to something new, repetition of melodic themes, choruses, or instrumental figures (riffs) will build instant familiarity into a song. Write a chorus that is totally and instantly understandable, simple, easily remembered, and that touches their hearts and/or their feet.

By the time the song is finished and the listeners have heard it three or four times, they'll know it and want to hear and sing it again.

The general objective is to have enough repetition without inducing boredom. It's sometimes difficult to determine how much is too much. Lyricists, in general, seem to get bored very quickly and even a very little repetition can make them feel guilty about not doing their job properly. On the other hand, a musician who's just found a great groove will tend to play it till the neighbors have him arrested. This supports the theory that you can get away with more repetition of a short lyric phrase if it's catchy and fun to sing, in other words, if it's "musical" by virtue of its meter, phrasing, rhythm, rhyme, assonance, and alliteration. "Chattanooga Choo Choo," "Little Latin Lupe Lu," "Gettin' Jiggy Wit It," and "Livin' La Vida Loca" all have those "catchy" qualities about them.

Obviously, the amount of repetition you use depends on the purpose of the song, what audience you're trying to reach: A ten-minute dance song can light up a dance floor but merely be annoying if you hear it on the radio while you're stuck in traffic.

Repetition of melody, I believe, allows listeners to focus more on the lyrics. If the melody changed in each of the sections and never repeated, we'd be too distracted to follow the lyrics. I think one of the reasons why the melodies in country music have such simple familiarity is because country music is very lyric oriented, and the familiarity helps the listener concentrate on the words.

Lyric repetition also serves to let the listener's mind rest. If, as a writer, you're giving listeners information in the verses, a repeated chorus coming up says, "OK, you'll only have to concentrate a little longer. When the chorus comes back, you can rest your mind and just groove. When it's over, you'll know just when to get ready to concentrate again." That mental set or preparation to pay attention is another psychology-of-learning principle. It's really the basis of the need, in both writing and production, to have "pickups" before choruses and verses, intros to songs, drum fills, any little figure or chord change, or something that telegraphs ahead that there's going to be a change. We like those when we dance, too. They help us to choreograph ourselves.

Repetition of words or short phrases, or the first part of a familiar melody or lyric, is a great tension creator in a song. However, in order to work, it has to pay off big. Otis Redding was great at that. "You got to, got to, got to, got to" and when he finally hits "Try a Little Tenderness," it's a release and a relief and feels good.

However, too much repetition can wear out your radio welcome fast. We all know songs like that. Pay attention to the ones that do it to you and figure out why. A chorus made up of the same short, repeated phrase throughout can be death. Ideally, a song should have a good balance of predictability and surprise without too much of either.

A song should have a good balance of predictability and surprise without too much of either.

Song Dynamics

Among the most powerful tools you can use to make your songs more commercial and to impress industry pros with your command of the craft is the use of contrasts and variations that I call "song dynamics." I've also observed that it's the tool most commonly overlooked and underused by amateur songwriters. In this section, we'll look at several devices you should have in your bag of tricks and why they work.

There are crucial points during a song at which the audience's attention must be dramatically and positively captured in order to make it effective on radio. I had a very valuable experience that confirmed my information about these factors.

Len Chandler (my partner in the Los Angeles Songwriters Showcase) and I were asked to produce demos of some strong commercial songs by a company that regularly tested records on behalf of producers and record companies. Every Saturday, four hundred young potential record buyers of several demographic groups (divided into age, sex, and racial groups) sat in a theater and turned a dial on the arm of their seats to indicate responses to a given song ranging from "don't like it" to neutral to "love it." As the song was played in the theater, lyrics were shown on the screen, and, simultaneously, a computer totaling the combined responses of each demographic group drew a graph of that group's reaction so that we could see how they responded at any given moment of the song. From watching those reactions and from the director's interpretations of what we saw, we learned the following:

1. Intros for ballads should be shorter in order to get the listener into the body of the song more quickly. Intros for up-tempo songs can be longer because people get involved physically almost immediately and don't need to wait. People reflect on ballad lyrics in a more passive way, which increases the need for a blockbuster chorus.

2. People will try to identify the voice when it's first heard. If it's familiar, it usually generates a positive reaction. People always feel more comfortable with a voice they know than one they don't, because they have to decide whether or not they like an unfamiliar singer.

This phenomenon also contributes to an unknown artist's difficulty in getting radio exposure. A good example was an unknown male artist with a beautiful but very high voice who got a negative audience reaction. We finally concluded that the audience was turned off because they didn't know whether to identify a male or female (the lyrics didn't immediately establish a gender). Remember that this wasn't Michael Jackson or Prince, both of whom have readily identifiable high voices. The problem here wasn't the high voice in itself; it was the lack of gender identity.

3. The reaction at the first sound of a voice is critical to the audience's continued reaction to the record. The longer it takes to respond positively, the harder it is to build interest through the rest of the song. In the absence of a familiar voice, the lyric content of the first line(s) is very important to the audience's response. This is the audience's first exposure to the song and artist, and there's an automatic tendency to pay attention when someone starts to sing, just as there is when someone starts to talk. If people don't under-stand, hear, or like what's being said, the reaction will be negative.

4. The "hook" chorus is another critical place in a song. If audience interest doesn't

increase perceptibly at the chorus's beginning and increase throughout, continued positive interest in the remainder of the record is unlikely.

In television, the pros say that there should be a new camera angle or other change at least every fifteen seconds to keep the viewer's interest. (In music videos, that time is considerably shorter.) This principle has an analogy to radio. We remember only a fraction of what we hear compared to what we see; therefore, we begin to understand why we're so easily distracted when we listen to the radio. The battle for people's attention on the radio is heavy, and songwriters need all the ammunition they can get. Now that we understand what has to be done, how can we create the excitement that solves the problem?

One of the main components of the "SuperLearning" techniques developed by Russian educators now being used in the West is that teachers vary the tone, intensity, and pitch of their voice frequently as they deliver the material. Those changes continue to stimulate the student's attention. This is the same effect you want to achieve in your listeners; therefore, you can use this principle by increasing and releasing tension, thus achieving contrasts between different segments of the song. Try some of these:

1. **Change the groove.** You could go from a straight "on the beat" feel in the verse to a more syncopated feel in the chorus or vice versa. In other words, go from emphasizing "1-2-3-4" to "1-**and**-2-**and**-3-**and**-4"—like a reggae beat.

2. **Change chords.** Initiate a whole new chord progression for the chorus and another for the bridge. Modulating up or down or playing the same progression in a different key are arrangement devices that can be built into your demos.

3. **Change time.** Don't change tempo or pulse if you're going for a radio or dance market record. It's been done by major artists (Paul McCartney on "Live and Let Die," Queen's "We Are the Champions"), but it's a very risky business, even to start slow and break into an up-tempo dance groove. Once you've engaged a listener or dancer in the pulse of a song, it's a solid base on which to build other dynamics. Against that solid base you can go from 4/4 time to a couple of bars of 3/4 time to increase tension like the Beatles did on "We Can Work It Out." It can make for an interesting transition between verse and chorus, for example, but be careful not to continue for more than a bar or two or you'll ruin the groove.

4. **Change melody.** A melodic change in the chorus is probably the most effective song dynamic you can use to make a song memorable and commercially viable. Generally, you'll want it to "lift" out of (up from) the verse melody by starting above the last note of the verse. That's not a rule, however, and there have been rare songs that have achieved a contrast by dropping down from the verse. A change in chord progressions will automatically induce you to change the melody in the chorus. Also, change the chorus melody before you work out new chords. Try playing and singing your verse melody until your chorus is supposed to come in, then stop playing and continue *a cappella*. Tape it so you can listen to it away from your instrument.

5. **Change lyric density.** The term "lyric density" is about how close together the

A melodic change in the chorus is probably the most effective song dynamic you can use to make a song memorable and commercially viable.

words are over a given tempo. You might have rapid-fire lyrics with one syllable per sixteenth note during the verse, then change to one syllable per fourth note in the chorus. Or just do the opposite while keeping the tempo the same. Many hit songs use that technique. The rest of the chorus continues in the same pattern, giving our minds another subconscious cue to remember the lyric and melody.

One of the factors that makes Lenny Kravitz's "Fly Away" work so well is the change in vocal phrasing and lyric density, going from short choppy phrases in the verse to the stretched-out words and the Beatlesque "ahhhs" of the chorus.

6. **Change the lyric meter.** Changing lyric meters from line to line or section to section is one of the most common techniques used in successful songs and is the most underused by novice songwriters. Though keeping the same meter through a verse can subtly build tension that can be released when you change it in the chorus, there is a risk of being too predictable. You can also alternate between two different meters every other line (and within the same line). There are many options.

> **TIP**
>
> If you can sing your verse lyric to your chorus melody, it's a good indication that your song could benefit from a new chorus lyric meter to help generate a new melody and provide more contrast.

Listen to any of Diane Warren's hits: "Un-break My Heart," "Because You Loved Me," "I Don't Wanna Miss a Thing," and many others. She's a master at changing her lyric meter and density in the middle of a line, at the choruses, or at the bridges in ways that feel natural and conversational. Matchbox Twenty's Rob Thomas is another writer who's great at that. Listen to the way you speak and pay attention to the natural rhythms of others. We rarely, if ever, hear people speak in iambic pentameter— "da-DUM da-DUM da-DUM da-DUM da-DUM" (five metric feet)—because it feels so stiff and predictable. When you write lyrics and music together, by yourself, whether for yourself as a singer or someone else, you have an opportunity to marry lyric and music in a uniquely conversational way. Collaborations can also have a very special magic when writers are in synch with each other. As a lyricist, the ability to express your own attitudes and ideas in a way that's natural for you is one of the best methods to create a unique song or singing style.

If you're a lyricist whose words will be set to music, employ changes in lyric density, meter, and rhyme scheme so that, eventually, your composer has a head start in creating musical contrasts. Writing lyrics against a metronome pulse or groove machine will help you hear those patterns in a useful context and have fun experimenting with the phrasing.

7. **Change the rhyme scheme.** You can have a different rhyme scheme in your verses than in your chorus and/or your bridge. Try not to use the same end rhymes in more than one verse. (See "Rhyme Schemes," chapter four.)

These devices have infinite variations and it's in their imaginative use that you exercise your creative muscles. They won't all work on all songs, but they're options you can try on each song. Arrangement devices such as dropping out and bringing in instruments, silence, and changes in intensity, volume, and texture can be used to further give your songs drama. These are devices to explore when you record your demo.

EXERCISE

Try this while you're listening to your favorite songs: Instead of singing along with the lyrics, pretend the words are part of the rhythm and just speak them, maybe substituting "da-da-da" for the words so you can get a sense of their meter or rhythm.

Rewriting

Before demoing any song, be sure it's the best it can be. Usually the first draft of any song can use improvement. So before your ecstasy about finishing it compels you to spend your hard-earned cash on a demo, put your song away for a few days. Being able to look at the song more objectively may spare you the frustration of hearing a publisher or producer say, "This is really good, but the second verse needs a rewrite," and knowing you'll have to spend even more to re-record the vocal. Not that a rewrite is a guarantee that it won't happen anyway, but at least you'll know you gave it your best shot.

It's often said that writing successful songs is 10 percent writing and 90 percent rewriting. In interviews with hundreds of hit songwriters, I have rarely heard them say that their hits came out all at once in their final version. The ones who can get close to the finished song the first time around have been at it so long that their creative flow and critical faculties practically work in unison. Even relatively inexperienced writers can occasionally write a song in fifteen minutes that's practically in its finished form. But for most writers, those times are rare.

It's often said that writing successful songs is 10 percent writing and 90 percent rewriting.

One of the differences between a pro and an amateur writer is that the pro usually recognizes from the beginning that he or she will probably be able to improve the song with rewrites. The amateur thinks that everything coming from the original, inspired state is wonderful and shouldn't be tampered with.

The latter attitude is the enemy of professionalism. Most writers go through this stage of development with great difficulty. The first time a publisher or producer rejects a song and suggests a rewrite, the writer usually rebels, thinking, "Who are you to criticize my work? Nobody knows better than I when it's finished or not!" I've watched many writers go through this stage, take the suggestions, rewrite, and be forced to admit that they really liked the changes they made and felt the songs had become much stronger. Once they have gone through that experience, they are much more open to change, particularly if the end result is getting a song recorded or published. This doesn't mean that every criticism you receive is valid because it comes from a so-called authority. It is necessary, though, to keep an open mind even if you eventually decide to leave the song unchanged.

Although it may be important to your livelihood that you rewrite for commercial considerations, it's most important to satisfy yourself that this is your best work. Hopefully, you want to create something that will be enjoyed for a long time. Five or twenty years from now, you don't want to be embarrassed to hear your song and know that if you'd just been a little harder on yourself, you'd be proud of it.

Sometimes it's valuable to imagine your toughest critic reading your lyric or hearing your song and picking it apart. You may notice flaws that you hadn't noticed before.

Here are some areas to view for possible rewrites:

1. Make sure your lyrics and music work well together and you haven't placed accents on the wrong syllables or tried to fit too many words together in a short musical space. Words need to be easily sung and comprehended.

2. Can you substitute an image, action, or dialogue line that will condense and heighten the song's impact? The less wordy a lyric is, the more room an artist has to phrase it in his or her style.

3. Is every line important and every word necessary? If you can omit a line or a word without affecting the meaning and flow of the lyric, replace it with a stronger one. Every line should contribute to the overall meaning.

4. Does your song contain all the dynamics necessary to hold a listener's attention? Does your chorus stand out melodically from your verses? Can you rearrange rhyme schemes or meter to enhance the difference between sections of your song? Try some alternate melody lines while imagining an appropriate singer performing them. You may find something better than your first idea.

Jack Segal, hit lyricist, super craftsman, and teacher, lays out some worthwhile tools for rewriting in his lyric class: reduction, inversion, insertion, and rhyme relocation.

| Reduction

Reduction is the shortening of sentences or lines; specifically, making fewer syllables and fewer metric feet. Let's take a line that's seven metric feet.

Aňd thére   Ĭ ẃas   jušt haňg—iňg ón   tŏ áll   thŏse ẃorn   oŭt liňes

Take out the useless words and cut it down to five feet with a one-syllable pickup:

Ĭ   wăs háng—iňg ón   tŏ áll   thŏse wórn   oŭt liňes

Always look for ways to streamline your lyrics. If the above line was locked into a musical pattern that accommodated the first version, the reduced version would lend itself to a variety of new phrasing possibilities that the first version didn't offer.

| Inversion

Inversion is a tricky form of rhyme relocation, reversing part of the line so that a new rhyme word emerges from the interior to the end position. It's important to preserve the natural, conversational flow of the line. If the inversion appears to have been done only to achieve a rhyme, it feels awkward.

"I loved you then, I love you still,
Break us up, they never will."

That's an example of a mediocre line gone bad. "I love you still" is an acceptable inversion of "I still love you," but the last line is one you'd never say in conversation. Obviously, the most natural line is "They'll never break us up." You could say, "They try to break us up, they never will." You'd then have two complete thoughts. If that possibility messes up your meter, go back to the first line and look for another end word to give you a new choice of rhymes. In doing so, you might use another form of inversion by inverting the order in the first line to "I love you still, I loved you then," giving you "then" to work with. In this case, you're also reversing the natural time order of "then"/"still," which weakens the line. You could also say, "I love you now" instead of "still," though it does have a slightly different meaning—an important element for consideration in this jigsaw juggle.

Sometimes it's better just to start over!

| Insertion

Insertion means filling in the blanks when the desired meter, number of syllables, and lyrical concept are known: You've got your verse or chorus written, your meter is established, you know what you want to say. You realize that there's a weak line in the middle that could be replaced. Now you have a real jigsaw puzzle.

Here's an example in something I wrote. The first draft:

She drifted past the mirror but she didn't even look.
A week ago she would have fixed her hair.
I could see that the spark had vanished from her eyes,
And she was too far in the ozone now to care.

I felt I needed to replace the third line with something about the emotional impact, the desperation the man was feeling.

She drifted past the mirror but she didn't even look.
A week ago she would have fixed her hair.
I was fading from her life and trying to hold on
But she was too far in the ozone now to care.

Even that line went through the same process, from "She was shut out of my life and I needed to break through" to "I was fading from her life and I needed to break through," which felt more vulnerable, to the final choice, which felt vulnerable but also more helpless.

Rhyme Relocation

Rhyme relocation is the flip-flopping of the rhymes to strengthen the power of the lyric and rhyme. The stronger rhyme-word of the two should come second whenever possible. Inversion is actually a form of rhyme relocation. You get more power out of placing the strongest word as the end rhyme. There are words that are obviously more powerful than others—said/dead, had/bad, dream/scream, well/hell. Obviously, the second word in each pair would evoke the strongest emotional response in the listener. If you have the strongest word first, reverse them. It won't always work and, ultimately, it's a juggle between the power of the line, power of the word, meaning, and flow. The overall principle is always to escalate toward the most powerful word, line, or idea.

If you're writing a story song, save the payoff until the last verse. The last line of every section is a power position because it's where the tension is released. If you blow it with a weak line, chances are that the listener will feel let down enough to have forgotten that brilliant line in the middle of the verse. In the case of lines, an interesting example is in George Michael's classic (Wham) hit, "Careless Whisper":

To the heart and mind
Ignorance is kind.

If you turned the lines around, you'd get a slightly more natural, conversational feel, but you'd lose considerable impact because "Ignorance is kind" is the real payoff line.

If you're writing the lyric first, you have the luxury of performing these changes without restriction. However, if the change gives you a different meter, follow through with the same meter in the rest of the verses or the rest of the choruses (if that's what you're changing). If you don't, you'll give your melody writer a nervous breakdown. At times, it's actually easier to make reductions when the melody and lyrics are already married. When you're able to sing it, you'll notice the awkward little spots where you could drop a word or two and give the singer more time to hang onto a word. It's also easier to feel when an insertion might help to enhance the rhythm of the lyric. Adding a word or two in the right place could help make the song "catchier."

There are obviously no hard-and-fast rules about this, but the general principle is that every word should perform a valuable function for the song. If a word does nothing to enhance the rhythm, meaning, or sound of the lyric, it shouldn't be there. Once you're used to working with these techniques, you'll find that you'll use them very quickly to explore the new possibilities they provide.

Writing on Assignment

Staff writers at publishing companies are often called upon to write on assignment; but even if you're not in that position, you'll hear about recording projects you'll want to write for. If you're a "project" writer (See "Creativity," page 7) who works best with specific guidelines, this is a great exercise, whether or not you've actually been given a project.

Tailoring songs for a specific artist is a calculated and methodical approach. You may have written down or taped some great ideas during the heat of inspiration; but now, in the light of what you'll learn about your target artist or project, you'll look at the ideas with a whole new perspective. Let's say you have a "prescription" to write. You know that the producer is looking for positive, up-tempo love songs for an artist. If you can, get information from the producer about the artist's vocal range, point of view, attitude, and philosophy. If it's not convenient to do that and the artist has previous albums, get them. Make a synopsis of the lyric of each song like, "He left me but I know I'll get over him," "I've had my problems with other women but I know she'll be different," "My friends think I'm crazy to love you but I don't care," "They all want you but I know what you want," etc. (See "Casting," chapter eleven.) See if the songs the artist records—particularly the successful ones—fall into a consistent pattern. There are artists who don't like "weak" or "victim" songs that say, basically, "You can walk all over me and I don't care. I'll still love you no matter what you do." Other artists have practically built their careers on songs with that attitude. Pay attention to the established image of an artist.

You can often get additional information from reading interviews with the artists in trade or fan magazines. When you hear their records, check out the kind of melodic passages the artist sings well. Does he/she have a great voice that loves to hold onto long notes and style them? Does the artist not have a great voice, coming off better doing story songs with lots of lyrics and short, choppy lines? Does the artist phrase well or have a stylistic trademark that you'd do well to accommodate?

Notice if the artist seems to prefer a particular form. Does he like a form that allows them a minute to "jam" on the hook during a fade? Does she prefer short, four-line choruses with lots of repetition or four different lines with a strong "payoff" line? Is the song for a group with more involved vocal parts, needing parallel lyric lines to intermesh? Once you've listened to enough of the artist, you can visualize him/her singing your lyrics and melodies, and it will become much easier to write for the style. A valuable exercise is to write a follow-up song to an artist's last hit, taking into consideration all the artistic factors you feel contributed to its success.

Some writers hate this approach to writing because they feel it's calculated, uninspired hack work. Other writers love it because they welcome the artistic challenge of saying something that comes from them but is tailor-made for someone else. They look at the parameters as an architect would look at building a house for a family's specific needs. Matching form with function is the challenge. If the music coming from this approach seems uninspired, the writer has no one to blame but himself. All those great inspired ideas you wrote on all those little scraps of paper or sang or played into a tape recorder should inspire you again.

Norman Gimbel had the phrase "killing me softly" in his notebook long before Lori Lieberman (who he and co-writer Charles Fox were producing) told him about her emotional reaction to experiencing Don McLean ("American Pie," "Vincent") in concert. They used (1) the need to write a song to fit her style, (2) the inspired phrase, and (3) Lori's own experience to put together a fresh and original classic that was later a hit by Roberta Flack and more recently by the Fugees (featuring Lauryn Hill). Many successful writers I've interviewed have felt that some of their best work was done under deadline or for a specific project.

If you write primarily for yourself, it can be artistically liberating to write for someone else and not be identified with your words, to be able to say something in a way that you wouldn't state it for yourself. You can expand the parameters of your craft, and that can't hurt. For nonperforming writers who depend on others to record their songs, tailoring is a valuable discipline to develop.

A possible criticism of this approach is that you may write a song that's too tailored to only one artist. If that artist doesn't record it, you may have a great song that no other artist could hear themselves singing. I don't agree. I believe that if it really is a great song, you'll find another artist to cut it, even if you have to rewrite or re-demo it. A great song is a great song!

chapter six

Writing Music

by Cat Cohen

Melody

Writing melodies for commercial songs is an art unto itself. Though there may be some similarity to classical composition, the priorities of pop melody writing are very different. The basis of most classical writing is building melodic ideas over an extended period of time. In pop writing, short melodic ideas are usually repeated and contrasted without much development and lead to the main chorus or hook section in a relatively short amount of time. The essence of pop composition is repeating these ideas with enough contrast and variation to keep the listener involved. The starting point of any melody is its initial idea or phrase. In 4/4 time, this can be anywhere from a half-measure (two beats) to two measures (eight beats) long. Occasionally, one may find a melodic idea that is four measures long in a slow romantic ballad, but usually this is a feature reserved for art song and classical writing. Short melodic ideas are easier for most people to remember.

Try tapping out one of the short melodic ideas running around in your head. Most songwriters seem to be blessed (or cursed) with these little bursts of inspiration. This is a great place to start, since what often has hooked your unconscious mind will have a tendency to hook others. The challenge of pop melody writing is expanding these ideas into song sections and then into complete songs. You can learn how to do this by using the techniques of repetition, variation, contrast, and development.

Take a look at a couple of melodic ideas and see how they can be expanded into songs. Here are two examples:

The first example is long, unfocused, and unworkable; while the second one is short and memorable, easy to develop into the kind of catchy, hooky phrases that sell a song. The basic reason that the first melody is unmemorable is a complete lack of repetition in the phrase, either notewise or rhythmically. See how the second melody takes the first three notes of the first measure and repeats them?

Now, take the second idea and see how it can be stretched out into eight effective measures.

Start with a one-bar phrase and simply duplicate it.

If it's duplicated four times, though, it might get a little too simple-minded.

Some people confuse being "commercial" with being mindlessly repetitive. Yes, you need enough repetition to get immediate recognition and familiarity, but Top 40 stations play the same songs over and over, and a song must have enough variety to withstand repeated listening. A better way to expand melodic fragments is to alternate between two melodic ideas.

Actually, the technique of alternating between melodic ideas is nothing new. It was derived from religious services where the priest, preacher, or cantor alternated singing with the choir or congregation. Contemporary gospel music is a great example of this "call and response." The same structure is also found in blues. Up-tempo music, from folk and square dancing to the "Hokey Pokey" to contemporary dance records, has always been based on this foundation, alternating between right and left, front and back steps.

Two ways of using this alternating technique are variation (with repetition) and contrast (with repetition). In variation, the second or "response" phrase is only slightly different from the "call" or original melodic idea. But this difference, no matter how slight, keeps the melody from becoming too predictable.

In contrast, a completely different melody is paired with the original, and the close alternation of the two ideas serves to link them quickly in the listener's mind.

A lot of pop recordings, especially dance records, are structured almost exclusively in this way. Listen and try to analyze "We Are Family" by Sister Sledge, one of the classic dance records of the late seventies, and see how it is composed of variation with repetition. Here it is spread out over an eight-measure section:

"We Are Family"

BY NILE ROGERS AND BERNARD EDWARDS

We are fam - i - ly;

I got all my sis - ters with me.

We are fam - i ly;

Get - up ev -'ry bod - y and sing.

Some pop styles use more complex phrasing than simple alternation. From Burt Bacharach to Michael McDonald to Barry Gibb to Luther Vandross, there is a whole range of more sophisticated approaches to commercial writing. Most of these writers have had some classical background, the kind of instruction that encourages the writer to develop and insert new material. It takes a lot more craft to develop more melodic ideas, somewhat like juggling with three or four balls instead of just two. It is easy to fall into the trap of taking a melody too far away without enough repetition to keep the listener involved. Inexperienced songwriters have a tendency to lose their audience by trying to say too much through melody or lyric in one song.

Inexperienced songwriters have a tendency to lose their audience by trying to say too much through melody or lyric in one song.

The song that follows here, "Torn," is an excellent example of a more complex melodic composition:

"Torn"

BY PHIL THORNALLEY, SCOTT CUTLER, AND ANNE PREVEN (NATALIE IMBRUGLIA)

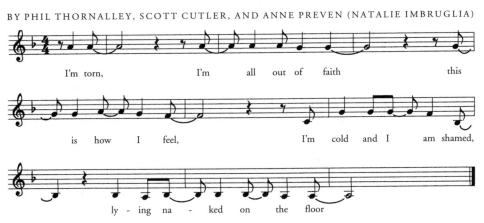

Once you get a handle on duplicating, alternating, contrasting, and developing melodic ideas, you can combine them to craft more distinctive song sections that still will be within the commercial ballpark. A song that combines these techniques is "What's Love Got to Do With It," which won the Grammy for Best Song of the Year in 1984.

"What's Love Got to Do With It"

BY TERRY BRITTEN AND GRAHAM LYLE (TINA TURNER)

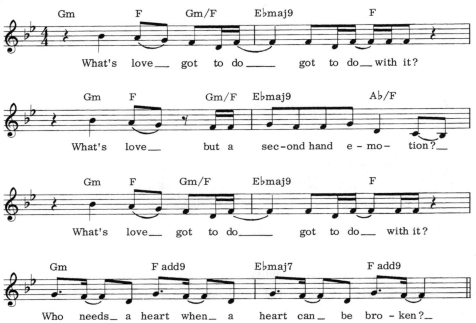

Completing Songs

Once you are able to write an effective eight-bar song section, the biggest challenge is then expanding it into a completed song. This is where most songwriters seem to get stuck. One of the best ways of writing an interesting, complete song is by using contrasting sections. Why do you need more than one song section in the first place? With few exceptions (remember "I'm Henry the Eighth I Am" by Herman's Hermits?), the record-buying public does not respond to simple one-section songs. To keep a listener involved for a full three minutes or more, you must depart from the main melodic material. Coming up with the amount of contrast appropriate to the song is perhaps the most difficult and crucial aspect of effective melody writing.

A good analogy to help understand how contrast functions is to compare a second song section to a vacation. If you stay at home all the time, life can get a little dull. A trip to another place or environment brings relief from monotony and the pleasure of returning home. A trip without much contrast (such as a dash to the supermarket and back) gives neither the enjoyment of leaving or returning. Similarly, a song with melodic departure and return keeps us involved and interested. A lack of change, and we tune out.

Here are some ideas to help you get more contrast in your song sections.

1. **Change the level of your melodic line.** Make the more important section (the hook section) higher in pitch, or use different time values (for instance, change to mostly sixteenth notes instead of eighths and quarters, use long half-notes instead of eighths, etc.).

2. **Change the phrase length.** If your verse is made up of long phrases (two bars or longer), then write shorter ones or vice versa. Nothing is more boring than a cookie-cutter four-line verse and a similar four-line chorus, all with the same pat phrase along the lines of:

I think that I shall never see
A thing as lovely as a tree
La, dee, dah, dee, dah, dee, dah
La, dee, dah, dee, dah, dee, dah . . .

3. **Change the rhythmic pattern.** If the verse has straight-ahead rhythm, make the chorus more syncopated or try the opposite. (See "Song Dynamics," page 93.)

4. **Define your sections with an appropriate transition.** The use of musical "punctuation" is very important to give the listener a clear sense of where the song is "at." You can accomplish this with a break, a stop, a build, or a musical turnaround. If you try to jump unexpectedly into a hook or second verse, the effect may be "arty," but you'll tend to lose your listener. Exceptions to this are album cuts from established artists whose fans look to them for new musical challenges. Top 40 formats don't have the time to let radio audiences figure out what seems puzzling in a song at first. Unless you are purposely going for an unusual song style, it's better to lead your audience carefully from one song section to the next.

Other considerations important in melody writing are *range* and *scale context.*

A song with melodic departure and return keeps us involved and interested. A lack of change, and we tune out.

Range

Every singer has a vocal range within which he or she can sing consistently and with professional control. Here is a guideline for ranges of different song styles and for different vocal abilities:

MODEST

Less than an octave. This is for the less-skilled singer, talk singer, or sing-along style performer. Country music and simple rock styles often feature performers whose personality far exceeds their ability to sing. Material written for them should never push them beyond their limited range.

AVERAGE

Octave and a third or fourth. Two or three notes above an octave is the typical range for most pop singers and styles. There is room for a few dramatic leaps or high notes, but nothing too demanding for the average performer.

WIDE

An octave and a fifth and beyond. This is for divas like Barbra Streisand or Whitney Houston or virtuoso singers like Lou Gramm or Larry Gatlin. Sometimes groups like Boyz II Men or The Backstreet Boys can handle a song encompassing a wide range.

Scale Context

Another important consideration is scale context. Without getting into an involved theoretical discussion, note that besides the key a song is written in (C major, G minor), the actual scale tones that are used in the melody have a great deal to do with the song's style. Here are a few examples of scale contexts:

MAJOR 7-TONE

"I Will Always Love You"

BY DOLLY PARTON AND RECORDED BY DOLLY PARTON, WHITNEY HOUSTON

"I Knew I Loved You"

BY SAVAGE GARDEN

MAJOR 6-TONE

| 1 | 2 | 3 | 4 | 5 | 6 – 8 |

"I Don't Want to Miss a Thing"

BY DIANE WARREN (AEROSMITH, MARK CHESNUTT)

"All Star"

BY SMASHMOUTH

MAJOR 5-TONE (PENTATONIC)

| 1 | 2 | 3 – 5 | 6 – 8 |

"My Girl"

BY WILLIAM "SMOKEY" ROBINSON AND RONALD WHITE (TEMPTATIONS)

"Streets of Philadelphia"

BY BRUCE SPRINGSTEEN

MINOR 7-TONE (NATURAL)

| 1 | 2 | ♭3 | 4 | 5 | ♭6 | ♭7 | 8 |

"Livin' La Vida Loca"

BY DESMOND CHILD AND ROBI ROSA (RICKY MARTIN)

"Be My Lover"

BY DONALD LANE MCCRAY, GERD AMIR SARAF, AND MELANIE THORNTON (LA BOUCHE)

MINOR 6-TONE

| 1 | 2 | ♭3 | 4 | 5 – ♭7 | 8 |

"Billie Jean"

BY MICHAEL JACKSON

"Bad Girls"

BY HOKENSON/ESPOSITO/SUDANO/SUMMER (DONNA SUMMER)

MINOR 5-TONE (PENTATONIC)

1 - ♭3   4   5 - ♭7   8

"Witchy Woman"

BY DON HENLEY AND GLENN FREY (THE EAGLES)

"Woodstock"

BY JONI MITCHELL (J. MITCHELL; CROSBY, STILLS, NASH, AND YOUNG)

RAGTIME

1   2   ♭3   3 - 5   6 - 8

"Signed, Sealed, Delivered, I'm Yours"

BY STEVIE WONDER, L. GARRETT, S. WRIGHT, AND LIL HARDAWAY

"Take Me to the Pilot"

BY ELTON JOHN AND BERNIE TAUPIN

"The Weight"

BY ROBBIE ROBERTSON (THE BAND)

BLUES

1 - ♭3   4   ♭5   5 - ♭7   8

"The Sunshine Of Your Love"

BY PETER BROWN, JOHN BRUCE, AND ERIC CLAPTON (CREAM)

"Fever"

BY EDDIE CODLEY AND JOHN DAVENPORT (PEGGY LEE, LITTLE WILLIE JOHN)

MIXOLYDIAN MODE

1   2   3   4   5   6   ♭7   8

"You Learn"

BY ALANIS MORISSETTE AND GLEN BALLARD (ALANIS MORISSETTE)

"Norwegian Wood"

BY JOHN LENNON AND PAUL MCCARTNEY (BEATLES)

DORIAN MODE

1   2   ♭3   4   5   6   ♭7   8

"Eleanor Rigby"

BY JOHN LENNON AND PAUL MCCARTNEY (BEATLES)

"Parsley, Sage, Rosemary and Thyme"

TRADITIONAL. ARRANGED AND RECORDED BY SIMON & GARFUNKEL

To summarize, pop melody writing is a specialized craft of balancing repetition and contrast. We can do this by duplicating, alternating, and developing melodic ideas. We then craft our ideas into contrasting sections. Writing within a suitable range and scale context helps pinpoint a song to its potential audience. A knowledge of these aspects enables you to write for specific styles and artists, which is what professional songwriting is all about.

Writing within a suitable range and scale context helps pinpoint a song to its potential audience.

Harmony

A knowledge of harmony is very important to a professional songwriter. A completed song includes not only lyric and melody, but a chordal accompaniment as well. Harmony is based on the concept of uniting pleasing musical sounds. The chordal sounds used to accompany and arrange our songs bring out their colors, their emotions. Think of a plain melody and lyric as a black-and-white sketch, a song with harmonization as a full-color drawing or painting. Very often, the imaginativeness of its harmonic setting is what gives a song its distinctive appeal.

Intervals

In order to understand how chords are constructed, they should be broken down into intervals. The basic unit of measuring intervals in Western music is the half-step. You can find a half-step easily on the piano by simply going up or down the keyboard to the next note, whether a black key or white key (C-C♯-D-D♯;-E-F-F♯; etc.). All intervals are measured multiples of half-steps, thus indicating the specific distances between musical pitches.

Here are the intervals inside the major scale, called *diatonic intervals*:

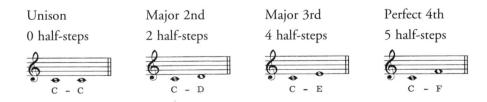

Unison   Major 2nd   Major 3rd   Perfect 4th

0 half-steps   2 half-steps   4 half-steps   5 half-steps

C – C   C – D   C – E   C – F

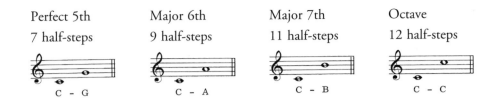

Perfect 5th	Major 6th	Major 7th	Octave
7 half-steps	9 half-steps	11 half-steps	12 half-steps
C - G	C - A	C - B	C - C

If you examine this chart, you will see that certain intervals have been skipped over. There are gaps in the major scale, tones that are considered to be outside the major scale. These are the minor intervals, colors that are used to form minor and exotic scales and chords.

Here are the intervals outside the major scale—*chromatic intervals*:

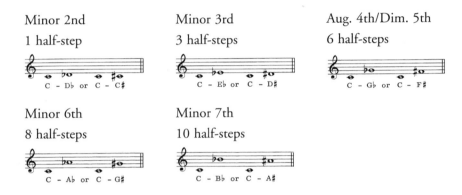

Minor 2nd	Minor 3rd	Aug. 4th/Dim. 5th
1 half-step	3 half-steps	6 half-steps
C - Db or C - C♯	C - Eb or C - D♯	C - Gb or C - F♯

Minor 6th	Minor 7th
8 half-steps	10 half-steps
C - Ab or C - G♯	C - Bb or C - A♯

The intervals on the unison, 4th, 5th, and octave are called perfect intervals because they rarely change, even when the scales change to minor or modal. The 2nd, 3rd, 6th, and 7th intervals are more coloristic, changing in order to form more interesting scale tone colors. They change from major (bright) to minor (dark), depending on the scale formula that one uses.

C Major	C Minor
Major third Perfect fifth	Minor third Perfect fifth

You can create a whole variety of chordal colors simply by building chords out of various combinations of intervals.

Three Levels of Chord Construction

When you play three or more pitches simultaneously, you have played a "chord," and harmony (or disharmony) is created. You can create a whole variety of chordal colors simply by building chords out of various combinations of intervals. The harmonies you may choose depend on the level of chordal sophistication your song requires. Rock, country, and folk styles use mainly simple triads (three-note chords), while jazz-influenced styles are written with more complex chords. Most pop and crossover styles tend to be made up of chords midway between these two extremes.

FIRST LEVEL OF HARMONY—TRIADS

The most common triad in pop music is the major triad, which has a specific formula of half-steps.

Major Triad   4 half-steps + 3 half-steps
                 (major 3rd)   (minor 3rd)

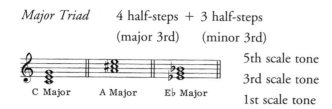

C Major	A Major	E♭ Major	5th scale tone 3rd scale tone 1st scale tone

Another regularly used triad in pop music is the minor triad, which lowers the middle tone, the 3rd, a half-step.

Minor Triad   3 half-steps + 4 half-steps
                 (minor 3rd)   (major 3rd)

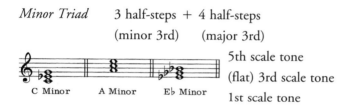

C Minor	A Minor	E♭ Minor	5th scale tone (flat) 3rd scale tone 1st scale tone

A third type of triad is especially common in rock music, the suspended triad (SUS), which "suspends" the use of the 3rd and replaces it with a 4th.

Suspended Triad 5 half-steps + 2 half-steps
                  (4th)   (major 2nd)

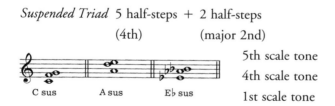

C sus	A sus	E♭ sus	5th scale tone 4th scale tone 1st scale tone

Many songs use chord progressions made up of triadic harmony like The Backstreet Boys' "I Want It That Way" (Max Martin and Andreas Carlsson):

| F#m | D A | F#m | D A | F#m | D A | F#m | E A |

Another example is in the chorus of the Eurythmics' "Here Comes the Rain Again."

| F | C | F | C | F | C | D | G |

SECOND LEVEL OF HARMONY—7ths

For simple styles, triads are all that may be necessary for effective harmonization, but in more middle-of-the-spectrum styles such as country-pop, R&B, and MOR, you'll need more sophisticated chords. For most of these styles, adding a 7th tone above the triads may give a fuller, more polished sound and lead the ear to a more interesting resolution.

Here are some formulas for building 7th chords:

Dominant 7th   Minor 7th   Major 7th

A dominant 7th chord is a major triad plus a minor 7th, a minor 7th chord is a minor triad with a minor 7th added, and a major 7th chord is a major triad plus a major 7th. It is common for more sophisticated song passages to be harmonized using *sus* and 7th chords as illustrated here in a chord progression from Diane Warren's song for Celine Dion "Because I Love You":

| D♭ | G♭ | B♭m7 | A♭sus | Fm7 | G♭maj7 | .... |

THIRD LEVEL OF HARMONY—9ths, 11ths, AND COMPLEX CHORDS

When you want to write in jazz-influenced harmonies such as R&B-pop, jazz-rock-fusion, Broadway, and pre-1950 pop standards, then even more sophisticated harmonies are called for. These include chords built on 9ths and above, as well as chromatically altered chords (with raised or lowered 5ths, 9ths, 11ths, etc.). This is much too demanding a subject to cover here, but don't be overly concerned. These chords are never used in 90 percent of the music on the charts. They are a specialized sound for a specialized urban audience. For those interested in studying jazz harmony, there are many excellent books on the subject, such as the John Mehegan Jazz Pianist series. The following song passage features complex harmonies and is used in songs like "Through the Fire," by David Foster, Cynthia Weil, and Tom Keene (Chaka Khan).

| A♭add2   C7 $^{-13}_{-9}$ | Fm7 E♭m7 A♭7 | D♭maj7 Cm7 Fm7 | B♭m7 E♭11 |

| Creating Chord Progressions

The true art of harmonization is more than knowing which chords to choose; it is often the order in which they progress through the song and how they relate to its melodic shape and emotion that determine their effectiveness. To get a better idea of how chords work together, you need to relate them to a scale context. Chords can be built diatonically (using only tones inside a scale) or chromatically (using tones inside and outside the scale).

DIATONIC CHORDS

Most songs can be harmonized entirely with diatonic chords. Here is how diatonic harmonies are formed inside a C major scale:[1]

These diatonic chords fall into two groups, primary chords and secondary chords. The primary chords are the ones most people refer to when describing three-chord rock songs such as "Twist and Shout," country-western classics such as "I Walk the Line," and traditional twelve-bar blues. Secondary chords are minor triads formed within a major scale, and they provide generally darker, more serious shadings of emotion and color. They allow you to give harmonic contrast in a song without having to change keys. Diatonic secondary chords can help achieve a sense of departure for our second song section without having to travel too far away harmonically. Diatonic secondary chords are used effectively in song passages like the chorus section of "Believe" recorded by Cher.

| I | | I | V | | I | ii | | I | IV | | I | I | V | | I | ii | | I | vi | | I |

MINOR DIATONIC CHORDS

You can do the same thing to the chords in the minor scale.

---

[1] Roman numerals are used in analyzing chords to show at a glance which scale tone the chord is built on; whether the chord is major, minor, or altered in some way; whether a 7th or 9th has been added, etc. The numeral corresponds to the scale degree that is the root of the chord. For instance, in the key of C, a iii chord would be an e-minor triad made up of E-G-B. "Capital" numerals are used for major triads and "lower case" numerals for minor triads. For the iii triad in C to be a major chord, the G would have to be raised to a G♯. But the IV chord—F-A-C—is a major triad automatically. A iii7 would consist of E-G-B-D. If a chord were built on E♭ (an exotic harmony), it would be notated as ♭iii or ♭III depending on whether the chord were major or minor. A degree sign is used after the Roman numeral to show a diminished chord—one in which there is less than a perfect fifth between the root and the "fifth" of the chord. An example in C Major would be the vii°. This triad is made up of B-D-F (while a perfect fifth would be B-F♯). The whole system of using Roman numerals can get rather complicated, but this basic knowledge of conventional symbols will suffice for the examples cited here.

Many songs make use of minor diatonic harmony as analyzed in the following chord progression from "Genie in a Bottle" recorded by Christina Aguilera. This gypsy-like sound is actually a simple four minor diatonic chord loop.

| i ♭VII | ♭VI vm7 |

CHROMATIC CHORDS

The Beatles were masters of using one slightly outside chord for temporary "shock value" in their songs with otherwise straightforward harmonization.

To get even more contrast and more unusual sounds, you may want to experiment with chords that use tones outside your scale context. Here is a list of chords that are "slightly outside," that use only one nonscale tone and do not take you too far out. The Beatles were masters of using one slightly outside chord for temporary "shock value" in their songs with otherwise straightforward harmonization.

Major
II, III, VI, ♭VII, iv

Minor
♭II, IV, ii

Song passages using slightly outside harmonies can be found in tunes like Otis Redding's "Dock of the Bay" (verse and chorus follow respectively):

| I | III | IV | II | I | III | IV | II |
| I | VI | I | VI | I | II | I | VI |

Exotic Harmony

For harmonic effects that are even "farther out," try using one of these chords. They contain more than one nonscale tone and take a song into strange, unexpected places. However, they have to be used carefully and sparingly or your listener may get confused and lose interest.

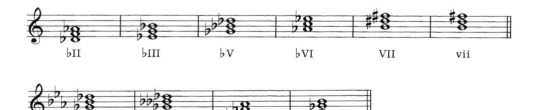

♭II   ♭III   ♭V   ♭VI   VII   vii

♭V   ♭v   ♭ii   (♭)iii

Chord progressions using these unusual harmonies are not uncommon in songs like "Do You Really Want to Hurt Me?" by Hay/Moss/Craig/O'Dowd (Culture Club).

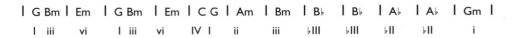

| G Bm | Em | G Bm | Em | C G | Am | Bm | B♭ | B♭ | A♭ | A♭ | Gm |
| I iii | vi | I iii | vi | IV I | ii | iii | ♭III | ♭III | ♭II | ♭II | i |

Vertical or Horizontal Construction

Now that you've seen how a variety of chords can be used to accompany pop melodies, don't overlook the fact that many pop recordings, especially dance records, do not rely on harmony as an important element. In fact, some contemporary records hardly use chords at all. Instead of the traditional vertical construction of a melody with underlying chords, you will find the horizontal construction of a melody accompanied only with a strong rhythmic background, countermelodic riffs and bass lines. That's right, no chords, just riffs!

Here is an example of a song that uses horizontal instead of vertical construction:

"Livin' La Vida Loca"

BY DESMOND CHILD AND ROBI ROSA (RICKY MARTIN)

Think of chords as coloring agents and learn to choose the appropriate simplicity or sophistication of harmonies to match the style of music you're seeking to write.

As you can see in this section, there are many ways to use harmony to make your songs more effective. Think of chords as coloring agents and learn to choose the appropriate simplicity or sophistication of harmonies to match the style of music you're seeking to write. A good way to get a handle on this is to listen to radio stations in your area and see which ones play songs mostly using triads, which ones play 7th chord songs, and which ones play songs using complex 9ths and above. In business, identifying a style of music and targeting the market audience it appeals to is called *demographics*. Why don't we coin a phrase and call this "harmonigraphics"? Whatever we call it, you can see that the more you know about chords and how they work together, the more versatility you can achieve in your songwriting.

Groove

Musicians have long referred to "groove" when describing the basic feel of a song, especially when it feels right. When Duke Ellington wrote "It Don't Mean a Thing If It Ain't Got That Swing," or when that infamous dancer on American Bandstand said that she thought a particular song was a hit because "It's got a good beat and you can dance to it," they were talking about groove. It is absolutely essential for a songwriter to learn what gives a song the kind of groove or feel that has "hit" written all over it.

Rhythmic Elements

In more technical terms, you can better understand groove by examining its rhythmic elements: pulse, tempo, meter, rhythmic subdivision, syncopation, and texture.

PULSE

A pulse is simply a regular, recurring beat. For instance, a march (hup, 2, 3, 4) is based on pulse. In pop music, an obvious example is the bass drum beat (1, 2, 3, 4) of the disco style.

TEMPO

The tempo is the speed of the pulse, the number of pulses per minute. You can understand this by comparing any music pulse to your heartbeat. At rest, our hearts beat at 72 to 80 times a minute. But get us excited (through up-tempo dancing, aerobics, or whatever) and watch our pulse race to 150 times a minute and beyond. Here is a chart showing the relationship of various tempos to pop music function and activity:

Heartbeat = 72 beats per minute: BPM

60 BPM	90 BPM	120 BPM	150 BPM
Slow Ballad	Mid-tempo	Up-tempo Dance	Hyper Drive
"I'll Make Love to You" (by Boys II Men)	"Crazy for You," by John Bettis and Jon Lind (Madonna) and "No Scrubs" (TLC)	"Smooth" (Santana)	"Livin' La Vida Loca" (Ricky Martin)

METER

Meter is the way in which pulses are grouped into measures or bars. Almost all pop music is grouped into 4/4 meter—four pulses (quarter notes) in each measure (or bar). Occasionally, one finds a 3/4 waltz meter with three pulses (quarter notes) in each measure.

Other meters like 2/4, 6/8, 2/2, or more complicated ones like 11/16 or 7/8 exist in classical music and jazz, but are seldom used in pop.

RHYTHMIC SUBDIVISION

The 4/4 pulse of a pop song is the basis for 95 percent of what we hear on the radio today. What's important is to differentiate the rhythms played on rock stations, country stations, soul stations, and easy listening stations. You may need more technical know-how to learn how rhythmic subdivisions help to define a song's style.

A 4/4 measure can be subdivided into any of the following:

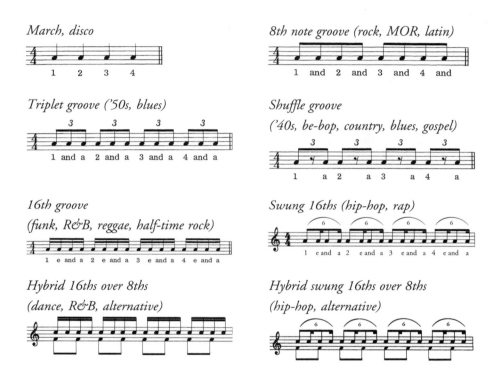

The swung 16th groove is played in a subdivision of six notes to the beat shuffled with the middle 16th of each group of three left out. This is very difficult to read. Consequently, it is usually notated in regular 16ths with an instruction above the first line of music to swing or shuffle the 16ths. It is counted the same way as 16ths but felt with a staggered rhythm, not an even rhythm. There happens to be a nursery rhyme we all know now that is counted in this beat: "one potato, two potato, three potato, four; five potato, six potato, seven potato more." The phrase "seven potato" fills in the whole triplet of that beat. I often refer to this groove as the potato groove because it can only be done while swinging the 16ths.

Both regular 16ths and swung 16ths are often played on top of a full 8th note feel. This results in two grooves at once, which I call a hybrid groove. Much of the pop music of the nineties has been played over hybrid grooves. Examples of straight 16th-8th hybrid include "Genie in a Bottle" by Christina Aguilera with the Backstreet Boys' "All I Have to Give." Hip-hop grooves are usually based on a swung 16th-8th hybrid and are common in today's R&B and alternative styles. Examples include "I Try" by Macy Gray and various cuts by Lauryn Hill and Alanis Morissette.

SYNCOPATION

Once you determine the rhythmic subdivision of a groove, the next most important feature that defines style is its syncopation. Syncopation occurs when there are rhythmic accents on the weak inner beats of a groove, *the beats between the pulses.* Dance music is full of syncopated patterns that use one or more of these accents to create rhythmic drive. Syncopated patterns can be found in the rhythm tracks and in the actual melodies of most of today's recorded music.

Examples within each of the six rhythmic subdivisions are listed below:

8th Note Groove
"Smooth"
BY ROB THOMAS AND ITAAL SHUR AND PERFORMED BY SANTANA

Triplet Groove
"I'll Make Love to You"
BY KENNETH "BABYFACE" EDMONDS AND PERFORMED BY BOYZ II MEN

Shuffle Groove
"With a Little Help From My Friends"
BY JOHN LENNON AND PAUL MCCARTNEY

16th Note Groove
"No Scrubs"

BY KEVIN BRIGGS, KANDI BURNS, AND TAMEKA COTTLE (TLC)

A scrub is a guy who thinks he's fly   and is   al - so known as a bus- ter.

"You Learn"

BY ALANIS MORISSETTE AND GLEN BALLARD

I   rec - om - mend get-ting your heart tram-pled on   to

an - y - one   yeah.

Hybrid 16th/8th
"I Knew I Loved You"

BY SAVAGE GARDEN

Hybrid Swung 16th/8th
"I Try"

BY MACY GRAY

TEXTURE

Once you understand how syncopation creates a danceable groove, you'll want to study the finer points of what makes one dance beat distinctive from another, even if they are made up of the same rhythmic subdivision. This can be a complicated study, but here's a simple concept that can make it easier to understand.

Each groove has its own unique "texture," from sparse to moderate to full. Some rhythm tracks move the beat along with just a few notes while others use many more. Here are examples of sparse and full grooves in eighth-note and sixteenth-note subdivisions:

Sparse 8th bass line

As in **"Livin' La Vida Loca"**

BY DESMOND CHILD AND ROBI ROSA (RICKY MARTIN)

Full 8th bass line

As in *"Like a Virgin"*

BY BILLY STEINBERG AND TOM KELLY (MADONNA)

Sparse 16th bass line

As in *"Purple Rain"*

BY PRINCE

Full 16th bass line (techno)

As in *"Heart of Glass"*

BY DEBORAH HARRY AND CHRIS STEIN (BLONDIE)

People in the record industry are looking for songs with the groove already built in. Knowing how to place your song in its best rhythmic setting will give your writing the competitive edge that says, "Play me on the radio!"

David "Cat" Cohen enjoys a multifaceted career as a songwriter, independent producer, keyboard teacher, and author. A songwriter with major credits (Cheryl Lynn, Syreeta, Freddie Hubbard), he is a member of ASCAP and NARAS. He has also placed songs in the HBO film The Rat Pack *and Universal Pictures'* Undercover Brother. *Cat teaches classes at UCLA Extension and the Musicians Institute in Hollywood. He regularly coaches and consults for songwriters in the L.A. area. He can be reached at his Web site at www.catcohen.com.*

chapter seven

Collaboration

Why Two (or More) Heads Can Be Better Than One

A substantial percentage of the world's most popular songs are collaborations. Consider the wealth of classic material that's come from teams like Lerner and Loewe; Rodgers and Hammerstein; Kander and Ebb; Bacharach and David; Rodgers and Hart; the Gershwins; Mann and Weil; Holland, Dozier, and Holland; Gamble and Huff; Lennon and McCartney; Goffin and King; Leiber and Stoller; Fleming and Morgan; L.A. Reid and "Babyface" Edmonds, and on and on.

In a January 2001 edition of *Billboard* magazine: the Hot Country Chart showed fifty-two of sixty songs were cowritten and of the remaining nine, six were writer/artists; on the Hot R&B/Hip-Hop Chart, eighty-eight of one hundred were cowritten and seven of those remaining were writer/artists; of the Hot 100, eighty-three were collaborations and of the remaining seventeen, nine were writer/artists. Today's song market is so competitive that professional writers can't afford to settle for less than the best, so they often elect to team up with other specialists.

Though this chapter is devoted to collaboration, it should be noted here that it isn't always the best or the only way to write. Hit writer Randy Goodrum ("You Needed Me," "Bluer Than Blue") has successfully written with and without a collaborator. Here's a quote from an interview I did with Randy:

First of all I'm not a collaborative writer as a rule. I started off writing for years and years on my own. Most everything that I have ever had that was big was written totally by me except for this year (1987) [Goodrum collaborated with Steve Perry on "Oh Sherrie," "Foolish Heart," and six others on an album]. But there are dangers with collaboration. At least from my experience, it can water down and lose a sense of uniqueness. I was in a seminar one time and somebody said, "Gee when I heard 'Bluer Than Blue,' I thought, how is he going to rhyme 'closet'?" I said, 'feel like it.' I rhymed '*it*,' not 'closet.' Well, if I had been cowriting, chances are we would have said, "Let's not use 'closet'." We would have thrown it out, yet it's a little bit more unique of a

Today's song market is so competitive that professional writers can't afford to settle for less than the best, so they often elect to team up with other specialists.

line than other songs that I've cowritten. Sometimes the art has to have a little bit of a rough edge in there, in a charismatic sort of sense. There has to be some abandon to it. You just rewrite and rewrite and rewrite and sometimes it's not logical what makes greatness. You know, it's just this little muse that comes along. He doesn't have a business suit on or anything, and it tickles. . . .

So I think with collaboration, it's good to get something that makes you just jump up and down, and if it can be better than what you can do on your own, that's incredible. Or if you can arrive at a place that neither of you can get by yourselves. . . . I wrote two songs with Michael McDonald for his solo album, and I am proud to say that neither of us has ever written anything like the two songs we came up with. They were totally in another place. So that's a nice way to look at cowriting also.

Though it's not the only way to go, there are several other good reasons why writers collaborate:

1. **A writer may have more talent as a lyricist than as a composer or vice versa.** It's important that you objectively assess your strengths and weaknesses. Obviously, if you're a good lyricist with marginal musical skills, you should look for a composer. Your ego may need to see only your name on the "words & music by" line at the top of the page, or maybe you just want all the royalties yourself. The bottom line, though, is that the song must be as good as it can possibly be, regardless of who did what.

Many talented musicians/arrangers can put the music together but don't feel the lyric is important enough to warrant a collaborator. They risk seriously limiting the artistic and commercial potential of the songs.

Writers often tend to get trapped in their own musical and lyrical clichés, and a collaborator can supply fresh ideas.

2. **Writers often tend to get trapped in their own musical and lyrical clichés, and a collaborator can supply fresh ideas.** When you pick up your guitar, your fingers automatically go through a familiar and comfortable set of chord changes, picking styles, or rhythm patterns. Out of these established patterns come melodies much like those you've written before. It's easy to get into a creative rut. At that point you need to get a chord book and work out some new chords and progressions, listen to the radio and discover some new grooves, or find a collaborator whose style you like.

Even professional writers aren't always productive and may need the input of other writers. They may write great ballads, but need to team up with someone when it comes to up-tempo songs or another style. In fact, there's always such a demand for up-tempo songs that if you do that well, it should be relatively easy to find cowriters.

3. **Writing with someone else disciplines your writing habits.** Many people seem to function better on deadlines and always wait until the last minute, while thinking up all kinds of other projects to avoid the task ("I can't possibly create with a dirty house/broken guitar string/out-of-tune piano."). This avoidance syndrome is a way of signaling and priming the subconscious to start working on the project at hand. At the eleventh hour,

when you have to produce, the brain sends a signal to the subconscious that says, "It's time to download all those ideas," and, like magic, they're there.

Many writers will avoid writing altogether if there are no deadlines. Those who function best on that kind of "crisis" basis set up deadlines for themselves. One good way is to find a collaborator and plan on a regular day to get together and write. You know you'll have to come up with some ideas to work on before that deadline, and that subconscious preparation process will operate on an ongoing basis if it knows that every week (or every day) that deadline will arrive.

4. **A partner will furnish a constant feedback and critique.** You're stuck for a rhyme and eager to finish the song. You put together the first thing to come into your head and say, "It's OK. I've heard stuff on the radio that rhymes 'rain' with 'again.' Maybe some British guy'll cut it." A conscientious collaborator is there to say, "Wrong! Let's see if we can find something else." Maybe you're a lyricist and your collaborator is a singer and can say, "I'll want to hold this note in the melody, so could we use another word instead of 'garbage'?" This feedback can keep you at your best and help you both grow commercially and artistically. (Though based on the above Goodrum quote, this could go either way.)

5. **The more collaborators on a song, the more people there are networking to get the song recorded.** Let's face it. There's also a political strategy to cowriting. If each writer has several industry contacts for whom he can play the song, you'll have that many more opportunities to get the song published or recorded as well as extend your reputation and your network of writers and industry people.

Meeting Your Match

Finding the perfect partner can be a difficult process. At best, no matter how you go about it, you'll have the same odds on finding the perfect collaborator right away as you'd have walking into a singles' bar and finding a marriage partner. The two situations have a lot in common. You're dealing with a whole range of personalities, personal habits, expectations, previous experiences, egos, and lifestyles. With collaborators you can add musical and literary influences, business know-how, and aggressiveness.

But there are a few ways to get started and narrow the odds. Like a singles' bar, you go to where other people are looking, too. You put an ad in a music-oriented periodical like *Music Connection* or the newsletter of your local songwriters organization. Placing an ad in your local newspaper is probably a waste of time because readers don't generally look for cowriters there. A better bet is to make little signs that you can put up on bulletin boards in music and record stores, the Musicians Union, or clubs that feature your kind of music. If you're a lyricist, it's also a good idea to put your signs on college music department bulletin boards so composition students can find you. Computer bulletin boards are also a good bet. Search under "song collaboration" or "music collaboration." Since it's possible to collaborate by exchanging audio files on the Net, distance is no longer much of an obstacle, though it's obviously not as spontaneous as being in the same room.

The more collaborators on a song, the more people there are networking to get the song recorded.

The ad or message should include the styles with which you're most comfortable, the instrument(s) you play, your favorite lyricists/composers, and your credits, if any. If you're looking for a lyricist and are in a working band, have a production deal, do your own publishing, or have an exclusive publishing deal, mention that, too. This tells the serious lyricists that you have serious prospects for their work.

Another approach is through professional organizations and services (www.musicianscontact.com has composer/lyricist listings containing relevant style and bio information). For an annual fee you can list your own information and be sent a list of potential collaborators. TAXI's www.musiciansjunction.com is a free service. (See Appendix for lists of songwriters' service Web sites.)

In Nashville, attend the weekly critique sessions by the Nashville Songwriters Association International (NSAI) or any of the many "writers nights" at local clubs. These are among the best opportunities to screen a writer's work before meeting in person. All workshops, clubs, and showcases offer that opportunity. Joining local or national songwriter organizations or music associations is also a great way to make contacts.

In any of these situations, you may hear a singer/songwriter whose music is excellent but whose lyrics are weak, or vice versa. You might, diplomatically, ask that person if he or she would consider collaboration.

"Writing Up"

There's a definite advantage in writing with someone who's out there exposing those songs to the public and the industry. It's also advantageous to your growth to write with those you feel are as good or, preferably better, writers than you. This strategy is called "writing up." If you've cowritten with an established writer, it provides entre to other pro caliber writers and to their publishers. One of the best positions to be in as an independent writer is to cowrite with a staff writer at a good publishing company and get a cut on a song you wrote together, particularly if you can keep your own publishing.

Try to meet as many people as possible in all areas of the industry. Publishers, though they seldom sign staff lyricists, often like to know of good lyricists that they can hook up with good composers or with other writers on their staffs. Producers may be working with bands who could use the services of a strong lyricist. Recording engineers are also good contacts.

A substantial number of successful collaborations today, particularly in pop and R&B/hip-hop, happen at the source of the project.

Writing With Artists and Producers

A substantial number of successful collaborations today, particularly in pop and R&B/hip-hop, happen at the source of the project. That encompasses three typical situations: writing with the artist, writing with the producer, or being a writer/producer yourself.

WRITING WITH THE ARTIST

This is a great strategy if you can do it. Assuming you come up with an exceptional song, the artist has a financial interest, as a cowriter, in recording the song. On an artistic level, the process can include: talking with the artist about what's going on in his/her life and getting song ideas from the conversation; taking the artist's lyric ideas and helping to structure them and finish them; initiating your own ideas lyrically or musically.

Here's what Jeff Trott (cowrote "Every Day Is a Winding Road," "If It Makes You Happy," and "My Favorite Mistake") told me, in an interview for United Airlines In-flight Entertainment, about his collaboration with Sheryl Crow.

My relationship with Sheryl is kind of like baseball pitchers. They have a starting pitcher and a closer. I'm really good at instigating ideas, but I'm not so good at finishing them. Sheryl's strength is being able to complete an idea. That's very difficult to do. It takes a lot of discipline. That's where our chemisty works. I get the ball rolling, and she's the closer.

These collaborations come about from personal relationships with artists, referrals by publishers, producers, managers, and other industry pros as well as other artists.

WRITING WITH PRODUCERS

The producer also has a financial stake in the success of the artist and usually a concept for the artist's sound and the type of material they want to record. So the producer may, along with collaborating with the artist, look for cowriters who have experience writing a specific type of song. If you're a writer/artist, teaming up with a writer/producer is a good strategy. Madonna's successive (and successful) collaborations with writer/producers Stephen Bray, Shep Pettibone, and Patrick Leonard are good examples.

BEING A WRITER/PRODUCER

Having the ability to produce artists puts a writer in a great situation. You can write and produce songs and shop them to specific artists. There is a distinct advantage to producing master quality tracks because there's a good possibility that if they like the song and the tracks, you'll also end up as a producer. That was the case with Steve Kipner, David Frank, and Pam Sheyne's Christina Aguilera breakthrough hit "Genie in a Bottle" (as well as 98 Degrees' "The Hardest Thing" and Dream's "He Loves U Not"). I interviewed Steve about the process of writing "Genie in a Bottle." Though he says he writes differently with different collaborators, this was a process that seems to be pretty common for pop and R&B/hip-hop writers who often start with groove tracks.

With "Genie in a Bottle," it was more of a track-driven song where David Frank knew that Pam Shayne was coming into town, so he got up, literally, at two in the morning, went into his studio, and just started coming up with very strange, interesting music. There's a kick-drum pattern in that song that's a very fast kick-drum. So what happens then is that you take that eight bars of music and just loop it around and around and it just doesn't stop. It just plays and you turn it up loud and all of a sudden, you just start singing something. So, I'll sing something or Pam would sing something, David would sing something. You're not really concentrating on anyone else, but you just sing stuff—stream of consciousness. You're not thinking about it. Whatever comes out. And someone will go, "What was that?" and you grab onto something. And so that gives you a little melody and all of a sudden, slowly but surely, everyone starts sort of like singing relatively the same melody.

There are no words at that point, but just sort of got a little melody. And then you're walking around and someone will go, "If you wanna be with me" . . . and someone says, "Wow, that's interesting." Someone will grab that and then the next line would come and then someone would say, "I'm a genie. I'm a genie in a bottle." Wow, that's good . . . let's try that. And someone else said, "You gotta rub me the right way." Wow, there you go, there's a new line. And so you try it again and it's almost like chiseling stuff away. And if something doesn't work, you change it. And you just keep literally knocking things around and molding it until you get an idea of what the song can be about. Once you've got the idea of "there's the right attitude"—first of all, when it's an up-tempo, aggressive sort of a song, it can't just be a namby-pamby sort of a lyric. It has to have an attitude that whoever's gonna end up singing the song has to have, has to believe in, and it has to be about something that people would want to be bothered with. And then you think, OK, now what can the verse be about? So the verses can be more of a sitting down and looking at the lyrics and what is this song about. What's the attitude we want to convey here? So it's actually done all of a sudden until you live in that little world in that thing, ya know, then all of a sudden a couple days can go by and you just keep working and it takes a long time, it's not that quick. Then after that's finished, you actually start to record and you customize it right to the end.

You can also find a great singer, write for (or with) and produce her, then shop her to record companies. You gamble your time and money on the quality of your writing and production, but it's a good strategy. When you shop the artist, you're also shopping your writing and production for future projects.

Can This Marriage Work?

After finding a collaborator who's stylistically compatible, you have the sometimes difficult task of developing a good rapport and business relationship with that person.

One successful songwriter says, "My ego is my biggest problem when I collaborate. I have to keep reminding myself that I'm collaborating with this lyricist because I really respect her work; and when she offers a suggestion or asks me to change part of my melody to accommodate a lyric, I should give it a shot." The ego problem in this example was caused, in part, by the fact that the writer had written both words and music to his songs for years and found it difficult to readjust his habits.

A negative and quarrelsome attitude can destroy any type of partnership, especially with people who are sensitive and involved with such emotional issues as exposing their vulnerable psyches. It's not always easy to deal with someone who tells you your "baby" is ugly. We all want to believe that because the baby comes from us, it's already perfect. Remember that you're both trying to make your song pretty. Even when you're writing alone, the ability to step back and look at your song objectively is a quality of professionalism. When you're working with someone else, that professional attitude becomes doubly important because criticism is a necessary part of the process. A good partner won't let you ignore a flaw. It is, in fact, one of the primary benefits of collaborating.

If you really do feel strongly about a line a cowriter has rejected, a few calm reasons why you think it works may convince your partner to leave it in. If you find yourself fighting too hard for it, it may be more productive to spend the time and energy looking for a new line. Famed lyricists Alan and Marilyn Bergman's rule is: If one collaborator doesn't like the line, it goes. With nearly endless alternatives, they're confident they'll eventually find a line they both like.

The one thing to keep foremost in your mind is that you're both trying to create the best song possible. All criticism and response should be directed toward that goal rather than to protecting your ego. Don't defend something just because you wrote it or because you'll get a bigger percentage if you contribute more (a good argument for a straight 50/50 split of writers' royalties from the beginning (see the following section, "Business Considerations").

You'll need to learn not only to accept criticism graciously but also to give it constructively. Critiquing is an art in itself. When you're beginning a relationship, it's crucial that any criticism be given as gently and positively as possible. As your routine develops and you get more comfortable and trusting with each other, you'll probably work out some shorthand to speed up the process. As you communicate better, you'll also get to know which buttons not to push. There's a big difference between saying, "What a dumb line!" and "Let's make that line stronger." The former is an unqualified putdown. The latter acknowledges a line could be better, offers a challenge, and implies faith in you and your partner. It's important that you continuously acknowledge your partner's talent and compliment good ideas. Criticism becomes much easier in an atmosphere of respect. If you find few causes for compliments, you should be writing with someone else.

Approaches to collaboration are as varied as the combinations of individuals involved. It's important to find out right away how your prospective partner likes to work. Here are some of the variables:

1. **Writing lyric or music alone and getting together later.** Some people are uncomfortable when their partner is in the same room. It disturbs their creative flow. They may be open to criticism and change later, but they need to get something to work from first. Some lyricists would rather write to a finished melody and vice versa. This method is well suited to correspondence. Some who write this way will send a melody or lyric to several writers in succession and say, "Take this lyric (or tune) for a week and see what you can

A negative and quarrelsome attitude can destroy any type of partnership, especially with people who are sensitive and involved with such emotional issues as exposing their vulnerable psyches.

come up with." It gives a writer a chance to hear several versions of his material. And it saves the hassle of waiting endlessly for a collaborator to finish a song—a very common problem.

To make that situation work, however, you should have an agreement in writing ahead of time that it won't be a complete song unless you both agree on the finished product. Otherwise, legally, it is a complete work. I should also mention that it's unethical to give a lyric or music to more than one potential collaborator at the same time without their knowledge. They should have the option to agree to that type of speculative situation or not. They may choose to spend their time more productively elsewhere, and it's disrespectful of you not to allow them the choice.

For yourself, it's always a good idea to ask if anyone else is working on the same assignment you've been given. Publishers have been known not to volunteer that information and writers rightfully resent it.

2. **Writing together in the same room.** Writers who work this way love the give-and-take of instant feedback. They enjoy the excitement and high energy level that can happen when two collaborators really start to groove. It's particularly good for artists who write both lyric and music, so ideas can be stimulated and shared in both areas. With this type of collaboration, your compatibility becomes more important. What is your most creative time of day? Can you work every day or once a week? Do you like each other and not feel intimidated (though a little tension is not necessarily a bad thing)?

Regardless of the approach, you'll need stylistic compatibility and also need to decide whether you or your partner also want to collaborate with others. It's generally understood that writers may collaborate with many other writers, particularly in Nashville, where it's part of the musical culture and business.

Pat and Pete Luboff (authors of *88 Songwriting Wrongs & How to Right Them* and hit songwriters: "Trust Me," the first single on Snoop Dogg's "Topp Dogg" album; "I Wish He Didn't Trust Me So Much," a No. 2 chart recording by Bobby Womack; "Body Language" by Patti LaBelle) have this to say about collaboration:

The paperwork is easy to deal with. The relationship with a creative partner is the hard part. The give-and-take process can be stimulating, which may be pleasant or devastating. To avoid the latter, it's important to collaborate from strength, not weakness. One of our cowriters says, "You have to feel you're very good to be able to collaborate, or you won't have the security to let things go. If you're not secure in your writing, you get that ego thing of trying to prove yourself with every line you write. You should collaborate to make it better, not because you can't do all of it by yourself."

The most important thing to keep in mind while writing alone or collaborating is that you're writing because you love it and the purpose is to have a good time. I go crazy every time I see Muppet character Don Music, songwriter on Sesame Street,

It's unethical to give a lyric or music to more than one potential collaborator at the same time without their knowledge.

banging his head into his piano keys and screaming, "I'll never do it, I'll never get that line." I've been there so many times myself. Fortunately, Don has Kermit the Frog to help him over the rough spots. All we have is our sense of humor and lots of patience.

It's a useful technique to play records of a specific artist while warming up to a song. This way, you create your own assignments. Check the label to make sure the artist does sing songs written by other writers. Playing the current hit single and trying to write the next one is a good job to take on.

Hit songwriter Harold Payne, who has written for Bobby Womack, Rod Stewart, and Snoop Dogg, among others, has these words of advice:

You can collaborate on an assignment or an organic basis. You should decide at the beginning if you want it to be commercial. If you do, what artist could record it? If you are writing a song that's more production-oriented, do you have the facilities among you to make the kind of demo that song needs? If we have a particular assignment to write for an artist, we do research, listen to something like it, and buy the artist's latest album.

If there's no particular assignment, we might work from a title. Both parties must be enthusiastic before looking at each other's ideas. It's chemistry that makes us go on a particular one. You should have a few different ideas, in case your first choice doesn't work, so someone doesn't feel forced to work on something they're not interested in.

Or you can just get together and have a conversation casually. I call that the organic approach. It's for the pleasure of it. It's an opportunity to stretch out a bit and establish rapport. Take whatever comes as a result of the interaction, no pressure. If something gets done, that's almost extra. It's also OK if you decide not to write together or not to write that particular idea. You have to be comfortable about saying, "That doesn't turn me on." It has to flow. Meet once a week; don't be afraid if there's no progress. Some obstacles are dislodged by just getting together.

A good way to start the collaboration going is to have a title session. We do this by talking about the world in general, what's happening in the news, what is happening to the way people relate to each other. Then we might decide whether we want to write an up song or a down one. Most of the time, we decide on the "up" side, because we want to be commercial, and positive songs tend to be more commercially acceptable. Then we might decide on a general area, like two people who have gotten back together after being split up. Then, we have to find a unique way of expressing that idea. We might throw around some titles of songs that have already been written on the subject, just to give a clearer idea of where we're heading. Or, we might just throw around titles on various subjects from lists that we've made on our own. Or, we might talk about something that

You can practice collaborating with the world's best writers before you approach your friend next door. How? Take any song that has been a hit or that you simply admire. If you want some lyric-writing practice, write new lyrics to the melody. If you want to try out your melody writing, put a new melody to those lyrics. Now, take what you've created to another writer without telling them how you did it, and she'll write the new missing part. The advantage of this trick is that while you're writing, you learn about how successful songs are structured, where rhymes go, where the title is placed, how long the song is, how many bars to each section, where the melody rises and falls, and other things we've discussed. And you know your finished product is based on a successful structure.

happened in the life of a friend that we feel would make a good story. These conversations over dinner make writing a pleasant social thing, rather than just another task to sit down to after a hard day of earning a living.

Business Considerations

Let's assume that you've found a lyricist and/or composer whose words or music feel like the magic ingredient you need to write great songs. You find that you can work well together and, first thing you know, you've got a fantastic song. You say, "Great, let's find a publisher!" Your partner says, "Oh, I guess I forgot to tell you. I've got my own publishing company, so I'd like to publish the song." At that point the song may be in trouble. You may rightfully ask whether your partner's company is capable of properly promoting the song. Does the company have the connections to get the song recorded? You're better off not having a publisher at all than to have the song tied up with an inadequate one. At least you'd be free to place the song with a good publisher.

If you find yourself in this situation, you might request that, if your partner's company doesn't get the song recorded in six months or a year, he give up his publishing interest and the two of you look for a publisher together. You might also set up your own company and split the publishing, but jointly agree to the time limit. Or you may agree to bring in a third publisher, at which point you both will give an equal share of the publishing (or all of it) to the new party. (See chapter ten, "Publishing," for more on this subject.)

The Splits

You also need to agree on a division of the writer's share of the royalties. Your collaborator may have supplied a title for a song, but you wrote the rest of it. You might feel you did most of the work and should get 90 percent of the money. Your partner may feel that without the title, which supplied the premise, there wouldn't *be* a song. You may both be right, but that kind of bickering could destroy a very promising collaborative effort. It's generally agreed that if you get together with the intention of writing a song or to establish an ongoing writing relationship, you split the writers' royalties 50/50.

Without an agreement to the contrary, all rights and percentages are split equally. Each writer owns an equal portion of the copyright, and each of the writers is empowered to grant a license to anyone who wants to record it.

If one of you is a lyricist and the other writes music, it's a pretty straightforward arrangement. It tends to get a little touchy if each of you writes music and lyrics or if the contributions are more difficult to quantify. There's more room for argument about who contributed the most. That's why it's always best to agree on equal shares ahead of time.

On some of the Lennon/McCartney tunes, one undoubtedly contributed more than the other on individual songs, but they just didn't want to fight over it every time, so they divided the royalties equally.

Here are some other possible situations you may have to deal with:

1. **You've written the song and you take it to someone else to "tighten it up," and that person contributes a new hook or changes the song's direction.** How much writer credit will he get? At the time you bring your song to the writer, you should try to work it out based on what you want him to contribute.

2. **You take your song to an artist who wants to "personalize" it and changes something.** For this he wants writer's credit. This is a very common and potentially volatile situation, with several factors to weigh:

   a. Is this an important cut? With an established artist, there's no question about it. But even with a new artist, the song could be a major hit or end up on a hit album. Any recording credit may therefore be important to you.

   b. How extensive are the changes? "Personalizing" the song by changing a "she" to a "he" does not warrant a writer's credit. If the artist wants more extensive changes and you want to accommodate him, offer to make them yourself. Get as much information as you can about what the artist is looking for and present several rewrites. If the artist seems unreasonably resistant to your changes, you may lose the cut unless you allow him to rewrite or just give him the credit. You can swallow your pride and walk to the bank, walk away with your pride (and your empty pockets), or tell the artist you can't change this song but suggest that you write something together from scratch. If it's just a matter of financial incentive for the artist to record the song, you also have the publisher's share of the royalties to offer if you publish the song yourself. (See "Negotiating," chapter eleven.)

   c. How badly does the artist want the song? If he thinks it's good enough, he's torn between wanting the writing credit and money and possibly blowing a potential hit. You're in the same position, too, except that you may also be motivated by anger that someone would have the *nerve* to demand credit for your work.

   While many artists wouldn't think of asking for undeserved credit (and royalties),

It's generally agreed that if you get together with the intention of writing a song or to establish an ongoing writing relationship, you split the writers' royalties 50/50.

others do it in a New York minute. You ultimately have to decide whether it's worth it to your career to give up a portion of those royalties and credits.

3. **A publisher suggests changes and wants a writer's credit.** Generally speaking, this is the publisher's job, and she shouldn't ask. It would depend, of course, on how substantial the contribution is. It can get a little touchy, but it should be your decision.

4. **Maybe you decide later that for some reason you want a new lyric to a song you've already written with someone.** Is it OK to change? Not without your cowriter's written permission.

5. **What if your melody writer or publisher wants a new foreign language lyric?** Do you still get paid? A decision has to be made whether you're going to say, "Words and music by _____," or "Words by _____ and music by_____." In the former, if a foreign subpublisher wants to commission a lyric translation, the percentage granted to the translator comes out of both your royalties equally. In the latter, it's deducted from the lyricist's half. In the former, if you're sued for lyric infringement, you both get sued. In the latter, the lyricist gets sued. In the former, if there's a successful instrumental version of the song, both writers get paid; in the latter, the lyricist doesn't. In the former, if a lyric is reprinted, you both get paid; in the latter, only the lyricist. Note that all these are also vice-versa and know that these questions can be worked out contractually. (See paragraph six of the Collaborators' Agreement, in the following section, "Preliminary Business Meeting".)

All these potential problems point to the need for collaborators to get all the business straight before they get into the music. There are few things more frustrating than knowing you've written a winner but can't do anything with it.

Preliminary Business Meeting

K.A. Parker is a professional lyricist, a five-time American Song Festival winner, and former staff writer for Motown's Stone Diamond Music who has taught lyric writing at UCLA, Musician's Institute, and throughout the United States. Her suggestions for conducting a business meeting and list of considerations for collaborators (which she uses in her classes) is the best I've seen. With her permission, I offer them to you minus the more extensive discussions of the ones I've already covered.

| Conducting the Business Meeting

Setting up a business meeting is like buying fire insurance: You may not think you need it until it's too late. The things that you'll be discussing will only be necessary if and when the songs you write with your collaborator turn out to be good enough to be published, recorded, and released. Of course, there's no way to know this until you actually start working together. But, assuming you believe in your own potential and in that of your collaborator (and there's no reason to work with another person unless you do), I am going to assume that you agree that a meeting of the minds on business matters is necessary before you begin work on music matters.

Don't fall into the trap of thinking that just because your potential collaborator is "nice," that ironing out the business will be a snap later on. Most of us are "nice" when we are trying to impress others. But greed does amazing things to people, and business is about money, after all. Ego, dreams, and money make a powerful brew. Many successful songwriters have ended up giving their royalty income to the lawyers who were left to sort out the disagreements between two "nice," talented people.

The business meeting has three basic rules:

1. **Never conduct a business meeting at the same time as a creative meeting.** You'll need to be organized, closed, and tough to do business. You'll need to be flexible, open, and childlike to be creative. Don't try to be both at the same time—it won't work. Conduct your business in a neutral place, like a coffee shop, on a day when you're not planning to write together. Sharing a meal is a nice idea. It softens the whole affair, limits the time frame (usually not more than an hour), and makes it easy to exit if you see that it's not going well. Of course, if things do go well, it helps to bond the relationship, too.

2. **Come prepared.** You may very well end up educating your new partner if she is less informed about the business than you are. Make copies of information you want her to read. Back up your opinion with resources. Take notes or tape the meeting for future reference. Make a checklist or agenda of the items you want to discuss. Be prepared to draw a letter of agreement for signature at a later date, based on the discussion. A business meeting is not a good time to be under the influence of alcohol or drugs of any kind. Have your drink when the meeting is over.

3. **Go in with a positive attitude.** Don't enter the meeting with tales about how you got screwed before and you're doing this to protect yourself. Assume good will and go from there. You're building a team and every team needs goals, guidelines, regulations, and direction. Don't be defensive. More than anything, the session should be an information-gathering interview. If you conduct it well, it should save you from any hostile confrontations in the future.

| Specifics

Now that you know the rules, what specifics do you discuss? Here's a list. You may want to eliminate some of these points or include some of your own, but all the basics are here:

1. **Is your information current?** Name, address, phone numbers, Social Security number, birth date, and affiliation (ASCAP, BMI, SESAC) of your partner should be up to date. This will go in your files and be used when you fill out the copyright forms on your songs. The minute you create a copyright (i.e., a song) together, you must keep up to date on this information. I remember vividly how I felt when a publisher greatly wanted a song of mine, but finally passed when my collaborator could not be found. Most publishers will not be interested in publishing half a song. Keep in touch! Note: I wait until I know I want to work with someone before I ask for his/her address and Social Security

Don't fall into the trap of thinking that just because your potential collaborator is "nice," that ironing out the business will be a snap later on.

number. Some people may be touchy about giving this info to a new acquaintance.

2. **How does your partner feel about publishing?** Does he have his own publishing company? Is it active? Does he want your publishing as well? How does he feel about working with the major publishers if they offer a contract on the tune? Is he interested in working with a small, untried publishing company?

3. **Does your partner have aspirations to be a recording artist?** Do you? Will either of you want to keep all the best songs for yourself? This is a source of major conflict with many collaborators and should be thoroughly discussed before the work begins. There is nothing more frustrating than holding back a great song on the chance that your partner might get signed—or seeing all your best songs go to another person, if you're the one with artistic aspirations. Be frank about this issue.

4. **When is a song completed?** Ideally, it's when both of you say so. That's OK if one of you isn't a perfectionist or a procrastinator. Clashes of temperament will be a sore spot here unless you come up with a set of rules. What if you disagree? How many times do you rewrite after a critique session? After the demo is complete, will you be willing to go back in and make major changes?

5. **How prolific are you?** How prolific is your partner? If one of you writes every day and one of you only writes when you're inspired, that can be very frustrating for the more prolific of the two. Do you or your partner need deadlines? Pressure? How long will you give a lyric or melody to your partner before you expect to see some activity on her part? What do you do when one of you wants the song finished and the other one doesn't want to finish it, or can't?

6. **When do you bring in a third party to work on the song?** Who will you bring in? Ideally, it's when you both agree you've reached a dead end. Again, in an ideal situation, it should be a mutually agreed-upon third party. But you need to discuss this thoroughly. *Never bring in a third party to work on a song without telling your partner.* You'd be surprised how often this is done, and it usually means the end of the partnership.

7. **What about splits?** This is a major bone of contention in many relationships where one party writes both words and music and the other party only writes one or the other. *Professional writers split everything right down the middle, no matter who does what. When a third party is called in, everything is divided into thirds.*

8. **What about demos?** Where do you do them? Who decides which songs to do? Who pays for them and how? Who produces, engineers, plays, sings? Generally, the fees are split exactly like the song, 50/50. But what if one partner owns a studio and can play all the instruments, etc.? Does he charge the other partner for the demo costs? This is an individual matter, and both parties should agree with whatever arrangement is made, regardless of how they work it out.

9. **What connections do each of you have?** Would either of you feel comfortable in using them? Is one of you more aggressive? Do either of you go to LA, New York, or Nashville on a regular basis? How will you get your songs heard by publishers, producers, or artists? Do either of you belong to professional organizations such as the Nashville

Professional writers split everything right down the middle, no matter who does what. When a third party is called in, everything is divided into thirds.

Songwriters Association, The Songwriters Guild, or Taxi? Would either of you be willing to join to get professional feedback, pitch songs to producers and publishers, and so forth? Most partnerships without goals die quickly. Once you spend the time and money required to write and demo your songs—then what? Are either of you prepared to move to LA, Nashville, or New York to better promote your work?

10. **How does each of you feel about songwriting competitions?** Who pays the entry fee and how will the winnings be split?

Creating music successfully with your partner will depend on the flexibility and willingness to work things out that each of you brings to the relationship. If the songs you produce are great, the incentive to work out the snags will be greater. It might help if you adopt the belief that people are more important than songs. If you don't believe that, then maybe you should write alone.

It might help if you adopt the belief that people are more important than songs. If you don't believe that, then maybe you should write alone.

Agreements regarding copyrighted musical compositions may be registered in the Copyright Office in Washington, D.C., if you know the original copyright registration number. This provides "constructive notice" of the agreement to the public so that anyone dealing with a writer acting in violation of the agreement is deemed to have notice of such a wrongful act. As to companies and individuals who conduct an actual search of copyright office records, a record of the agreement will discourage any transfers or licenses in violation of its terms.

Writing As a Band—Working It Out

Occasionally you'll pick up a record by a group and see five or six writers (group members) listed after a title. You think, "Do they expect me to believe that all those writers contributed equally to the writing of that song?" There are, in fact, groups in which all members create lyrics and/or music together; but in most group situations, one writer (or two) usually contributes more than the rest. Maybe the lead singer or keyboard player is responsible for the melody, or someone else has the lyric concept or writes most of the words. Many bands are formed around a writer/artist or team. There are bands in which several members contribute their own songs or write with another group member.

So why, then, should a group decide to share writing credit with all its members if those members *don't* contribute to lyrics or melodies? For two main reasons: the first financial, the second artistic.

| Financial Reasons

On the financial side, there are five major areas in which a group member can make money: (1) record royalties (2) live performances (3) merchandising (4) songwriting royalties (5) publishing.

1. In record royalties (not writer/publisher royalties), the cold reality is that recording costs, advances, video production and other expenses are recouped by the company from

The following is a cowriters' contract with comments to help you tailor it to your own situation. (There is a copy of this agreement at *www.johnbraheny.com*.)

COLLABORATORS' AGREEMENT

This Agreement is entered into on _____ 20 __ with respect to the following musical composition(s):

_____

_____

The undersigned songwriters have collaborated in the creation of the aforementioned song(s) with the following understanding:

1. No songwriter shall be responsible to any other songwriter for expenses incurred in the preparation or presentation of the song(s) unless agreed upon.

2. All sums received from exploitation of the song(s), as well as all approved expenses incurred, will be divided as follows:

   Writer's name   Percent share

   _____   _____

   _____   _____

   _____   _____

3. _____ wrote all of the lyrics to the song(s).

   _____ composed all the music to the song(s).

   [NOTE: If the writers have made varying contributions to the music and lyric, and there is no precise split in responsibility for each, an attempt to identify individual contribution is of virtuality no use.]

4. If the song(s) are not [*signed to a publishing agreement/commercially recorded/commercially released*] by __-__-__ we may each withdraw our respective creative contributions to any song(s) not meeting such requirement, and the other(s) shall have no remaining claim to income from any use then made by the creator thereof. [NOTE: Again, there is little purpose to this clause unless the division between lyrical and musical contributions is clearcut.]

5. [One or more of *the writers*] shall have the only right to issue licenses for any use whatsoever of the song(s). [*or*] All of us shall have equal rights to issue licenses for any use of the song(s), but must pay appropriate shares of any money received as specified in Paragraph 2 above. [*or*] Any of us may grant licenses for any use of the song(s), but only after obtaining written approval of all of the others.

6. [One of the writers] [All of us] Any of us with approval, etc., may authorize changes to the lyric or melody of the song(s) and may reduce the shares of all of us in equal proportion to compensate any new songwriter(s) adding such creative changes. [NOTE: If there is a definite division between lyrical and musical contributions among the original writers, reductions for changes may be appropriately categorized by the type of change and assessed against that writer.]

7. [One of the writers] is hereby granted full power of attorney [*or*] [All of *the writers*] are each granted full power of attorney to assign any rights or grant any licenses respecting the song(s) in the event that the others are unavailable to give their approval for any period in excess of _____ days.

COLLABORATORS' AGREEMENT CONTINUED

[NOTE: In some circumstances, where one writer may be far more knowledgeable in music industry matters or where one writer insists on reserving a song for his or her performing group's use only, it may be appropriate to grant that writer the exclusive right to grant licenses and assign rights without approval of the others.]

8. In the event of any dispute between us regarding the song(s) or this Agreement, we will submit the matter to binding arbitration in (the largest nearby city) under the rules of the American Arbitration Association or any local arbitration association upon which we otherwise agree.

Signature _____

Soc. Sec. Number _____

Address and Phone(s) _____

Although it's not critical, you may wish to have this document notarized. In many states, notarization is required for any power of attorney. Check your state laws as to how a power of attorney is legally granted.

---

your meager *artist* royalties. So most group members never end up receiving any artist royalties (from the record company) beyond the original advance unless they're very, very successful.

2. Regarding live performances, even subsequently successful groups usually take at least two years from the start of a recording contract to begin making any kind of decent money performing. "Opening act" status and at least two hit singles are needed to bring in enough revenue to do more than pay touring bills. The exceptions to this are the bands that can tour constantly, or who got their record deal because they had already built a following by touring.

3. Merchandising of T-shirts, etc., at concerts can be lucrative, but this business also takes time to build and the band may have to sell merchandising rights to get advances to help defray their costs. Concert venues and promoters also get percentages of merchandising.

4.-5. So, the only relatively reliable sources of income left are from writer royalties or income generated by self-publishing. The songwriting royalties will be earned whether the songs are published by a company outside the group or by a company the group sets up to publish its own songs. The second option, setting up a publishing company for the group and splitting the publishing half of the income with the band members, is a good way to reward nonwriting members of the band with mechanical and performance royalties. In that case, an individual or company is hired to administer the group's publishing company for a fee (see "Self-Publishing" and "Administration Deals," chapter eleven), and the remaining royalties are divided among the group. This, of course, assumes that the band didn't have to give up their publishing as part of the record deal.

Artistic Reasons

On the artistic side, the philosophy is that everyone in the group contributes his own individual talent toward creating the final product and therefore deserves a share of the credit. The final and unique sound of the group is not dictated by the writer/artist/lead singer, etc., but by the interaction of all the members. In other words, if one member left the group, this philosophy says, the sound would be audibly altered.

But, you might ask, "What if the bass player doesn't write lyrics or melodies? How does he justify receiving royalties?" To answer that we have to ignore our traditional concept of the songwriter. Instead I reiterate that the group may not be writing just a song as we know it, but creating a *sound*, an element frequently as important to the commercial success of a record as lyrics and melodies, particularly in pop, rock, and R&B/ hip-hop. So it's not only important what the bass player plays, but how he plays it, what sound modification devices he chooses to use and when. If he's also a singer, it's important how his voice sounds, how he uses it, and what parts he creates for the vocal arrangement. He may create an instrumental hook in the form of a bass riff that gives the tune a unique identity or serves as the basis (so to speak) for the whole song. So although he hasn't written a word or a note of actual melody, his contribution can be extremely important to the success of the record and, ultimately, the group.

It may occur to you that, depending on the situation, all the above musical contributions can be and often are made by others. The studio musician, arranger, or producer are all paid in other ways and are free to solicit work with anyone else. A group member whose first commitment is to the group doesn't always have these options.

Dividing writer royalties doesn't work with everyone and may give rise to jealousy from those who feel their contribution was more important, especially after the big money starts rolling in. So if you're writing with a band, it may be worth considering sharing the credit, especially if you want to attract creative people to your band and if everyone can perceive each other's contribution as being equally important.

As you can see, collaboration is an option to be seriously considered. It offers many positive advantages, both artistically and commercially. The difficulty in finding a compatible partner and keeping your business straight can be more than compensated for with increased productivity and quality.

The Business

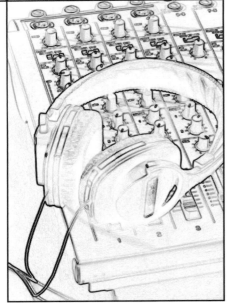

Protecting Your Songs

The Importance of Taking Care of Business

Now that you've put so much soul and perspiration into writing those great songs, I hope you're not looking at the rest of this book and saying, "Oh, that's just the business stuff. I don't have a business kind of mind. I think I'll skip that part." Or "I'll just get a manager who can take care of all that." Those words have a sad echo for a lot of people I've met over the years whose creativity has been drained and their careers put on hold while they tried to undo by legal means the damage caused by their own ignorance.

There was a time not long ago when there were no books from which someone (who wasn't an attorney) could learn about the business. Now you have no excuse. The following chapters are an introduction to some basics of the music business. It doesn't pretend to teach you everything, but it will give you plenty of streetwise information about the business that you don't have to be a Ph.D. to understand. At the bottom of it all, as you might have suspected, are common sense and human nature. Don't forget that the *music business* is also very creative. You can exercise your creativity every bit as much by figuring out fresh approaches to getting your songs recorded as you can by writing a song, and succeeding at it can feel just as good.

Your songs and talent are your babies. You want to know that when they go out in the world, they have every advantage. You want them to be protected, to be with people who care about them, to have a chance to do something good in the world, and if they're special, to pay your rent in your old age. Reading the rest of this book is a major payment on an insurance policy you owe to those babies.

I'll show you many options in this section, just in case you thought there were only one or two. There are many different ways to deal with your business, and your personal situation may use a combination of them.

Many wonderful, honest, hard-working people exist in this business who want to see you succeed and who are motivated every bit as much by seeing their creativity pay off for you as they are by the financial rewards they'll receive by helping you do it. They take great pride in their work and go through as much frustration and aggravation in their

You can exercise your creativity every bit as much by figuring out fresh approaches to getting your songs recorded as you can by writing a song, and succeeding at it can feel just as good.

jobs as you do in yours. Reading the rest of this book will help you find those people and get some idea of what happens on their end of your business. That knowledge will help you make the best kind of business deals, the ones in which everyone is rewarded for his efforts and knows how to work as a team. And it will help you avoid the dishonest people and poor business deals.

Your Song Is Your Property

One of the most important business considerations is protecting your songs. While you may be emotionally attached to your "baby," you have to think of it as a product or commodity—an "intellectual property."

Our government (and others around the world) have agreed that an artist deserves to retain ownership of his own creations. To encourage creative expression, legislation was enacted so that an artist could expect to be compensated by whoever sought the "right to copy" his work. A creator can assign different rights to different people for different purposes. A sculptor gives a gallery "the right to display." A songwriter can license (or assign) the rights to her song to a music publisher to obtain recordings of her song, reproduce those recordings, and distribute them to the public.

Now we come to the need for a "right to copy," or copyright: How can someone acquire something from you until they are sure it is yours to begin with? Anyone can show me "his" car, even take me for a ride in it, but if there were ever any legal questions regarding that car, we would need to see some proof of ownership.

Countless stories have been told about songwriters who have written some of America's most famous and successful songs and either did not know how to register their own works or depended totally on someone else to give them proper payment as the creators. Years later, as these songwriters became more educated regarding copyright protection procedures, they realized they had blindly signed over all of their rights to earn any income from their songs.

Fortunately, today there are books (like this one), songwriters organizations, classes, seminars, and other learning opportunities available to help people learn about their rights as creative artists. When a songwriter puts so much work, worry, and love into his art, it seems irresponsible not to know how to protect it.

Before I knew better, I had a fantasy about the Copyright Office in which, when they received my new song, a piano player played it for all the employees just to make sure it was really original. He'd say, "Hey, have you guys ever heard this one before?" In the fantasy, I'd break out in a cold sweat as I prayed that I hadn't accidentally written part of something I'd heard on the radio or in a club somewhere. One by one, the copyright "experts" (who I knew had heard everything) would shake their heads and somebody would say, "Wait a minute! Play the last four bars of that bridge again. No, I thought it might have been 'Earth Angel,' but it's OK. Let it pass," and I was home free.

If you have that fantasy, you can now wipe it out in favor of cold reality. The Copyright

Office processes more than 600,000 registrations every year. Needless to say, they don't listen to those songs, but they do check over the forms to make sure you've filled them out correctly. If you haven't, they'll send back your application. They also don't check to see if the song is original, since the copyright registration is only a proof of the *date* of registration.

Copyright registration is only a proof of the *date* of registration.

According to the Copyright Revision Act of 1976, which went into effect on January 1, 1978, *original* (original with the creator of the work) songs are entitled to copyright protection from the time they're "fixed" in a tangible medium of expression. This means on paper or "phonorecord," which includes vinyl, tape, compact disc, or digital audio file. At the time it's written or recorded, it's considered to be *created*. If you sing your song "live" for an audience (before it's in "fixed" form), it is not automatically protected. Technically, it's only considered protected when it's recorded or written. Consequently, it's a good idea to record the song and put the copyright notice on the tape/CD with the date and even better to obtain a copyright registration before performing it in public. Ideas, concepts, titles, chord or rhythm patterns are not protected—only the specific form of their expression.

Length of Copyright Protection

The length of copyright protection is described by the Copyright Office as follows:

WORKS ORIGINALLY CREATED ON OR AFTER JANUARY 1, 1978

A work that is created (fixed in tangible form for the first time) on or after January 1, 1978, is automatically protected from the moment of its creation and is ordinarily given a term enduring for the author's life plus an additional 70 years after the author's death. In the case of "a joint work prepared by two or more authors who did not work for hire," the term lasts for 70 years after the last surviving author's death. For works made for hire, and for anonymous and pseudonymous works (unless the author's identity is revealed in Copyright Office records), the duration of copyright will be 95 years from publication or 120 years from creation, whichever is shorter.

WORKS ORIGINALLY CREATED BEFORE JANUARY 1, 1978, BUT NOT PUBLISHED OR REGISTERED BY THAT DATE

These works have been automatically brought under the statute and are now given federal copyright protection. The duration of copyright in these works will generally be computed in the same way as for works created on or after January 1, 1978: The life-plus-70 or 95/120-year terms will apply to them as well. The law provides that in no case will the term of copyright for works in this category expire before December 31, 2002, and for works published on or before December 31, 2002, the term of copyright will not expire before December 31, 2047.

WORKS ORIGINALLY CREATED AND PUBLISHED OR REGISTERED BEFORE JANUARY 1, 1978

Under the law in effect before 1978, copyright was secured either on the date a work was published with a copyright notice or on the date of registration if the work was registered in unpublished form. In either case, the copyright endured for a first term of 28 years from the date it was secured. During the last (28th) year of the first term, the copyright was eligible for renewal. The Copyright Act of 1976 extended the renewal term from 28 to 47 years for copyrights that were subsisting on January 1, 1978, or for pre-1978 copyrights restored under the Uruguay Round Agreements Act (URAA), making these works eligible for a total term of protection of 75 years. Public Law 105-298, enacted on October 27, 1998, further extended the renewal term of copyrights still subsisting on that date by an additional 20 years, providing for a renewal term of 67 years and a total term of protection of 95 years.

Public Law 102-307, enacted on June 26, 1992, amended the 1976 Copyright Act to provide for automatic renewal of the term of copyrights secured between January 1, 1964, and December 31, 1977. Although the renewal term is automatically provided, the Copyright Office does not issue a renewal certificate for these works unless a renewal application and fee are received and registered in the Copyright Office.

Public Law 102-307 makes renewal registration optional. Thus, filing for renewal registration is no longer required in order to extend the original 28-year copyright term to the full 95 years. However, some benefits accrue from making a renewal registration during the 28th year of the original term.

For more detailed information on renewal of copyright and the copyright term, request Circular 15, "Renewal of Copyright"; Circular 15a, "Duration of Copyright"; and Circular 15t, "Extension of Copyright Terms."

Filing for renewal registration is no longer required in order to extend the original 28-year copyright term to the full 95 years.

| The Copyright Notice
FORM OF NOTICE FOR VISUALLY PERCEPTIBLE COPIES

The notice for visually perceptible copies should contain all the following three elements:

1. The symbol © (copyright symbol), the word "Copyright," or the abbreviation "Copr."; and

2. The year of first publication of the work. In the case of compilations or derivative works incorporating previously published material, the year date of first publication of the compilation or derivative work is sufficient. The year date may be omitted where a pictorial, graphic, or sculptural work, with accompanying textual matter, if any, is reproduced in or on greeting cards, postcards, stationery, jewelry, dolls, toys, or any useful article; and

3. The name of the owner of copyright in the work, or an abbreviation by which the name can be recognized, or a generally known alternative designation of the owner.

Example: © 2000 John Doe

The "C in a circle" notice is used only on "visually perceptible copies." Certain kinds of works—for example, musical, dramatic, and literary works—may be fixed not in "copies" but by means of sound in an audio recording. Since audio recordings such as audio tapes and phonograph disks are "phonorecords" and not "copies," the "C in a circle" notice is not used to indicate protection of the underlying musical, dramatic, or literary work that is recorded.

FORM OF NOTICE FOR PHONORECORDS OF SOUND RECORDINGS*

*Sound recordings are defined in the law as "works that result from the fixation of a series of musical, spoken, or other sounds, but not including the sounds accompanying a motion picture or other audiovisual work." Common examples include recordings of music, drama, or lectures. A sound recording is not the same as a phonorecord. A phonorecord is the physical object in which works of authorship are embodied. The word "phonorecord" includes cassette tapes, CDs, LPs, 45 r.p.m. disks, as well as other formats.

The notice for phonorecords embodying a sound recording should contain all the following three elements:

1. The symbol (the letter P in a circle); and

2. The year of first publication of the sound recording; and

3. The name of the owner of copyright in the sound recording, or an abbreviation by which the name can be recognized, or a generally known alternative designation of the owner. If the producer of the sound recording is named on the phonorecord label or container and if no other name appears in conjunction with the notice, the producer's name shall be considered a part of the notice.

Example: 2000 A. B. C. Records Inc. Form of Notice for Visually Perceptible Copies

Copyright Registration

In general, copyright registration is a legal formality intended to make a public record of the basic facts of a particular copyright. However, registration is not a condition of copyright protection. Even though registration is not a requirement for protection, the copyright law provides several inducements or advantages to encourage copyright owners to make registration. Among these advantages are the following:

1. Registration establishes a public record of the copyright claim.

2. Before an infringement suit may be filed in court, registration is necessary for works of U.S. origin.

3. If made before or within five years of publication, registration will establish prima facie evidence in court of the validity of the copyright and of the facts stated in the certificate.

4. If registration is made within three months after publication of the work or prior to an infringement of the work, statutory damages and attorney's fees will be available to the copyright owner in court actions. Otherwise, only an award of actual damages and profits is available to the copyright owner.

In general, copyright registration is a legal formality intended to make a public record of the basic facts of a particular copyright.

5. Registration allows the owner of the copyright to record the registration with the U.S. Customs Service for protection against the importation of infringing copies. For additional information, request Publication No. 563 "How to Protect Your Intellectual Property Right," from:

U.S. Customs Service
P.O. Box 7404
Washington, D.C. 20044
www.customs.gov (for online publications)

Registration may be made at any time within the life of the copyright. Unlike the law before 1978, when a work has been registered in unpublished form, it is not necessary to make another registration when the work becomes published, although the copyright owner may register the published edition, if desired.

| Registration Procedures
ORIGINAL REGISTRATION

To register a work, send the following three elements in the same envelope or package to:

Library of Congress Copyright Office
101 Independence Avenue S.E.
Washington, D.C. 20559-6000

1. A properly completed application form.

2. A nonrefundable filing fee of $30 (effective through June 30, 2002) for each application. NOTE: Copyright Office fees are subject to change. For current fees, please check the Copyright Office Website at www.loc.gov/copyright, write the Copyright Office, or call (202) 707-3000.

3. A nonreturnable deposit of the work being registered. The deposit requirements vary in particular situations. The general requirements follow. Also note the information under "Special Deposit Requirements."

    a. If the work was first published in the United States on or after January 1, 1978, two complete copies or phonorecords of the best edition.

    b. If the work was first published in the United States before January 1, 1978, two complete copies or phonorecords of the work as first published.

    c. If the work was first published outside the United States, one complete copy or phonorecord of the work as first published.

    d. If sending multiple works, all applications, deposits, and fees should be sent in the same package. If possible, applications should be attached to the appropriate deposit. Whenever possible, number each package (e.g., 1 of 3, 2 of 4) to facilitate processing.

WHAT HAPPENS IF THE THREE ELEMENTS ARE NOT RECEIVED TOGETHER

Applications and fees received without appropriate copies, phonorecords, or identifying material will not be processed and ordinarily will be returned. Unpublished deposits without applications or fees ordinarily will be returned, also. In most cases, published deposits received without applications and fees can be immediately transferred to the collections of the Library of Congress. This practice is in accordance with section 408 of the law, which provides that the published deposit required for the collections of the Library of Congress may be used for registration only if the deposit is "accompanied by the prescribed application and fee. . . ."

After the deposit is received and transferred to another service unit of the Library for its collections or other disposition, it is no longer available to the Copyright Office. If you wish to register the work, you must deposit additional copies or phonorecords with your application and fee.

Applications and fees received without appropriate copies, phonorecords, or identifying material will not be processed and ordinarily will be returned.

RENEWAL REGISTRATION

To register a renewal, send:

1. A properly completed application Form RE and, if necessary, Form RE Addendum, and

2. A nonrefundable filing fee of $45 without Addendum; $60 with Addendum for each application. (See previous note on Copyright Office fees.) Each Addendum form must be accompanied by a deposit representing the work being reviewed. See Circular 15, "Renewal of Copyright."

NOTE: Complete the application form using black ink pen or type. You may photocopy blank application forms. However, photocopied forms submitted to the Copyright Office must be clear, legible, on a good grade of 8½-inch × 11-inch white paper suitable for automatic feeding through a photocopier. The forms should be printed, preferably in black ink, head-to-head so that when you turn the sheet over, the top of page two is directly behind the top of page one. Forms not meeting these requirements may be returned, resulting in delayed registration.

SPECIAL DEPOSIT REQUIREMENTS

Special deposit requirements exist for many types of works. The following are prominent examples of exceptions to the general deposit requirements:

1. If the work is a motion picture, the deposit requirement is one complete copy of the unpublished or published motion picture and a separate written description of its contents, such as a continuity, press book, or synopsis.

2. If the work is a literary, dramatic, or musical work published only in a phonorecord, the deposit requirement is one complete phonorecord.

LOW-BUDGET COPYRIGHT REGISTRATION

The least expensive way to register your unpublished songs is to combine them under one title. Here are the guidelines from the Copyright Office:

> Under the following conditions, a work may be registered in unpublished form as a "collection," with one application form and one fee:
>
> The elements of the collection are assembled in an orderly form;
>
> The combined elements bear a single title identifying the collection as a whole;
>
> The copyright claimant in all the elements and in the collection as a whole is the same; and all the elements are by the same author, or, if they are by different authors, at least one of the authors has contributed copyrightable authorship to each element.
>
> An unpublished collection is not indexed under the individual titles of the contents but under the title of the collection.

The practical application of this last information is that if someone hears your song and wants to initiate a search of the Copyright Office for it, they won't find it under the title of the song if they don't know what you titled the collection. Also, if someone wants to publish the composition/song and you give them the existing copyright number, the number will be for the collection; so be clear on the contract that it's for a specific song included in the collection called "y," registration # "y."

Effective Date Of Registration

A copyright registration is effective on the date the Copyright Office receives all the required elements in acceptable form, regardless of how long it then takes to process the application and mail the certificate of registration. The time the Copyright Office requires to process an application varies, depending on the amount of material the Office is receiving.

If you apply for copyright registration, you will not receive an acknowledgment that your application has been received (the Office receives more than 600,000 applications annually), but you can expect:

A letter or a telephone call from a Copyright Office staff member if further information is needed or a certificate of registration indicating that the work has been registered, or if the application cannot be accepted, a letter explaining why it has been rejected.

Requests to have certificates available for pickup in the Public Information Office or to have certificates sent by Federal Express or another mail service cannot be honored.

The *poor man's copyright* is the process of sending yourself your song by registered mail. It's the least reliable "protection" since it could be argued that, with it in your possession, you could have opened it and altered its contents. Also, if your house burned down, you may have no proof at all that those songs were yours. The next level above the "poor man's" method is to send the registered letter to someone else who can swear to keep it in their possession. Another option is to use an online service to register it. Several companies including *www.copyright.net* are developing those services.

WHY IT'S BEST TO REGISTER WITH THE COPYRIGHT OFFICE

No matter how reliable or unreliable any of these methods may be, what they don't do is:

   1. Allow you to sue someone for copyright infringement in Federal Court if you've registered your song within three months of the date of first publication or before the infringement occurs. Otherwise you'll have to pursue it in Civil Court. Tough to prove the date of creation and very expensive and difficult to obtain compensation for damages.

   2. Allow you to automatically collect statutory damages (if you win) of up to $100,000 plus attorney fees and court costs depending on the type and degree of infringement as decided by the court. (See "Awarding Damages" later in this chapter.)

So, in the long run, you're much better off dealing with the government on this one.

Copyright Infringement/Plagiarism

One of the most common fears of songwriters is that they'll have a song stolen. Although it's happened, plagiarism is less common than the paranoia would indicate. Publishers would rather publish a song than plagiarize it. They'd rather be in line for your next hit than be in court defending themselves in a copyright infringement case.

   The more concrete fear is that another writer will steal an idea. Since neither an idea nor a title can be copyrighted, the possibility is greater that another writer might borrow an idea or title and use it as a basis for a new song. There's no real protection for lyric ideas. Throughout the history of literature and music, writers and musicians have borrowed from each other quite blatantly with no apologies for doing it. The originators of musical and literary forms are well documented and the forms are still in use. The storyteller is said to have a choice of thirty-six basic plots. Beyond that, he's dealing with variations. The idea itself is not as important as how he develops it. The language, characterization, and imagery are what make a story or a song special.

   If you do come up with a new idea or an unusual variation, but don't craft it well, it is unlikely that it will spark interest. There is, however, the chance that another writer will realize you had a good idea but you didn't do it justice. That person may have the craftsmanship and perseverance to make it work and would have every right to develop the idea in her own way. If the writer took your idea in a totally different direction and used none of your actual language, it would probably not constitute copyright infringement.

| Copyright Infringement

Copyright infringement is a federal crime that occurs when any of the copyright owner's exclusive rights are violated. Those rights cover reproduction, adaptation, publication, performance, and display.

In order to prove copyright infringement, two things must be established:

1. who has ownership of the copyright
2. whether the alleged infringer actually copied the song.

A copyright registration number for that song from the Library of Congress can be admitted as evidence that the song belongs to the person filing the suit.

Whether the copyright is registered before or after the infringement will influence the type of damage compensation for which the plaintiff (the one suing) is eligible. The plaintiff also must prove that the song was infringed upon. If a witness cannot testify that he or she saw the defendant actually listening to and copying the song, the plaintiff has to prove (1) access and (2) substantial similarity.

ACCESS

Access is really "the opportunity to have heard" a song or a "reasonable possibility that it was heard" by the defendant. If you prove that a song was widely known, the courts will assume the defendant heard it. "Widely known" is obvious with recorded songs, particularly hits. Where it gets really sticky is in a case where a writer/performer is traveling around the country singing his/her songs. Though no publishing or recording deals are involved, it's possible that the song could be taped or taught to another writer/performer and a chain of listeners created over which the original writer has no control. If you played a concert in the defendant's town, he could have both "opportunity" and "possibility," but it would be difficult to find any kind of proof.

SUBSTANTIAL SIMILARITY

A popular myth says that more than four bars need to be copied before it constitutes infringement. Not true!

The crucial question is, of course, how similar was the defendant's song to that of the plaintiff? This is where we get into the question of whether it's OK to copy "a few bars" of another work. A popular myth says that more than four bars need to be copied before it constitutes infringement. Not true! On the one hand, there are probably a lot of songs with four-bar passages that are technically the same, but they sound so much different that one would not remind you of the other. But there are other songs that are instantly recognizable in just four notes, such as the first four notes of the old "Dragnet" theme, which establish the identity of the song so strongly that using them would constitute a "substantial taking."

The court uses two tests to determine the degree of similarity. Expert witnesses such as musicologists are brought in to testify about whether the actual melodic construction is the same and whether the general idea of the two works is similar. The other test is for a jury to decide whether, after listening to both songs, they sound alike, or close enough that one could be mistaken for the other, or that the impression to "the reasonable person" is similar. If you listen to George Harrison's "My Sweet Lord," you will understand why he lost the infringement suit by the owners of "He's So Fine." Though it was decided that Harrison didn't deliberately plagiarize the song, he was still found guilty. "I didn't mean to do it" is not a defense.

Sampling is another potential area of infringement. (See "Sampling," chapter nine.)

Illegal File-Sharing: The New Infringers

The protection of all kinds of intellectual property is an ongoing battle. Challenges generated by ease of communication provided by the Internet are the latest. People who use Napster and other file-sharing technologies that allow the downloading of songs without compensation to the creators and without their permission are copyright infringers regardless of how they may justify their actions. The rationales go like this:

1. **We're helping to promote the artists.** Answer: In some cases, particularly with new indie artists, that has, in fact, proven to be true. "Viral marketing," the concept of one fan turning several others on to the artists and those friends doing the same is a very effective technique. It is also true that record companies' control over distribution and airplay has left few other ways, aside from constant touring, for independent artists to promote themselves.

Having said that, the key issue is that it is the right of the creator of the music to determine to whom and how his music will be distributed. If that artist intentionally releases an audio file of a song as part of a campaign to promote his CD, that's his prerogative, his right. If not, nobody else has that right.

The key issue is that it is the right of the creator of the music to determine to whom and how his music will be distributed.

2. **Record companies are ripping us off.** Answer: I find it difficult to be an apologist for major labels, but most music fans know nothing about the economics of the music industry. What they don't see is the money that goes into making them aware of the artists they love and want to download. They want to do it as a result of the labels having done their marketing job effectively. The artists they're successful with are the ones who pay for the 90 percent they lose money on.

3. **The artists are rich and don't mind.** Answer: You don't know how much they make or owe. You'd be surprised at how many artists are still in survival mode after selling millions of records. Most music fans are also ignorant of the fact that many artists don't write their own songs and when fans download those artists' recordings, they're depriving writers of their royalties regardless of the success of the artists.

4. **Music should all be free.** Answer: Only those who have never spent substantial time, effort, and creativity at risk to their well-being, livelihood, and sanity to create and perform their music could make an argument like that. It is only because of commercial success, or the promise of it, that artists and songwriters can afford to continue to create and those in the music business will continue to invest in the gamble. Intellectual property is one of our main exports, valued around the world. When it is no longer able to support artists and songwriters, there may be nothing left that's worth stealing.

The Copyright Office, the Recording Industry Association of America (RIAA), the Songwriters Guild of America, National Music Publishers Association, songwriters and artists who are fighting illegal distribution of intellectual property will, I believe, prevail. When they do, everyone who creates music will be able to enjoy the rewards that new distribution technologies are creating.

Public Domain

Often, a defense in an infringement case is that the defendant did not copy the plaintiff's song, but copied part of a "public domain" song that existed long before the plaintiff's song. A song is in the public domain if, like classical works and traditional folk songs, it was composed before there were copyright laws or no one knows who wrote them. They're also in the public domain when their copyright term has expired.

Posting your work on the Internet does not put it into the "public domain" and downloading others' work does not constitute fair use.

Posting your work on the Internet does not put it into the "public domain" and downloading others' work does not constitute fair use.

Fair Use

Some uses can be made of the works of other writers that don't constitute infringement. These are covered by the doctrine of "fair use." These include criticism (for example, reproducing part of a lyric in a record review), comment, news reporting (using a small portion of another's work as a basis for an editorial comment or a news story that relates to it), scholarship or research (using portions of other works for a thesis or term paper, for instance), and teaching. The latter is the fair use area that most concerns songwriters and composers. Several major music publishing and music educators associations have worked out guidelines for the photocopying of sheet music for classroom use.

Four guidelines help define what constitutes fair use:

1. the purpose and character of the use, including whether it's for commercial or for nonprofit educational purposes;

2. the nature of the copyrighted work itself;

3. the amount and substantiality of the portion used in relation to the work as a whole;

4. the effect of the use on the potential market for, or value of, the copyrighted work.

Parody is another category that can be considered fair use. I say "can be" because it also is subject to the above qualifications; and if, for instance, you use too much of the original work, you may be on shaky legal ground. "Weird Al" Yankovic has made a career of parodying hits but always obtains permission of the copyright owners for the use of their melodies. It's clearly the safest course of action. In some cases, it amounts to more of a professional courtesy than anything else, but at least you're covered. Fair use legal problems are decided by the courts on a case-by-case basis. Decisions of the courts can then be cited as precedents in future cases.

Awarding Damages

What can the plaintiff expect to receive if she wins an infringement case? If it can be established how much profit was made by the infringer or how much monetary damage has been done, it can all be recovered. The plaintiff will probably fare better if it can be proven that the person willfully infringed than if it was unintentional.

It's very difficult to prove damages, though, so the plaintiff can elect to seek "statutory damages," an amount set by law to encourage copyright registration. (They figured that if they offered a cash reward, they could keep you from being your own worst enemy.) The amount can range from $200 to $100,000. In order to be eligible to collect statutory damages and recover the attorney fees spent on the trial, the copyright registration must have been obtained before or within three months of the date the infringement occurred.

What I've discussed here is a simplification of the subject. If you would like to pursue this further or have other questions answered about copyright, call your local bar association and locate a copyright attorney. I also highly recommend *The Musician's Business and Legal Guide* by Mark Halloran, (see Bibliography) or contacting the U.S. Copyright Office for the circulars listed.

Online Resources

- The U.S. Copyright Office: www.loc.gov/copyright/

It's all here: forms, basic info, legislation updates, and international copyright info. It also presents updates (in nonlegalese) of the ongoing court cases and Copyright Office rulings regarding use of music on the Internet, Webcasting, challenges to copyright laws, and more.

- The Copyright Web Site: www.benedict.com

Includes resources, famous court cases, and other fascinating info.

- Copyright and Fair Use: http://fairuse.stanford.edu

A Stanford University Library site that's an amazing repository of facts, articles, opinions on copyright, multimedia, intellectual property in general, Cyberspace law.

Avoiding the Songsharks

"Songsharks" are companies and individuals who charge a fee to publish your song or collaborate with you, most commonly to write music to your lyric, which they like to refer to as a "songpoem." Others, under the guise of publishing companies, ask you to submit material, then inform you that it just so happens that they've found an album project that your song is perfect for. Actually, the "publishing" company sends your song to another branch of their own company that is the "record" company. The latter writes to say that the song is perfect—they just need some money from you first to make sure they can do a good job. You're "double teamed" to make sure the sharks get your money.

Many "songshark" letters have been forwarded to me from songwriters who were concerned about getting ripped off. The most common story is that, out of nowhere, they received a letter asking them to submit material for "review." "Where did they find out about me?" is the common question from writers who've received letters out of the blue from a notorious "record company" who wants to record their material. They're always flattered that someone knows about them. Sorry to burst the bubble, but they get your name and address from the Library of Congress, where you copyrighted your song (and via the Freedom of Information Act, that copyright information is then available to the public).

The next most common story is that the writer responded to an ad in a magazine. In either case, they received a letter much like the one that follows, a composite of several I've seen from "record" or "production" companies. Their offers usually contain the same catch phrases. Only the names have been changed. I've highlighted the most common statements and sales pitches:

As a songwriter, *you've probably considered having a song recorded* at one time or another. *If you've been disappointed* and you're about to make that decision to just let that song sit unrecorded, Songshark Music Productions would like you to consider submitting it to us.

Recording companies need new songs. Without them, they would cease to exist. Just think how many new songs you hear on the radio, television, and records. *Some day one of them may be yours! Just compare your efforts with songs on the market today.*

Many writers, perhaps like yourself, produce some really good songs. *Your song may be excellent and worthy of recording.* We are interested in ALL types of material: popular, country western, gospel, rock, ballads, etc.

We employ professional arrangers, musicians, and vocalists to help you accomplish that commercial production that was, before, out of reach. Best of all, after Songshark Music Productions records your song on a commercial record, *we will ship records to disc jockeys and record stores and pay you a ROYALTY for each record sold.*

Songshark Music Productions will record songs of any style, with or without melody (leadsheet). *If you have lyric only, it will be completed with a commercial tune by our professional arrangers.* If you have a completed song, rest assured our arrangers will adhere to your lyric and melody as much as possible. If you send a tape, make sure it is accompanied by the lyrics or leadsheet along with a self-addressed stamped envelope for its return.

Have no fear in sending us your uncopyrighted songs or poems. Songshark Music Productions is a recording company and is not in the business of stealing songs or poems. However, if you wish to stay on the "safe side," have your material notarized and/or send it *Registered Mail through the United States Post Office.* You may have real ability and *you must act now, today!* Let us look over your work, so that we may give you *our honest opinion.* Don't just let your poem or song sit around. *Let us help you get it recorded.*

What a great offer! Songshark Music Productions came along just in the nick of time to save your creative life. But take a closer look at this letter and you'll find clues to tip you off to their questionable business practices.

First they use "If you've been disappointed" as an attention-grabber. Who hasn't been disappointed? Sounds like they're going to get your song recorded for you!

Next the pitch gets heavy. The "just compare" line is typical—and effective. There isn't a writer alive who hasn't heard a song on the radio and said, "If that can get on the radio, my song is a cinch!"

Notice that the letter makes no mention of R&B. "Country Western" is a phrase seldom heard anymore. That alone tells you this company is behind the times.

Next they actually promise that *after* they record your song on a *commercial* record (they're already assuming it will be good enough), they'll ship records to DJs and record stores. They'll probably actually do this. They could fulfill this promise by sending it to *two DJs* and *two* record stores. The reality is that they're hoping that *you* will buy the albums, along with all the other writers whose songs are included on it. Songsharks have no real illusions about their ability to get airplay on an unknown artist on a compilation record (containing several different singers). They know that even if a radio station did play one of the cuts from this album and it got good listener response, it would go nowhere because the listeners couldn't buy an *album* of *that* artist. So why should they play it instead of the superstar product from major record labels they're being pushed to play? They wouldn't. If they will play unknown artists, they'd rather play new artists from legitimate small independent record companies.

Songsharks have no real illusions about their ability to get airplay on an unknown artist on a compilation record (containing several different singers).

Notice how Songsharks capitalize "ROYALTY" in the letter as though it's an added bonus, as if they want very badly to prove to you that they're really honest and wouldn't think of ripping you off. Receiving royalties for each record sold is a matter of course, and specific percentages are always negotiated upfront.

Many writers are confused by people who tell them that if they can't write musical notation, they haven't "written" the melody. Songsharks want you to believe that "melody" means "lead sheet" or the melody written down. In truth, if someone has created a melody in his head and can sing it into a tape recorder, he's "written" it. When someone else essentially puts chords to the melody, writes a chord and/or melody chart, and wants writer credit and half the writers royalties for it, the first writer must decide if that contribution warrants cowriter credit.

If someone has created a melody in his head and can sing it into a tape recorder, he's "written" it.

But Songshark isn't looking to share the royalties with you as would a legitimate collaborator who believes her contribution is valuable enough to deserve a royalty split. A legitimate collaborator works on your song because she honestly believes you can make a potential hit together, not because a company pays her to write a melody for "any" lyric she's not otherwise motivated to work with and for "any" lyricist she's never even taken the trouble to talk to.

The Songshark letter assures you the company is "not in the business of stealing songs or poems." Songsharks often refer to lyrics as "songpoems," knowing that the world is full of frustrated poets who think their poems could be used as song lyrics. They might be quite sincere about not wanting to steal your song, but they're being tremendously irresponsible about it. The worst possible protection is the so-called "poor man's copyright," sending your work to yourself by registered mail. It's been proven to be legally weak. You notice they didn't suggest you actually obtain a legitimate copyright registration through the Library of Congress. They could just as easily have given you the phone number of the Copyright Office. But they don't care about you. It's in *their* best interest that you don't take time to think about it or check with anyone about this letter.

The last paragraph urges you to hurry and let them help you. This is a prime setup that makes you think this is really an exclusive deal. This actually makes it sound as though you have to be good enough to be able to make use of their services. You're nervous when you send it in, hoping against hope that you have something they'll think worthy to record.

Typically, the next step is that they send you a second letter that says:

Congratulations! Out of all the hundreds of songs we receive, (title) has been chosen to appear on our new (title) album which will be *distributed to radio stations around the country. Just send $400* to cover production costs so that our experienced and creative *team of singers, musicians,* and producers can record your song with the *best possible quality for commercial release.*

There's the zinger. You actually think something might happen and you send your $400 (or much more). Another letter arrives to tell you there's yet another album you could get your song on if you send more money. Once you send your first money, they know you're gullible. They know you're not aware that NO legitimate record company would ever charge you to have your song released on their record. No legitimate publisher, record company, or demo service writes melodies for a fee.

Demo services, by the way, are legitimate businesses (and demo production seems to be a part of the activities of this songshark company).

In the legitimate music industry, publishers and record companies gamble *their* money on your talent. If you lose, they lose. In the songshark "industry," only you lose. They don't gamble.

Some sharks will make a demo of your song under the guise of releasing your song on a record. Demos can usually be done much cheaper elsewhere with your participation, though demo services may legitimately charge for arrangements, lead sheets, or chord charts. However, before dealing with any demo production service, you should hear samples of their work. (See Demo Production Services, page 252.)

Songsharks are very inventive in coming up with new ways to separate you from your money. They'll "publish," "promote," "record," and charge you large "screening" fees, explaining that screening is a standard practice in the industry. Screening is a standard practice, but charging for it is considered unethical. In the legitimate music industry, publishers and record companies gamble *their* money on your talent. If you lose, they lose. In the songshark "industry," only you lose. They don't gamble.

Songsharks usually do operate within the letter of the law. Strictly speaking, they *usually* do what they promise. But everyone in the legitimate music industry considers them unethical because what they promise and deliver is not what you think it is. Their carefully worded letters create an illusion that bears little resemblance to how the real world of music publishing works. They prey on ignorant people who don't know how to get good information or who would rather harbor their illusions than deal with hard reality.

The songsharks argue that those people don't want to deal with the music industry. Songsharks say they're satisfying a need for people to hear their songs in a "finished" product. If that's the case, then sharks are essentially the equivalent of a "vanity press" for poets and authors, another legitimate business, but one that doesn't pretend to be anything else. If songsharks operated like vanity presses, they'd say it costs X amount to produce a master of your song, X amount to press X number of records, and then *you* do what you want with them. If you want them to actually promote your record, they'd tell you it will cost X amount *if* they thought the record were promotable.

Legitimate promotion is expensive. Major labels regularly spend $100,000+ on a single. Just sending records to radio stations is not promoting a record. Promoting records that you don't believe in is the quickest way to get radio program directors not to take your calls and to totally lose your credibility.

When songsharks promise to get your songs played on the radio, they deliver that, too. They buy time on small stations in small markets that typically play your song at 3 A.M. You'll receive no performance royalty because the station can't log the airplay. BMI and ASCAP don't recognize songsharks as legitimate publishers, so songsharks can't put BMI or ASCAP next to the title of your song on their record. You thought that, when they said they'd "get it on the radio," they meant everywhere. *No one can promise that,* even promoters for major artists, unless they're also delivering payola. If they were honest, they'd tell you exactly what they do and how they do it, but songsharks are not in the honesty business.

Where Your Money Comes From

One of the most confusing things to new writers is the source of income from their songs. Though it's not important until one of your songs gets recorded, most of us want to know how much money we can make and how we can get it. "How much money" is impossible to predict because there are so many variables. A song may earn nothing or it may earn millions throughout the life of the copyright. How we get paid is quite simple. There are four major income sources from songs—*mechanical, performance, synchronization,* and *print.* The Royalty Sources Flow Chart in this chapter illustrates how these sources relate to the songwriter and others who may also get a slice of the pie.

Methods of Payment

Mechanical, synchronization, and *print* royalties are collected by the publisher, who takes his share and sends you your share, usually quarterly or semiannually. The *performance* royalties are collected by the performing rights organizations—BMI, ASCAP, and SESAC. They will send a quarterly check and statement directly to you and one to your publisher, the amounts divided according to the terms of your publishing contract.

For example, if you have a *standard 50/50 writer/publisher split,* the publisher's half of the performance royalties will go directly to him, and your half will go directly to you. If you have a *50/50 cowriter split,* half of the *writers'* share (25 percent of the total) will go directly to you, the other half to your cowriter. Maybe you're splitting the publishing as well. If you have a *50/50 copublishing split* and you're the only writer, the other publisher would get a check for 50 percent of the publishing (25 percent of the total). Your own publishing company would get a check for the other half of the publishing (25 percent of the total). As the writer, you'd get a check for all of the writer's share (50 percent of the total). In the end you have two checks comprising 75 percent of the total.

The following diagrams illustrate the way income is divided between publishers and writers, based on contract clauses that may limit what the writers actually earn. Keep in

The 50/50 division is "traditional" and is not an absolute, though the writer should not accept less than 100 percent of the writer's share.

mind that the 50/50 division is "traditional" and is not an absolute, though the writer should not accept less than 100 percent of the writer's share. I use 200 percent as a basis because the publisher's share is nearly always referred to in terms of 100 percent, i.e., "100 percent of publishing," "50 percent of publishing," etc. The "writer's" share may be divided between any number of writers and the "publisher's" share may be divided between any number of publishers.

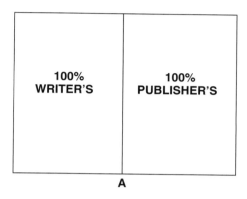

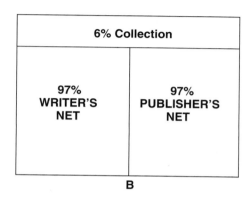

Figure A represents a 50/50 split of gross income. Figure B is the royalty split you get when the contract calls for a 50/50 split of gross income "less costs of collection." The 6 percent shown here as an example, is the current fee charged by the Harry Fox Agency for collection of mechanical income only. Other mechanical rights organizations charge different fees. Ideally, for the writer, this cost should be paid by the publisher (Figure C).

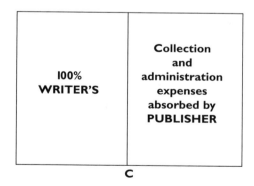

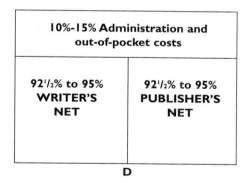

Figure D represents a 50/50 split of gross income "less administration" and out-of-pocket costs (copyright registration, photocopies, postage, etc.) directly connected to the exploitation of that specific composition. In this example, those costs are shared by the writer and publisher by being taken "off the top" before royalties are divided. However, the publisher should absorb those costs as in Figure C.

Split Publishing or Copublishing

Figure E shows the division of income for a writer who gets "half the publishing." In this most common situation, the "other publisher" usually absorbs costs of collection and administration. In other cases, such as when two writers with their own publishing companies split the income, an independent administration company may be hired. In such a case, the writers' companies should both share those expenses.

```
┌─────────────┬─────────────────────┐
│             │   OTHER             │
│             │   PUBLISHER         │
│             │   50%               │
│   100%      │                     │
│   WRITER'S  │                     │
│             │   WRITER'S          │
│             │   PUBLISHING        │
│             │   COMPANY           │
│             │   50%               │
└─────────────┴─────────────────────┘
              E
```

Mechanical Royalties

Mechanical royalties come from the sale of things mechanical—audio records, tapes, compact discs, and, more recently, video discs—to the general public. The current mechanical rate, called the "statutory rate," set by the Copyright Royalty Tribunal as of January 1, 2000, is 7.55 cents per use for compositions that are five minutes or less; for songs over five minutes, the rate is 1.45 cents per minute or fraction thereof of playing time, whichever is greater (the rate is updated every two years). So, if you have ten songs on an LP, the record company owes the publisher 75.5 cents. For the years 2002 through 2003, the statutory rate will be increased to 8.0 cents per song (or 1.55 cents per minute).

At times, you may be able to negotiate a contract for part of the "publishing" (the traditional 50 percent publisher's share in addition to your 50 percent writer's share). This can occur most often if you're a recording artist or a hot writer with a proven success record. A publisher will make that kind of split if he's excited enough about your songs, is in competition with other publishers for your songs, or if you can convince him/her that you'll personally be very aggressive about pitching the tune to producers and artists.

Collecting the money is a very important part of the publisher's job and often a difficult one. Most publishers contract with agencies such as Harry Fox, who issue licenses and collect both domestic and certain foreign mechanical royalties for a fee.

Because the agencies collect on behalf of many publishers, they have some power, and they audit the record companies regularly to make sure the publishers get all the royalties

Because the agencies collect on behalf of many publishers, they have some power, and they audit the record companies regularly to make sure the publishers get all the royalties they've earned.

The following are the commissions retained by the Harry Fox Agency on royalty payments to its publisher principals (as of 1/2001):

Mechanical Licensing: 6% of royalties distributed.

On Synchronization Licensing for Motion Pictures: 10% of royalties distributed with a maximum of $250 per composition.

On All Other Synchronization Licensing (Broadcast and Standard Cable TV, Home Video, Commercial Licensing, etc.): 5% of royalties distributed with a maximum of $2,200 per composition.

On Electrical Transcription Licensing (Syndicated Radio, Background Music, In-flight, etc.): 5% of royalties distributed with a maximum of $2,200 per composition.

On Import Licensing: 4% of royalties distributed.

they've earned. There is a lot of "creative bookkeeping" in record companies and publishing companies. Their objective is to hold on to the money for as long as they can so they can make a substantial amount of money from the interest on your royalties.

The major mechanical rights organizations that publishers will most often work with are listed here:

NMPA/Harry Fox Agency

711 Third Ave.

New York, N.Y. 10017

Tel.: (212) 370-5330 Fax: (212) 953-2384

Web site: www.nmpa.org/hfa.html

In L.A.: (323) 466-3861

In Nashville: (615) 242-4173

Canadian Musical Reproduction Rights Agency Ltd. (CMRRA)

56 Wellesley St. West #320

Toronto, Ontario Canada M5S 2S3

Tel.: (416) 926-1966 Fax: (416) 926-7521

Web site: www.cmrra.ca

So how do the numbers work out? A little arithmetic shows that one song on a million-seller CD or CD-single will bring a total of $75,500. When you have a song as a single, you can figure it will be on the CD album, too. Often a CD-single will also contain several mixes. For example, the Ricky Martin hit, "Livin' La Vida Loca" CD-single contained the following remixes: (1) Album version, (2) Scissorhands push & pull English house mix, (3) Track Masters remix, (4) Pablo Flores English radio edit, (5) Pablo Flores Spanish Dub-apella. Each of those remixes are also licensed at the same mechanical rates. $(5 \times 7.55$

= 37.75 cents) unless some are over five minutes, in which case it will be more.

If you have a hit single, then down the road you may also be involved in "Greatest Hits" and other compilation CDs, the record clubs, and TV packages like "The Top Hits of 2002," etc. Producers of these will usually want you to give them a lower "rate," commonly three-quarters (¾) that song's rate. Their philosophy is that it's an extra market for you—a bonus—and they may sell hundreds of thousands of records after the peak sales period of your original release. (See "Publishing," chapter ten)

The Compulsory License

The first time a composition is recorded, the copyright owner has total control over who records the song and what they're charged.

The first time a composition is recorded, the copyright owner has total control over who records the song and what they're charged. Theoretically, copyright owners could charge even more than the current statutory rate for that first recording, but they never do. That first-time control is the reason a producer and artist can be granted a "hold" by a publisher and promised that no one will be allowed to record the song before they do.

After a record of a song has been manufactured and distributed the first time, the copyright law allows anyone else to record the song as long as it avoids changing the basic melody or fundamental character of the work. In other words, no one can do an arrangement of your song and get their own copyright on it. Those who record the song after the first recording must obtain a "compulsory license" and agree to pay the statutory maximum mechanical rate unless they can negotiate a lower rate with the copyright owner. Failure to obtain a compulsory license constitutes piracy.

In addition, they must file a "notice of intention" with the copyright owner and the Copyright Office before they can distribute the records. The licensee is required to make payments and accountings (signed by a Certified Public Accountant) each month for records made and distributed during the previous month and to designate the name of the copyright owner or agent on the record or tape label or container. If this is not done and not remedied within thirty days, the license is defaulted.

The licensee doesn't have to pay if there is no record of copyright registration filed at the Library of Congress.

Compulsory licenses are only granted for records, tapes, and CDs primarily intended to be distributed to the public for private use.

Controlled Composition Clauses

If you're a self-contained writer/artist, group, or writer/producer looking for a record deal, you should be aware of the almost universal practice of record companies to demand a reduced mechanical royalty rate on "controlled compositions" (songs and other musical material in which the copyrights are controlled by the artist). The current practice is to ask for 75 percent of the statutory rate or less. Your ability to resist their "take it or leave it" approach is entirely dependent on your or your manager's or attorney's assessment of your bargaining power in that particular situation. New artists are particularly vulnerable and frequently give in with the philosophy that any deal is better than no deal.

Record companies may also tell an artist or producer that even if they choose "outside material" (songs controlled by a publisher or writer other than themselves), the record company will still pay only 75 percent of the statutory rate and often limit that to ten songs, forcing the artist to negotiate for a lower rate from the other "outside" publisher and writer or make up the difference from his own pocket on those in addition to any songs over the ten-song limit. The obvious effect is to reduce the willingness of the producer and artist to record "outside material," possibly reducing the quality of music on the album because the producer or the recording artist must rely on their own material rather than use possibly better-written songs by other writers.

From the record company's point of view, it's expensive to produce, market, and promote a record, particularly if they have to front the money for a video. They want to cut expenses any way they can.

From your point of view, the record company makes their money from selling records. You make yours from that royalty; and without that song, there wouldn't be a record! So though writers and publishers unanimously condemn the practice, it's a reality that you will have to deal with either as writer/artist or as an "outside" writer.

Sampling

In addition to the above, be aware that if your "outside" song is on an album that contains samples (pieces of compositions and/or sound recordings used from other songs), the artist will have to pay another copyright owner *and* record company additional licensing fees, further reducing their ability to pay additional mechanical fees for *your* song.

Sampling of *your* work, in general, could be looked at as an additional source of revenue. For example, in the early days of the sampling craze, publisher Jay Warner, as soon as he realized his writer, funkster Rick James, was being frequently sampled, began sending compilations of James's recordings to rap artists, inviting them to sample them. He also provided them with forms to fill out listing the cuts they sampled, length of samples, etc., capitalizing on this new source of income.

If you're a recording artist who wants to sample someone else's recording, you must contact *both* the owner of the copyright on the song (usually the publisher) and the owner of the recording (usually the record company) for permission *before* you release your record. Samples aren't subject to the compulsory license (the previous page), so you'll have to negotiate based on the length of the sample, how you're using it, the number of times it's used, and the importance of the sample to the potential success of the recording.

Sampling of *your* work, in general, could be looked at as an additional source of revenue.

For example, if you use a whole chorus of someone else's song, it's obviously very important and you'll have to share all royalties with the writer, publisher, and record company and probably credit the writer on the record.

Depending on the criteria above, you may be required to pay a flat fee, fee plus mechanical royalty, and/or performance royalty. If you wait to seek permission until after your record is released, you're in deep trouble and are in the worst possible negotiating position. You could be sued for copyright infringement and the copyright owners could even get an injunction against distribution of your record. So you *must* negotiate for the use of samples before releasing your record, and preferably at the time you decide you want to use them in a specific song. If the price is too high, you'll have time to replace it with something else.

If you wait to seek permission until after your record is released, you're in deep trouble and are in the worst possible negotiating position.

Performance Royalties: BMI, ASCAP, and SESAC

Performance royalties are a major source of income for a writer. They're not to be confused with the money a performer makes directly from public appearances. Performance royalties are monies the copyright owner(s) and songwriter(s) receive when their song is performed publicly. According to the copyright law, nobody can publicly perform a copyrighted song without permission of the copyright owner. (Don't panic! It doesn't mean if you sing somebody's song in a club, you have to find him and ask permission. See below.)

The most common uses of music in public performance are familiar to us: radio, network and local TV, jukeboxes, music services like Muzak, and live performances. When your songs are played in any of these venues, you, as the writer, and the publisher (whoever owns the copyright) are entitled to get paid for its use. The obvious problem is how to go about collecting the money. Do you call the radio and TV stations all over the country to pay you each time they play your song? Do you send a bill to a club owner because you heard someone play your song there? How do you find out how many times they played it? How do you get them to pay? How do you give them permission to play it there in the first place? The mind boggles at the enormity of the task.

The performing rights organizations—BMI, ASCAP (American Society of Composers, Authors and Publishers) and SESAC (no longer using their original title, Society of European Stage Authors and Composers)—are the entities that take care of these problems for you. Through membership in ASCAP or affiliation with BMI or SESAC, you grant them permission to license *nondramatic public* performances, "small rights," of your compositions. (Dramatic performances, or "grand rights," are those contained in musical theatre, ballet, operas, operettas, etc., in which the story line of the song is dramatized with sets, costumes, props, and so forth. The licenses are granted directly by the copyright owner.) A writer or publisher may collect from only one of these organizations for the same song.

You may only belong to *one organization at a time in the United States*. You can switch from one organization to another depending on the length of your contract period with that organization. You may, however, simultaneously belong to a U.S. and a European organization such as PRS (United Kingdom), SACEM (France), or GEMA (Germany), though you generally have to be generating a substantial amount of airplay in those countries for it to be worthwhile.

How do these organizations collect the money?

Generally speaking, radio and TV stations and networks pay annual "blanket license" fees negotiated by the performing rights organizations on behalf of their writer and publisher members. Blanket fees give radio and local and network TV permission for unlimited use of the compositions. Fees are based on a percentage of the advertising revenue received by the stations or networks. The philosophy is that if a station has a 50,000-watt clear channel signal, it's reaching millions of people, enabling them to charge top dollar for advertising.

For a list of performance revenue sources, see the Royalty Sources Flow Chart.

Revenues collected from dance clubs are charged according to their maximum legal

Blanket fees give radio and local and network TV permission for unlimited use of the compositions.

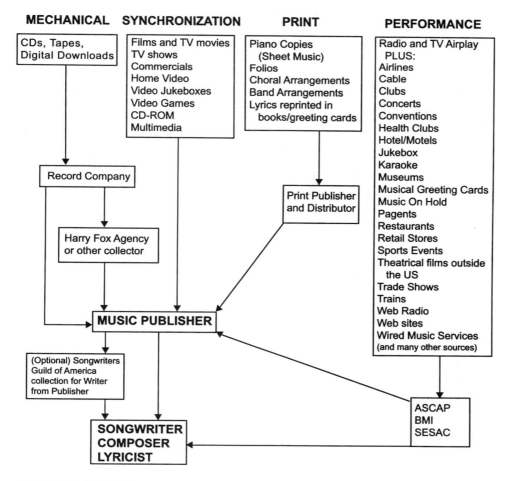

ROYALTY SOURCES FLOW CHART

ADDITIONAL SOURCES
Grand Rights - for musical theatre performances

room occupancy. Other clubs are charged a fee based on their annual entertainment expenses. Concert halls' charges are based on seating capacity and ticket prices. The American Hotel and Motel Association, The American Symphony Orchestra League, The Amusement Machine Operators of America, and The National Ballroom Operators Association all negotiate for their respective types of licenses. There is an annual fee for every jukebox. That money goes into a fund and is divided between the organizations. The organizations also license cable TV, colleges and universities, airlines, retail stores, and many other music users.

How do they know how many times a song is played?

Each organization has its own method of determining the number of performances. BMI chooses a representative cross section of stations to sample each quarter. The stations supply a written record (log) of all music performed. The logs are put through an elaborate computer system that multiplies each performance listed by a factor that reflects the ratio of stations logged to the number of stations licensed. They then make a statistical projection that gives them a figure to approximate the number of "plays" on all stations. Different types or classes of stations are weighed in different ways.

ASCAP uses a method involving a combination of station logging and taping selected stations for a given period of time, sending the tapes to a central place where expert listeners pick out the ASCAP songs, tally them, and make the statistical projections.

Both methods have been developed by statistical experts, with the goal of finding cost-effective ways to get the information. The organizations strive to spend less money so that more may be distributed to their writer and publisher members. Both organizations operate on a nonprofit basis, distributing to their members all money not used for overhead. Both monitor all network TV performances by direct census from producers' cue sheets. For local TV, they use a combination of sampling, cue sheets, and program. All organizations distribute foreign performance royalties through reciprocal agreements with foreign performing rights societies. Though there are differences in the way they monitor and determine royalties, the methods of all three organizations are constantly evolving as they each attempt to compete with each other for writer members.

SESAC, the smallest of the three, is a for-profit company and pays based on a formula that factors in singles chart positions, nationally distributed releases of albums, and TV performance data. They also have a method for computing and making "post chart" payments. SESAC was the first (in 1993) to directly monitor airplay with Broadcast Data System's (BDS) computerized tracking system.

A visit to Broadcast Data System's Web site at www.bdsonline.com [(800) 688-4634] will give you:

1. the reporting stations for specific genres;
2. the top artists scanned in each genre;
3. direct links to more than fifty record companies.

How much do you make each time it's played?

It varies in both BMI and ASCAP according to the amount of income generated from all sources during the year or the quarter. Each has an equation that gives it an overall per-play figure based on the type of station, number of plays, and the overall amount collected from user organizations based on periodic negotiations of blanket licenses. Performance income for publishers and songwriters will generally amount to a great deal more than the money earned from mechanical royalties (which can continue for many, many years). All organizations have embraced Internet technology that facilitates licensing, including online filing of cue sheets for film and TV uses.

Do performing rights organizations give advances to writers and publishers?

BMI and ASCAP are not officially giving advances. The advances, based on anticipated airplay, were a risky business for the organizations. They walked a fine line between giving you your money in advance of earning it and literally shortchanging other writers (collectively) by advancing you money that may not be recouped. They had to know if your song was a single or album cut with a major or new artist, if there was a major promotional effort and other factors to determine how much performance income you'd earn in the future. It is possible, in some cases, to have BMI or ASCAP co-sign a loan for you if they know there's already money in the pipeline for a song that's already generating considerable airplay.

How else do the organizations help songwriters?

The more songs licensed by an organization that are receiving airplay, the more money that organization can command in negotiations from the various users. The more money they receive, the more they can distribute to their members. Consequently, the three are in competition with each other for actively productive members. So it's in their interest to try to help you before you need to decide which organization to join. If your material merits being published or produced, whether you're an individual writer, writer/artist, or a self-contained group writing your own material, they can help you connect with publishers, producers, or record companies. Their representatives are always looking for great new songwriter, writer/artist, and film composer talent.

All three organizations sponsor local industry showcases, seminars, and workshops in most popular music genres that can be very helpful for generating networking opportunities and industry attention. Contact the organizations or go to their Web sites, where they list schedules of their events around the country, FAQS (frequently asked questions), informative articles on the music industry, and interviews with their writer and artist members.

Which is the best?

That's the toughest question to answer because there are so many variables—one of the most important being your own needs. The big question is usually "Who pays more?"—a complicated question that depends somewhat on your unique situation. Talk to them all. Believe me, they'll leave no questions unanswered. But remember: How much they each

Performance income for publishers and songwriters will generally amount to a great deal more than the money earned from mechanical royalties.

pay may be the biggest question, but it's not the only one. How do they treat you? Is there someone there you can relate to? Do you feel comfortable calling with a question? Those are the considerations that precede your making money at all. The organization you join is your decision alone. Some publishers will automatically put you in one or the other (if you're not already affiliated) because they feel one or the other is paying more at that time. I've even known publishers to make that choice for you for the mere reason that they prefer filling out one form over another. It's an important decision, however, so don't let anyone else make it for you.

Is there a charge to join?

There is a $10 annual fee for a writer to be an ASCAP member. There is no fee to affiliate with BMI or SESAC. (Membership in SESAC is by invitation only.)

What else do I need to know?

Report any new songs that you have published or recorded to the clearance departments of your performing rights organization.

Report any new songs that you have published or recorded to the clearance departments of your performing rights organization. The publisher should also do this, but make sure it's done and done with the correct cowriting or copublishing percentages, if applicable.

BMI and ASCAP members may cowrite with one another. If the song is licensed by both organizations, each will pay its own writers and publishers. If there is no publisher involved in a song, a BMI writer can collect the full writer and publisher share of performance royalties.

Be sure to notify your organizations immediately of any change of address so that you'll be sure to get your royalty checks!

ASCAP

New York—One Lincoln Plaza, New York, NY 10023   Tel.: (212) 621-6000
   Fax: (212) 724-9064
Los Angeles—7920 W. Sunset Boulevard, Third Floor, Los Angeles, CA 90046
   Tel.: (323) 883-1000   Fax: (323) 883-1049
London—8 Cork Street, London W1X1PB England   Tel.: 011-44-207-439-0909
   Fax: 011-44-207-434-0073
Nashville—Two Music Square West, Nashville, TN 37203   Tel.: (615) 742-5000
   Fax: (615) 742-5020
Miami—844 Alton Road, Suite 1, Miami Beach, FL 33139
   Tel.: (305) 673-3446   Fax: (305) 673-2446
Chicago—1608 West Belmont Avenue, Suite 200, Chicago, IL 60657
   Tel.: (773) 472-1157   Fax: (773) 472-1158
Puerto Rico—510 Royal Bank Center, 255 Ponce de León Avenue, Hato Rey,
   Puerto Rico 00917   Tel.: (787) 281-0782   Fax: (787) 767-2805
Membership—Atlanta PMB, 400 541 10th Street NW, Atlanta, GA 30318
   Tel.: (404) 635-1758   Fax: (404) 627-2404

BMI

New York—320 West 57th Street, New York, NY 10019-3790   Tel.: (212) 586-2000

Nashville—10 Music Square East, Nashville, TN 37203-4399   Tel.: (615) 401-2000

Los Angeles—8730 Sunset Boulevard, Third Floor West,
   West Hollywood, CA 90069-2211   Tel.: (310) 659-9109

London—84 Harley House, Marylebone Rd., London NW1 5HN, England
   Tel.: 011-44171-486-2036

Miami—5201 Blue Lagoon Drive, Suite 310 Miami, FL 33126   Tel.: (305) 266-3636

Atlanta—P.O. Box 19199 Atlanta, GA 31126   Tel.: (404) 261-5151

Puerto Rico—Suite A-262, East Wing, Royal Bank Center, 255 Ponce de León
   Hato Rey, Puerto Rico 00917   Tel.: (787) 754-6490

SESAC

Headquarters—55 Music Square East, Nashville, TN 37203
   Tel.: (615) 320-0055   Fax: (615) 329-9627

SESAC—421 W. 54th Street New York, NY 10019
   Tel.: (212) 586-3450   Fax: (212) 489-5699

SESAC—501 Santa Monica Blvd., Suite 450 Santa Monica, CA 90401-2430
   Tel.: (310) 393-9671   Fax: (310) 393-6497

SESAC International—6 Kenrick Place, London W1H 3FF, England
   Tel.: (020) 7486-9994   Fax: (020) 7486-9929

For more in-depth analysis, I recommend Jeffrey Brabec and Todd Brabec's *Music, Money & Success* (see Bibliography) and investigate each organization directly.

Synchronization Royalties

Another important area of income for writers and publishers is the licensing of the right to record the music or song in synchronization (timed to the pictures in a film or TV movie) and the right to perform publicly (that is, show in theaters, etc.) the music that's recorded under that "synch" right.

The film or TV producer is responsible for negotiating the synchronization and performance license with the copyright owner (usually the publisher). The Harry Fox Agency, Inc., in New York; The Clearing House in Los Angeles; and many independent attorneys with expertise in this area negotiate synchronization rights between film/TV producers and music publishers.

How much money can be made from synch royalties?

It's totally negotiable and depends largely on the previous popularity of the song and the way it's to be used. At the bottom rung are instrumental pieces used as background music. Next is "source music," the songs that come from a recognized source in the film such as a car radio or music in an elevator. Then there are featured performances in which we watch a rock band in the film perform a song or listen to a theme that's prominently featured over the intro or end credits. If the song has already been a hit and it's a perfect selection for that particular film, it's worth a lot. If it's an unknown song and there's a soundtrack album as well, it may be perceived in the negotiation that a lower "synch fee" might be worked out because the film's exposure of the song may benefit record sales, print, or other promotional areas. Fees are also based on the length of the song and whether it's used in a network or syndicated program.

The negotiations involve a producer's desire to obtain rights to *as many* possible uses for the *longest* possible time in the *most* territories. The copyright owner negotiates to limit them or obtain higher fees for additional time and uses. If you need an in-depth discussion of synchronization licensing, including the information on foreign usage, consult *Music, Money & Success* (see Bibliography).

The most common situation is that a film or TV producer asks you to compose a score or songs as a "work for hire" in which the production company becomes the "author" and publisher and which also automatically gives them the "synch rights." This doesn't mean, though, that you won't receive screen credit. That and the fee you receive are a part of your contract negotiations. You will also receive performance royalties for domestic and foreign TV and performances in foreign movie theaters. It's possible, but very difficult, for an unknown writer to retain publishing rights for music in a film. Film companies will fight hard to get them and may not use the song at all if it looks as if they can't get them. From their point of view, having the rights saves them future negotiations for future uses and gives them lots of extra money if their movie helps to make your song a hit. Most of the cases I know in which the writer retained at least some publishing rights were those in which a well-known writer was approached to do the song or score and his/her "clout" helped or the film company neglected to negotiate rights before mixing the music into the film, leaving the writer in a great negotiating position.

(For more info on marketing your songs to film and TV, see "Film and Television" in chapter fourteen.)

It's possible, but very difficult, for an unknown writer to retain publishing rights for music in a film.

Music in Print

Most writers know little about print music. If you write mass-appeal songs, particularly adult contemporary, pop, or country, you'll be able to take advantage of a potentially lucrative print market. With the possible exception of the education print market, though, the songs will have to become very popular records to make all those piano bar singers, cover bands, and other print buyers want them. Ronny Schiff, an independent agent for print projects, has worked for some of the biggest print companies, including Warner Bros. Music and Hal Leonard Publishing. Here's her rundown on the types of print music publishing:

1. **Sheet Music:** piano/vocal arrangements, often with chord designations for other instruments, and "easy piano" sheet music.

2. **Personality Folio:** collections based on a name artist, e.g., "The Songs of . . . ," "The . . . Songbook." These involve an additional contract called a "name and likeness" contract, which allows the print publisher to use the artist's or writer/artist's name and/or picture. For example, Carlos Santana could negotiate a "name and likeness" contract if someone wanted to do a personality folio that included not only songs he wrote but songs by other writers that he'd popularized. The philosophy is that his picture on the cover will sell that book.

3. **Matching Folio:** music matching a particular album or musical theater show. These may also involve a "name and likeness" contract.

4. **Mixed Folio:** collections based on concepts like "Easy Piano Tunes," "Greatest Hits of 200__," etc., involving songs from several writers.

5. **Educational:** included in this category are arrangements for choruses, marching bands, concert bands, jazz bands, and orchestras. These are obviously sold to schools, drum and bugle corps, etc. This market gives music great exposure beyond actual sales. How many times in school have you heard the same songs being practiced by the chorus or band? Multiply that by the number of listeners in schools and/or attending sports events, and you get an idea how much exposure is available there. Writers also might receive royalties if their songs are used in a televised event or parade.

The educational print market can be very lucrative, especially for jazz and pop writers; one thousand copies for a marching band is a big sell. It doesn't sound so big until you realize that arrangements go for $40 to $50 and a song will earn 10 to 12½ percent of the retail selling price. Choral arrangements of songs can be a good source of revenue, too. Some choral composers can sell fifty thousand copies per year of songs that haven't even been recorded! It's not unusual for popular choral writers to net $7,000 (10 percent of $1.40 retail $\times$ 50,000) for a single tune.

There are also freelance opportunities to compose and arrange for concert, jazz, and marching bands. Schools regularly buy arrangements of original songs as well as hits, but for this you need an understanding of the proficiency levels of different student groups so the parts aren't too difficult for them.

Another area of the educational market is "how to" books, especially in the areas of guitar, combo, and electronic instruments. This is a market for the songwriter who also has teaching skills to use. There's also great demand for guitar and bass note-for-note transcription books with tablature.

6. **MIDI Sequences:** an area handled by both print publishers and companies who create and market MIDI sound and song files. Often, MIDI sequenced versions of songs are packaged on disks along with the print versions. Some may also be full professional arrangements that can be used in performance.

What does the publisher get in print royalties?

Retail prices for print music, like everything else, continue to rise. Currently for sheet music, print publishers will pay your publisher up to 20 percent of the retail selling price.

Folio publishers will pay about 12½ percent of the retail selling price. In cases where the folio contains songs by various writers, this income is prorated according to the total number of copyrighted songs.

What does the writer get?

Often, she gets the short end of the stick. The longtime practice in "standard" publishing contracts has been to offer the writer a "penny" value on sheet music sales, currently about 6 to 10 cents per copy. This means that if your publisher can renegotiate his deal with the print company after a new version of your hit becomes popular, you may still be getting pennies a sheet from your old deal while his share goes up.

Try to negotiate 50 percent *of all royalties received by your publisher from all your print sales.* That way you remain equal partners in all royalties received. The 50 percent is based on a standard writer/publisher split, but should you be able to negotiate one more favorable to you, the print deal should reflect the same split. Publishers have no justification for giving you less than a 50/50 split on your print deal. In some situations, a publisher may have to lay out some legal fees to negotiate a difficult deal with a print publisher, but that's part of the expense of running a publishing company, just like producing demos is yours. If you can't get 50 percent of publisher's print income, check the Songwriters Guild of America's guidelines for print royalties. (See "Negotiable Contract Clauses," chapter ten.)

Try to negotiate 50 percent of all royalties received by your publisher from all your print sales.

Researching Print Music Deals

If you're a self-published writer or a music publisher, you'll need to have some idea of how to go about looking for and sizing up a prospective print publisher. In the early days, the primary avenue of exposure for songs was selling sheet music and arrangements to the "big bands" and to artists who sang live on radio. With the growing popularity of records, sheet music became dependent on the popularity and style of the recording. As music publishers became more involved in the recording industry, they became less interested in print music and began to contract with those equipped to specialize in print marketing and distribution. Print publishers are further specialized in two major areas: pop, which includes sheet music and folios; and education, which deals with arrangements for chorus, marching bands, orchestras, school jazz groups, and the like.

Print expert Ronny Schiff believes the best research method in looking for an effective pop print publisher is to drop in on a few sheet music stores and ask some questions:

1. How frequently are they serviced with new hit songs? You want a print publisher that calls the stores weekly and provides them with a list of the latest acquisitions. (There's heavy competition between print publishers for the rights to new hits.)

2. Does the print company keep sheet music in print, or does it let it lapse after the song has peaked on the charts?

3. Do they use the song in a variety of book and educational formats?

4. Do they supply retailers with promotional aids, displays, and so forth?

From an artistic standpoint, you'll want to consider the accuracy of the piano/guitar/vocal copies or guitar tablature copies. Compare them to the record. You'll want to work with a company that is consistently accurate. In negotiating a print deal, try to get a clause that grants you approval of the arrangements, but be reasonable about it. Don't hold up production if you're out of town.

It's possible to negotiate an educational print deal separately from the pop print contract. To research the effectiveness of those educational market specialists, call on some high school and college band and choral directors and ask them which companies provide the best service and the best arrangements. When you talk to the educational print companies, ask if they do marching band and choral arrangements and ask to see the promotional packages they send to the schools. You'll want to be sure they'll promote your music aggressively.

A maze of deal points can be negotiated in both pop and educational markets, and all print companies have structured a variety of deals for a variety of situations. It's to your advantage to find an attorney or publisher who's knowledgeable and creative in the print area to help you negotiate your deals.

New Income From Digital Sources

One of the upsides of the changes wrought by new digital distribution systems is the possibility of more income for songwriters, publishers, and recording artists via new copyright legislation. Here is an excerpt from Jeffrey Brabec and Todd Brabec's book *Music, Money & Success* that explains the legislation.

THE DIGITAL PERFORMANCE RIGHT IN SOUND RECORDINGS ACT OF 1995 (DPRSRA) AND THE DIGITAL MILLENNIUM COPYRIGHT ACT OF 1998 (DMCA)

The 1995 DPRSRA created a public performance right for artists and record companies in certain sound recordings when they are performed by audio transmissions. Previously only songwriters and publishers enjoy the performance right. This new right is a limited one and covers subscription (statutory license) and on-demand transmissions but exempts transmissions by FCC licensed broadcast stations. Webcasting (audio streaming of recordings over the Internet) was included under this limited right by the 1998 DMCA. License rates and terms are to be decided by voluntary negotiation or compulsory arbitration. The first CARP royalty decision for the fees for non-exempt-, subscription digital services was 6.5% of gross revenues resulting from residential services in the U.S. with 50% of the royalties going to artists (45%), nonfeatured musicians (2.5%) and non-featured vocalists (2.5%) with the remaining 50% going to record companies.

The 1998 DMCA implements the WIPO (World Intellectual Property Org.) Copyright Treaty and the WIPO Performances and Monograms Treaty that deal with copyright protection for works in a digital form and that require countries to give protection to foreign works no less favorable than the protection afforded to domestic works. The DMCA also creates civil and criminal penalties (up to a one million dollar fine and 10 years imprisonment) for the circumvention of the technological measures used by copyright owners to protect their works as well as the tampering with copyright management information (title of work, author, copyright owner, conditions or terms, etc.). Limitations on the copyright infringement liability of OSPs (online service providers) is also included with the steps set forth that OSPs must follow when they either detect or are notified of infringing transmissions. These include disconnecting repeat offenders; removing infringing material on the internet and identifying infringers to copyright owners based upon subpoenas.

chapter ten

Publishing

The Copyright Law broadly defines "publication," as it refers to songwriting, as the reproduction of a song in the form of any kind of product, printed or recorded, and the offering of those products for sale to the public. The practical concept of music publishing, however, is a lot more complex than any legal definition or theory.

Mention "music publishing" to someone outside the business, and they're likely to associate it with print in the same way they'd think of a book publisher. The business of music publishing in America did, in fact, begin with the manufacture and sale of sheet music copies and piano rolls for player pianos. But through decades of social, economic, and technological changes, the business continues to evolve with the times. Currently, the sale of sheet music is only a small part of music publishing, and its actual manufacture and sale is carried out by a handful of "print publishers" licensed to print and distribute by music companies whose duties, as we'll see, are now much broader.

Leonard Feist's book, *Popular Music Publishing in America*, traces the fascinating history of the business. Feist chronicles the role of the "songplugger" from the early 1900s in New York's "Tin Pan Alley," where most of the music publishers had their offices. In those days, they performed the songs for vaudeville troupes who were putting together shows for their tours; for employees of music stores who, in turn, performed the songs for potential sheet music customers; and for anyone else who might influence sales.

Today, songpluggers are still in the front lines, only now, since the business centers mainly around records and films, they're playing demos of songs for managers, record producers, recording artists, record company A&R personnel, and film music supervisors. Today they're called "professional managers" (Don't confuse them with "personal managers."), and songplugging is just one of their duties.

It's important to understand all that publishers do, whether you want them to pitch your songs to their contacts or if you pitch your own songs but want to avail yourself of the other services publishers provide.

What Publishers Do

Many different levels and types of activities come under the label of "publishing."

At its best, publishing demands imagination, creativity, intuition, tenacity, and good business sense. A publisher must be willing to make mistakes and face daily rejection of songs he believes in. A knowledge of how the music industry operates and a familiarity with the work of a great variety of recording artists (both established and new) are also required. It's a special combination of ingredients that makes a great publisher, and few have it all. In your own situation, you may not need all of these services or a publisher with all those qualities.

Publishers' activities fall into four categories: creative, promotional, business, and administrative.

1. Creative endeavors include screening new songs, meeting with new writers, attending concerts, going to night clubs and recording studios to hear and make contact with new and established artists, critiquing and working with staff writers and upcoming independent writers, reviewing songs already in the catalogue, producing demos, initiating or suggesting collaborations between staff writers or lyricists and producer/writers or artists, and conceiving new uses for songs.

2. Promotional duties include contacting producers, managers, agents, and A&R reps to learn what songs they need for their artists; reading music, film, and advertising trade magazines, periodicals, and tip sheets to discover projects that may need material; mailing demos; conducting casting meetings with professional staffers and writers to determine which songs are appropriate for certain projects; maintaining files on producers, the songs they liked (or didn't), the songs they're "holding" and for how long; making calls to radio stations, record companies, and managers to work out ideas for promotion.

3. On the business side, publishers also hire personnel; establish company policies; negotiate contracts with writers, subpublishers, music print publishers, and producers, artists, managers, or film/TV production companies; initiate and maintain contacts with foreign subpublishers; make decisions on "holds"; and negotiate and grant licenses to users.

4. Among administrative duties, they file copyright forms; file notices with BMI, AS-CAP, or SESAC for songs released for airplay; file notices with agencies that collect mechanical royalties (for sales of recordings) or make collections from record companies themselves; do general accounting, financial planning, and tax accounting; compute and pay writers' royalties.

Additional Activities

There are other tasks that warrant a little more explanation:

CATALOGUE EVALUATION AND PURCHASE

This is the level at which the "heavy-duty" deal-making machinery gets into gear. Companies merge or one major company buys another. Companies also acquire the catalogs (groups of songs owned by one company) or estates of individual writers. Some catalogs

It's a special combination of ingredients that makes a great publisher, and few have it all.

contain "standards" that will probably make money forever. Any time you turn on the radio, you'll hear "oldies" that are obviously still generating lots of performance royalties. Companies that own those songs are always being assessed by experts to determine their future earning power and looked upon as potential investments not only by other publishing companies but by international financiers.

I'll editorialize here to say that one of the great tragedies involved in catalog acquisition is that the purchasing company all too often looks at the move as a way to cut expenses by combining staff. In practice, it often means the termination of the staff at the acquired company, the very ones who are most familiar with the history and the songs in that company's catalog. To see the name of a song in a company's database is not the same as having a person on staff who actually remembers the song. New technology is impacting this problem for the better, though. All companies are attempting now to get audio files (like MP3) of the songs into databases that can be searched by a number of criteria such as style, tempo, lyric content (including the actual lyric), male or female cast, history of past recordings, etc.

The people involved in mergers and acquisitions aren't generally the ones who are assessing new talent off the street (so you won't have much contact with them), though some "street" experience in evaluating the commercial potential of songs is valuable to those predicting the future value of any catalogue.

WRITER/ARTIST DEVELOPMENT

Investing in the production of master recordings and the signing of new writer/artist talent is another level of activity that's becoming more and more common for those companies who can afford it. The companies look to sign promising writer/artists and self-contained bands. They'll produce masters and shop them to record companies. Obviously, if they get a record deal, they'll own part to all (usually half) of the publishing on all the songs their artist records, which guarantees them an outlet for the songs and helps them expose the songs to other artists.

In a case like this, a publisher is often acting like a combination manager, producer, and publicist and A&R person all rolled into one. In fact, many publishers have their own A&R representatives since most of the duties described here are the same as those of record company A&R reps. Trying to find the right producer for an artist involves a knowledge of the work of many producers, playing the writer/artist's preliminary tapes for them, scheduling the project, negotiating the contracts and choosing the songs, studio, and musicians if necessary. After the masters are completed, it involves making appointments to play the tapes for key record company A&R people and film music supervisors, putting together press kits, setting up showcases, and following up. It can also involve finding the artist a manager.

Writer/artist development deals are most often a strategy limited to major publishers who have the cash flow to be able to afford to gamble.

Development deals usually involve a 50/50 split on the publishing (meaning that you get 100 percent of your writers royalties plus half of the publisher royalties = 75 percent for you), and the publisher has six months to a year and a half after completion of the masters to get you a record deal.

These publishing/production deals can be a viable alternative for a writer/artist or group, depending on your situation. (See "Where Do You Start?," chapter thirteen.)

WRITER/PRODUCER DEVELOPMENT

This is also a successful strategy of publishers. With the advent of sophisticated and reasonably priced home recording technology, prolific songwriters find it cost effective to learn to produce and arrange their own demos. In the process, they get valuable production experience. At some point, they may decide to find artists who they can write for/with, a strategy that can pay off massively if they produce a successful artist. Writer/producers are among the world's most successful writers. Naturally, to have a writer who can perpetually get their songs onto a succession of successful albums because they're *inside* those projects, makes it an appealing package for a publisher to invest in. In this case, publishers can act as an agent to help their writer/producers find hot new artists to produce.

WRITER DEVELOPMENT

As opposed to writer/artist or writer/producer, this is another important aspect of a publishing company's work. The most common way that publishers do this is to sign writers exclusively to their staffs. (For more information, see "Exclusive Staff Writing Positions" in this chapter.)

Exploring the Possibilities

There are major companies who hire people to do individual tasks, and small independents that must, to some degree, do it all. Still others seem to be publishers in name only and, in effect, serve as "holding companies." This is often the case with managers, producers, or film/TV production companies who use a song once with a particular artist or project and have no staff or time to exploit the song beyond that first use.

Uses of songs are limited only by lack of imagination and perception.

Uses of songs are limited only by lack of imagination and perception. The bottom line for any publisher is to make money by finding as many uses as possible for the song. Obviously the big ones are through sales of records, tapes, and CDs; synchronization (the use of songs in films, TV, and commercials); and airplay. If a song is successful in these areas, sheet music can be an additional source of revenue. The song might be suited to a choral or band arrangement for high schools and colleges. It also might have value in advertising as part of a radio or TV commercial. Manufacturers of autos, audio equipment, and the like compile special CDs to demonstrate auto sound and stereo equipment. Public places such as restaurants, hotels, doctors' offices, elevators, and supermarkets use collections of songs for which royalties are paid. Manufacturers of music boxes, musical toys, and video games are also licensed to use appropriate songs. Greeting card manufacturers use song lyrics and electronic melodic devices, and there are more uses on the horizon.

It's not always enough just to be aware of those possibilities. A creative publisher will *initiate* uses for songs already in the company's catalogue and even generate new songs. For instance, the publisher might hear of a new children's book being written and have his writers or outside writers tailor songs for an album that would be compatible.

New technology has introduced uses for music that were not even dreamed of a short time ago. A good publisher will keep abreast of all these new uses. It's up to you, with the help of some advice, to assess your needs (they'll differ at various points in your career) and determine which kind of publisher works best for you or if you should consider self-publishing. (See "Self-Publishing," chapter eleven.)

New technology has introduced uses for music that were not even dreamed of a short time ago.

Finding a Publisher

Though finding a publisher who believes in your material can be difficult, it could be your most important music industry contact.

Several organizations are listed in the following section, "Checking Out the Publisher." Beyond that, even outside the major music centers, if you hang out at songwriter organizations and events and college music business seminars, you'll get information from instructors and fellow songwriters. Read the trade magazines' (*Billboard*, *Radio and Records*, and *College Music Journal*, for example) list of publishers of hit songs. *Songwriter's Market* (published by Writer's Digest Books, available online and through most bookstores) will give you profiles of companies open to listening to new songs, including contact names, what they're looking for, and how to submit tapes.

Major Publishers vs. Independents

In looking for a publisher, the most important elements to consider are the individual's credibility, whether he or she is independent or works for a major publishing company, and your own relationship with that person. Has she earned the respect of producers by consistently bringing them high-quality, appropriate songs for their projects? Does she respect you, love your songs, and believe you'll be successful? Those are the key questions.

Sometimes it's easier for a professional manager (with the emphasis, when you say it, on "professional") to open the doors of producers and artists if they have the name of a major company behind them. A major publisher may also have the cash flow to invest in the development deals mentioned above if you're a writer/artist/band or writer/producer. The debate over whether to go with a small or large publisher usually gets around to the well-worn axiom that "A small company can give you more individual attention. You'll get lost in a big company." That's not always the case.

Depending on the ratio of professional staff to staff songwriters, you can get individual attention at major companies (if, in fact, you want it). By the same token, a small company may have so much to do that they don't have much time to spend working with you on a personal basis. It all depends on the company and the individuals there.

There are many small but aggressive independent publishers with great contacts and experience. Many independents formerly worked for major companies but wanted the autonomy of making their own business decisions or got laid off after a corporate merger. They may not have the cash flow to hire staff writers, but can do a great job on a song-by-song basis.

Major publishers are also interested in hearing new songs even though most of their "new" material comes from their own staff writers or from re-demoing old songs already in their catalogue. They're interested in keeping in touch with the "street" to get a feeling about new trends and to make sure they're not missing out on any hot new writers, writer/artists, or writer/producers, though many count on the networking of their own writers to do that. You may, however, find them less accessible than independents.

Most major publishers are affiliated with record companies. Is this a positive or a negative? Do the publishers hold off pitching songs to artists on other labels in favor of those on the affiliated label? No. Each of those companies has its own financial bottom line. Though the publisher will certainly attempt to get songs to artists on the "home" label, it's in his best interest to aggressively pitch them to other artists, as well. (There's also no guarantee that an artist on the affiliated label will record the songs, though there are companies who offer bonuses to affiliated producers to record songs in their catalogs.)

Checking Out the Publisher

You're offered a contract by a publisher. Maybe you've submitted a song by mail. Questions rush through your mind. What if this publisher is a rip-off? What if she doesn't do anything with my song? How do I find out about her? Relax! If you want to know what the publisher has done in the past, you have every right to ask. She'll be glad to brag about her success. If she wants your song, she should be able to sell you on her abilities.

She may tell you who she wants to pitch the song to, but sometimes she won't. She's afraid you'll pitch it yourself, or she may not be able to reveal privileged information. Don't necessarily take reluctance as a sign of deviousness. You can negotiate a reversion clause in your contract (see "Negotiable Contract Clauses" on page 185 under the section "Single-Song Contracts") so that if the publisher is unable to get your song recorded, you'll get it back.

If a publisher is just getting started and doesn't have much of a track record, it doesn't mean he can't do the job. Just ask him why he thinks he can do a good job for you, and get a reversion clause of two years or less. If he has few songs to pitch and is serious about the business, he'll be aggressive and, hopefully, will soon be able to give you a list of projects he's pitched your song to.

If you want to check out a specific publisher, call one of the national songwriter organizations. Check with the Nashville Songwriters Association in that city and BMI, ASCAP, SESAC, or The Songwriters Guild of America at their respective offices. (See Appendix.) There may be someone in those organizations who can give you feedback about individual publishers or companies. There is no "Good Housekeeping Seal of Approval" for publishers except that songsharks (see page 155) (those who charge to publish your songs) are not allowed to be affiliated with ASCAP, BMI, or SESAC.

You can talk to other songwriters who have worked with the company. The problem with seeking someone else's approval, however, is that one writer may trash a publisher for not getting a song recorded, and the next writer may praise the same publisher because her song did get recorded. It's hard to sort out these types of subjective evaluations when you don't know all the details. In the end, you have to do as much research as you can, use your own best judgment, and choose a publisher who suits your individual needs. Also there's a lot to be said for trusting your own intuition, your "gut" feeling, about somebody. Unless you're just incredibly paranoid about everybody anyway, if it doesn't feel right, it probably isn't.

Writer/Publisher Q&A

Is it good to send songs to a publisher by certified mail?

No, it scares them to death. They feel they're being set up for a lawsuit and they don't feel it's worth it to take a chance on accepting them. It's also inconvenient for both parties.

May I show my song to several publishers at once?

Yes, and you should. It is an ethical and common practice. You have a song you believe in and want everyone to have an opportunity to hear it.

What if more than one publisher says she wants it?

This is a "problem" you hope to have. Get more information from each of them. What are their recent successes? Will they give a reversion clause, pay for a demo, give you an advance? Who do they envision recording the song? Can they get to those artists? Let them know who else is interested. (Don't lie. They may know each other.) If you get satisfactory answers to all your questions but want to check them out further, tell them you want to think it over. If a publisher pressures you to sign a contract immediately, walk away. Call other writers they publish and ask about their reputations.

If I have a publisher, is it OK if I also pitch those songs to producers?

Yes, you should. The publisher will probably appreciate the help. After all, he gets his percentage whether he gets the song recorded or you do. Remember to let him know what you're planning so you don't both promise the same song to different producers. There may also be a reason why he may not want you to pitch it to

There's a lot to be said for trusting your own intuition, your "gut" feeling, about somebody. Unless you're just incredibly paranoid about everybody anyway, if it doesn't feel right, it probably isn't.

If a publisher pressures you to sign a contract immediately, walk away.

a certain producer and he may have a game plan that you'll mess up. The publisher may also be able to help you get in the door or provide useful info about the producer you want to pitch to.

Getting Feedback From Publishers

I often ask writers how they've been received by publishers I know. Though I've heard stories about publishers who were long on ego abuse, in all fairness, that's a rarity. It's not as rare, though, for publishers to avoid offering any feedback or constructive criticism. More often they give a stock answer: "That's not the type of song we're looking for," "I wouldn't know who'd record a song like that," "I don't think the song is marketable." All those lines, though probably true, don't help you know how to write better or more marketable songs. I decided to ask some publishers why this is the case and got some fairly typical responses.

One publisher said, "I won't give writers a critique anymore unless they're very close to writing hit songs and I know I want to get involved as their publisher. Otherwise, it's more hassle than it's worth. I used to do it all the time because I wanted to help, but I stepped on too many egos and got into arguments. Songwriters don't really want to be criticized. Even when they ask for it, they just argue with me."

On the other hand, he said, "Bob [a writer we both knew] is the kind of writer I will work with. He's come a long way because he listens. The first time I heard his tunes, I knew he had a basic grip on how to write a good song. I told him one of the tunes was close, but I thought it would be stronger with a bridge. Next day he came back with two different versions of a bridge and we published it and got it recorded. He didn't say, 'What do you mean, it needs a bridge? I wrote it without a bridge and it sounds OK to me!' He just gave it a shot and because he did, we both won."

Another publisher explained, "Hey, if I wanted to spend all my time teaching people how to write songs, I wouldn't have time to deal with the songs I'm already committed to. Besides, most writers don't even want to hear it!"

Len Chandler (my Los Angeles Songwriters Showcase partner) and I once suggested to a writer a change we felt would clarify a particular lyric. The writer couldn't believe his song was being critiqued and replied incredulously, "But I wrote that song in Topanga Canyon!" To that writer, the act of writing the song was akin to receiving a sacred message from the Great Spirit. To suggest any change by himself or someone else was unthinkable.

I'm not going to tell you that it's wrong to feel so personally about your songs or that you should operate with the attitude that there's something wrong with your songs and all you have to do is find some publisher to tell you what it is. That's destructive to your self-esteem and, in music, you need all the self-esteem you can get. But it's also self-destructive to assume you have nothing to learn from anyone. Nothing will stop your creative and professional growth more surely than that. You need to be able to look at feedback from industry pros as an *opportunity to learn* either or both of two important things: (1) You can learn something valuable about improving that song, about writing in general or writing more commercially in particular; (2) You can learn about the needs and tastes of that particular person, so even if you decide not to act on the criticism, you'll have learned what to bring or what not to bring that publisher or producer next time.

In any case, you need at least to be *receptive* to criticism and to know that most industry people won't even bother to give it unless they think you have enough talent to begin with. If you're defensive and argumentative, you may have a problem finding a publisher who will want to work with you. There are simply too many other good writers around who are open to criticism and willing to rewrite.

There's another angle to this that should also be brought out. Publishers aren't infallible, and you don't need to believe their every opinion as gospel. You'll definitely find, in going from one publisher to another, a great diversity of tastes and opinions. Pay attention to the criticism and don't let their experience and willingness to help go to waste. You may learn more from those you disagree with than you will from those who see things the way you do. You need them both. Those who agree will give you support and confidence. Those who challenge you, especially if they're articulate about it, can give you the opportunity to grow.

Uncontracted Songplugging

Songplugging without a contract is a practice that writers occasionally ask me about and wonder how to deal with. Most publishers want a contract, at least a letter of intent, before they commit their time and energy to pitching your song. But for those who don't, here's how it works.

A publisher might say, "Just let me run with your song for a month, six months, or whatever you agree to, without a contract, and see what happens. If I can get you a record on it, I get the publishing. If not, you've got the song back." The publisher may suggest this for a variety of reasons:

1. He doesn't want to sign your song, not be able to do anything with it, and have you hounding him forever.

2. He's not sure enough about the song to commit his money or his company's money to do demos, copies, and all the attendant things that go with it.

3. He has a specific artist in mind for the song and if it's rejected, he doesn't know anyone else who would cut it.

In any case, he trusts you not to take it to another publisher and is allowing you to get the song back if he can't get it recorded. The danger of not having the deal on paper is that one of you may forget the terms of the agreement. Make sure you clarify what happens if an artist or producer puts a *hold* on the song (asks that the publisher not show it to anyone else for a period to give him a chance to cut it or decide if he will cut it). The producer may want to hold the song for longer than you had originally agreed with the publisher. Fairness would dictate that you wait, along with the publisher, until the producer makes up his mind. Since the publisher made the initial contact with the producer, it would be unethical of you to take it to other publishers or publish it yourself. Remember that the music business is like a small town, and word gets around if you abuse the trust people place in you.

Remember that the music business is like a small town, and word gets around if you abuse the trust people place in you.

It often happens that a publisher won't ask you not to show it to other publishers because he assumes you know the ethics involved and doesn't want to insult you by suggesting your ignorance. But writers who know little about the publisher's job, or the industry in general, may not even consider that there are ethics involved here. They actually may look at the situation as an adversarial relationship rather than a partnership built on mutual respect. (See "Ethics in the Biz," chapter thirteen.) I've run across several writers in the past who told me, quite innocently, that they planned to let several publishers try to market the song or said, "I'll let publisher 'A' run with the tune for a couple of weeks and if he doesn't get anything happening, I'll take it to publisher 'B,' who's also interested." The problem was that he hadn't told publisher "A" that he intended to do that.

Imagine what would happen if both publishers pitched the song for the same project. In other words, they'd both be doing their job as publishers on your behalf, using their hard-earned expertise and credibility. Suppose the producer likes the tune for his artist and wants to cut it immediately. If the producer realizes that both publishers pitched him the tune, he'll probably call both publishers and tell them. They aren't going to be happy about your game; but if you don't have contracts with either, they both might want you to sign one immediately. There's also a good chance that the producer will want to sign the song to his own company.

Who will you choose and what do you tell the other publisher, who may have worked as hard for you? If you had a contract with "A" and none with "B," then "A" is the winner and "B" is mad at you for using him unethically. "B" assumes you knew your contract with "A" gave "A" *exclusive* right to publish your song. (He may also decide that he'll never pitch a song again without a contract.) If you're unfortunate enough to have signed contracts with both "A" and "B" on the same song, you're in serious legal trouble, because you lied on the contract when you gave exclusivity to two publishers at once. Would you sell your car to two different people? Basically, the rule of thumb is "Be up front." Let everyone know what's going on. If a publisher wants to plug your song without a contract, agree on a specific period in which no one else will plug the song, and stick to it! (See "Independent Songpluggers" and "Self-Publishing" chapter eleven.)

Single-Song Contracts

Songwriter-publisher contracts covering one song are the ones you'll come in contact with most frequently as a songwriter. I use the plural because there are probably hundreds of different single-song contracts that say "standard" at the top of the page. Publishers obtain these contracts in various ways. Some come right "off the rack" from music supply stores.

NEGOTIABLE CONTRACT CLAUSES:

Songwriters Guild of America's (SGA)

Ten Basic Points Your Contract Should Include

THERE IS NO STANDARD SONGWRITER CONTRACT. Deals vary from publisher to publisher and often from writer to writer within a publishing company.

EVERYTHING IS NEGOTIABLE. You should not attempt to arrange any sort of long-term agreement without the help of someone with experience in dealing objectively with the issues involved in negotiating contracts between writer and publisher. The following are basic points that each contract should include.

1. WORK FOR HIRE—When you receive a contract covering just one composition, you should make sure that the phrases "employment for hire" and "exclusive writer agreement" are not included. Also, there should be no options for future songs.

2. PERFORMING RIGHTS AFFILIATION—If you previously signed publishing contracts, you should be affiliated with either ASCAP, BMI, or SESAC. All performance royalties must be received directly by you from your performing rights organization and this should be written into your song contract. (The same goes for any third party licensing organization mutually agreed upon.)

3. REVERSION CLAUSE—The contract should include a provision that, if the publisher does not secure a release of a commercial sound recording within a specified time (one year, two years, etc.), the contract can be terminated by you.

4. CHANGES IN THE COMPOSITION—If the contract includes a provision that the publisher can change the title, lyrics, or music, then this should be amended that only with your previous consent can such changes be made.

5. ROYALTY PROVISIONS—Basically, you should receive fifty percent (50%) of all publisher's income on all licenses issued. If the publisher prints and sells his own sheet music and folios, your royalty should be ten percent (10%) of the wholesale selling price. The royalty should not be stated in the contract as a flat rate ($.05, $.07, etc.).

6. NEGOTIABLE DEDUCTIONS—Ideally, demos and all other expenses of publication should be paid 100% by the publisher. The only allowable fee is the Harry Fox Agency collection fee, whereby the writer pays one half of the amount charged to the publisher. Today's rate charged by The Harry Fox Agency is 4½%.

7. ROYALTY STATEMENTS AND AUDIT PROVISION—Once the song is recorded and printed, you are entitled to receive royalty statements at least once every six months. In addition, an audit provision with no time restriction should be included in every contract.

8. WRITER'S CREDIT—The publisher should make sure that you receive proper credit on all uses of the composition.

9. ARBITRATION—In order to avoid large legal fees in case of a dispute with your publisher, the contract should include an arbitration clause.

10. FUTURE USES—Any use not specifically covered by the contract should be retained by the writer to be negotiated as it comes up.

The Songwriters Guild of America is available for members to seek the proper information before they sign a contract. LET US HELP YOU GET THE BEST POSSIBLE CONTRACT!

You should remember that we already have a contract that we recommend to writers, which you should certainly try to present to your publisher. Copies are available at the SGA office or online at http://www.songwriters.org.

Some publishers will get a contract from their attorney and work out modifications based on that publisher's philosophy of doing business. Well-established companies will have contracts that they've developed over the years. The only things you can count on as "standard" are that, if a publisher hands you a contract, it will be biased to the publisher's advantage and that it will be negotiable. Never believe that because a contract's typeset and says it's "standard," that it can't be changed.

How contracts are worded and how they can be negotiated are very important areas to explore. Paranoia is common among songwriters due to a lack of understanding about contract clauses and how to negotiate them. Most of that fear persists because songwriters don't understand the reasons why some of the clauses exist. Many deals have gone out the window because a writer has been told never to accept this or that deal point.

| Comments on SGA's Recommendations

These are all great recommendations and most are absolutely essential. Ability to obtain these recommendations depends on the bargaining strength of the writer. I'll add that I'm not an attorney and, not knowing your individual situation, I can't advise you about what clauses I think would be more or less important in your specific circumstance. I can discuss what I feel are the important issues from both sides so you can look at this agreement with some perspective. The best advice is to have a music business attorney look over your contract. Also keep in mind that although a single song contract is important, unless you think this is the only publishable song you'll ever write, it's not exactly the end of your creative career if you can't get all the clauses recommended here. You will need to be flexible.

What makes negotiating so crazy is that it's difficult to get any perspective about your bargaining strength. Even if you've been successful in the past (which definitely gives you an edge), your current material will be judged for its commercial potential in today's market. The only thing you can do is try to negotiate these clauses to your own advantage and hope for the best, keeping in mind that the best contract is one in which each party's needs have been addressed and neither party feels he's been "had."

Here are my commentaries on the SGA's recommendations:

The best contract is one in which each party's needs have been addressed and neither party feels he's been "had."

1. WORK FOR HIRE

When you receive a contract covering just one composition, you should make sure that the phrases "employment for hire" and "exclusive writer agreement" are not included. Also, there should be no options for future songs.

Pretty straight ahead, "exclusive writer agreements" are "staff" deals in which you're not allowed to write for anyone else for a period of time. Those deals usually include "work for hire" agreements, which means that everything you write during that time considers the "employer" (publisher) to be the "author," for copyright purposes. It still means you'll get paid and credited according to your contract, however.

2. PERFORMING RIGHTS AFFILIATION

If you previously signed publishing contracts, you should be affiliated with either ASCAP, BMI, or SESAC. All performance royalties must be received directly by you from your performing rights organization and this should be written into your song contract. (The same goes for any third party licensing organization mutually agreed upon.)

Most contracts include this clause to acknowledge that they (the publishers) won't be sending your writer's share of performance royalties to you—that you'll receive them directly from your performing rights organization.

3. REVERSION CLAUSE

The contract should include a provision that, if the publisher does not secure a release of a commercial sound recording within a specified time (one year, two years, etc.). The contract can be terminated by you.

The reversion clause in songwriter/publisher contracts was pioneered many years ago by The Songwriters Guild of America, in their model writer-oriented contract. Reversion clauses have been a bone of contention with publishers, but nearly all publishers accept it in order to remain competitive. It also keeps disgruntled writers off their backs if they're not getting their song cut.

The length of time granted to the publisher is a major negotiating point in this clause. It can be any length you agree on, but it commonly runs as short as six months or as long, in current practice, as three years. Personally, I feel that two years should be adequate. Six months or a year is not always enough time for publishers, for several practical reasons. It frequently happens that an artist may be interested in a song but won't be recording again for another six months. Touring commitments or other circumstances may delay the recording or even the release of the record. If that were to happen, then technically, the writer could get her song back and take the publishing herself after the record was later released, leaving the publisher with no reward for the job done. That fact soured publishers on short reversion periods, unless they know they're hitting the one or two artists most likely to cut the tune at a time when they're in the studio and looking for songs.

A producer also may put a "hold" on the song, asking the publisher to refrain from pitching it to anyone else until a final decision is made. That "hold" may last weeks or months. (See "Holds," chapter eleven.)

The producer also may have collected fifteen or twenty songs as possibilities for the project, whittled them down to ten, and your song got whittled out. Or, it actually might get recorded but fail to live up to the expectations of the producer, artist, or label and end up "in the can" (not released), as they say. The record might be released someday, but by that time, the reversion period is up and the publisher has had to return the song to the writer.

So, you see, publishers face problems with short reversion periods. Given that, I feel it would be fair to negotiate a one- or two-year reversion clause with the stipulation that the period be extended for the length of time a producer has the song on "hold." (This, of course, would require an agreement in writing between the publisher and producer as well.)

By the time the reversion period is up, the writer should also have had adequate opportunity to assess the amount of activity the publisher has expended on the song. If the writer sees that the publisher has been taking care of business, she could grant the publisher an extended reversion period.

Early in the history of this clause, some publishers would subvert its intent by pressing up a few copies of the demo, sending them to radio stations, and saying, "OK, I released the song on a record, so that means I can keep the publishing." Currently, the wording goes an extra step by saying the publisher is responsible for the song's "commercial recording and release for distribution and sale to the public."

There are other reasons you can include in a contract for a song to revert back to the writer besides the inability of the publisher to get it recorded. The clause can prevent the publisher from reassigning your copyright to another individual or company without your consent or you also can have the song revert back to you if the publisher refuses to allow you or your representative to audit his books regarding royalties. I would suggest that you state that at the end of the reversion period, the song "reverts to you *automatically*" without requiring you to send a registered letter by a certain time to demand it (which most contracts request). They may count on your forgetting to do that. Here's an example:

Within two (2) years from the date hereof, commercial recordings of the musical composition must have been released for either (a) sale to the public on records, tapes, CDs or other recorded products; (b) synchronization in the sound track of a theatrical motion picture released to the public; (c) synchronization in the sound track of a television program broadcast to the public; (d) synchronization in the sound track of a home video program for sale to the public; or (e) other recordings consistent with this agreement that are released and/or sold to the public.

If at the end of two years from the date of this Agreement, a commercial recording has been secured but a commercial release or usage shall not have occurred, Publisher shall have the option to extend the term of this agreement for an additional twelve months (for a total contract term of thirty-six months). If none of the foregoing recordings have been released within said thirty-six-month time period, this contract shall terminate.

Upon the termination of this agreement, all rights in and to the Composition and in and to any and all copyrights secured thereon shall automatically revest in and become the property of the Writer, and shall be re-assigned to the Writer by Publisher free of any and all encumbrances of any nature whatsoever.

The following example is simpler and doesn't include the option for the publisher to extend the contract, which, as I stated above, is not a bad thing to do. What I like about this is that it also (i) qualifies what "released" means and keeps them from getting around it by having their own in-house record label release it (a common songshark tactic). Of course, if it's Warner/Chappell Music and their "relate" third party is Warner Bros. Records, this would be fine.

Note that paragraph ii allows you to fill in a minimum amount you'll take for any other

a. Notwithstanding anything contained in this Agreement, this Agreement shall terminate automatically and any and all rights in and to the Composition shall revert to the Writer, if Publisher shall not secure, within twenty-four (24) months from the date set forth in this Agreement, the following:

i. A commercial sound recording of the Composition to be recorded and released in the recording industry's customary commercial channels along with a Mechanical License issued for the Composition by an unrelated third party, or;

ii. Any other agreement for the exploitation of the Composition which derives an initial agreement fee and/or payment due in excess of the amount of _____ dollars ($ _____).

use, which will include film synch license, etc. Remember that the "initial agreement fee and/or payment" will be interpreted as a payment to the *publisher*, of which you'll get half. I like this because it can keep the publisher from holding your song for a five dollar use. You can also specify in the reversion clause that it needs to be released by an artist signed to a major label, an artist with a previous Top 20 hit or anything else you want to put in.

4. CHANGES IN THE COMPOSITION

If the contract includes a provision that the publisher can change the title, lyrics or music, then this should be amended that only with your previous consent can such changes be made.

Here's a scenario that illustrates the value of this type of clause. You have a contract with a publisher on a song. The publisher pitches the song to an artist. The artist wants a piece of the publishing before he records the song, but the publisher refuses. The artist says, "I basically love the song and I'll record it, but I think the second verse is weak and I'd like to rewrite it. Of course, I'll have to have half of the writer's royalties to do that." The publisher says to himself, "What the hell. I still get all my publishing and the writer should be grateful that he gets cowriting credit with this famous artist. I'll go for it."

Your second verse may not have been bad at all. The artist may write a terrible second verse and destroy the integrity of your song (which you would have to live with) or make it so personalized that no one else would want to record it. If the publisher had refused and had stuck to his guns, the artist might have recorded it anyway. If the artist genuinely felt the second verse was weak and could explain why, you should have been offered the first opportunity to rewrite it. This publisher has just deprived you of half your writer's share of royalties and will come back to you and say, "100 percent of nothing is nothing. I thought you'd be glad to get half of what could be a big writer's royalty." This may be a compromise you're willing to make, but the fact is that without this clause in your contract, he has every right to do just what he did *without your permission*.

There have also been cases in which a publisher/writer with greed and a big ego wants his name on your song as cowriter and will put it there on the flimsiest of justifications. He may decide to change your title, change a couple of words here and there, change a melody line, and cut himself in as a cowriter without your permission. The publisher may also insist on unnecessary changes in your song if he's getting flak from his staff writer(s) for signing an "outside" song (from a nonstaff writer). To appease them, he might have one of them "rewrite" the song and take cowriter credit!

Those are some of the situations that happen. When those types of proposals are made *before* the song is signed to a publisher, you have the choice to forget it or to go along for the sake of your career. The reason to include a "no change" clause is to make sure you still have that choice after the contract is signed. And if a cowriter is still forced on you under any of the above circumstances, there should be at least a clause that provides that no more than 50 percent of your writer's royalties can be split with anyone else.

Sometimes a publisher will want to take writer credits himself. It's part of a publisher's job to help inspire, guide, edit, critique, and make suggestions for writers. If you, the writer, feel that the creative contributions of the publisher are substantial enough to warrant inclusion as a cowriter, then you should offer it. There are times, of course, when the publisher does deserve a writer credit. So if you see a publisher's name on a song, you should reserve your judgment about how it got there until you know the real story.

You might ask why a publisher would not want to give you a "no change" clause if he's such a good guy. Well, here's another scenario. The publisher gets a tip that a major artist is finishing up an album and a couple of her songs didn't turn out so well at the session, or the artist decides the songs weren't right after all. The publisher remembers your song and rushes over. The producer loves it and so does the artist *except* that: (a) she wants the melody to be a little more rangey to show off her voice; (b) it was written as a man's song, so a couple of lines need to be changed; and (c) the title has to be changed, too, to reflect all the other changes. They want to do it right now. The publisher calls the last number he had for you and it's disconnected or you're in an ashram in India and can't be reached. The publisher, at that point, has to risk losing the cut and incurring your wrath for it or risk your taking back the copyright because he allowed the change without your permission. Chances are the publisher will risk the latter and pray that you don't turn out to be an ungrateful person. A publisher could cover himself on this one by stating he'll make his best effort (like a registered letter) to contact you.

Another situation where this applies is when a publisher assigns a writer to create a lyric for your instrumental composition without your consent. It's very seldom that an instrumental becomes a hit unless it's a movie theme. The commercial viability of the piece may be enhanced appreciably with a great lyric. The right lyric is very important, though. Some great instrumentals could be trivialized and cheapened by any lyric, let alone a bad one. Many dynamic orchestrations can be written for an instrumental without having to be conscious of "leaving space" for the vocals. Also, without language barriers, an instrumental can be internationally successful. So there are a lot of factors to consider. I believe the original writer, with the input of the publisher, should have the last word on which lyric, if any, should be written for his or her melody. (See "Lyric Translations" in chapter eleven.)

5. ROYALTY PROVISIONS

Basically, you should receive fifty percent (50%) of all publisher's income on all licenses issued. If the publisher prints and sells his own sheet music and folios, your royalty should be ten percent (10%) of the wholesale selling price. The royalty should not be stated in the contract as a flat rate ($.05, $.07, etc.).

We're seeing the development of digital delivery systems we could only imagine for audio and visual creations at the time I wrote the first edition of this book. Vinyl records, except for a small group of die-hard enthusiasts, are obsolete. Audiocassettes, as a medium for distributing music, are about to follow. CDs prevail and digital audio files are on the way up. Some predict they'll rule by 2006. The entire industry is playing catch-up trying to figure out how to track their distribution and collect from users. I don't doubt they will, to the extent that they can. Publishers are at the forefront of the quest. The bottom line here is that, as a writer, no matter what the new uses they collect for, you should get 50 percent of what your publisher collects. It's in your best interest to make sure your contract includes *"any other use now existing or used in the future from which the publisher receives royalties."* Or if they give you a list, add a clause saying, *"and all other uses not referred to in this agreement."* If that clause isn't there, the publisher doesn't have to pay you for a use that's *not listed* on your contract.

As a writer, no matter what the new uses they collect for, you should get 50 percent of what your publisher collects.

6. NEGOTIABLE DEDUCTIONS

Ideally, demos and all other expenses of publication should be paid 100% by the publisher. The only allowable fee is the Harry Fox Agency collection fee, whereby the writer pays one half of the amount charged to the publisher. Today's rate charged by the Harry Fox Agency is 6%.

Publishers should assume all administration costs except the Harry Fox Agency fee for collection of mechanical royalties. An exception to their assuming all administration costs would be in the case of a copublishing agreement between the publisher and the publishing company owned by the writer, in which case, those fees could be split.

Regarding demo costs, what's happening now is that writers are approaching publishers with good, appropriate demos—complete and already paid for. In that situation, I think the publisher should pay you up front for all, or at least half, of the demo costs you incurred. Your negotiating position on this point may be weakened if you're also asking for a reversion clause. Most publishers are reluctant to lay out cash on a song if there's a chance they'll have to give the song back to you. They'll have to spend money to promote the song, and they want to minimize their risk. I believe that a reversion clause is more important than front money in general, but that depends on how badly you need the bucks. If you can't get them to pay you for your demo right away and give you a reversion, negotiate to have them reimburse you 100 percent or at least not less than 50 percent for your demo when they get the song recorded.

7. ROYALTY STATEMENTS AND AUDIT PROVISION

Once the song is recorded and printed, you are entitled to receive royalty statements at least once every six months. In addition, an audit provision with no time restriction should be included in every contract.

This is pretty standard. Many publishers, however, pay quarterly. New royalty accounting software has streamlined this process considerably, so it's not such a labor-intensive problem anymore. But the incentive for publishers to prefer semiannual rather than quarterly payments is that they collect interest on your royalties for three more months. Not much for a small company, but for the majors it really adds up.

The audit provision with no time restriction is difficult to get. If they don't include it, by California statute, you'd have four years to sue them, six years in New York. So they try to get you to agree to the finality of a royalty statement within a year or two. That means that if you find something wrong with your statement, you only have that long to object. Try to get at least three.

My recommendation is that you join the Songwriters Guild of America. They offer these contract recommendations and, for a small percentage, will check your royalty statement (you have your statements mailed to them directly), and forward it to you immediately. They check it against your contract, which you send them when you join, and if they find a discrepancy, they call the publisher immediately and try to straighten it out. If they can't, chances are there are other members who are having problems with the same publisher and SGA will audit them on your behalf. Usually, it's an accounting mistake on the part of the publisher and it's easy to remedy. (Hey, we'll give them the benefit of the doubt—the first time!) The problem is that, without someone knowledgeable checking it, you'd never know about it. I suspect that there are a few of you who have trouble balancing your checkbook, let alone analyzing a royalty statement. I have several successful writer friends for whom SGA has gone after royalties and has gotten them money they didn't know they had, and in one case, *did* know they had but couldn't afford to pursue. Essentially, SGA performs the same functions for writers that the Harry Fox Agency performs for publishers in collecting from record companies. They've been doing it for a long time and do it very well. Reach them at: www.songwriters.org.

New York—(212) 768-7902   SongNews@aol.com
Los Angeles—(323) 462-1108   LASGA@aol.com
Nashville—(615) 329-1782   SGANash@aol.com
Administrative/Executive office—(201) 867-7603   Lbachman@aol.com

8. WRITER'S CREDIT

The publisher should make sure that you receive proper credit on all uses of the composition.

Publishers don't object to this, but in some cases it's hard to guarantee. They want it, too, but if they're dealing with film and TV synch uses, it's sometimes hard to get unless you have a featured song that plays over the title or end credits or is part of a film that contains many songs and everybody gets credited.

9. ARBITRATION

In order to avoid large legal fees in case of a dispute with your publisher, the contract should include an arbitration clause.

THE SONGWRITERS GUILD CONTRACT ARBITRATION CLAUSE

Any and all differences, disputes or controversies arising out of or in connection with this contract shall be submitted to arbitration before a sole arbitrator under the then prevailing rules of the American Arbitration Association. The location of the arbitration shall be New York, New York, if the Writer on the date of execution of this contract resides East of the Mississippi River, or in Los Angeles, California, if the Writer on the date of execution of this contract resides West of the Mississippi River. The parties hereby individually and jointly agree to abide by and perform any award rendered in such arbitration. Judgment upon any such award rendered may be entered in any court having jurisdiction thereof.

Pick California or New York and use this if the contract offered doesn't have an arbitration clause. (SGA Contract is available online at *www.songwriters.org.*)

10. FUTURE USES

Any use not specifically covered by the contract should be retained by the writer to be negotiated as it comes up.

(See no. 5, page 193.)

| Other Negotiable Contract Clauses
REDUCED MECHANICAL ROYALTY RATES

Try to get this clause: "A publisher may not grant a licensee a rate lower than the current statutory rate without the prior consent of the writer." (See chapter nine, "Where Your Money Comes From.") It's wise to have such a clause added to the contract. This practice of allowing a company to pay you less than the current statutory rate is called "giving a rate." The "rate" refers to the current mechanical rate effective at the time the license is granted to the record company for use of the song.

Here's the problem situation that prompted this clause. Let's say, hypothetically, that your publisher has interested an artist in your song and the record company says, "We'd like Sally Superstar to record the song you brought us, but we don't want to pay the current statutory mechanical rate." The most prevalent reason for that is that Sally, in her recording contract, has a "Controlled Composition Clause" (see chapter nine) that requires her to get a "rate" from you if she wants to record your "outside" song. Otherwise, she'd have to pay you out of her own artist royalties. If Sally's record, with your song on it, is a hit, the quarter of the rate given up could add up to a lot of rent money. You can usually trust that your publisher will be reluctant to give up anything less than full statutory rate. Remember, he'll be losing money too, unless it would be worthwhile to accept a reduced rate because of a substantial amount of projected sales (e.g., a compilation of hits that can almost guarantee half a million sales).

One thing publishers object to about getting your permission is that they may not be able to find you. (See no. 4, page 190.) Be sure to notify your publisher and performing rights organization of your new address as soon as you move.

If you can't get the clause, you should at least get one that limits the reduction to a three-quarter rate. The clause should also state that "no less than the full statutory rate should apply to licenses granted to any person or business entity owned, controlled or affiliated, in whole or in part, by or with the publisher," because there's the chance that a publisher might give a very low rate to an affiliated record label.

Sharing in Advances

If your publisher receives an advance, for example, for the inclusion of your song in a collection for which he gave a reduced mechanical rate because of the volume of units projected to be sold (a common practice), you should share in the advance. Make sure you share in all advances based *specifically on your song*. Publishers will also get advances on their entire catalogue, say, from a foreign subpublisher. They can't pay you out of that because they would be hard-pressed to figure out how much of the advance is based on *your* song.

Commercial exploitation of your demos should not be allowed without your consent.

Commercial exploitation of your demos should not be allowed without your consent. You've just become a big star and your publisher releases an album of your old demos that you recorded ten years ago when you weren't nearly as wonderful a writer or singer as (you think) you are now. (This recently happened to Trisha Yearwood.) You should have had the clause that says, "Publisher shall not commercially exploit any demonstration records embodying the performances of writers without writer's written consent."

Clauses and Wordings to Watch for in Single-Song Contracts:

1. **"No royalties will be paid for . . . *copies disposed of as new issues.*"** It's common practice in print music to send *new issues* of all new sheet music to dealers to let them check it out. Publishers will be paid for it by the print publishers with whom they subcontract; but, with this clause, you, the writer, won't. This clause is usually connected with a clause that mentions not getting paid for *promotional copies* of records, which your publisher *will not* get paid for, so it's all right to leave it in. But make sure *new issues* gets deleted.

2. **"Publisher shall *reasonably* prorate such royalties . . ."** Watch out for vague language. "Reasonable" to the publisher may not be reasonable to you. Proratio formulas should be specifically defined, for example: "In such event, the royalties payable to writer shall be computed by a fraction, the numerator of which shall be one (representing the

writer's song) and the denominator of which shall be the total number of copyrighted musical compositions contained in the (folio, book, etc.)."

3. **"A royalty of _____ percent of the *net* cash proceeds . . ."** Always make sure that you have spelled out what "net" means. Does it mean after *administrative* costs? If so, forget it. It's the publisher's job to administer and those costs should *not* be deducted "off the top" (from the gross) before your writer's royalties are paid. If you're copublishing the song, though, it's certainly fair to split the costs between your company and theirs. Does net mean after demo costs? After promotional costs? Be sure to get it spelled out.

Your Chances for Advances

First of all, never quit your day job figuring you'll make a living from advances on single-song contracts. But since writers always seem to be interested in this, here's the info. An advance is, essentially, money paid to you before it's been earned. One of the big questions when you negotiate any contract (whether a single song, a staff writing contract, or recording contract) is "How much of an advance can I get?" A couple of general philosophies operate regarding advance money, which apply more to record deals than single songs because of the huge amounts involved. One is that the more money a company puts out in advances, the more committed they are to recouping it, so naturally they'll work harder. But only to a point. And once a company decides that your project is a loser, another philosophy may kick in called "don't throw good money after bad." They'll just stop trying. An advance may be the only money you'll see on the deal if they drop your project.

A philosophy you'll hear from small independent publishers is "instead of giving you an advance, I will or plan to spend that money doing great demos and other things that will help us both make more money in the long run." He's got a point. In that situation, you have to rely on a most important consideration, which is whether you feel the publisher can do the job for you.

| Variables Regarding Advances

Here are some variables to consider regarding cash advances in a writer/publisher deal. In reality, this is a moot point unless they really want your song.

An advance is money paid ahead of time against future royalties, not a payment for the song. The money they give you now comes off the top of any future royalties due you. Despite this fact, I'm surprised at the writers I talk to who are very upset a couple of years down the road when their statement from the publisher doesn't yield them a check. They've conveniently forgotten that the publisher will pay himself back for the advance. The computer doesn't forget!

Reversion clauses in your publishing contract may be affected by an advance. So how does it relate to advances? Here's the basic principle. The more money a publisher puts out in front, before actually getting a record cut on the song, the more he gambles. So he is not going to want to give you back the song *and* lose the money if the song doesn't get

Never quit your day job figuring you'll make a living from advances on single-song contracts.

recorded. Oh yes, he can just write it off, but of course, he'd rather not. If the song never earns money, you're not expected to pay back the advance. So he will probably tell you that he can't give you a reversion clause if he gives you an advance. That's just a good business practice. However, you should try to get both.

Remember, though, that if someone working for a major publishing company offers you an advance, it's not their own money and there's a company budget for those expenses. A small, independent publisher doesn't get a salary. If he doesn't get songs recorded, he doesn't eat (OK, I exaggerate), and that advance would come directly out of his pocket. He's less likely to give you one for that reason. You may be able to get both an advance and a reversion clause if you agree to return the advance if the song reverts. Some publishers will even want you to pay back their demo expenses on reversion.

Going in with a good demo enhances your chances. Based on the same principle as above, if you go to a publisher with a good, usable demo and that saves him the cost of producing it ($500 to over $4,000), you're in a much better position to ask for an advance. You're also in a much better position to ask for a reversion clause, but you still may have to decide between the clause and an advance. It's a good idea to ask for at least enough of an advance to cover your demo costs.

It's a good idea to ask for at least enough of an advance to cover your demo costs.

If you want to keep a part of the publishing, they're unlikely to want to give you an advance. Here again, you're reducing the potential income for them because they'll now be keeping only a portion of the publishing royalties. In fact, they're likely to ask you to split the demo costs if you want to split the income. Not unreasonable at all, because you'll be business partners.

How much of an advance can you get?

Whatever you can negotiate, but five hundred dollars for a single song is probably on the top end. Ultimately, everything depends on how badly the publisher wants the song and how much he feels he can afford to give you. The risk for him is that you'll take it somewhere else if he doesn't give you what you want. If you need an advance, you should ask for it, but the enthusiasm of the publisher and his willingness to give you a reversion clause are ultimately worth more. The publishers' ability to assess the commercial viability of your song is their game, and if you raise the stakes, they lose more if they're wrong. Bear it in mind since they're bound to hit a limit at some point. Be prepared to be flexible.

Exclusive Staff Writing Positions

A staff writer may be at one company for several years. During that time, all the songs he or she writes become the property of the publisher, generally with the standard 50/50 writer/publisher royalty split, though copublishing deals are also quite common, particularly if you already have a successful track record. The writer is paid weekly (or monthly, quarterly, or annually) advances against future royalties, rather than a salary. The publisher gambles that he'll be able to recoup that money by getting some of those songs cut. If the songs never recoup the investment, the writer doesn't owe the publisher and the publisher loses his investment.

So, why would a publisher gamble like that rather than sign songs off the street? A writer signed to a staff position is likely very talented, dedicated, and prolific. Having a writer under contract for several years makes it worthwhile to invest a considerable amount of time and money in developing that writer's career. During that time, the publisher hopes that a substantial catalogue of material is developed that will continue to be recorded. That writer's resulting success attracts other good writers as well. And having these writers under contract also prevents their songs from going to another company.

Contract Issues

You should *never* sign an exclusive long-term staff-writer contract without the counsel of an experienced music industry attorney. However, you can get a general idea beforehand of what the publisher will usually want from you. Here are a few points:

1. **The publisher will want to publish all the songs you've already written that aren't already published.** She'll want to have (at least) "first refusal." You can argue that any advances in the deal are for future writing services only and that a separate payment should be made for back catalogue, especially if the publisher will be using the demos you paid for yourself.

2. **Some publishers will expect a certain quota of songs per month or year (twenty per year is common).** Others feel if you deliver a great song every now and then, they won't be pushy. You both need to have an understanding of your creative habits. Some writers need deadlines. Some need to be left alone. Sometimes a publisher will set a quota of "acceptable" songs. This is not a good idea for you, especially if they can extend your contract indefinitely until the quota of "acceptable" songs is fulfilled. For purposes of fulfilling your quota, they usually consider that two 50/50 cowrites equal one song, etc.

3. **The publisher will want a one-year contract with at least four one-year options.** *Their* options. Try to limit it to three. You can build performance clauses into your contract that keep them from picking up the option unless, for instance, they secure a certain amount of recordings during the previous year. You can also negotiate to have your weekly advances increase every time they pick up the option.

4. **Advances range from $1,000 to over $4,000 a month, depending on how successful you've been or (they think) you will be.** Advances of more than half a million dollars have been made for already established writer/producers. These are "advances" against future royalties. There may be someone out there getting a straight salary (on a standard 50/50 writer/publisher deal) that's not recoupable from future royalties. But if there is, it's extremely rare because, by the time you're a valuable enough writer to command that kind of a deal, you either don't need the money or you're better off just getting an administration deal for your own publishing company.

You should *never* sign an exclusive long-term staff-writer contract without the counsel of an experienced music industry attorney.

Benefits of Being an Exclusive (Staff) Writer

The following are benefits that may or may not be offered by publishers and are listed as the benefits you'd find in an ideal situation.

1. You're often provided a work space with instruments and recording equipment. This is great if you don't already have a good setup elsewhere.

2. You're given a weekly "draw," an advance against future royalties so you don't have to worry about the rent.

3. The publisher may pay for all your demos or give you a specific demo budget.

4. You're in an environment where you're encouraged and expected to be productive. Being around other productive writers can help your motivation.

5. You'll receive critical feedback that will, hopefully, help you grow as a writer.

6. You'll be made aware of upcoming recording projects so that you can tailor songs for those artists.

7. Your publisher will hook you up with film and TV assignments, album projects, and collaborators—often artists or producers with projects of their own.

8. If he feels you have artist potential, he may be motivated to find you a producer, a manager, and a record deal.

9. Because of his belief in you and his financial investment, he'll do all he can to promote your career. (See "Writer/Artist Development" in this chapter.)

10. Publisher as bank. There are writers, writer/artists, and writer/producers for whom few to none of the above benefits are as important as having their projects financed and getting huge advances.

Drawbacks of Being a Staff Writer

Though the staff writer situation can be wonderful and productive (and certainly has been the best way to go for many hit writers), it's a mistake to assume it's the best situation for everyone. Many staff writers and ex-staffers complain about company policies that they knew about ahead of time but thought that "if the money's good enough, I can deal with it." They later found they couldn't. Some problems could not have been anticipated and were the result of personality conflicts or policy or personnel changes. It's often difficult to fix the blame, but here are a few complaints:

- **"My publisher hasn't placed any of my songs. I got all the cuts myself."** Maybe they signed you because they realized you *could* get your own cuts. If so, maybe you should have split the publishing. Hopefully, you signed with the company because they offered other services beyond securing recordings of your songs. Publishers often can do their most valuable work after the song is recorded by securing additional covers and uses of the song and by making sure you get paid for all those uses.

- **"My publisher demands that the company gets 100 percent of the publishing when I collaborate with another writer, even when that writer has his/her own publishing company."** That's one you should know about going in. The bad thing about this policy is that it seriously restricts the number of outstanding writers you can cowrite with since the best so often have their own companies and naturally are reluctant to give up their publishing royalties to your company.

Most publishers are more liberal, though, and are willing to do a 50/50 split with the other writer's publisher. The belief is that another strong company involved in the song provides more contacts to get it recorded. You run into problems when you collaborate with a great writer who has his own company and your publisher doesn't think it's worth giving up half to someone who may not be actively pitching the song.

• **"The company seems to have lost interest in my songs, but they won't let me out of my contract."** Occasionally the person at the company who was responsible for signing you (and was the most enthusiastic about your material and your potential) leaves. Others at the company are pitching their favorite writers' songs because they feel more accountable to the writer they signed. Since you can't force someone to like either you or your material, it's sometimes a losing battle. It usually happens with writers who aren't getting many cuts yet (another good reason for you to be pitching the songs yourself). It's much more rare for this situation to develop with a writer who's a consistent money-maker for the company. Sometimes a company won't let you go because they've invested a lot in you and figure you'll hit with something eventually. What they risk is that you'll stop turning in songs to force them not to pick up your option. This tactic has been used before, but it's not a great idea. It's self-destructive to stop creating deliberately for that reason. If you continue to write songs without turning them in to your publisher, you may find yourself in serious legal difficulty later since they legally own everything you write during the time you're under contract to them. If you're having problems, it's time for a serious heart-to-heart talk.

• **"My company is great with my pop and rock songs but doesn't seem to know what to do with my country material"** (or vice versa). It's possible that you're not nearly as good at country writing as you think you are and that's the real reason they're not pitching those songs. It's also possible that your publisher doesn't know a good country song when he hears one. Or maybe he does and sends it to the company's Nashville office where *they* may think your publisher doesn't know what he's talking about.

In general, the major publishers have a pretty good ability to deal with a variety of styles, though, as always, it depends on the contacts and expertise of the *individuals* at the company.

• **"My publisher's criticism is destroying my self-confidence and killing my motivation."** Positive, constructive criticism, given sensitively, with encouragement by someone whose opinions you respect, can help you develop very quickly. There are publishers who can do that. You need to find them if you feel you need a nourishing situation to help you be a better writer. If you don't need that, it's not important. Among publishers, as among the public at large, there is a wide spectrum in individual talents for giving good criticism. Some publishers, though they're very definite about what they like or don't like, don't seem to have the vocabulary or the frame of reference to be specific about why or what you could do to improve your song. For them to say, "It just doesn't get me," won't help you to be a better writer.

Consistently, though certainly not exclusively, the best critiquers are those who've been writers, musicians, or producers; have had good criticism; and have experience in restructuring songs. An inability to critique doesn't make someone a less effective song-plugger, but it does make him an ineffective developer of writers.

A publisher can also overcriticize. Hit writer Alan O'Day ("Angie Baby," "Undercover Angel") had a great metaphor for this syndrome: "When you're a hammer, everything looks like a nail."

An inability to critique doesn't make someone a less effective songplugger, but it does make him an ineffective developer of writers.

- **"There are songs I believe in but my publisher doesn't. I can't stand to see them orphaned."** One of the problems with the basic staff deal is that they won't want to give you reversion clauses that give you back the song if they don't get it recorded. You can negotiate for all the songs to revert back to you that haven't been recorded by a certain number of years after your contract ends. The publisher will attempt to limit this to the catalogue you brought with you when you made the deal and only ones from that catalogue that haven't been commercially promoted. These deals and contract clauses may be very difficult to negotiate unless you're already a successful writer. Also, if you love the songs, you should always be out there pitching them yourself.

- **"I wrote fifteen songs last month and they only demoed one. I'm getting discouraged. Why should I keep writing when they don't even demo what I give them?"** It may be hard for you to accept that everything you write may not sound like a hit to them. There also may be budget problems. Someone in the company has to decide which songs are worth spending the money on, and there may be several other staffers turning out fifteen songs a month. Figure a bare *minimum* of $500 per song and they're into big bucks. One possible remedy for this problem is that, if a certain number of "acceptable" songs have to be turned in each month, you have a clause in your contract that any songs rejected from that "quota" become your property, free and clear of any interest of the publisher.

Advantages of Independence

Along with the relevant advantages and disadvantages of being a staff writer, you should consider the following:

1. As an independent songwriter, you're free to offer financial incentives to individuals who can help you place your songs (see "Negotiating," chapter eleven) that, if you were under contract, your publisher may not be likely to offer unless it's for a major film theme that looks like a good investment.

2. If you can publish the song yourself, you're looking at a lot more potential income.

3. You're never in competition with other writers on the publisher's staff (unless, of course, you're pitching songs to that publisher) as to whose songs get pitched to a particular producer.

4. You can pitch an individual song to any publisher you think can do the best job.

For more information, see chapter eleven.

WHAT PUBLISHERS REALLY WANT

My friend, Ralph Murphy, Nashville hit writer and ASCAP Assistant Vice President, (and Mark Ford) assembled an informal survey that polled fourteen Nashville music publishers. (This is an excerpt. Get the whole story at: www.ascap.com/nashville/murphy.html.)

Each publisher, within the past twelve months, had placed a hit song on the charts and had signed a new staff writer. The publishers ranked each of the following attributes from 1 to 10 (with 1 being *least* important and 10 being *most* important) based on the last writer they signed, not on any particular "wish list." [Note: Averages for each question appear in brackets.]

Attributes That Motivate a Publisher

10. Track record [4.9]

9. Persistence pursuing the deal [5.1]

8. Living in or near Nashville [5.3]

7. Record deal/artist potential [6.0]

Tied for 6th place:

6. Ability to cowrite [6.2]

6. Ability to perform songs live [6.2]

5. Affordability (amount of draw) [6.3]

("I was surprised that track record, affordability, and record deal did not score higher."—Ralph Murphy)

The Big Four

According to our survey, the following four were the top deal-maker qualities:

4. Ability to write alone [7.5]

3. Ability to write great melodies [8.7]

2. Personality/compatibility with the company [9.0]

1. Ability to write great lyrics [9.6]

How Staff Deals Happen

Dreamy-eyed writers who've written ten songs come to me and say they're shopping for a staff-writing deal. Far be it from me to discourage them. In fact, if all (or even some) of those songs sound like hits and the writer also has great artist potential, he/she is likely to have offers.

More often, songwriters and publishers build a relationship one song at a time. Don't let your dreams keep you from getting a day (or night) job so you can afford to let that process take place in its own time. It's important for you to work with a variety of publishers on a song-by-song basis to find those individuals whose opinions and business practices you respect and who are aggressive about pitching your songs. It's also important for a publisher to have the opportunity to size up your creative output, your willingness and ability to rewrite, your mutual personal chemistry, and, obviously, the reaction to your songs from producers. It also can't hurt your negotiating position to have more than one company wanting to sign you. This "sizing up" process is very important in any long-range partnership. Very few marriages succeed when you go to the altar after knowing each other a week. The mutual personal chemistry aspect was more important than I would have guessed among the reasons publishers sign staff writers, according to the survey on the previous page. Remember, though, that this was done in Nashville, where writers come to the publishers' offices to write on a regular basis. In close quarters, the staff likes to be glad to see you.

The mutual personal chemistry aspect was more important than I would have guessed among the reasons publishers sign staff writers.

chapter eleven

Self-Publishing

Why Publish Your Own Songs?

In the last chapter I discussed what a publisher does. Now let's discuss the advantages of having your own publishing company. It's important, because the publisher's share of royalties could represent a lot of money. The information in this chapter is primarily geared to those of you who want to be your own publisher and actively pitch your own songs and possibly those of other writers. However, there are a lot of situations for which you'd want to self-publish without getting into it that deeply. You may have the occasion to self-publish a few songs. You may, by a stroke of luck, get a song recorded and not be asked for the publishing by the producer or artist, or the recording of the song may be released only in the United States or with a minor artist for which the collection could be handled easily by an administrator. (See "Administration Deals," in this chapter.) In those cases, only a part of this information may apply to you.

Here are some other reasons why you might want to publish your own songs and some qualities that would help you do a good job for yourself.

• **You are a good commercial songwriter whose tunes are very coverable** (suitable to be recorded by other artists) and you already have a lot of contacts among producers and artists who are interested in your songs. In other words, you're in a position to fulfill one of a publisher's major functions: getting covers. You should be aware, though, that it takes a lot of time, and follow-up is very important.

• **You have the ability to "sell" yourself.** Some people represent others better than themselves. You should be an aggressive self-starter. You should have the ability to be both creator and businessperson. (Yes, it can be done, and yes, it's a myth that creative artists always make poor businesspeople.)

You have a great casting sense that lets you present the right song to the right artist at the right time. Publishers' reputations are built on their credibility.

• **You have your own production company or record company** and you're releasing your own product.

• **You are a recording artist who is recording your own songs** and therefore already doing part of a publisher's job.

- **You already have written commercially successful songs** and it is easy for you to get in those doors.
- **You are writing with someone who does well as his own publisher** and you can negotiate a portion of the rights for your own company. If your cowriter is a staff writer with a major company, this is a great situation for you. However, you may find it very difficult to defend not giving your publishing share to your cowriter's company unless you also have great contacts and are aggressive about pitching your songs. In other words, you would be an equal partner in the promotion of the song.
- **You are a writer/artist whose style is so unique that your songs are unlikely to be recorded by other artists.** You don't need a publisher to get your songs recorded. Be sure not to sell yourself short on the potential for other artists to record your songs, though.
- **You're independently wealthy or have financial backing.** You write coverable tunes and you can afford the alternative of hiring someone with experience and contacts to promote your songs.

If you're capable of hustling for yourself, you'll have the satisfaction of knowing that someone with your best interest at heart is on the job. You will not be constantly wondering whether the publisher is "sitting on your song" or why he is avoiding your calls. If someone is not on the case, you have only yourself to blame. Can you handle that?

Start Your Own Publishing Company

Assuming that, for whatever reason, you feel your best plan of action is to start your own company, here's how to proceed:

1. Choose a name for your company. Remember that you cannot have a company with the same name (or very close) as another publishing company. People don't want to confuse your company name with someone else's and send *them* your royalties. (Yes, it does happen, and no, they are not perfect.)

2. You must clear the name you've chosen for your publishing company with BMI, ASCAP, or SESAC. You are eligible to have BMI, ASCAP, or SESAC process your application as a publisher if: (a) a record is being released containing a performance of the song; (b) a motion picture is being released that includes the song; (c) a television program will be or has been broadcast using the song; or (d) a radio program has been broadcast that played the song.

3. Unless you intend to publish the songs of other writers who may belong to other performing rights organizations, you need only set up a company with the one you are affiliated with as a writer. The reason why you see hyphenated publishing company names (Warner/Chappell, Sony/Tree, etc.) is that one is a BMI-affiliated company and one is an ASCAP-affiliated company. If you do want to have a company in each organization (ASCAP, BMI, SESAC), clear the company names with each. Give them three alternate company names in order of preference. If your first choice is already being used by someone else, they

will select the next choice that is not already taken, so be creative and pick something unusual.

If you're a writer representing your own songs, it is a good idea not to use a version of your own name (unless you're already famous) because, if you're pitching to producers and record companies, it signals to them that this is a "hip-pocket" company and not a "real" company and they'll automatically assume the publishing is up for grabs. Not that this tactic gives you a great edge, but sometimes it's a factor in your favor if they think they'll have to fight for it.

There is a $50 annual fee for being a publisher-member of ASCAP. There is a one-time $100 publisher administration fee to be a BMI publisher and no annual fee. There is no fee for SESAC publishers.

4. Once the name(s) has been cleared, obtain the forms from your local county clerk's office to register a Fictitious Business Name Statement, also known as a d/b/a (Doing Business As _____). Then open a bank account under your new business name. Your county clerk will refer you to a local publication that will publish a "fictitious business name" statement that gives the required notice that you are now officially doing business as "Crass Commercial Music" or whatever you've chosen. The notice must be published once per week for four weeks in a paper of "general circulation" in the county where the business is located. You can use the same d/b/a to list more than one company if you want to add another publishing company, production company, etc. The process and cost of publication varies from city to city and county to county but is generally under $50.

A name using the legal name of the individual owner, as long as the business name does not imply other owners, does not require a d/b/a, regardless of the insistence of some misinformed bank employees. "John Braheny Music" would not require any fictitious name registration. "Braheny & Associates Music" or "Braheny & Company Publishing" probably would.

5. Copyright all the songs you wish to have in your company on a PA form assigned to your publishing company. (See "Copyright Registration," chapter eight.) If you already have obtained copyright registrations on your *unpublished* songs, register them again as *published* works. Why would you want to do that? Because if you (or your heirs) ever wanted to sell your catalog, it would have to be proven that your *company* actually owned your songs.

6. For songs being released on records or for songs that will be or have been performed in a motion picture, television program, or radio program (regardless of whether the song is included on any recording), fill out both the writer's and publisher's clearance forms from the performing rights organization involved (BMI, ASCAP, or SESAC). These forms notify the organization that a specific song is being released in a specific medium so that, when it's performed on the radio, TV, or elsewhere, the organization will know who to pay, what percentage to pay the writer and the publisher, and where to send the checks. Directions are included on the forms and in publisher's manuals provided by the organizations. All are also available online (See Web sites in Appendix.) Keep a photocopy or printout of everything related to a particular song in its own file.

If you (or your heirs) ever wanted to sell your catalog, it would have to be proven that your *company* actually owned your songs.

7. Matters such as the legal entity under which you should operate your publishing company (e.g., as a corporation, partnership, or sole proprietorship), whether you need to obtain any kind of business license, and whether you need to obtain a federal (or state) employer identification number and report wages and withhold taxes for employees can be complicated issues and are beyond the scope of this book. Consult an attorney or accountant for such matters. Regulations vary from state to state.

8. Organize yourself to keep track of your "song shopping."

Business Expenses and the IRS

You'll incur many expenses in the process of setting up and maintaining your business, both as a songwriter and publisher. Keep records of all your expenses (receipts with date, vendor's name, amount of purchase, plus sales tax, if applicable) and income records. Use your business checks and arrange for a separate business credit card, if possible, for those expenses. The IRS will allow you to deduct these expenses for three years without seeing any business-related income. After that, they figure it's just a hobby and won't allow the deductions.

Here is a combined list of both publishing business and songwriting expenses you can deduct.

- **Services of a graphic artist** and printing for company logo, j-card inserts, labels, business cards. Costs vary. You'll save a lot in the long run by buying computer programs and a good color printer.
- **Bank account** and check printing, service charges for business account—$100+.
- **Subscriptions** to trade magazines, books and tip sheets, online services, between $300–$1000+ per year.
- **Music business and songwriter organization dues.** (Some people belong to several.) Costs vary.
- **Postage** for letters and demos mailed. FedEx, UPS, message services. E-mail and a Web site can save you this.
- **Photocopies** of lyric sheets, cover letters, lead sheets, forms, business correspondence, and anything else you'll need to copy. A printer and well-organized database will save you this in the long run.
- **Stationery**—letterhead, envelopes, mailing labels, mailing envelopes, card files, business cards. Good software available for most of this.
- **Copyright registration**—$30 each and may go up again.
- **Demo recording costs**—about $200 per song minimum depending on where you are and how elaborate you need it to be.
- **Blank media**—Buy in bulk to save money.
- **Tape and CD duplication**—Costs vary. Save money and invest in a CD burner.
- **Audiovisual equipment**—cassette/CD/DVD/VCR decks, home and auto systems—insurance, maintenance, and repair of all of these.

- **Purchase (and rentals) of CDs and videos** to research artists you want to pitch your songs to.

- **Nightclubs and entertainment events,** concerts, movies, theater—You'll need to document this for the IRS.

- **Business meals**—also need to document for the IRS.

- **Business gifts**—up to $25 per person. Also gift flowers, greeting cards, holiday and thank-you cards.

- **Promotion and advertising**—newspaper and magazine ads, fliers.

- **Computer costs**—If you write, keep records and accounting ledgers, and research with your computer, or Personal Digital Assistants (Palm Pilot, etc.), you can write them off as well as related equipment including computer stand, printer, etc. (Check with your tax service.)

- **Software**—for composing, recording, and mixing your music—for organizing your networking, accounting, correspondence, and other business.

- **Travel expenses**—for that trip to L.A., Nashville, or New York to meet with publishers, producers, or record companies. Includes airfare, luggage and travel gear, lodging, tips, car rental and gas, laundry, taxi, buses, subways, upgrades to business class. Keep good records of gas, mileage, food, lodging.

- **Auto expenses**—gas, oil, repairs, tires, insurance, DMV, AAA, wash/wax, tolls, parking, lease payments can be deducted based on the percentage of work-related travel. Keep mileage and repair records.

- **Home office expenses**—based on the percent of square footage of your office space relative to the square footage of your home. Includes rent, interest payments, property taxes, insurance, and utilities. Some cities have special regulations and taxes regarding home offices. Check it out.

- **Phones**—home, cell, pager, DSL, or cable modem. If you're aggressive, these can run $600+ per month. Check out the lower-cost long-distance services. Installing a second phone for business helps tremendously to document those expenses for the IRS.

- **Answering service or machine**—to make sure you don't miss any calls.

- **Attorney fees**—to put together contracts that reflect your business philosophy and protect your interests, you'll need publisher/writer single-song and copublishing contracts.

- **Accounting fees**—Find an accountant experienced in the music business to make sure you get all the deductions you're entitled to.

- **Business filing fees**—Check with your city or county clerk.

- **Seminars, classes, workshops, songwriter-related showcases,** and other educational activities (including those on how to run your business better).

- **Web site maintenance**—building, maintaining, and promoting your site.

- **Musical instruments,** amps, P.A. system, insurance, maintenance, and repairs.

NOTE: The amount you can deduct for computers, office equipment, sound systems, instruments, etc., can be deducted on a diminishing depreciation scale over several years.

Casting

"Alanis (or Celine, Ricky, etc.) could sing this song really great!" This statement, and the ignorance behind it, has been the cause of countless unnecessary rejections of songs. Though it's certainly not the only cause, it ranks right up there with poorly crafted songs. But for the sake of this discussion, let's say both the demo and song are excellent. Are they *appropriate*? It's not a question of whether they *could* do it. They could make the phone book sound good. But, from the artist's point of view, it's about whether they *need* to record your song.

The history of pop music is filled with songs written by self-contained artists who had no idea their songs could be hits by other artists.

If you're writing for yourself in a band or solo artist context and don't think this information applies to you, don't stop reading just yet. The history of pop music is filled with songs written by self-contained artists who had no idea their songs could be hits by other artists. Someone had the skills to recognize that those songs were right for those other artists. Wouldn't it be better to develop these skills yourself rather than reward skillful publishers/managers with a substantial percentage of your income for it?

The skill is called "casting," knowing which song is appropriate for which artist. First, there's a process of elimination. Forget about artists who write their own songs. Not that they wouldn't ever record a song they didn't write; but generally speaking, they're not motivated financially to record "outside" songs (written by someone other than themselves or their producer). With substantial royalties for sales and airplay on a hit, they'd rather fill their CDs with their own songs, for better or worse.

Who *Not* to Pitch To—Playing the Odds

If you're playing the odds, you'll leave self-contained artists until last. First, you'll read the *Billboard* magazine charts to find those artists who record "outside" songs. How can you tell? You look at the "Hot 100" chart and your favorite genre singles chart: "Hot R&B/hip-hop," "Hot Country," or "Hot Latin Tracks." (The other charts don't list writers.) You look to the left under the name of the song, and the first name is the producer's, the second (in parentheses) is the name(s) of the songwriter(s). If the same name is in both places, the producer is the writer. Then if you see, in the column to the right, that the artist's name is the same as the writer, you know the odds are bad. You may have a hard time telling who wrote the songs when the artist is a group. Though if there are four or more writers listed, you can often assume the group did or they're using samples of other songs.) Go online to their record companies and look up the artists' bios. If they wrote the songs, they'll want everybody to know it.

You'll end up with a list of about 25 percent of the hits (on the "Hot 100") on which the artist sings an "outside" song. About two-thirds of those will be country. On the Hot Country chart about 60 to 70 percent are "outside" songs. Check the charts periodically. Tape "countdown" radio or cable TV shows (MTV, BMT, CMT) of current hits so you can listen more than once and analyze them without having to stay tuned all day. Keep your *Billboard* handy for reference.

Doing the Research

A critical step in casting is to get all the information possible about the artist to save yourself the embarrassment of pitching something totally wrong. Your best move is to buy the CDs of any artist in your style who records outside songs. Listen to each cut on the album with special emphasis on the successful singles and determine the following:

1. **Style.** If it's rock, is it influenced by pop, blues, funk, punk, metal, or world music? If country, is it on the rock side, traditional, pop, Texas swing? You may find different influences in different songs on any given CD, but they'll give you some boundaries outside of which it may be futile to venture.

2. **Are there any songs the artist *did* write?** Pay particular attention to the style of these. Also try to determine the common factors of the "outside" songs. Chances are, the artist or producer had some input into those choices.

3. **Lyric message.** The shaping of an artist's image is based largely on their personal philosophies and attitudes about life and love, how they handle disappointments, etc. Those attitudes show up in their song lyrics regardless of who writes them. Read or listen to the lyric of each song and answer the following:

    a. Is the lyric positive or negative, up or down, do the down songs show some hope in the end? Are the songs in first, second, or third person? Are they about winners or losers?

    b. Does the lyric have a payoff, a final "moral"? Is it based on a high concept (Steve Wariner's "Holes in the Floor of Heaven") or just a straight-ahead love song?

    c. Is the artist young, naive, inexperienced, hopeful, or more mature, experienced, a little world-weary, sexy? I heard a song pitched for a former gospel artist looking for secular songs for a new project. The song was a sex-oriented song that would have worked great for Keith Sweat but definitely not for an artist who didn't want to lose his gospel following altogether. I heard a song that was pitched for an established country star, but it was about how he had to return to his little town in defeat because he had *not* attained his dream of stardom. Remember that a successful artist is singing your song, needs to believe the lyric, and it has to reflect the artist's self-image. Songs that say "I'm a terrible human being" don't work unless you're apologizing to someone you've done wrong.

4. **Lyrics as vocal platforms.** In addition to vocal range, you need to consider whether your lyric allows the artist room to sing. When I see a lyric sheet literally covered with lyric and hear the words sung so tightly that there's no space for the singer to "style" the song in his/her unique way, I know it's going in the reject pile. Great singers love to hold notes (particularly vowels at the ends of lines) and play with them, embellishing the melody. It may be a wonderful story and brilliant lyric but may be so much a product of your own unique style that it won't work in their style. A group like Third Eye Blind, for instance, writes unique songs that other artists would have difficulty covering without sounding like them.

5. **Who is the artist's audience?** Pre- to early teens (Backstreet Boys, Britney Spears, Brandy)? Listeners in their mid to late teens generally become more genre specific (rock, pop, alternative, rap, hip-hop, country) and tend to fragment along those styles. Gear your song and demo to that style or recognize whether or not you write in that style or for that audience.

6. **Vocal range:** Listen to the song with the highest and lowest notes and you've got the range. Does the artist have a wide vocal range like Celine Dion? Odds are she'll choose a song that will show it off. If the artist has a limited range, a two-octave stretch won't work. Also, look for a place in the artist's range that they favor because there may be a unique quality or timbre there. It's been referred to as a "sweet spot." Make sure the song allows them to use that spot.

7. **Structure:** Do the artist's successful songs use a repeated chorus, pre-chorus sections, classic AABA (verse-verse-bridge-verse *a la* "Yesterday")? AABA structures are rarely recorded except by self-contained artists. The reason is that it's easier for a listener to learn a song with a repeating chorus, so verse/chorus songs are seen as being more commercial and usually will be preferred.

Along with analyzing the song, collect articles about and interviews with the artist from fanzines, trade magazines, and the artist's personal and fan Web sites. You can find some great clues to the artist's image and values. Don't send a recovering alcoholic or drug addict your great song about the bottle being your best friend; but the song about getting your life together might work. It may help to know that the artist is a father/mother, donates money to organizations that help kids, just got divorced, is a womanizer, feels women deserve more respect, feels women should stay at home, is a born-again Christian, etc.

Another level of casting expertise involves projecting, based on past success and artist image, where you feel the artist *could* go. This is a common strategy of writer/producer/arrangers and publishers who can conjure a vision of the artist's next step and, in the process, become the artist's producer, at least on the producer's own songs. This requires a thorough knowledge of the artist and, in the best case, the ability to produce tracks that would provide the artist with a fresh sound. There is a point in a very successful career where an artist looks away from the too familiar and into adventureland. You can either anticipate that move or help to create it.

Regardless of all the homework you do on an artist, you can still strike out, though the odds will be considerably better if you've done the research. A major benefit is that you now have a great frame of reference when you talk to the manager, record company A&R rep for the artist, or the new producer who may be taking the artist in a different direction. In my experience, those people speak to and listen to demos from so many writers who are clueless about their artists, that they welcome a conversation with someone who knows what makes their artist special. It also gives you a level of confidence in that call or meeting that communicates that you should be taken seriously.

There is a point in a very successful career where an artist looks away from the too familiar and into adventureland.

Successful Pitching Strategies

1. **Establish priorities.** Research the trade charts and tip sheets and compile a list of currently successful artists who record the style(s) of songs you write and who record songs by other writers. Choose a particular song and determine which of those artists would be appropriate to send the song to. Make those artists your "A" list. Make other lists of artists in order of priority. These might include:

B—new artists with record deals.

C—new artists and former hit artists who have production deals with established producers but no record contracts.

D—recording artists with past hits but no recent success, no producer or record deal.

E—new artists with new producers and no record deal.

F—new artists with no producer and no record deal.

Even though this is a logical priority list in terms of playing the odds and spending your time, energy, and money accordingly, the music business isn't known for succeeding on logic. In this case, the situation with any artist on any of those lists could totally change on any given day. "A's" become "D's," "D's" become "A's," and "F's" become "A's" overnight.

Don't underestimate the value of pitching to new artists. We didn't get a great turnout at the L.A. Songwriters Showcase when Arista Records' reps were looking for songs for a new, unknown artist named Whitney Houston. "Whitney who? Never heard of her. I'm saving my best stuff for superstars." There's a lot to be said for the personal and political rewards of being there when they need you, when nobody else will take the chance. It's also easier to get to new artists, and you're more likely to be heard when they're desperate for hit songs because the major publishers may not be giving them their best material.

2. **Surround the act with demos.** By that, I mean get the song to their manager, attorney, producer, recording engineer, A&R person at the record company, musicians, roadies, hairdresser, chauffeur, secretary, gardener, relatives, lovers, anyone who is a potential contact. But don't do this unless you've done your homework very well and feel confident that this is an outstanding and appropriate song. It will annoy them to no end to keep getting the wrong song.

3. **Check the club and concert listings** in your local paper and try to find out where the acts are playing. Go to the club early when the act does a sound check and try to connect with the artist, road manager, or musicians. You should be aware that for their legal protection, many writer/artists are cautioned by their attorneys not to personally accept any unsolicited demos. With artists who don't write, it's not as much of a problem.

4. **Introduce yourself to some recording engineers at the hot studios in town.** Several of the major trade magazines have sections on who's recording, where, and the names of the engineer(s) (*Billboard*'s "Pro Audio" section and *Music Connection*'s "Studio Mix"

Introduce yourself to some recording engineers at the hot studios in town.

section, for example). Let them hear your songs and offer them financial incentives if they can place songs with acts that record there. You may, in fact, make an offer to any of the above-mentioned contacts. Ten percent of the mechanical royalties on a recording they secure for you is a good place to start, but higher percentages are not necessarily out of line. Use your best judgment and offer whatever feels right. (See "Negotiating," in this chapter, for more information on this.)

5. **Be aware of the successful bands in your area.** Maybe there's a great "cover" band in which none of the members write. They may want a record deal but have no original material. You might be able to cowrite with someone in the band. Pay particular attention to the lead singer and keyboard player. It's always a good idea to look for bands that are good enough to have a shot at a record deal. (Look for the qualities described in "Getting a Record Deal," chapter fifteen.) If they hit with your songs, it may result in a long and lucrative relationship.

6. **Get involved in every musical project you possibly can,** including student films and video projects, background music for a play, commercial jingles, church choir, anything! In every project, you may meet someone who likes your work and likes working with you and who will refer you for another project. It's called "networking," and it's one of the best ways to develop a reputation and contacts. When you find good musicians, singers, or writers, refer them to projects. What you give comes back! (Though you can count on the fact that it doesn't always come back from those you'll give it to.)

7. **Think of some creative ways to stand out from the crowd.** There are legendary stories about writers and publishers pulling outrageous stunts like dropping tapes from helicopters or by parachutes or delivering them via strippers or in cakes. A friend of mine sent demos to A&R departments in sealed soup cans with the songs listed as ingredients. Very clever, but he neglected to send along can openers. Some probably still sit unopened in A&R offices as a lasting testament to his ingenuity.

Those are the stories that get passed around in the industry and usually end with, "Yeah, fantastic! If only the *song* had been good!"

The point is that if you can think of an imaginative way to present your material, you'll definitely make a lasting impression; but it's useless to you unless the people who receive your package are also excited about the music.

8. **Make your packaging as professional as your song.** Let's assume your music is worth pitching. You need to know what you can do to make an eye-catching professional-looking package. I know a writer whose trademark is hot pink—the color she uses for lyric sheets, cover letter, tape label, and j-card insert. Publishers or producers can pick it out of a stack or basket of tapes immediately. Using good graphics with a logo and an artistic layout with possibly a picture on the tape/CD insert (particularly for performers) can strengthen your presentation. There are great graphics programs available like Adobe Photoshop, Pagemaker, Illustrator, and InDesign that will give you spectacular results. (See "Presenting Your Demo," chapter twelve.)

Regarding logos, a common question comes up: *If I have my own publishing company, should I send materials out under company letterhead?* If you're sending songs to publishers, no, unless you're suggesting a copublishing agreement in your letter. If they're going to record companies, yes. In sending songs to producers, you have this to consider. It might help to get your song through the door, or it may make the producer skittish. A producer usually has his own publishing company and will prefer to record a song he at least partially owns. He may opt to pass on your song if he thinks the publishing rights are not available. However, it all depends on how good the songs are. If he wants to record them and also wants a piece of the publishing, he'll definitely try to negotiate. So, use your company logo and take your chances.

9. **Be prepared.** Never leave the house without demos and lyric sheets. If possible, carry a portable player and headset. You never know who you're going to meet.

Negotiating

A writer I know happened to get to the manager of a major R&B/pop crossover group. The manager loved her song and felt it was so good that the group wanted to record it despite the fact that they usually wrote their own songs. He asked her if the group could have the publishing if they recorded it. She said, "No." He said, "Good-bye." She told me later she was totally unprepared to deal with the situation and had no idea what to say. She was excited that he liked it, but when he wanted the publishing, she thought he was trying to rip her off.

There are three schools of thought on this situation.

1. The first is, "Right, don't let them have the publishing. You did right! You did the job of a publisher by getting it to the group in the first place. Does anyone seriously believe that the manager is going to do anything with that song beyond this group's recording of it?"

2. The second is, "My God, do you know that there are writers who'd sell their kids for just an album cut on that group? The writer's royalties alone are worth thousands, especially if it's a single. So what if you do give them the publishing, if you can get a guaranteed release? If you give it to a 'real' publisher, it might never get cut because they're not going to give up *their* piece of the action to that group. Either way, you wouldn't have been able to keep any of the publishing anyway! It's just one song and it'll help build your career."

3. The third point of view is, "Why didn't you negotiate?" She answered, "I don't know. I didn't even think of it. What's to negotiate? Either you give them the publishing or you don't, right?" Wrong!

Let's look at each of these attitudes. The first is certainly defensible and, in fact, it is important to analyze whether this manager (or producer or artist) has an active publishing company with employees who will spend time trying to get other recordings of your song, even after the group has recorded it. If he does, it might be a good situation. If not, you'll know that any subsequent covers of the song will be entirely up to you and though you'll get your writer's royalty, you won't share any of the publisher's royalties for doing the publisher's work. If they insist on owning the publishing, you could point out that you'll want to be actively pitching this song to other artists after this recording and try to get them to split the publishing with your own company. If that doesn't work, see if they'll give you a portion of the mechanical or performance royalties on any new recordings of the song that *you* are responsible for placing.

Even active publishers (as opposed to holding companies) have different philosophies about splitting the publishing with an artist or producer in order to get a recording. They range from "Under no circumstances will I give up anything. I'm doing the work and I deserve the royalties," to "I'll give up what I have to get the tune recorded." It depends a lot on the individual circumstances. How important is this recording? Is this the only artist who could cut the tune? Would this cut be very important in the development of the writer's career in generating interest in the rest of his/her catalogue? If I give this producer a piece of the action, am I setting a precedent with him that I'll regret later? And always, how badly do they want this song? If you're going to be your own publisher, these are some of the questions that you'll have to consider.

The second attitude is also defensible. This may be a major act and your first recording. One hundred percent of zero is zero. If the manager or producer is adamant about having the publishing and you know it will make you a lot of money for the writer's share of the royalties, it might be best to let them have it. Is this the last or only good song you'll ever write? If they want it that badly, chances are the song is good enough that you should have more confidence in your own ability. Maybe you won't need to make a deal like that with your next song because you'll be in a better bargaining position if this one turns out to be a winner. There is a danger in being too attached to a song, too protective. It's the classic situation of the bird in hand. If you do decide to give them the publishing, however, and the company is basically a holding company and not an active publisher, *make sure that you have it in writing* that the publishing doesn't get assigned to them officially until the record is actually released. That way, if they decide not to record the song after all, it doesn't end up in limbo because they own it but won't do anything with it.

But don't give it up so fast. There are other negotiating positions you can take.

Two major sources of income (mechanical and performance royalties) are negotiable without transferring your ownership of any of the copyright. Generally, when someone says they want "the publishing," they want ownership of the copyright. In the "standard" writer/publisher agreement, you assign the copyright to the publisher in a contract that gives you half the total income as writer, the other half going to the publisher. But the publisher owns the song and can sell it to anyone else if he wants to (unless the agreement includes a nonassignment clause). A good businessperson will always want to own the copyright. A copyright's value will increase with the song's degree and length of popularity. So you can't blame them for trying to get as much as they can. They're not trying to rip you off. They're just looking out for their own interests. You need to do the same.

A copyright's value will increase with the song's degree and length of popularity.

"Mechanicals" are the income from the sale of records, tapes, and CDs. (See "Mechanical Royalties," chapter nine.) As the writer, you'll take half off the top right away and from the remainder (referred to as the "publisher's share of mechanicals") you can offer percentages as an incentive for someone to record the song. The advantages of offering a percent of the "publisher's share of "mechanicals" on *that particular recording* is that you still own the copyright and you give them incentive only for their limited use of the song. This is referred to as a "cut in" or a "participation agreement." If someone else later records the song, you still own the copyright so you can make a better deal. You can get all the publisher's and writer's royalties for future recordings.

Performance royalties is another negotiable item. This term applies to all the money received through BMI, ASCAP, or SESAC for the performances of your songs on radio, TV, jukeboxes, and in clubs. Those organizations, called performing rights organizations, pay directly to the publisher and to the writer. This is a different situation from "mechanical" royalties that are paid directly to the publisher. If you have a hit song, particularly one that gets played on the radio long after it's been a hit, your "performance" royalties can amount to considerably more money than your "mechanicals."

For the purpose of negotiation, another important difference exists between "mechanical" and "performance" income. When you receive your quarterly earnings statement from BMI or ASCAP, they don't note which recording of your song you're receiving royalties from (SESAC does, however). You can't say, "I'll give you X percent of the publisher's share of the performance income on this particular record," since, in some cases, two different versions of the same song (e.g., a country and a pop version) have been on the charts at the same time. You could say, "I can give you X percent participation in the publisher's share of performance income:

a. for the first _____ quarters in which royalties are received;

or

b. until the quarter before the next recording of this song is released."

Another approach is to negotiate a percentage of the mechanical or performance royalties until a *specified maximum dollar figure is reached.* In other words, "I'll give you X percent of the money up to (until you've received) X dollars." Here are some other points to keep in mind when negotiating with anyone regarding mechanicals and performance income:

1. The percentage or dollar amount you offer is totally negotiable. There are no set rules. You may offer any percentage of the income from the song that you want to offer and still maintain ownership of the copyright.

2. On an album cut, your performance royalties won't amount to much unless it's a piece that radio DJs take particular interest in. With the exception of the small percentage of stations that specialize in playing albums, radio will play singles. There are times, though, when an album cut unexpectedly gets enough radio excitement going that it forces the company to release it as a single.

3. On a hot act with good album sales, mechanical royalties on album cuts are worth a great deal. Singles are still worth more because your song will appear on both the single and album and because the single will earn performance royalties if it gets airplay. Remember, too, that each different mix of the same song on a CD-single makes the same royalties as the other so you may have two different radio mixes and two club mixes—four times the mechanical rate, plus the album cut, plus eventually a "greatest hits" CD and other compilations.

4. On pop records (including R&B/pop) by established artists, you'll get the highest mechanical *and* performance royalties. On country records, mechanicals are low because sales here are usually low except for country/pop crossover superstars like Faith Hill and Trisha Yearwood and a few other top sellers. But performance (airplay) royalties on a country *single* can be very high because of the great number of country radio stations. These are generalities to give you a rough estimate of the relative popularity of styles, but the bottom line is determined by the popularity of the individual artist.

5. It may be wise to offer one percentage of royalty participation for an album cut and an additional percentage if it becomes a single. This approach may work for a situation in which the artist or producer to whom you're offering the incentive can influence the choice of the record as a single. Their increased financial participation, if your song is chosen as a single, could be a factor in that decision.

6. Make sure the "cut in" or "participation" goes into effect only upon *release* of a specified record by a specified artist on a specified label. If you choose to deal with producers and artists directly and they want some financial incentive, just keep in mind that "there's more than one way to skin a cat" or "everything is negotiable."

A word of caution in making these deals: If the person to whom you're offering this incentive is employed by a record company and makes this agreement without the permission of the company, your deal may constitute commercial bribery. Check it out!

"Holds"

If a producer (or record company or artist) feels your song is right for his recording project, he'll ask for a "hold" on it. It means he'll want to have the first opportunity to record the song. He doesn't want you to pitch it to anyone else in the meantime because he doesn't want to spend the money to produce the song, only to have his release beaten out by another artist. Producers commonly have exclusive holds on more songs than they need to put on an album because it frequently happens, as I've mentioned before, that even if they get around to recording a song, it may turn out to be less exciting than they thought it would.

Aside from that, there are several other reasons why your song may not end up on an album. A writer/artist may have written new songs since yours went on hold and the artist will decide to record those instead of yours. Maybe it was decided that other writers' songs chosen since yours were stronger or better suited to the project. It also happens that a musical direction or concept for the project may emerge from the material that's gathered and it inevitably becomes clear that certain songs just don't fit with the others, no matter how good they may be. There aren't enough ballads, or (more often) too many. The artist, producer, or A&R person at the record company may change his/her mind about the song at the last minute.

Since any of those things can and do happen and because selecting the right songs is crucial to an album's success, you can see why a producer wants to hold on to as many songs as possible until the project is finished.

On the other side we have the writer and publisher, who may want very much for the producer and artist to record the song. In granting a hold to the producer, there is a risk for them that the producer does not share. It can't hurt the producer if he decides not to record the song, but the publisher may be forced to turn down some other equally good, if not better, offers in honoring the hold. In being your own publisher, this is a situation you'll have to deal with and with great diplomacy.

There are several different attitudes among publishers regarding holds:

1. "If I think the project is worth it, I'll always let them hold it. In the process, I'm building my relationship with the producer."

2. "I never give holds. They all know that if they want the song, they'll have to hurry up and record it. I'll stay in touch with the producer and let him know about any other interest in the song as it comes up, and I'll let him know I want him to record it, but I'll keep pitching it."

3. "It depends on my relationship with that producer, how long he wants to keep it, and whether I know if he'll be honest with me about the status of the project—not lead me on by telling me it'll be just a little longer when he knows he'll need a lot more time."

4. "I'll tell them they can have a hold, but if another major project comes along, I'll give it to them, too. I know the odds are that when it gets down to it, only one of them will end up wanting to record the song anyway." Be careful with this one. You could burn some bridges if they discover you've given them both holds, particularly if one of them has spent some of his budget to record it.

If more than one producer wants to hold your song, ask yourself some questions: Is one of the acts likely to sell more records and get more airplay than the other? Is the song to be released as a single or an album cut? Do the producers plan for a major artist or a newcomer to record your song? Is it being considered for a country artist (good for performance royalties but not so good for mechanical royalties, as country music fans aren't avid record buyers) or for a crossover artist (good for performance and mechanical royalties)?

How long do they each need to hold it? If one will be able to tell you in two weeks whether he's cutting it and the other needs six months before his act is ready, off the road, or on the wagon before he can get into the studio, tell him you'll let him know in two weeks! Stall for time.

Through the years, publishers and artists have tried to organize a united front to get record companies and producers to pay "option fees" like screenwriters do for keeping a script out of circulation. It's never worked because, though screenwriters have a union, writers and publishers don't, so there's no way to enforce it. The only bright light is that recently a major country artist started offering many thousands of dollars to hold a song. She has a major commitment to finding great songs and will put her money where her mouth is. Now if we can only get *that* bit of wisdom to spread.

Foreign Subpublishing

The international market for American songs has grown tremendously in the past several years.

Foreign subpublishing has become an important aspect of the publisher's business. It's estimated that 60 percent of the world music market is outside the United States. The international market for American songs has grown tremendously in the past several years. A publisher with any chart success at all and a strong catalogue of songs to back it up won't miss the opportunity to capitalize on it in other countries. Most publishers, including the small independents, have affiliations with foreign publishers in countries where their songs are viable. In simplest terms, it works like this: American publisher "A" contacts foreign publisher "F." "A" has done research that shows him that "F" has had success with songs similar to those in "A" 's catalogue. He's also learned that "F" is very aggressive about getting cover records, promoting the songs of their U.S. affiliates, and collecting the money.

Publisher "A" contacts "F," often at MIDEM (the international music industry conference held in France each year), and gets together with "F" to play him the catalogue, listen to "F" 's catalogue, and get a sense of the activities of "F" 's company, their personalities, and business know-how. "A" needs to feel that "F" is genuinely excited about the songs and has good ideas about which artists in his country would be likely to record them. "F" is also interested in having "A" represent his songs in the United States, though this doesn't often happen.

Assuming that both publishers are in tune with each other, a contract for a number of years (usually three) is worked out, usually including an advance from "F" to "A." (This is unless "F" 's commission is low, e.g., 10 percent, in which case, no advance is paid.) The amount of the advance is based on several factors, including "A" 's track record, current hits, and the strength of the overall catalogue, particularly the number of songs that would be viable in "F" 's territory.

The musical tastes of listeners and record buyers can be very different from one country to the next.

The musical tastes of listeners and record buyers can be very different from one country to the next. Check out the international charts in *Billboard* and you'll see what I mean. Part of the jobs of both publishers may be to come up with a translation of the song for a new artist or a translated version by the original artist. Most major artists produce foreign language versions of their hits.

In cases with lyric translations, often the lyric translator is considered to be an author and "F" takes part of the copyright ownership of the new version, often with a new title to make the separation of royalties easier. The original writers should always try to get a clause in their contract that gives them approval of translations and agreement that no more than 50 percent of the writer's royalties will be lost to the translated version. The best situation is for the subpublisher to pay a flat fee to the translator, but it's tough to get that.

Royalty splits in such cases vary from 90/10 to 75/25 for "A" and "F," respectively, including both performance royalties from that country's version of BMI or ASCAP and mechanical royalties from local record companies collected by "F." That is the case for songs by the original American artist or cover records obtained by "A." If "F" obtains a new cover of the song by an artist in his territory, "A" and "F" usually divide the royalties received from that recording anywhere from 70/30 to 60/40. The higher "cover splits" are easier to obtain if the overall deal split is in the higher range. That, by the way, is the reason why you receive a lower royalty from foreign recordings on your writer/publisher contract. You're only getting 50 percent of *what the publisher receives in this country.*

It's possible to lose out on an enormous amount of money on an international hit if the foreign subpublishing deals are not in place or are not good ones. Foreign royalties may be generated that you won't even know about. It's one of the areas that gets neglected by writers who retain their own publishing rights and have a big hit. It's well worth the trouble for you, your attorney, or other representative, particularly if you have a hot catalogue, to go to MIDEM, do your research, and choose publishers from Japan, England, Australia, Italy, Scandinavia, Argentina, and other countries where you think your songs are viable. The advances you could receive from the deals you make could more than pay for the trip. Next best is to contract with another American publisher, or attorney, who has already set up foreign subpublishing contracts, to make that trip on your behalf and have them deal with all other countries, excluding the United States. Don't attempt to negotiate foreign subpublishing deals without the assistance of an attorney experienced in that area. There are many potential difficulties caused, for instance, by constantly shifting currency exchanges that need the advice of an expert.

To find foreign publishers on your own, check the international charts in *Billboard* to see which hits are stylistically compatible with yours and in which countries they're popular. You can get lists of publishers in those countries from *Billboard's International Buyer's Guide* and the annual *Songwriter's Market,* but there's no substitute for personal recommendations and meetings with prospective subpublishers.

A creative foreign publisher can be valuable by helping to set up tours and TV exposure for the U.S. writer/artist or group whose songs he represents. The more popular he makes the act and songs in his territory, the more money he makes. He can also arrange interviews on radio, TV, or in newspapers, provide interpreters if necessary, concoct promotions that would work in his own country, but maybe not the United States, find the best lyric translators and adapters, or maybe even facilitate cowriting situations with his own writers.

Obviously, the agreement works both ways. U.S. publisher "A" will also become familiar with the songs in "F" 's catalogue and advise him as to what type of songs "A" could get recorded over here, maybe assisting "F" in finding an American record deal or producer for one of "F" 's hot local writer/artists. The agreement also gives "F" the opportunity to sign songs in his country that may not be viable there but that could get recorded in the United States. It's always important to remember that the whole world loves a great song.

A good way to learn more about performance and mechanical royalties in other countries (where they're usually collected by the same organizations) is to go to the English language Web sites of their Performing Rights Organizations via the National Music Publishers Association list (www.nmpa.org/links.html#Rights).

Administration Deals

If you want to publish your own songs, don't need advances on royalties or any other benefits of a copublishing contract, but want to find someone else to take care of the business end, your best course of action is an administration deal. An administrator doesn't (in most cases) own the copyright or any percentage of it. He is paid a fee of 10 percent to 25 percent of the gross income from all sources in a contract usually of three to five years. In order to make it worthwhile for an administrator to work with your catalogue, you'll need, of course, to have recordings that are generating income.

Here's the way the cash flow goes:

- First, the administrator pays the writer(s) 50 percent of the gross;
- Then deducts the administration fees and expenses;
- Then sends the rest to the publisher(s).

Some major "full service" publishing companies with their own in-house administration departments will administer your catalogue for a fee. There are also independent administrators, attorneys, or accountants who will charge you for their services on an hourly basis.

WHAT ADMINISTRATORS DO

These tasks vary depending on your needs:

1. The paperwork of issuing mechanical (recording) licenses and negotiating synchronization (film/TV/commercials) licenses, registering copyrights domestically and internationally, royalty accounting, and paying writers and copublishers. There is also some wisdom in the "Third Party Rule," which is that it's usually better to have a third party negotiate on your behalf, particularly if you're not totally confident of your understanding of the issues or your bargaining position or you're dealing with a personal friend.

2. Digging up royalties that you may never have received from previous recordings of your songs worldwide.

3. Subpublishing, setting up publishing or administration affiliates in foreign countries to pitch your songs locally and assist in royalty collections there.

4. Collecting money from record companies. Most hire the services of a mechanical

licensing organization such as the Harry Fox Agency and some do the collections themselves. (See "Mechanical Royalties," chapter nine.)

5. Pitch your songs to producers and artists. Some administrators won't do this at all and are basically accounting firms. Others consider that the more action they generate on your catalog, the more income their percentage earns. Since they don't own any of the publishing rights, they can't look down the road and say, "Someday this tune will get recorded and make me money for a long time." They're working for you on a short-term contract and need to make your songs pay off now. Some administration companies will pitch songs actively for an extra overall percentage of the entire catalogue, for a percent of the publishing royalties on any recording they secure, or for partial copyright *ownership* if they get a cover recording that earns more than a predetermined amount.

Caution!! Administration is a very complex business and requires great expertise and experience, particularly in collecting foreign royalties. While it's possible to have your attorney do the paperwork for you, unless administration is a *primary* area of his expertise, I'd advise you to look for a specialist such as Bug Music (www.bugmusic.com) or Copyright.net. (www.copyright.net). Also consider the Songwriters Guild of America (SGA) Catalog Administration service, which charges 3 percent for collection of performance income and 9 percent for all other income. Contact them at www.songwriters .org/services2.htm#CATALOG.

Administration is a very complex business and requires great expertise and experience.

Independent Songpluggers

For writers who don't want to tie up their publishing and can afford to hire someone, hiring an independent songplugger is a viable option. Independent songplugging has also been a good way to enter the music business for someone with good ears, personality, and lots of perseverance. If you're successful at it, you'll most surely get offers from established publishing companies who would rather have you as an employee than a competitor.

If you're pitching your own songs and making good contacts in the industry as a result, you might consider pitching songs of other writers for extra income and to keep your contacts fresh by having another reason to call them periodically. If they like your songs and encourage you to come back with more (even if they can't use your songs for the projects at hand), it's a good idea to be able to pitch them the appropriate songs of other writers that you believe in. Nurturing those industry contacts makes you infinitely more valuable as a collaborator. You also become more valuable to your industry contacts if they know you'll bring them great songs regardless of who wrote them.

Indie songpluggers have always been around but have been, as might be expected, a constant part of the Nashville scene because of the greater percentage of artists who record "outside" songs.

Based on her reputation as one of Nashville's best, I interviewed Liz Rose to shed some light on the subject. Among her many indie Top 10 successes are no. 1 singles by Garth

Brooks ("She's Gonna Make It") and Faith Hill ("The Way You Love Me"). She's also a staff songwriter for Jody Williams Music/Sony/Tree. Below is the interview:

Who are typical clients of indie songpluggers?

Indie pluggers are usually hired by (staff) writers from large companies that need more exposure, companies that have catalogues that aren't being worked enough, writers that don't have deals but have big cuts and want to keep their publishing or have copub deals. There is also the writer that has had no success but hires a plugger so that they can keep the publishing. This is great for the writer if they don't need the draw from the publisher and the money for demos.

How do you establish the credibility to get you through the doors the first time?

Most independent pluggers like to have a name writer with cuts or a company behind them. Especially for a new plugger that has no contacts. When I started out, I was fortunate enough to have the support of writers like Kent Blazy, Will Robinson, and Jason Blume. Their names helped me get in doors where no one knew who I was. I have worked for companies, hit writers who have their own companies, and new writers who are trying to break in. I've worked with publishers in town and out of town and (pitched) my own catalogue, King Lizard Music.

What do you like about plugging?

I love plugging and being independent. It gives me more freedom as to what I pitch. I am very fortunate to be working with some of the best catalogues and songwriters in the business. I work songs and catalogues that I believe in and feel have a chance of getting cut. The competition is incredible. With all the closings and mergers of publishing companies, there seem to be more independents and more creative ways to work catalogs. It's an interesting time to be independent. I love working with songwriters.

What kind of agreements do you have with your clients?

I don't really do single-song deals. I'll work single songs if I believe I can get the song cut and prefer a mutual verbal agreement and trust. I don't like to tie up a writer's songs on single-song contracts. I prefer a year commitment. A year is a good length to see how a song will do, whether you still believe in it, or give up. I have an agreement with my clients to have only a certain number of clients so they are properly exploited.

Are periodic reports a part of the agreement?

I keep a pitch log, but I am available any time to discuss pitches. I talk to my clients all the time especially when there is good news!

What are your fees?

My fees are different depending on the catalogue, number of writers and songs. My bonuses depend on how many records the artist sold the last time, how many they sell on this record, and whether the song is a single and its chart position. I do get a percentage of royalty participation without ownership. In some instances, there is the opportunity for copyright ownership. I own two other catalogs. Most successful pluggers want a piece of the copyright. After all, it takes a great plugger to get a song cut these days, and a miracle, without the plugger the song would just sit there and the writer, with no publishing contract, that owns all their publishing, should work some kind of fair deal with the plugger. If they signed a publishing contract, they probably couldn't keep any of their own (publishing) unless they have major hits behind them.

Do you guarantee a specific number of pitches?

I don't agree to a number of pitches because I don't know what my meetings will be. I exploit the songs I believe I can get cut and no matter the company, the writer, or just a single song. I play what is appropriate at the time of the meeting. The name of the game is not how many copies of songs you throw out there; it's how many you get cut. I usually meet with artists and producers and A&R that don't want to go through ten songs a meeting. I usually play sometimes one and maybe up to four.

How do writers find pluggers?

I would say check around town and ask about them. Find out how many and what cuts they have secured, who they have worked with. And if it's a new plugger, go with your gut about how they react to your songs and what contacts they have. Everyone starts somewhere.

Are there any situations writers should be cautious about?

I would say avoid pluggers that require a large sum of money and have very little track record, unless it is going to be fairly exclusive and the two parties really feel a great connection.

A version of this interview first appeared in my SongSense column in Music Biz Magazine *(www.musicbizmag.com).*

Demos

Why You Need Them

Demonstration recordings, "demos," are used to show your songs to publishers, producers, record companies, club owners, and other music industry people who may want to use your songs. These people will rarely look at a lyric without music, and even the few who can read music won't be able to get the full impact of the song by just looking at a lead sheet (lyrics with musical notation). Since the end product (the recording) is to be heard, they need to evaluate your song by hearing it. So you're left with the options of performing the song for them live or giving them a demo. Most publishers feel a live audition of a song is impractical and inefficient. To paraphrase what many publishers have said to me, "My major responsibility as a publisher is to devote myself to the songs I've already signed and to the writers on our staff. There's not much time for me to schedule appointments in my workday. The few appointments I make are referrals from people whose 'ears' I respect. I know there are some great tunes just walking around out there looking for a publisher and sometimes I'm too busy to see the writer. So in order to be able to listen to new songs, I need to have tapes or CDs. Then I can listen when my head is into it and I'm not distracted. What I'm actually listening for is a song that will be a hit record, so it's easier for me to hear it on CD since I won't be distracted by watching the performer."

So unless you have good contacts in the music business, you probably won't get an appointment to sing your songs "live" and will need to make a demo. Even if you can get a live audition, your contact will want to have a demo to listen to later or play for someone else at the company.

A very practical reason why publishers prefer a demo is that it allows them to listen to a lot of songs in a short time. It's hard for any sensitive person to shut you down thirty seconds into your song while you're looking at him (though it's certainly been known to happen). So handing them a demo is both a time-saver and a convenience.

A demo can benefit the writer in other ways, too. Creating a demo is an education in itself, whether you're actively producing it or observing someone else putting it together. If you're producing your demos at home, you can learn about the recording process at your own pace. You can experiment and work out arrangements without the pressure of paying for studio time.

The more familiar you become with the finished product, the better perspective you have on the writing process. You can more easily imagine a singer performing the song. You learn more about the use of space and density in your lyric writing and become more conscious of the role that arrangements play in enhancing a song's emotional impact.

One of the great thrills of songwriting is to watch your song bloom into a full-blown musical production, to make it fulfill your vision or surpass it. Your failures as well as your successes become great teachers.

On the business side, demos are efficient. Once you get a good demo of your song, you can make an unlimited number of copies and within a couple of weeks have them in a hundred different offices (more later about whether you *should* do that), assured that everyone will hear the same top-quality rendition of your song. That's quality control.

Types of Demos

Different kinds of demos serve different needs.

Basic song demos—A most basic kind of guitar/vocal or keyboard/vocal with maybe the addition of a bass or groove machine (depending on the equipment you own or have available) or, at its simplest, *a cappella* (unaccompanied) vocal. These can be used as a kind of "dummy demo" to be critiqued before spending money on a more elaborate version; to show the energy on the emotional and rhythm "feel" of your song as a guideline for musicians or demo production services who may do a more elaborate production; to play for publishers or producers who you already *know* will accept simple demos. Often what you play in this "dummy demo" will actually become part of the finished demo or master.

More elaborate song demos—Studio demos or more elaborately produced home demos either (a) produced by the writer to play for publishers or to pitch directly to producers and artists or (b) produced by the publisher to pitch to producers and artists. These demos usually have a groove (sequenced, looped, or live), bass, guitar or keyboard, lead vocal, and sometimes background vocals. What goes on the demo, in addition to that, is based totally on the writer's or publisher's perception of the artist's style and the "ears" and personal tastes of the producer making the demo. Also, the demo can be mixed in several different ways (strings replaced by steel guitar, for instance) to accommodate different styles.

Artist demo—One used by an artist or band to shop for a record deal, manager, or producer. It highlights the strengths of the artist, including not only the songs but the arrangements, performances, vocals, instrumental virtuosity of individual members, and the overall style and energy of the group. Even in the case of an individual writer/artist, this is almost always a demo using a group in order to show the artist in the musical environment that best suits her style. This is a studio demo but, depending on the style of the group and how well rehearsed they are, it could be done with a minimum of expense.

Master demo—The same function as an artist demo, but with the high quality of studio, engineering, production, and attention to detail that would make it acceptable for release as a record or to be included in a TV or film soundtrack.

Who Gets What and How Elaborate Does It Need to Be?

In creating your demo, it's important to know what purpose you want it to serve. One way to sort it out is to decide who's going to get it. These are the major groups of people to whom you'll be sending demos.

| Publishers

Though it used to be considered part of a publisher's job to produce appropriate demos to pitch to producers (and is still done in Nashville), the reality is that you'll need to produce your own demos well enough for the publishers to use. Even if you have a staff writing deal, the publisher will probably deduct at least part of the cost of the demo from your future royalties. So you end up paying for it either way.

One of the advantages in presenting well-produced demos to publishers is the increased ability to negotiate reversion clauses (see "Negotiable Contract Clauses," chapter ten). Publishers are reluctant to return songs they've had to lay out money for, and demo costs represent a good share of the initial expense. (Major publishing companies usually have in-house studios for their staff writers to use, but independent companies watch their recording budgets very carefully.) If you give them a high-quality demo, that expense is eliminated (unless, of course, you're asking them in your contract to reimburse you for them up front).

Another advantage is that your chances of interesting a publisher in a song based on a simple guitar/vocal or piano/vocal demo are slim. Though some publishers can "hear through" such a sample, others need more elaborate production to help them imagine how the finished product might sound. In most cases you won't know ahead of time what a particular publisher needs to hear. Your basic demo is likely to be sandwiched between two or more elaborate demos that sound like records, and yours will suffer in comparison.

There are exceptions. Country music publishers are still accustomed to hearing guitar or piano/vocal demos, and since the focus of most successful country songs is the lyric, a simple demo will work with a *great* lyric. A word here about country publishers. Though they say they'd rather hear a simple demo, the songs they pitch to producers are typically produced using the best musicians available. (And Nashville overflows with great musicians.) After interviewing a few publishers about this apparent contradiction, the best answer is that they get tired of hearing spectacularly expensive demos of spectacularly bad songs. They figure they'll "hear" a great song demoed simply and they'll spend the money on the demo. But even with mid- to up-tempo songs, it's good to have enough rhythm track to give them the "feel" you want them to hear, particularly as there is more pop influence in country than in the past.

In another arena, keyboard/vocal demos of pop ballads can work if you have an excellent lyric, melody, keyboard player, and singer. Those are exceptions, though, and no longer the rule. If you have any kind of rock, R&B, pop rhythm ballad, or up-tempo song, you need a basic groove, i.e., drums or loops, bass and keyboard, synth or guitar, because the groove and energy are essential ingredients in its appeal.

| Producers

Record producers come from a great variety of backgrounds. Some evolve into producers from having been recording engineers and their skills may be focused on how records sound. Others are former studio musicians who may focus mainly on getting the right players and putting together great arrangements. Others, closer to the function of film producers, excel in the overview. Their skill is in putting together the magic elements— the artist, the arranger, the musicians, the engineer, the studio, the money, and most importantly, the songs.

No matter what their backgrounds, their success depends on recognizing great and *appropriate* songs for the artists they produce. However, as you might guess, their initial impressions, when hearing your demo, may vary based on their own particular areas of expertise. An engineer/producer may have a negative reaction to a poorly recorded demo (though he'll know how to fix it). A studio musician/producer might cringe at an out-of-tune vocal or guitar, though he may be more adept at hearing the arrangement possibilities of a rough or simple demo. The "overview" type of producer may not have the musicians' sophisticated ability to visualize a finished production—he may just know what he likes when he hears it. Obviously, these categories are oversimplified for the sake of illustration, and any individual producer will possess his own unique combination of tastes and skills.

The point is that, in order to deal with that diversity, your best approach is to make sure your demo is technically "clean" and well arranged. I've heard a successful musician/producer say, "I can hear it from a piano/vocal," and at another time say, "The demo sounded just like the artist—the right key, the musical hooks, and everything was right there. I hardly had to do anything, so we recorded it." One statement doesn't necessarily contradict the other but illustrates the fact that the more you give them, the more easily they'll hear it. Of the utmost importance in pitching a song to a producer for a specific artist is that the song is appropriate for the artist. (See "Casting," chapter eleven.) Do your research!

If you're an artist or band looking for someone to produce you, it's most important that the producer hears your best *performance* and your best *material*. He should be able to hear all the voices and instrumental parts clearly. A well-recorded live performance will work just fine if the vocals can be recorded cleanly.

Record Companies

In most cases, the person at the record company you'll be pitching tapes to is the A&R person. A&R stands for "artist and repertoire," and in times of old, when almost nobody wrote his own songs, they were the ones who told the artists what they would record. For better or worse, those days are gone. A&R executives have a wide variety of tasks to perform and, like producers, come from diverse backgrounds. Different record companies have different philosophies in hiring them. Each of these philosophies has potential advantages and disadvantages. Some companies want people who know music intimately, such as musicians, producers (in some companies all the A&R executives are producers), music journalists, and critics. Producers may become "studio bound" and lose touch with "the street," though they usually have the respect of the artists, managers, and other professionals they deal with and a decent ear for raw talent.

Others ascribe to the "man on the street" theory and hire an opinionated young rock fan to be their rock A&R representative, maybe a kid who works in a record store. That philosophy sees an A&R person as a "general public record buyer." The "man on the street" who has been exposed to finished records and masters all his life may have trouble "hearing" less-than-finished product and, because of a lack of music or production experience, may not easily gain the respect of artists.

Other companies tend to hire from within the company. The former secretary of a producer (who screened all his material anyway) or the guy from the mailroom who used to hang out in the A&R department may be next in line for the job. The advantage is that he or she pretty much knows how the company operates and the company knows them. There's no dealing with an outsider who already has his own methods and philosophies, which may clash with the company status quo (unless the company wants a change). Each of the above philosophies, by the way, has produced outstanding A&R people.

A&R reps have always (and will always) take a lot of flack for not having "ears," and the "man on the street" variety is probably the most vulnerable to it. But if he's the one who signs you, he's brilliant; if he passed, he's deaf. It goes with the territory.

The basic functions of an A&R department today are to find new talent and sign it; when needed, to find the artist a manager, booking agent, or band members; to supervise and oversee production and budgets of recording projects; and to find suitable hit songs for the artists signed to the label.

The legendary former president of Arista Records, Clive Davis, relied heavily on great artists who weren't writers (Whitney Houston, Aretha Franklin, etc.) and on his own ears to find them great songs. That philosophy is still more the rule than the exception in country music. A&R representatives also look for hits for artists on their labels who do write, though they may not write enough songs or commercial enough songs. So the record company is an important target if they have nonwriting artists or if you're pitching yourself as an artist. Again, here you need well-produced demos and the song must be right for the artist for whom they need songs.

Never waste postage by sending a song to an A&R department "just in case they might have an artist who could do this song." Target a specific artist, know the artist's work, have the correct label, and know the song is right or don't bother. If you're pitching the song to a specific artist, write "for Britney Spears" or whomever on the package *and* in a cover letter *and* on the demo. They'll either turn it over to the artist's producer without opening it or listen and decide for themselves whether to pass it to the producer or send it back unopened. (More about circumventing that situation in "Getting Through the Doors," page 283.)

If you're pitching yourself or your group to an A&R department as an *artist*, the best way is to go in with two to four finished masters of the best songs you can write or find in your style and an uncompromised, passionate performance. Regardless of their technical quality, excuses like "I know I can do it better, but I had a cold that day," or "Our regular bass player went on the road, and this new guy only had one rehearsal," just don't make it. This may be your only shot, and it's better to postpone your session till your cold is cured and your bass player is back. You can't expect a record company to sign you if they don't know exactly what they're getting. It's not absolutely necessary, but if possible, include the following with your demo in order of importance: your personal bio or bios of group members (see "Presenting Your Demo," in this chapter); photos (if they're really good ones); a press kit with reviews, list of clubs played, a graphic design or logo on your press kit cover and a tape/CD. All this says, "We're ready and we're serious!"

Club Owners

If you're looking for a live gig in a club, your demo should be live, too. Most club owners won't trust studio demos alone because they've been burned so many times by hearing a great studio tape of a band that sounded very different once they got on stage. It doesn't hurt to include studio cuts, but your demo should contain at least part of a live set with your "between song" rap, audience interaction, applause, etc., intact. Along with the tape, send them photos and bios with a list of clubs previously played, letters from owners of other clubs where you've worked. If it's a "cover" gig where you're playing "the hits" and requests, include a list of the songs you're prepared to play. If you have a live video, it's much better than a live audio tape, but it's ideal to have both.

What You Can Do at Home

Once you've decided what kind of demo you need and who you're going to submit it to, you have to plan the actual production of the demo itself. It's important to plan ahead because you can waste a lot of time and money going into a recording project cold. One of the ways many songwriters cut the expense of demo production is by doing their own recording at home.

Recording at home has many obvious advantages. Sometimes you don't only get a great idea for a lyric, you also hear that groove and a bass line. Sometimes inspiration hits at 2 A.M. when your left brain is winding down and your right brain is starting to talk to you. If you've got your studio in the next room, you can plug in your headset, turn on the drum machine and keyboard, crank it up, and catch that idea before it gets away! Within hours you not only have a new song, but you've got the demo done the way you heard it in your head. You didn't have to teach other musicians your song, worry about whether everybody would show up on time for the session, talk the guitar player out of doing a solo, buy lunch for the band at rehearsal, spend your time in the studio watching the clock tick away dollar signs, or worry about what's growing on the coffee cups. These advantages alone may make it worthwhile for you to invest in your own home studio, particularly if you write a lot of songs. For what it would cost you for a few demo sessions in a pro studio, you could buy a good little home studio setup.

You will, of course, be saddled with maintenance of the equipment, the learning curve of getting control of the technology, and the ever-present desire to buy the next piece of state-of-the-art gear to upgrade your setup. No matter how convenient and versatile your equipment, there will always be something you want to be able to do with it that you just can't achieve without one more gadget. Another problem also goes with the territory: getting hung up in the engineering, forever fiddling with equipment to get the right sound. This will actually rob you of spontaneity. There's always a trade-off. Your individual needs will be the key to your decision to have your own studio. But you have a lot of options to choose from to let you enjoy the best of both worlds.

If you're a musician with even minimal skills, present-day technology (which is increasing at a dazzling rate) can make it possible for you to create master-quality demos at home. Companies like DigiDesign (ProTools), Roland, Kurzweil, Yamaha, Korg, Kawai, Casio, Sequential Circuits, Fender, Akai, Ensoniq, and others manufacture synthesizers, sequencers, and samplers (which record any rhythm, chord, or melodic pattern you create) and drum machines programmed to digitally reproduce actual drum sounds, or "samples." As the digital components become easier to mass-produce, their cost comes down and their versatility increases.

Digital recording allows you to perform most of the functions of a major recording studio using your personal computer and specially developed software programs. Included in the new instruments is the capability to program/record one note of the melody at a time (called "step time"), which later can be electronically played back in its entirety at any speed. This is a great boon to those with limited keyboard skills because it can make you sound like a virtuoso. If you rush or are a little late on a beat, it can also correct your time (called "quantizing"). The drum machines can be inspirational, especially if you're having a hard time getting into writing an up-tempo groove.

Other computer-assisted capabilities include the ability to digitally sample any sound, correct single notes, change pitch, transpose to another key without changing tempo (and vice versa), and change the duration of a note after it's recorded. To take advantage of this technology, you need equipment with MIDI (Musical Instrument Digital Interface) capabilities. There are also adapters available that will convert or retrofit any instrument to MIDI.

A recent development is software-based instruments—samplers and synths that exist only inside your computer. The day is coming when the computer will provide everything that MIDI instruments provide today.

Developments in digital technology for composing, arranging, and recording occur so fast that I can't be specific about what to buy—the equipment will be obsolete by the time this book hits the stores. The best thing you can do to keep up with the latest developments, along with a visit to your local musical instrument retailer, is to subscribe to or periodically pick up a copy of *Keyboard, Guitar for the Practicing Musician, Guitar Player,* or *Electronic Musician* or visit those magazines online.

You might think, "That's great if you write synth-styled songs, but what if I want to write acoustic country songs?" Again, technology makes it easy. Fostex, Teac, Yamaha, and others make very portable, easy-to-use, hard disc recording equipment. They've also developed educational books to help you get the most out of them. The books deal not only with recording techniques, but with shaping the acoustic properties of your home environment.

It's possible to record and make copies of your demo from start to finish in your own home studio. But many writers choose to record at home using just those electronic/ digital instruments that don't depend on the use of microphones and an acoustic environment. Then they take what they have to a professional recording studio, transfer it to the studio tape, and use the studio's selection of microphones and outboard gear (reverb, limiters, compressors, etc.) to record acoustic instruments and vocals and to mix the tracks. This method can save a lot of money and still produce a high-quality demo. It allows you to spend your creative, experimental time at home without the studio pressure and to plan the best use of your studio time. If you can get the rhythm tracks down at home with groove machines and sequencers, you can also give your singer a chance to work with the tracks before the studio session.

The digital recording you can do at home is usually so clean it can be used in studio masters. Today it's not unusual to create many components of master tracks outside the studio and then combine them with the advantages of the studio environment and technology. Most studios have the equipment to "read" what you bring them. In fact, the old joke about the studio musicians "phoning in" their parts is, in fact, a reality. Many writers and producers are now "mailing" tracks to each other over high-speed DSL, cable, or T1 lines, adding more instrumental parts or vocals, and mailing them back with no loss of fidelity.

Choosing a Studio

Many songwriters use the facilities of a professional recording studio to put the finishing touches on their demos. Other writers like to work in a studio from the start. If you should decide to do all or part of your recording in a studio, there are several factors to consider in choosing one. It's very important to pick a studio where you can get the services and equipment you need to achieve the sound and quality you want.

Between the pro studio and the home studio is the project studio. Project studios are set up to do anything a pro studio can do without the "big room"—the large recording areas that require large amounts of real estate. Project studios will usually have full MIDI production capabilities (something pro studios often do without) as well as high-quality audio recording and editing. Project studios are small enough to be in homes or commercial spaces.

Your first move should be to decide what kind of demo you want and how much recording you'll do there. Then you want to decide what you need from the studio in order to do it. The amount of money you have to spend is also very important, though we'll discuss other options later. How do you decide what you need? Here are some points to consider:

1. **What style of music do you play?** If your music is primarily electronic (electronic drums, keyboards, etc.), some studios have excellent facilities for plugging "direct" into the recording equipment but offer little if you need an acoustic environment for vocals or instruments that you'd record with a microphone. It may be best to go elsewhere to do your acoustic recording.

A small room is adequate if you play quiet, acoustic music. If you play loud rock and roll, decide whether you want a big, open concert–style sound, for which you'd look for a big, high-ceilinged room (also good for live string sections), or the tight, "present" sound you get in a smaller, acoustically "dead" room. Most studios, however, offer some versatility by the use of "baffles" (also called "gobos"), which are movable pads that can be placed between instruments or amps. The baffles often offer a choice of sound-absorbent or reflective surfaces to give you a choice of "live" or "dead" sound. The studio may also give you a choice of curtains or reflective walls or rug-covered or hard floor surfaces to achieve the same effects. The baffles can also isolate the sounds from "bleeding" into the mikes of other instruments.

The way songs are miked, recorded, and mixed is different in each style of music, so no matter what your style, you'll want to find an engineer who's experienced with that type of music, or make sure that the studio allows you to bring in your own engineer.

Note that some engineers are better at tracking (recording the music) and others are better at mixing—two distinctly different skills.

2. **Do you want to record demos or masters?** You really don't need masters unless you're shopping your project to record labels or film and TV and you are (or have) a good producer and a very clear idea of how you want to sound on record. Otherwise, go for more simple demos. If you're producing masters, you're going for a "radio-ready," finished product. Consequently, every detail of the recording must be the best—the sounds of all the instruments, the arrangements, performances, audio quality, everything.

While the capabilities of digital recording make it possible to get a master quality sound and quickly fix problems that might occur in the recording, those fixes take time to tweak, and that extra time is what you spend on a master.

"You get what you pay for" is a good maxim to keep in mind when you shop for studio time. If you find a studio with unusually low prices, don't feel awkward about asking them how they can afford to offer such inexpensive rates. Ask if they have a maintenance person on duty. If they say, "No, but we have someone we can call if anything goes wrong," determine how that might affect your session. If it's just you and a couple of buddies who don't have anything else to do but wait to see how fast those repairs can happen, it may not matter to you. If you have fifteen musicians all getting union scale who have another session booked after yours, you're in very big trouble and may end up having to pay them and not get anything recorded.

3. **Don't book too much time in a single block.** Sometimes you can get a better deal if you book a large block of studio time, but there's a "burnout factor" that takes place after long periods of tension and concentrated listening, particularly if you're into a time period that runs counter to your "biological clock" (e.g., 4 A.M. if your regular bedtime is 11 P.M.). You may actually waste money by the mistakes you make because your perceptions and high-frequency hearing are not operating efficiently. Avoid the temptation to use drugs to compensate. They only damage your perceptions further and can make you less aware that you're not functioning at your peak. Make sure your engineer is also working at his peak. It's a good idea to take an "ear break" every hour or so.

The number of tracks a studio offers should not be the basis of your choice. More is not necessarily better. Studios can offer anywhere from two to forty-eight tracks to serve many different needs. I've heard "live" two-track demos of bands that rival the excitement of a twenty-four-track master because they have more "presence."

Hard disk recording, either stand-alone (Alesis, Mackie, Tascam) or computer-based (ProTools, Logic, Cakewalk, Performer to name a few), is the new standard, primarily because of flexibility in editing. It is normal for live instruments and voices to be edited ("tweaked") to fix mistakes in otherwise good parts to achieve "perfection" in timing and pitch or to create new parts out of bits of original performances.

4. **Can you bring your own recording tape or other media or are you required to buy from the studio?** They'll charge you more than you'd pay at a recording supply store. You may live in a place where you have no choice, but if you're in a major recording center, buy outside the studio. If you do that, however, check with the studio first to find out what media you need. Compared to other expenses, media is cheap. Don't cut corners using cheap blank CDs that fail in one or two months or a hard drive that is too small or too slow. (More disk speed = more tracks.)

Always count on using more recording media than you think you'll need. It's better to be prepared. You can always use what you have left over at another time.

| Studio Deals

If you do decide to work in a studio, you can make special deals to lower your costs, but be careful not to let your eagerness get you into trouble.

In your search for your next career break, you encounter local studio owner Harry Sessions. He says, "I like your tunes and you're a good performer. I think you've got a shot at getting a record deal. I own a studio and I'd like to take you in and cut some of your tunes just to see what we could come up with."

This is just what you've been waiting to hear. You've been trying to see A&R people at the record companies with your home demos and getting nowhere. Even though they say they can listen to a simple demo, you know they're listening to finished radio-quality masters every day and that those probably have a competitive edge. You've been waiting for a deal like this to come along and say to yourself, "Just do it, don't ask questions."

You finish the four-song project with help from your (or Harry's) musician friends who learned, rehearsed, and recorded the songs with you. You've got no written or verbal contract regarding the ownership of the masters. You figure Harry is a friend helping you out and in some kind of way he'll get paid when you make a deal with the record label. But then he drops the bomb: "Of course, you understand that I get the *publishing* on all these tunes. I assume you're hip enough to know that's the way these deals are done. I get the production points[1] and the publishing."[2]

You're a little shocked, but you don't want to appear unhip, of course, and Harry has been so nice to you that you don't want to seem ungrateful. You're behaving exactly the way he wants you to. Now he wants you to sign the contract.

This is a familiar scenario and periodically someone calls me and asks, "Do I have to give him my publishing? He says he has a right to it because he did the masters." The answer is NO, assuming that you made no written or verbal agreement before the sessions regarding the publishing or production points. However, in order to preempt Harry from making the claim that he cowrote the songs with you, be sure to put your songs in some tangible form, whether you write them out or record them on a simple tape recorder before working with Harry.

Another situation you'll run into is when a studio owner offers to produce your demos or masters "on spec." The studio owner "speculates" that the time and sometimes the money that he, as producer, puts in will be recouped when you sell your master to a record label. He hopes he'll end up as (a) the producer of the whole album project, (b) your producer for the life of your record contract, and/or (c) publisher of all the songs he produces for you. That's Harry Sessions's maximum payoff and he'll need a production and publishing contract with you to achieve it.

Many producers have been burned so often that they've coined the phrase "Spec = (ex)spec(t) not to get paid." At minimum, without a production contract, the producer/

---

[1] A percentage of income earned by the producer paid from your artist royalties. If we assume that your artist royalty is 12 percent of the suggested retail price of the record, 3 to 5 percent of the suggested retail price is the customary producer royalty. The latter is referred to not as percentages, but as "points," to avoid the impression that it's 3 percent of 12 percent. Therefore, 3 points to the producer with an artist royalty of 12 percent actually amounts to 25 percent of the artist's royalty. However, the producer royalty is typically "prorated" by the number of tracks the producer contributes to the album in relation to the overall number of tracks on the entire album.

[2] Ownership of the copyrights and 50 percent of the income from the songs.

studio owner hopes the record company would like *you* and the production enough that you'll "buy out" the masters (with your record company advance) with enough money for a profit beyond what he put into the tapes. He also hopes he'd get production points and credit on those recordings the label eventually releases. If he does a great job, he deserves that, particularly if he can also make some valuable industry contacts for you, though, to be fair, that's not his responsibility unless you've previously agreed to it. Many reputable producers with strong industry contacts simply want to find new artists to develop and produce rather than wait for the record companies to hire him. He will be more concerned with producer points and his producer advance than profiting from a buyout or publishing.

Unfortunately for less reputable or unknown producers, if the record company likes you as an artist but doesn't like his production, without a production or publishing contract between you and him, you may get a record deal and he won't get anything. Ironically, it is often the lesser-known producers who present the more onerous "spec" contracts in order to avoid getting burned. In fact, because the record company may want you produced by someone *they* choose, you should *never* guarantee that the "spec" producer will be hired by you or the record company to produce any product released in your future record deal. Usually, the agreement should say that you will "use my best efforts" to get the producer involved. This also assumes that the recording experience was good for you, creative and productive, you felt supported artistically, and you want to continue this relationship.

Legally, if he doesn't present you with a production contract until after the masters are complete and you don't like the deal he presents you with then, you're under no obligation to accept. If the studio owner hasn't gotten together with you ahead of time and laid out the conditions under which he's speculating his time and facilities, then he's gambling that you'll like his work enough to go along with him or that he can intimidate you like Harry Sessions.

The reality is, though, that if you walk away, you won't be able to take your demo with you. The producer/studio owner physically owns the tapes. He doesn't have to give you the masters or copies. After all, he figures, why should you be able to use the results of his production expertise and time without his being compensated for it? He can't release the tapes without your permission or sell them to a label without owning the rights to your performances unless you later sign with a label who wishes to buy them from him or unless he has actually paid you to perform on the masters. If you later publish and release those songs, he can't collect any royalties on your publishing without a specific contract to do so. Obviously, without a record out, there aren't any royalties anyway, but writer/artists often worry that some time in the future someone will make a claim based on this studio situation.

In this case both the studio owner/producer and the writer/artist are responsible for the unpleasant situation because they didn't let it be known what they both expected from the deal in writing before the recording took place.

The preceding example is one I come across more than I'd like to, but many other studio deals can be made that are fair to both the studio and the writer/performer. With an agreement up front in writing, this could have been one of them. The fact is that you're also speculating that all the hard work and time you put into this project will pay off for you, too. If you're happy with what you accomplished in the studio together and enjoyed working with the producer, you don't want those ugly, unexpected, after-the-fact business realities to damage a promising relationship.

Making "Sound" Deals

Now that we've got an idea of what can go wrong in negotiating a special studio deal, let's talk more constructively about a better way to approach this situation.

As I said earlier, you have to decide whether you need demos or masters, whether you need a "state-of-the-art" studio and engineer, or if you can get by with lower quality and less experience for less money. If you can get by with a less expensive demo, you may not need to worry about making a deal.

If you decide that you need a more elaborate demo than you can afford to pay for outright, the next question to ask yourself is, "What do I have to offer that a studio owner/producer or an engineer/producer might want?" The variables are cash, services, or participation. Musicians sometimes barter services in exchange for studio time. Maybe you're a builder or painter, decorator, graphic artist, electrician, secretary, or have some other skill that would be of use to a studio owner. As a musician, you might play on some of his other in-house productions. You may also own a piece of outboard equipment or a unique instrument you could exchange for studio time.

If you just need a demo, don't give away percentages of production or publishing.

Participation refers to percentages of the income stream generated by you as an artist or writer and gets a little more complex. In the case of an artist, by "participation" I mean production points as discussed in the previous section. In the case of a writer or writer/artist, I'm talking about ownership of your copyrights or receipt of royalties (without ownership) from your songs. Generally speaking, if you just need a demo, don't give away percentages of production or publishing. The only exception I can think of is if you're making a deal with a major producer with a great track record who can walk into a record company, play them a demo, and get a budget on the strength of his reputation.

If you're a writer with limited funds, you may encounter studio owners or engineer/producers who will ask for your publishing even for producing a simple song demo. The problem with engineer/studio owners acting as publishers is that even though they'll sometimes come across opportunities to pitch a tune in their studio to a producer who needs a song, they may not actively be publishers on a daily basis. That's why it would be better to offer them a percentage of the publisher share of mechanical royalties on any record they secure, but *only on that record*, without giving them ownership of any percentage of your copyright. (See "Negotiating," page 215.) If their involvement is very limited, such as merely handing your song demo to one person, you may want to ask for a cap on the amount they can receive from your mechanical royalties rather than a perpetual participation.

If you're recording masters as an artist (ready to be pressed and radio quality) and determine that the studio is equipped to give you master quality, you'll need a producer unless you're already a good, experienced producer and have the rare ability to be objective with your own work. It's only fair, in lieu of cash, to offer a producer production points. In fact, he usually gets both. But in a "spec" deal, the cash in front is what he's giving up. A percentage (usually half) of the publishing (ownership) on *only* the tunes he produces is also a common deal in lieu of cash. This, for a full-time publisher/producer, is called a "development deal." With either of those deals, though, make sure there's a time period involved in which you are returned your copyrights and that you have the option to work with another producer if the record deal doesn't happen. The period ranges from six to eighteen months and is most often a year (but ultimately, whatever you agree on) after the masters are completed. The studio or independent engineer will still own the actual master tapes (unless you paid for them), so that if a record company wants to use something you've already done, they can buy the master, giving the studio or engineer the opportunity to get back their investment. If they insist on owning the masters, you should agree on a buyout price in the event that you secure a record deal. They may also want to be compensated if the tapes are used to obtain a record deal, even though the masters are not bought by the record company.

A "spec" or development deal may be separated into its speculative components. For instance, depending on what the studio owner/engineer/producer contributes, you may agree on all or a combination of the following: a preset rate or price for use of the studio facilities to be paid out of your advance; best efforts to continue using the producer on the first album under your record deal; a percentage of your advance or "buyout" if the producer "shops" the masters and helps you secure a record deal; and/or producer points for those tracks actually used on your first album. Since there are many contingencies to these agreements, you should always have an experienced music industry attorney help you negotiate them.

You should also be aware, and wary, of exclusive production agreements. These agreements involve providing your exclusive recording services (and often publishing) to a production company and are more similar to a recording contract than a "spec" or development arrangement. Under these agreements, it is anticipated that the production company (not you) will ultimately sign with the record company and furnish your services to the record company. These agreements should only be considered when the person or company is very reputable, has a proven track record and strong industry ties. The issues to be negotiated can be just as complex as a recording agreement and should only be done with the advice of an experienced music industry attorney.

Studio Rates

Whether you're paying cash or bartering services, these are always flexible. When you call a studio for rates, they'll always give you their "book" rate, so dig a little deeper. Here are some of the factors involved in lowering that rate.

BLOCK BOOKING

The more hours you can guarantee them, the cheaper you usually can get studio time. As I mentioned earlier, though, spending hours in the studio when you're overtired can be counterproductive.

LATE HOURS AND DOWNTIME

You can make a better deal if you can work at the studio's convenience. If you let the owner know that you'll be able to come in on short notice in their "downtime" (when the studio isn't booked), it helps them by keeping money coming in and they're liable to give you a better rate. Tell them to call you if someone cancels and the notice is too short to book another session at their full rate or if the studio has to cancel a session because a piece of equipment broke (just make sure you don't need to use that particular piece of equipment). In some of these deals, the studio reserves the right to bump you out when they get a "book rate" session in your time slot. Late night or early morning hours can also be cheaper in some studios.

Up-front cash will get you better rates. The more you can give the studio in advance of the session, particularly if you've blocked out a large number of guaranteed hours, the better the rates you'll get.

RECORDING ENGINEERS

The one you choose will have a bearing on your studio costs. Some engineers are still in training and some are well-experienced pros. If you're doing a simple demo, it may be cheaper to hire a beginner (if you can get him to admit it). What you have to weigh is the possibility that a beginner's mistake may cost you time/money.

If you bring along your own favorite independent engineer, it may involve extra time for him to learn the idiosyncrasies of a new studio, though you're saving time by using someone you've established communication with. Another advantage is that he may have a relationship with a studio that will give him a lower rate for bringing in your business.

Make sure when you use any engineer that he hasn't already been working for twelve hours and is too burnt out to react or hear properly. Engineers work more hours under stress than is healthy for human beings anyway. So always find out how long your engineer has worked before your session. If their own staff engineers are unavailable during the hours you want to work, most studios can recommend independent engineers who have worked in their studio before.

Though most seasoned engineers are fairly versatile, some have experience primarily in country music, R&B/hip-hop, heavy metal, or some other style and are more familiar with the way instruments and vocals are recorded and mixed in that style. Find one who will understand how to record your style of music.

When you're pricing a studio, you may be quoted the studio time rates *without* the engineer, though most demo studios include it. Engineer fees vary from city to city, time of year (January and February are traditionally slow.), and even project to project. In other words, the same engineer might change half his regular record company rate for a January demo. Engineers in L.A. and New York cost more than a similarly skilled engineer does in Kentucky. The range of fees is so wide—from nearly free (what everyone wants to pay) to thousands a day plus points—that rather than my quoting figures, it's more important to know the engineer's skills. Can she handle MIDI gear? Digital editing? How does she interact with musicians and singers (people skills)? Engineering is much more than pushing buttons. The best at all levels will want to keep you happy, since it's easier to keep you as a client than to find new ones.

Find out exactly what the fees are and figure them into your budget. Independent engineers are usually paid separately, and staff engineers are paid with the same check you pay the studio. Get it straight ahead of time. In fact, talk to the engineer you'll be working with before the session so you both can feel a little more relaxed and confident about what you intend to do.

Pro studios will include a second engineer in your price. These are usually minimum-wage employees who do the "scut work"—notating track sheets, answering the phone, and handling the patchbay—all things that will save your engineer time.

Many demo studios advertise "production assistance," but people are sometimes disappointed by the minimal assistance actually available.

If you know nothing about production, hire a demo producer who specializes in the type of demo you need. Ideally, you should be at the sessions so that you'll learn how it's done and you can express your opinions *before* recording begins. Being there is especially valuable to help make sure your singer gets your lyric and the vocal phrasing right.

Ask the studio exactly what is meant by "production assistance." Is it five minutes with the engineer before the session, or is it playing your songs for someone and discussing a musical direction, musicians, and budget? Regarding the latter, remember that the studio is in business to make money and, therefore, may be inclined to make suggestions that will result in your use of more studio time than you need. At least try to determine whether a simple or a full-blown production is appropriate before talking to the studio. The more "overdubbing" or "tracking" (adding instruments or vocals to the initial recording) that's done, the more studio time you need. Playing the instruments yourself and building the tracks one by one is most time-consuming.

When you work out your budget, decide whether it's cheaper not to pay other musicians and spend the money on more studio time or use less time and pay more musicians. The other trade-off is that with good musicians, you'll get parts that may be better than what you'd think of or be able to execute.

EQUIPMENT

The cost of the studio time is also determined by the equipment you need. If you're doing a piano/vocal, you may only need an analog two-track studio. Cheap! The bare minimum for a digital recording would be eight tracks, an ADAT recorder, and a mixer. Of course you'll also need to decide if you want an acoustic piano and what kind. If you're cutting masters with a big production, you may want twenty-four or more tracks with automated mixdown capabilities. You will need some signal processing devices that the studio may or may not have available for the quoted hourly rate. This is referred to as "outboard" equipment and includes such things as phasers, flangers, limiters, compressors, various types of reverb and delay, harmonizers, DBX or Dolby noise reduction, graphic or parametric equalizers, and many others. Though these are basic items to most studios, discuss your needs for this equipment *before* the session so you aren't surprised by, "Oh, you want to do that! You need a thingamajig and we don't have one, but we can rent one for you for $100 a day!" Don't be fooled by the brand names of outboard equipment that many studios advertise, unless they specify the model number and you're familiar with that model. The brand name alone doesn't tell you if they have the specific piece of equipment you need.

Getting all the info before the session will save you money in the end. In fact, knowing what questions to ask ahead of time and knowing what everyone needs to make them happy on the business end are the keys to saving your peace of mind during and after the session.

The Recording Process

Once you've decided on a studio, engineer, and necessary equipment, keep in mind the following suggestions about the recording process:

1. Remember to double your estimated recording time (for listening to playbacks).

2. Test your mixes on your car stereo/cassette or CD player. (CDs are preferred and any decent studio will have a CD burner.) Switch back and forth between your song and the radio or a familiar tape for comparison. Listen for the clarity of instruments and vocals.

3. If you have several days in which to record, in the first session, record your basic drum, guitar, bass, and keyboard tracks with a temporary "scratch" vocal. That temporary vocal allows the musicians to create parts that support but don't get in the way of the vocal. At the end of the first session, "scratch" (eliminate) the vocal and do a rough mix. "Mix" refers to the relative volumes, placement (right, left, or center for stereo), and "EQ" (equalization), the amount of treble, bass, and midrange emphasis, on each of the instruments. You'll then take home a tape/CD with which the vocalist can rehearse her performance and with which you can work out and rehearse "overdubs," additional parts such as instrumental solos and harmony parts, background vocals, orchestral parts, etc. During the next session, record the vocals and the overdubs and get a rough (quick) mix or two of that session. Take them home and listen to the mixes so you can make decisions about them at your leisure outside the pressure of the studio. It's generally not a good idea to do more than a rough mix at the same session in which you record. It's difficult to have a good perspective on this important process when you and your ears are fatigued.

This is a common, though not necessarily the best, approach to the recording process. If you're a self-contained group, you're well rehearsed, and want to preserve a spontaneous sound, you'd record everything "live" at the same time, though it still may be advisable to have a separate mixing session. You may not have the luxury of recording over a several-day period. If you must do it all at once, prepare very well, rehearse the musicians and singer(s), and make sure your engineer knows ahead of time what you want to do and how you want to do it. The best idea is to visit the studio first to meet with the engineer.

Saving Money by Being Prepared

The best way to cut down on time, aggravation, and expenses is to have a solid idea of what you want for your demo and a good plan for getting it. In preparing for the session, there are some things to consider that will save you a lot of time and worry.

Choose the right musicians and rehearse ahead of time. One of the most difficult aspects of doing demos is choosing the right musicians. Demos require musicians with an ability to exercise restraint, to control their egos, and to control the desire to "show off." Some are too wrapped up in learning their instrument to be able to direct their creativity toward playing something simple that fits and complements the whole arrangement or supports a vocal.

The ideal in choosing musicians is that you've had an opportunity to work with or listen to a lot of them and can afford to pay $100+ (varies from city to city) per tune. You may have to pay them extra to overdub other parts. You'll then choose them according to the style of songs you're recording and the way you'll predict that they'll interact with other musicians when left to their own creativity. The goal is that you want to exercise a minimum of direction and get maximum creative contribution from each of the musicians involved. In fact, you'll ideally want to find a number of musicians who play together in the same group or at least have played together often enough that they have their own communication well tuned. Also, a good producer will help you choose musicians he's worked with in the past and knows their capabilities, eliminating the need to rehearse.

What if you don't have that much money and you can't afford to be choosy? You should know, then, that there are a lot of musicians around looking for something to get involved in and willing to do sessions for the experience or "on spec" (on the speculation that if and when you get paid, they get paid). Make signs explaining your situation, the type of music you're interested in, and put them on bulletin boards in music stores, colleges, music departments, and clubs. Advertise in musicians' magazines. Contact musicians' services that match musicians in your area with opportunities and with each other. Here are two good ones.

Musicians Contact Service

www.musicianscontact.com

Taxi's Musician's Junction

www.musiciansjunction.com

Offer to trade your own services as a musician, singer, or whatever. You're bound to go through some trial and error to find the right people, but that's what you need to do.

When you find the musicians you want, rehearse with them as much as possible before doing the session, if you're insecure about your arrangements, and you're looking for something out of the ordinary. It'll save you lots of money in studio time. Agree on the fees before the session and pay them promptly. You'll feel much better about directing them if you've taken care of business and, psychologically, you'll eliminate bad vibes and have an eager team working with you.

Prepare master rhythm charts of the songs for each musician before you rehearse or before the session if there's no rehearsal. Master rhythm charts don't necessarily need to have the melody written out, but should contain a "road map" of the song; the chord changes and all the directions you've thought of ahead of time, such as when certain instruments enter or exit, a specific bass line you want to hear, etc. If you don't have the groove written out, bring recorded examples of what you want. Singers who can sight-read music should have a "lead sheet" that contains melody line and lyric. They *must* have a neatly typed lyric sheet.

The Nashville Number System is used universally in Nashville (surprise!) and extensively outside of Nashville as a valuable song-charting shorthand. Say you get the singer in the studio and realize at the last minute that his key is wrong. Zap! Transpose the key instantly and all the musicians immediately know the new chord changes. It substitutes numbers for chord letters. It's a universal "language" for studio musicians and very helpful for songwriters. To help you learn, there are a variety of books and software packages. Search the Internet under "nashville number system" or get Chas Williams's book, *The Nashville Number System* (Corner Music (615) 297-9559), which will teach you several different styles in use.

Have your musicians check their instruments and amps before the session to eliminate unwanted hums, buzzes, noisy pedals, or other obnoxious sounds. Listen up-close to the amps where the mikes will be placed. This is frequently a problem with musicians who are used to playing live. A slight hum in an amp that might ordinarily go unnoticed in a live situation will make you crazy when it's miked and magnified in the studio. You may end up spending lots of costly time trying to fix a buzzing guitar string or having to call an instrument rental company to send over a new pedal.

Get your "sounds" established on the instruments during rehearsals. Do you want the bass and guitar to be mellow or biting? "Tune" the drums the way you want them for the song or the session. For the studio, producers may or may not prefer the snare to be deadened somewhat with pads of cloth and masking tape near the edge of the head. It depends on the style. They'll also deaden the kick drum as well by removing the front head and pushing a pillow against the inside of the head. This is, however, a matter of personal taste. Those creative decisions should be made as much as possible before the session. You may change your mind later when you hear them over the studio monitors, but at least you'll have a concept to start with. If you're using a drum machine, program it for each song before the session.

It's part of the engineer's job to "get a sound" on the instruments before recording, and you should be prepared to explain the concept you're going for. (Try bringing examples of the drum, bass, or other instrument sounds from CDs you like to show the engineer what you want.) Find out in the initial meeting with the engineer whether this procedure is included in "setup time" before the clock starts running on your session. Sometimes it is, but usually it's not. Know in advance how much setup time you're allowed. (It varies from one-half to one hour.) Make sure your musicians understand this and don't waste time setting up.

Everyone should have spare strings, drum heads, batteries, etc. I don't know a professional musician who hasn't learned that lesson on his first gig, but I thought I'd bring it up anyway, just in case.

Decide the order in which you want to do the songs. Is one song more difficult and another more fun? Find out how the musicians feel about it, assuming you have time to do them all. Be careful to figure realistically how much you can get done. The engineer can help you decide when you meet with him before the session.

Make sure the musicians know exactly where and when the session is, how long it'll take them to get there, and that they all have transportation. If you're using different musicians for different songs, try to schedule as accurately as possible so they don't have to wait more than a half hour.

Choosing the Songs

Whether producing your demos at home or in the studio, there are a few decisions that must be made before you begin. Your most obvious decision is choosing which of your songs to record.

All the songs you write don't have to be commercial, but the ones you present to publishers and producers must be. Many writers have difficulty determining the commerciality of their songs. How do you know?

You start by asking your friends, most of whom will be so knocked out that you wrote a song that they'll automatically love it (unless your friends are also writers). Tell them to be critical, and don't try to explain the song before playing it.

Can they sing the chorus back to you?

Can they tell you what the song is about?

Did they understand all the words? ∎

Do they remember any lyrics?

Can they name the title without your having told them?

Which of your songs do they like the best?

Which do they remember? Why?

Which ones can they sing the melodies to?

Those songs are your best shots.

Get as many opinions as possible. If the critique is negative, thank them and don't get defensive. Keep a cool head and know that they're not attacking you personally. The rewards of letting them help you grow and find success in your craft far outweigh the short-term ego damage. Treat criticism like clothing. Try it on and see if it fits.

What if you write a lot of different styles of songs and get good critical response on all of them? Your decision is then based on whether you have the desire or the potential to become a recording artist. You have the best chance at it if you have an easily identifiable voice and style. (See chapter fifteen, "Getting a Record Deal.") If that's your direction, limit your selections to the style you feel most at home with. If you love to sing rhythm and blues-styled tunes, but also write good country songs, stick with R&B for demos to show record companies. It's confusing to them to hear a lot of different styles from one artist and it presents a marketing problem: "Do we market this artist as country or R&B?" Will the people who buy your R&B-styled CD be turned off by hearing a country song on it? It's good, however, to show some variety within the style.

For publishers, it's different. Though they're happy if you specialize, it's a plus for you to be able to write well in many different styles. So it's OK to present them with your best songs in several different musical genres.

Make sure you have the final version of your song or you'll end up spending money to change it. My friend, Hank Linderman (producer, engineer, guitarist, songwriter, and author of *Hot Tips for the Home Recording Studio*), tells this story:

I was recording and coproducing a song with a songwriter (Erik Andrews) I had done several demos for. This particular song was a pop ballad, and this version was country, so we decided to hire a singer (Walker Igleheart) with a very clear tenor—perfect for the song. After finding the correct key (over the phone with the singer), we constructed a beautiful track, sent out a copy to Walker, and got ready for the vocal session. When that day came, Erik and I were prepared—the mic was set up, the headphone mix was ready, everyone had lyric sheets, pencils, and water. After two hours of work, we had a great vocal. Erik paid Walker, and that was that.

The next morning I got a call from Erik—he had rewritten the second verse. Could we set up another brief vocal session? After reaching an agreement with Walker for a reduced rate, we booked the session.

Once again, we were prepared. Once again, Walker nailed it. Erik paid Walker, and Walker left. Within minutes, Erik was shaking his head—he was concerned with the bridge. He said he'd get back to me.

Once again, after Erik made his changes, we brought Walker in for what hopefully was the final session. When Walker arrived, Erik apologized for the situation and thanked Walker for his good attitude throughout the process. Without skipping a beat, Walker replied, "Erik, we're gonna get this song right if it takes every last dime you've got!"

The final piece of the story is that though the country version was never cut, Erik and I re-recorded the song as an R&B ballad, and Erik got a cut.

Arrangements

We'd all like to believe that a great melody and lyric are all that's necessary to make people pay attention to a song. In some cases that may be true; but in most cases, the melody becomes more appealing in the context of the harmonies and countermelodies around it, and the meaning of a lyric can be conveyed even more strongly by framing it in the most effective way.

In recording demos or records, you can do several key things to make them clean and powerful.

One of the most common problems in demos is the conflict between vocal and instrumental tracks. Demos are uncomfortable to listen to if the vocal is buried under the instrument tracks. It sometimes seems that the writer or artist is so insecure about the lyric or vocal that it's intentionally obscured. Or whoever mixed the demo knew the lyric so well, there was no perspective left about whether anyone else could understand it. One of the functions of a producer is to provide the right perspective to the mix. If you don't have a producer, let the engineer do it or call in someone who doesn't know the song when you're close to the final mix. Ask him if he can understand the words. This is the reason so many records are mixed by a separate engineer.

Another good way to avoid this problem is to run a "vocal up" mix in addition to the full mix. You may also want a "no vocal" mix (handy for singing "live" to track), a "lead vocal only" mix (with reverb and effects still on), a "backing (background) vocal only" mix, and a "no lead vocal" mix (mixed as though there is no lead vocal). These mixes give you versatile options, particularly for TV use or for pitching to production music libraries (see page 319).

If you're recording a band, letting the whole band (or any one member) mix the tracks will cost you money in studio time because everyone will want his own instrument to be loudest.

The arrangement is also crucial in achieving clean vocals. Some important considerations are:

- **Melodic movement of instrumental parts relative to the vocal melody.** One of the things that makes demos sound busy or cluttered is the conflict of too many melody lines moving at the same time. Our natural tendency as listeners is to focus on the vocal melody. A harmony on that melody (instrumental or vocal) may enhance it, but a different single line melody on, say, an electric guitar at the same time may be distracting. A slow-moving chordal "pad" of strings or synthesizer will work fine because they don't command our attention like a single-line melody. Rhythm instruments and repeated short rhythm parts on the instruments aren't usually a problem because once your brain realizes that they'll keep repeating, you take them for granted. Your body responds automatically, but your mind focuses on the movement of the melody.

Cutting basic tracks or overdubs without being able to hear the vocal phrasing or melody can produce a busy, cluttered sound. That's why it's best to use at least a "scratch"

One of the most common problems in demos is the conflict between vocal and instrumental tracks.

vocal (to be removed later) during a "head" arrangement (not written previously) and during production of both rhythm tracks and overdubs. That way you can tell if your arrangement works and if any of the instrumental parts are competing with the vocal melody. If there are any problems, they can be fixed while the musicians are still there.

• **Linear placement of instrumental parts relative to the vocals.** The idea is to make a "window" for the vocals, to highlight them and to create expectation and tension. Drum "fills" perform this function going into a chorus, for instance. Instrumental "fills" should "bracket" the vocals, ending when the vocal phrase starts and starting when it ends. In the diagram below, the top line represents the vocal phrase (with accompaniment), the notes represent the ongoing pulse, and the bottom line represents an instrumental "fill" that picks up where the vocal stops and drops out where the vocal begins again. If, for instance, you have a two-bar, eight-beat phrase and the vocal phrase takes the first five beats, the fill might start as early as that fifth beat. Even if a vocal is holding a single note past that point, a fill will work because the melody line isn't moving.

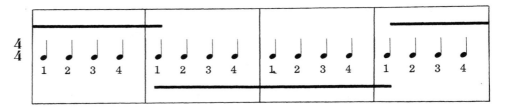

• **Vertical placement of the instrumental parts in the audio frequency range relative to the range of the vocals.** Again, rhythm instruments and parts aren't usually a problem, but with melody instruments, you can make cleaner tracks and highlight the vocals more by separating the ranges in which the instruments are played. Keyboards and guitar commonly get played in the same midrange area as the vocals. Experiment with moving the parts up or down an octave or two to keep that vocal "window" uncluttered. (See the diagram of instrument ranges.) Other ways to enhance that window are to mix the volume of the instruments lower in that range, to de-emphasize the EQ (equalization, treble/bass/midrange frequencies) in that range, and to pan the instruments (place them apart from each other in the left/right/center spectrum).

If you have a lot of tracks available, there's a tendency to think of ways to fill them. There are always ways to fill empty tracks, but "less is more." Try to have fewer parts and make each one sonically interesting.

The emotional impact of a vocal may well be *the* most important factor in the effectiveness of a demo.

Vocals

The emotional impact of a vocal may well be *the* most important factor in the effectiveness of a demo. Most writers who can sing automatically assume they should be the one to sing on it. Sometimes it's a simple question of economics. You feel it costs too much to hire another singer. Or it could be simple ego. You figure you know the song; you feel the emotions that went into it. It's part of you. Who could do it better? Even if you're

THE CRAFT AND BUSINESS OF SONGWRITING

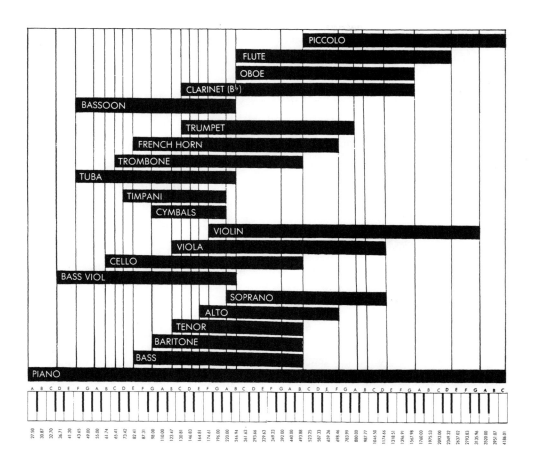

not a great singer, you feel you can at least do it adequately. You may be right. Then again, you may be wrong. You'll never know if the performance of a great singer could have made the difference between acceptance and rejection. Have faith that if the song has emotional impact, a very good singer (with your direction) should be able to put it across. So the rule of thumb is: *If you know anyone who can sing the song better than you, he or she should be singing on the demo.* Make sure that the singer is comfortable with the song's musical style. Classically or musical theater-trained singers may be out of their element doing country or hip-hop, for instance. Stylistically, it must be believable.

The singer should avoid improvising too much on the melody. Stylistic inflections are OK, but vocal gymnastics that tend to obscure the melody are not. What you get is a showcase for the performance and not for the song, making it difficult for an artist to hear what they could do with the song without re-creating your demo singer's performance. To highlight both, have the singer stick to the melody till the last chorus and maybe do a chorus repeat at the end in which the singer improvises to demonstrate some stylistic direction.

If your song could be sung by either sex, do you choose a male or female for the demo?

The consensus seems to be that it's much easier for a female artist to hear herself singing a male demoed song than for a male artist to imagine himself singing a song he hears from a female singer. Too bad those sexist attitudes still exist, but your odds are better with a male vocal in these cases. Obviously, if it's practical for you, do both male and female versions.

There are a wide range of fees for demo singers depending on how good and how fast they are, how well they sight read (or how quickly they learn), and how much in demand their services are. Again, if your funds are low, you might suggest barter. Share studio time and assist the singer with producing her own demo. Remind her that she can put your song on her own performance demo and that you'll be pitching your song, with her vocal, to producers. Many major artists have been discovered through their exposure on demo tapes. You may find a great cover group that needs originals to pitch to record companies. Your songs may be just what they need.

Intros

How you introduce your song on a demo depends on who your audience will be. In *song demos* for publishers or producers, you *must* keep intros short. Get to the vocal/lyric fast. They consider intros a waste of their listening time because they're only listening to the song. In *artist demos* to producers and record companies, that's not the case because you're creating a finished product and the creativity of that intro is part of what you're selling.

The length of an intro will vary from song to song. Generally, though, it should be kept under four bars for a ballad because it's more difficult to sustain interest at a slow tempo. An up-tempo dance song that involves a listener's body will generate more excitement simply by increasing the speed of his heartbeat. Consequently, those intros can be longer.

Short or long, an introduction creates an immediate first impression that sets up the listener's expectation for the whole song. It sets the mood, the emotional tone, and ultimately, on a record, becomes the "signature" that sets it apart from all other songs. When you go to a concert or hear a live recording, you'll hear the audience cheer in recognition of their favorite songs after only a few notes.

So, in producing your demo and writing the song, pay special attention to developing a unique intro. Some writers have a tendency to throw away that opportunity by "vamping" (repeating the same thing) for four or eight bars between two chords. To bore your audience before even getting into the song is deadly. I've seen publishers angrily push the "stop" button on their cassette or CD player after eight bars of boredom.

Here are some possibilities to explore:

1. Use a variation or mutation of either your verse or chorus melodic theme as an intro.

2. Work backwards from the first vocal melody to discover a melody or progression that might heighten the impact of the vocal entrance. A big dynamic buildup to a soft, quiet vocal entrance might work well or maybe a gradual build to a strong vocal entrance.

3. Use an interesting repeating instrumental riff that will be heard later under the verse or chorus (e.g., the Stones' "Satisfaction" or Stevie Wonder's "Superstition").

4. Explore your acoustic or synthesizer instruments for a unique sound or blend of sounds.

5. Introduce a new instrument or part every bar or two to thicken the texture and increase tension. This is fairly common, but if your instrumentation and melody are unique, it can be a very effective intro.

6. Develop a groove by starting with the simplest component and adding the other rhythmic parts as you go. Sometimes it's easier to develop the whole groove first with drums, bass, rhythm guitar, and other rhythm parts, then figure out later which of those components to start the intro with. If you've layered them onto separate channels of a recorder, experiment by punching various combinations in or out every bar or two. You might start with the bass line, then bring in the drums, then the rhythm guitar or vice versa, whatever works best. Try all the combinations you can think of.

7. Consider the possibility, particularly in a ballad, of having no instrumental intro at all, just starting with the lead vocal or an interesting background vocal part.

The bottom line is that, no matter how long it is or what devices you use to create interest, the intro must sustain a listener's attention. Some long ones do and some short ones don't. See page 259 for an intro exercise.

Consider the possibility, particularly in a ballad, of having no instrumental intro at all, just starting with the lead vocal or an interesting background vocal part.

Solos

Solos, like intros, are generally considered by publishers and producers to be a waste of their listening time in *song demos*. If they're judging the song, they don't care if Eric Clapton is playing on your demo. No solos. Just the song, please. Publishers and producers commonly hit the "stop" button on a demo because of interminably long and self-indulgent intros or just because they know they're going to hear a solo. Most people include long solos only because they don't have enough lyric and want to fill the space or some friends are helping with the demo and get to show off with a solo as a compensation for their time. Don't do it! It doesn't help you.

That's not to say that a short solo of a couple of bars that serves a definite function as a transition or a dramatic tension-builder can't be very effective in a song demo. Just don't use a whole verse or chorus worth.

If you're cutting masters or *artist demos* to sell a self-contained band to a producer or record company, the above does *not* apply. They *need* to hear the talents of the group, but that long guitar solo better be a killer!

Endings

With endings you have two choices: Work out an ending or fade. The fade is usually done to allow you to keep grooving on an exciting riff or repetitive vocal phrase or "the hook," without bringing down the energy level and intensity of the music. On a fade, you only bring down the actual volume. You leave the illusion that the band is just going on down the road and even though, after a while, you can't hear them, you know they're still groovin'. A fade works if you have something great to go out on that feels like it has a natural momentum. Commercially speaking, it's always a good idea for the "hook," or chorus, or whatever you want an audience to remember to be the last thing they hear. With a fade you also give DJs a chance to talk over the ending, which excites them as much as talking over the intro (even though it doesn't necessarily excite us). It also lets them do their own fade, which may be considerably shorter than yours. Keep in mind that unless you're playing a dance gig, long, repetitive fades tend to get tedious, so the shorter the better. This is particularly true for demos, presentations to record companies, and showcases.

As for working out endings, it all depends on the song. The only thing I can say is: Please see this as an opportunity to show your originality. I'll grant you that there are times when the best ending for the song is one that has already been well worn. Just try to give it the care you give the rest of your song.

Demo Production Services

If you've decided that all you want to do is write songs and producing your own demos is way too much of a hassle, never fear! Demo production services have sprung up into an industry of their own. These services advertise in music trade magazines including *Music Connection, Billboard, American Songwriter, Performing Songwriter*, etc., and the newsletters of songwriters' organizations all over the country. Also, you can also find their Web sites on the Internet where you can immediately hear samples of their work. (Search under "song demo.") Here are some guidelines for dealing with them.

• Only deal with demo production services if you can check out their product ahead of time. Some will send you a free tape or CD sample of their work; others may charge a nominal fee, but it's worth it to know what you're getting into.

• Only deal with those who will tell you exactly what you'll get for your money. They should send you a rate sheet that gives you a choice of options from guitar/vocal to full-scale productions with strings, horn sections, and so forth. Extra rates for lead sheet preparation, copies, and other services should be spelled out. In other words, no surprises. Some companies, on their demo tapes or CDs, will give you a choice of singers.

• Don't deal with companies who offer to compose music to your lyrics for a fee or to publish your song for a fee. By the rules of BMI and ASCAP, they are not allowed to be members of those organizations. Therefore, if by some remote chance they actually got airplay on your song, you'd never be able to get paid for it. (See "Avoiding the Songsharks," page 155.) You can always call or write your nearest BMI or ASCAP office to check them out or go online to www.BMI.com or www.ASCAP.com and search their publisher databases.

Occasionally there is some confusion among songwriters who think that if they can't write musical notation, they're not "writing" music. If you "think up," "make up," or "compose" a melody that you can sing into a tape recorder, you have "written" the music.

As a JPFolks.com mentor, I addressed the following question from a member. JPFolks .com is an international songwriters organization that I highly recommend.

Q. If I have written a song, words, and music and I ask someone to play it for me for a demo and if they create an intro and a lead guitar break, do they own the music to the intro and the break? I have tried to explain to this person that that's what's called "arranging," but he insists that he "owns" the music to the intro because it's like a separate song (although it wasn't written until he created it for my song). How do I get it across to this guy that it's part of the "arrangement" of the song? He's a great entertainer and he's not a stupid guy, but we have argued about this and he cannot seem to understand that he doesn't own any part of the song. Can you clear up this confusion once and for all?

A. This is a common situation that I've dealt with many times as a consultant. If you have written both lyrics and music and go to a demo producer/arranger for their services, that arrangement IS their service and they deserve to be paid for it. I don't know any legitimate demo production service that asks for writer credit. If they do, they'll soon be out of business. If you hire a guitar player to play on your session, regardless of what they play, they have no ownership of the song. However, if you say ahead of time, "I want you to help me with this melody and I'll share writers' credit with you," that's a different story, of course. It's all about agreement making/agreement keeping. If this is his philosophy, he should have told you up front so you would have had a choice to reject working with him. To change what is a customary practice in the industry (that demo producers, arrangers, musicians don't share song ownership) *after the fact* is a very bad business practice.

It has traditionally been the policy that if you write words and music, you've written the song. That's no longer necessarily true, however. There are those whose specialty is dance music, hip-hop, and R&B in particular, who are experts at creating grooves. When you write with these people, even though they didn't write any actual melody or lyric, they usually receive credit. Lest this get too confusing (since part of the arrangement IS creating grooves), it usually involves creating the groove first, then writing the melody and lyric over it. It's a common way for hip-hop writers to create a song/record. The bottom line, however, is that this agreement is made before you write the song.

Let me clarify one more thing. This time it may be on your guitar player's behalf. Musicians and singers on your demo DO have ownership/copyright interest in their *performance* (though not the song itself). When they play or sing on a demo, there is an understanding that it is only to be used for "demonstration" purposes. Consequently, it only becomes a problem when you decide to use it as a master to be sold to consumers or used in a TV show or film in which you are paid for both the use of the song (synchronization fee) and use of the master recording (master use fee).

If you "think up," "make up," or "compose" a melody that you can sing into a tape recorder, you have "written" the music.

Legally, since it is something that directly creates income for you, you now owe those musicians and singers part of the income you receive (unless they waive that right) from their performances. That's why it's always a good idea to have the musicians/singers sign an agreement that determines how (or if) you'll pay them in the event that you receive income from your demo.

For a copy of a demo-musician release agreement, go to www.johnbraheny.com.

Some demo production companies offer special services like having lead sheets made for you. A lead sheet looks like printed sheet music, but contains only the melody and lyrics. (Translating your melody into music notation is called doing a "takedown.") It's important to note, however, that lead sheets are *rarely* used to pitch songs to anyone.

Takedown or a Nashville Number System chart is usually included in the demo cost because they may need to do it anyway in order to get a roadmap from which to build the arrangement. Arrangement, too, is usually included in the overall cost of the demo.

Most demo services are mail-order businesses, though many will let you be on the premises, and some will even let you do your own vocals. Most services welcome any creative input you have about how you would like your demo to sound. They thrive on repeat business and pride themselves on giving you what you want. If you like some sound you've heard (i.e., on a record) and are looking for something like it, send it with your song and it will help them zero in on your needs.

Tape/CD Copies

When you've recorded a demo you're happy with and you're ready to make copies to send out to the pros, be professional yourself. Today's music industry operates mostly on cassettes and CDs. CDs are cheaper to mail and easier to handle. Most industry people have CD or cassette players in their cars where they can listen relatively uninterrupted.

Don't buy cheap, low-quality tape. It's a bad way to cut corners because it's noisy, subject to dropouts (places on the tape where you'll lose the sound), and may subliminally turn people off. Save money instead by teaming up with other writers and buying high-quality bulk-loaded cassettes and boxes in volume. Find ads for bulk tape in music magazines and trade papers. Write to them for a catalogue and samples. Most companies who deal in bulk-ordered tapes can also custom wind tapes to any length. Buy ten-, twenty- or thirty-minute lengths. Or buy some of each depending on the number of songs you'll be putting on each tape. Remember that a thirty-minute tape has fifteen minutes per side, usually enough for four songs. Put all your songs on one side. Know that you won't get most of your tapes back, so consider it an expense you'll have to "eat."

Also, if you're burning CDs, make sure you get good quality CDs. There is a lot of difference from brand to brand and price to price. Ask for a recommendation from the studio.

Check your local phone book for tape duplicating services if you don't have a high-quality copying setup at home. Using studio time to make copies (except for one master cassette or CD from which you can copy) can be very expensive. Check with the studio to find out if they have a copying service at lower than their regular studio rates.

Presenting Your Demo

I think it's always enlightening to get a scenario of what happens behind the scenes in the office of a person who listens to demos. Here's a sample from my own experience and that of friends who torture their brains and eardrums in the all-too-often futile search for that killer song or sound.

You should know that if 5 percent of the songs are in the ballpark, they're doing very well. They engage in this masochism because they know that when they find that one-in-a-thousand song that brings tears to their eyes and makes the hair stand up on the back of their necks, they'll forget about all the bad ones they just listened to. The rejects aren't even all bad. Some have lots of imagination and no craft and some have lots of craft but little originality. The right combination of ingredients is rare, but they know it's there somewhere. They're anxious to find it as soon as possible. Some listen in the order they receive the tapes/CDs. Most others don't. What they do is look for the most likely candidates.

First, they look for the names of writers they already know are good. That's where the odds are best. Next, they listen to tapes referred to them by other industry people whose tastes (or power) they respect. Next, when faced with a stack of anonymous tapes, they look for a package that is professional, neat, and imaginative. They hope the songs will show those same qualities. The odds still aren't great, but they're several points above the lowest. The least-likely candidates are the ones that look like the sender doesn't care. The lyric sheets, if any, are scribbled illegibly on the back of a menu and the cover letter with no return address says, "I no thees songs wood bee grate for Garth. Pleez sen them to him." What are the odds that they're going to find a really "grate" lyric here? It's not about bad spelling, but about not caring enough to find someone (who can use a "spell-checker") to check the spelling. It's easy to get the impression that this person doesn't care enough to find out how to write a good song (or a good letter, for that matter).

Though the above scenario is most common, don't get the idea that *all* pros listen in the same way. I've heard stories from A&R reps who were actually intrigued enough by that funky-looking package to open it first and who have actually found something worthwhile. If you want to play the game with the odds in your favor, however, you'll pay attention to these guidelines.

Remember: With the advent of reasonably priced CD burners and CD players in the car, this medium has lots of advantages. They're light, easy to mail, and more convenient to listen to. Ask before you send, but when in doubt, send cassette tape. Audio files, however, are the *most* convenient. (See no. 3 below.) Don't send DAT tapes unless specifically requested.

The following checklist will maximize your chances of getting heard and respect the listener's time.

1. **Never send more than three songs unless specifically requested** otherwise. Demo listeners like to watch the "in" pile diminish and the "out" pile grow as quickly as possible. If the listener has a limited time to listen, which is usually the case, the tendency is to listen to a tape/CD they know they can complete. So if you send a demo with ten songs on it and someone else's demo has one song, you can bet that the "out" pile will grow quickly with one-song demos. There's also the psychology that implies, "I've sent you *the* song you need!" This is particularly true in pitching songs to producers for a *specific* artist. Along those same lines, most people resent getting tapes/CDs with twenty songs and a letter that says, "I know you'll like at least one of these, so just pick out what you want." They want *you* to do that and send them three songs or less—songs you totally believe in. If you're not far enough along to be able to decide, you're not ready. When sending CDs with more than three songs, *highlight three* you want the listener to focus on first and include the *numbers* of the cuts in your cover letter and lyric sheets (so they have a reference while the CD is on their player and they can't see the label). If they like those, they'll listen to the others. And please remove the shrink wrap!

2. **Place your best and most commercial song first.** If you have a strong up-tempo song, start with that. If they don't like the first one, it may be the only shot you get. If you're sending a cassette, put all the songs on the same side and put the label only on the "play" side. TIP: Put a couple more songs on the other side of a cassette, but *don't list them*. If you get a call that they'd like to hear more, tell them to turn the tape over.

3. **Never send your original master tape or CD.** You will never see it again.

4. **Always cue your tape to the beginning of the first song.** You don't want the person to start listening in a bad mood because you just wasted his time making him rewind your tape. When you make your copies, leave four seconds between songs. Most cassette decks have an automatic search feature, which finds the silence between songs, stops the fast-forward, and automatically starts playing the next song. Obviously, this isn't a problem with CDs. If your CD contains more than the first four you want heard, clearly mark on the on the CD *and* printed insert which ones you want them to hear.

5. **Send a neatly typed or printed lyric sheet.** Letterhead is impressive. It says "This is my business and I take it seriously." Some don't like to look at lyrics while they listen, but most do. It's a time saver to be able to see it all at once and to see the structure of the song graphically laid out on the page. Lead sheets (with melody and lyric together) are *not* sent out with demos. They're good to have at the point where a producer wants to record your song and you want to be sure he/she has the correct melody. (Since the current copyright law permits tapes or CDs to be sent for copyright registration, the

importance of lead sheets has diminished.) Lead sheets are bulky to mail, it's too difficult to follow the lyric and visualize the song's form, and many industry pros don't read music anyway. It also pegs you as a songwriter over fifty who has no experience in submitting demos, since this practice went out of style about twenty-five years ago.

When you type your lyric sheet, separate the sections of the songs with a space and label each one (verse, chorus, bridge, etc.) at the upper left side of the section. Do not type your lyrics in prose fashion. Lay them out with the rhymes at the ends of the lines so the structure and rhyme schemes of the song can be seen immediately.

6. **Make sure there's a copyright notice** (© 2001 I.B. Cool, All Rights Reserved) on the bottom of the first page of the lyric sheet and on the tape or CD label. Technically, this isn't necessary, but it alerts everyone that your song is protected, whether it's registered or not. (See "The Copyright Notice," and "Copyright Registration," chapter eight.)

7. **Cover letters should be short and to the point.** Let the music speak for itself and avoid hype. A professional presentation will do more to impress someone than "I know these are hit songs because they're better than anything I've ever heard on the radio," or "I just know that we can both make a lot of money if you'll publish these songs." Avoid the temptation to tell your life story, and don't explain how you have a terminal disease, you're the sole support of your ten children and if these songs don't get recorded they'll all be homeless or worse. In fact, don't plead, apologize, or show any hint of desperation. It only gives the message that you have no confidence in the ability of the songs to stand on their own.

Here's what should be in your cover letter:

a. It should be addressed to a specific person in the company.

b. It should state your purpose in sending the demo. Are you looking for a publisher, a producer, a record deal for you as an artist? Do you want the listener to pay special attention to your production, your singing, your band, or just the song? Is it targeted for a specific artist?

c. List any significant professional credits that apply to the purpose of your submission. If you want your song published, list other published or recorded songs, contests won, etc. If you're a performer submitting an artist demo, resist the temptation to grab at weak credits: "I played at the same club that (famous star) played." Tell them what drives you, what inspires you. Keep it short. List real sales figures. Don't lie.

d. Include any casting ideas you might have if you're pitching to other artists.

e. Ask for feedback if you want it. Odds are you won't get it, but give it a shot.

f. List the songs enclosed and writers' names in the order they appear on the tape/CD. (Lyric sheets should also be enclosed in the same order the songs appear on the demo.)

g. Thank them for their time and attention.

h. Include your address, phone number(s), Web site, and e-mail address (if you have them).

8. **Send a self-addressed stamped envelope (SASE)** if you want your tape or CD back. There are two schools of thought about this. On the pro SASE side, if you don't want to

lose all those tapes, you can't expect to get them back without it. There's another school of thought, though, that if you say you want it back, you're assuming they won't like it. There's no guarantee that you'll get them back even if you do send an SASE, in which case you're gambling even more money. Worse could happen than letting your tape or CD sit around a producer's office. Your decision may depend on how many tapes/CDs you can afford to lose.

9. **Put your name, address, and phone number on the tape or CD box,** and on every lyric sheet. It seems like such common sense. In fact it would be embarrassing even to suggest that you might forget to do it, but I see it happen constantly. The problem on this end is that, between listening sessions at the office, the car, and home, it's so easy to separate the tape from the box or lyric sheet. Once they've gone to the trouble to find your hit song, not finding *you* is a fate they don't deserve.

10. **Be sure you have adequate postage.** Also, don't send your tape in an ordinary stationery envelope. It's risky because rough postal handling could force the edge of the tape box through the envelope. Use a special envelope with an insulated lining. Some people also prefer the soft "bubble" tape box because it doesn't have sharp edges and it's lighter to mail. CDs have an obvious advantage as there are very lightweight sleeves available for them.

The main thing to remember is to make your demo submission as easy as possible to deal with.

Using the Internet: Your Demo as Audio File

An increasingly popular strategy is sending your demo as an audio file. It's rare these days that a record company, producer, or manager doesn't have a high-speed Internet access line. Obviously, many of the above suggestions don't apply to sound files.

Giant Records A&R Executive, Craig Coburn, in a *Music Connection* magazine interview, said:

In the future, I would love to see people soliciting the record labels—whether it's artists, managers, or lawyers—using the Internet. I'd like them to send me a letter asking me to check out their Web site rather than sending me the music.

We're not getting that many electronic submissions yet and I'd like to. When I'm talking to people, I encourage them to send MP3's. The quality of MP3 is not exactly up to the quality of a CD, but it's close enough for an A&R person to hear the music and to know if it's something that excites us or not.

The most popular formats are MP3 and RealAudio. The fidelity is not quite CD quality but still adequate to show them what you do. There are a couple different procedures for this:

1. Send an e-mail with the audio file attached. Follow the suggestions listed above for cover letter. Include phone number(s). Also include your Web site address so they can click it and go directly to it. When they get to your site, they'll hopefully find additional bio material, photos, and lyrics.

2. Just send them an e-mail intriguing enough to get them to go to your site and hear your music there.

Indie marketing consultant Tim Sweeney (coauthor of *The Complete Guide to Internet Promotion for Musicians, Artists, & Songwriters*) suggests that, because of the limited amount of time someone may want to spend at any site and their various online access speeds, it's important to help them decide quickly which of your songs may be of most interest to them. You can help by providing a short description like the one below provided on the site of Franklin Spicer and Valerie Ford's Pegasus Project, a New World Music (World Beat, Smooth Jazz, New Age) group.

ONE PEOPLE

The first song Franklin ever heard from Val was a reggae tune she had recorded called "One People." He really liked the positive message and the infectious chorus. Franklin talked her into doing a rewrite and making it a Pegasus Project tune. They wanted to share a positive message of how we all are part of one global family. This song was shaped from a number of African musical influences, including the Tuku style. The huge chorus backup vocals were done in two days of recording using seven different singers.

Note that the description includes information on the style, what it's about, why it was written, and how it was recorded. Their site also includes lyrics to all the songs.

Your demo will introduce you to the eyes and ears of many music industry professionals. Take this introduction very seriously. It's your job interview. It should look good, have something important to say, and say it well. There are a lot of other applicants for the job. The pros are looking for the best. Be it!

EXERCISE

When you listen to the radio, check out the intros. Ask yourself if they keep you interested and note how they are done.

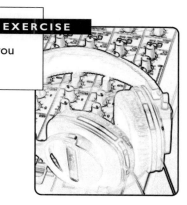

Marketing Yourself and Your Songs

Where Do You Start?

Whether your sole goal is to be a songwriter or whether you also have aspirations to be a performer, one of the most common and frustrating problems for a novice is not knowing where to start. Do you approach publishers first or go right to the record companies? Should you find an independent producer or look for a manager?

The first answer you'll get from anyone is "It all depends." No single approach works the same for everyone and that one step-by-step formula you want so badly just doesn't exist. In this section I'll cover some of the assessments you'll need to make of your own personal situation to help you sort out a direction. The best way to find your path is to get a realistic evaluation of your chances through some professional feedback.

Do you want your songs to be and are they suitable to be performed by other artists? You may have developed a songwriting style that's too lyrically personal or musically unique to interest artists in recording your songs. However, that uniqueness can be a valuable thing if you also perform your own songs. Some of the most exciting artists write so uniquely that it's difficult for another artist to record their songs without sounding like imitators.

The next consideration is to assess your potential as an artist. Do you want to perform your own songs? Do you have the talent record companies require? Do you have a unique vocal identity? Bob Dylan isn't a great singer, but you always know who he is when you hear him. Randy Travis, Reba McEntire, Macy Gray, and Matchbox Twenty all have strong vocal identities and very distinctive styles.

Don't kid yourself about whether you have those qualities. Get specific feedback about it. If you don't, your odds for becoming a performer are poor, unless you can create a unique group sound or concept or have fantastic commercial songs. In other words, to be a successful artist, you need to provide as many ways as possible for the audience to identify and remember you.

Some people may tell you that you don't have artist potential and others may tell you that your songs aren't "coverable." They may be right, but don't let one or two different people make that assessment for you.

There are many different publishers with a variety of tastes. Publishers generally want songs that offer a variety of possibilities for recording. If there's only one artist your song appears appropriate for and they fail to get the artist to cut it, they may have a dead song on their hands. Try your songs out on several publishers and others who will give you honest, critical feedback about your songs' overall potential.

If you're an intelligent, perceptive writer who's willing to spend some time on your craft, you can learn to write more coverable songs without sacrificing the factors that make you unique.

The following are some of the potential routes you can take, depending on your own special combination of talents and aspirations. They are, of course, generalizations. Your situation may fall in the cracks somewhere, but it should give you a rough idea.

Publisher

If you have coverable songs but don't quite fill the bill as an artist, finding a good publisher who will shop your songs to artists may be the best approach. If you want to be your own publisher and contact producers and artists yourself, that's another option.

If the feedback you get is that you're both a topnotch singer and writer, find a publisher who is also willing to put up money to record and shop masters of you as an artist. Many publishers have production companies through which they'll finance masters and shop them to record labels. These are called "development deals." If they get you a deal and they own half of the publishing rights to your songs (the standard deal) in the bargain, it's gravy for them. In other words, they don't need to go out and try to get other artists to record the songs (though they often do after you record them).

If you approach publishers first, you will certainly bargain away a part (if you have the clout) if not all of your publishing rights. But in exchange you'll get: (1) someone working very hard on your career (since they have a vested interest), (2) a company who can possibly get you a record deal, and (3) someone who can pitch your songs to other artists. (See "Publishing," chapter ten.)

Record Company

If publishers aren't exactly shoving contracts in your face when they hear your songs, but most people feel you've got what it takes to be an artist, or if your songs work well for your unique style, but aren't the kinds of songs publishers think they can place, go for the record companies first.

If your own songs aren't strong enough or you don't have enough potential hit singles to approach a record company, look for great songs from other writers. Though record companies would prefer to sign a totally self-contained artist, the next best thing is that you or your producer know how to pick the right songs. The bottom line is that, one way or another, you have to have material that's considered hit potential by the company. They want to at least feel confident that there's a radio format receptive to the artist's material. (See "Getting a Record Deal," chapter fifteen.)

One of the advantages of being signed directly to a major record label is that you stand a better chance of keeping your own publishing rights, which, if you become successful, could amount to a considerable income. If you want to make a publishing deal later, you're in a great negotiating position if you already have a record deal, particularly if you've had hits as an artist. Some labels, however, will want to acquire all or part of the publishing rights for their affiliated publishing companies. Small, independent labels will be especially interested in your publishing. If the company operates on a narrow profit margin, the publishing royalties from the songs could make it a better gamble for them. But don't give anything up unless you're satisfied with what you're getting for it.

| Producer

For a writer/artist, finding an independent producer is another option. (There's no point in doing this if you're solely a writer unless you're collaborating with a writer who *is* an artist.) If the producer is putting up the financial backing for demo/masters or an album, he may want half the publishing. It's not uncommon, but restrict it to the songs he records within a time period (six to eighteen months after completion of the masters). If he fails to secure an acceptable record deal, all rights should revert back to you. The producer will still own the masters (if he paid for them) and will recoup his money if you get a deal later if the record company wants to use those masters. If he does get you a deal, you're signed to his production company with that producer. If the producer is respected by the record company and dedicated to your career, he can work to your advantage. If not, it can hurt your career because, if you're signed to the production company rather than directly to the label, the label does not have an option to get you another producer without buying out your contract.

Be careful about signing with a producer who has a contract to deliver a certain amount of product annually to a particular label. It's not necessarily a bad deal, but if that producer is guaranteed a certain amount of money per album, his temptation is to record the album as cheaply as possible, put the "override" in his pocket, go on to the next act, and neglect to follow up on your project at the label. If you don't have strong management and enthusiasm for your product at the label to act as a check and balance in that situation, you're at a severe disadvantage. At a major label you may be competing with more than one hundred other acts for optimum release dates when the company isn't focusing all its publicity and promotion attention on its superstar acts. If that producer/label team doesn't seem to be looking after your best interests, you may be better off trying to get out of your deal so you can pursue another one. Your attorney will include "performance" clauses that nullify your contract if certain sales figures or other terms aren't met and can protect you from some of these problems.

I recommend reading Moses Avalon's book, *Confessions of a Record Producer: How to*

Survive the Scams and Shams of the Music Business. He runs down a litany of cautions in all these deals. Or visit his Web site at www.mosesavalon.com.

| Manager

If you don't have very good artist potential and aren't already a very successful writer or writer/producer, it doesn't make much sense to look for management. You can pay an attorney a fee to negotiate your deals rather than pay a manager 15 percent to 20 percent of your income. As in the case of producers, if you're solely a writer, you should approach a manager only if you wish to pitch songs to his artists.

At what point a manager should become involved in an artist's or writer/artist's career is subject to debate. A manager might tell you it's very important that your career be guided correctly from the start. They're right: It's important for an artist to have someone to help make career decisions and to coordinate publicity campaigns and club bookings, but does it take a manager to do that? You can do a lot of it yourself. Also, some very good industry attorneys will perform the management functions of shopping your tapes to labels, negotiating deals, and offering career advice. They may not always be right, but no one else is either.

At what point a manager should become involved in an artist's or writer/ artist's career is subject to debate.

If you don't already have a manager, many record company A&R and artist development departments, after you're signed, perform some management functions for you such as securing booking agencies and coordinating promotional appearances and will also help you find a manager.

It's usually difficult to get a good manager when you're starting, since most of them only want to get involved with artists who already have record deals or who are touring extensively. Remember that managers get paid a percentage of what *you* get paid and if you're not making money and they have to help finance your career until you get to that point, there is a natural reluctance to get involved. If you can find one who's knowledgeable, resourceful, aggressive, honest, and is willing to gamble with you, grab him now, because he won't be available for long.

It frequently happens that a friend of the artist with a minimum of music business experience and an abundance of faith takes on management duties. I've seen some of these situations work out very well, particularly if the manager is aggressive about learning the business. However it does happen that the artist or manager realizes that the latter's lack of expertise and industry clout is holding back the artist's career. A viable option at that point is to look for a comanagement deal with a major management firm. The novice manager obtains the power of the established firm and a great opportunity to learn and establish contacts. The major company benefits by having someone who can deal with details and the artist's needs on a daily basis.

"Where to start," as you can see, involves a lot of variables, and it's important to know what they are before getting started. Still, it's a good idea to test the water in all directions before committing to a course of action. Professional feedback is what you'll need to make a good decision.

Writers, Writer/Artists, and Writer/Producers in the Marketplace

You'll often hear songs on the radio that you feel are below your standards and wonder how they got there. You feel your own songs should surely have a chance. You may be right, but you may also be misunderstanding a basic fact of life. You're judging your standards as a writer against industry standards of making a record. (See "A Song Is Not a Record," chapter three.)

Some writer/artists have high standards; some don't. But they all have access to "the record-making machinery" that allows them to put their visions on vinyl and use production and arrangement to compensate for the dynamic factors that writers who aren't artists need to build into their songs. Usually, it's not a question of songwriting standards of excellence, but about the greater degree of creative latitude available to writer/artists and writer/producers who have a much larger canvas and more colors and brushes with which they can paint that final picture. In other words, they have arrangement, sound, and production techniques as further ingredients to help them make an appealing product.

An example that comes to mind is writer/producer Jim Steinman's "Total Eclipse of the Heart," a hit by Bonnie Tyler in the eighties and again by Nicky French in the nineties. The song took an uncommon amount of time to get to the chorus, yet Steinman heightened tension with that long verse while providing the necessary repetition of "Turn around bright eyes" by the background vocals.

This is a prime example of a song that publishers would have had a hard time accepting because of its unorthodox form. They'd sign Steinman in a minute as a writer/producer because of his versatile talent, but if a songwriter who was not an artist or producer brought in the song in a bare form, they'd be hard-pressed to think of an artist who'd record it, despite the wonderfully original title/concept. They'd undoubtedly ask for a rewrite to "get to the hook faster" (which may also have worked fine). As a producer, Steinman didn't have to change it, giving himself an opportunity to be innovative. He continued his success in the same unorthodox way as a writer/producer with several monster Meat Loaf hits.

More and more writers are opening up new creative fields by learning to produce and arrange, finding a singer (if not themselves) as a vehicle, and producing masters or demos that indicate the production possibilities strongly enough to stretch the forms and show them to be "workable." If you're a writer who doesn't have production and arrangement skills, you face the challenge of finding creative ways to express your ideas on a more limited canvas. You need, to a greater extent, to work within established song forms (and variations) and to use your creativity to develop well-crafted lyric concepts and exciting, memorable melodies. Whether or not you ever develop arranging or production skills, you'll have the confidence that you can write a great song.

Researching the Music Industry

If you were making a cross-country drive on a tight timetable and weren't sure about how to get to your destination, would you just start driving in the general direction and hope everything would work out somehow? No way! You'd be studying maps trying to find the best roads, figuring out when and where you'd be sleeping, and researching any other information that would make your trip as fast, pleasant, and efficient as possible. (You might even stop to ask somebody for directions.) But it's surprising how many songwriters will make a blind trip into the music industry and spend years just wandering around and going nowhere. They seem to feel that crafting and marketing their songs is one of the few professions in the world that they don't have to know anything about to do successfully. Since you're reading this book, I know you understand the need to learn a lot more about this fascinating and ever-changing business and learn how to improve your odds of success.

It's quite common to hear industry pros say that when they've had an "open door" policy regarding unsolicited material, over 95 percent of the songs they received were not even "in the ballpark" for the artist. It was clear that those writers didn't even bother to listen to the artist or find out the special needs or strengths of the company soliciting the songs. The fact is that there are many ways to research the information and learn about the industry that will put you in that remaining 5 percent.

| Music Trade Magazines

One of the things a serious songwriter should do is read the music trade magazines. They are a music industry education. If you can't afford to subscribe and don't have an Internet connection, you can go to the public library every week and read them. (Libraries also have Internet access.) If they don't have them, gather a group of others to formally petition the library to subscribe. They may not be getting the music trades because they don't think anyone is interested. Most are weekly magazines and they're very expensive ($250 to $300 per year), but if you feel you're ready to begin your assault on the industry, they're one of your best investments. Some music trade magazines follow:

Billboard www.billboard.com

Gavin Online www.gavin.com

Hits www.hitsdailydouble.com   Charts not as strong as above but articles, gossip, opinion, and analysis with attitude!

Radio and Records www.rronline.com

Music Connection www.musicconnection.com   No charts but great industry interviews and features.

Music Row www.musicrow.com is dedicated to the Nashville music industry. If you write country, don't be without it. Monthly and weekly editions.

Country Music Today www.country.com/countrymusictoday/

One of the most valuable features of the "trades" is the charts. *Billboard* is the most valuable to writers because their pop, country, and R&B/hip-hop "singles" charts list the producer, writer, label and release number, distributing label, publisher, licensee (BMI, ASCAP, SESAC), and sheet music supplier. Though the other singles, album, airplay, and sales charts don't list writers and producers, they are still a valuable barometer of the popularity of artists, records, and record companies.

Album charts feature: Blues, Contemporary Christian, Gospel, Heatseekers (emerging artists), Independent, Internet (sales report), Kid Audio (children's CDs), The Billboard Latin 50, Pop Catalog (albums more than two years old that have fallen below no. 100 on the album 200 chart, and reissues), R&B/hip-hop, Reggae, World Music, Country, Inspirational (including all styles of Christian music), Classical, Classical Crossover, New Age, Jazz Latin, Hits of the World, Album Rock Tracks (i.e., which cuts from rock albums are getting the most airplay), Modern Rock Tracks, Jazz, Jazz/Contemporary.

Note that the charts of the smaller genres of music don't appear every week.

Singles Charts feature: The Billboard Hot Hundred (the granddaddy of them all), Adult Contemporary (AC), Adult Top 40, Country, Dance/Club Play, Dance/Maxi-Singles, Hot Latin Tracks, R&B/hip-hop, Rap, Rock/Mainstream Rock Tracks, Rock/Modern Rock Tracks, Top 40 Tracks. ("Tracks" refer to album cuts.)

They also feature Top Video Sales and Rentals.

Charts are tabulated with SoundScan, which reads the bar codes on every album sold via reporting retail stores and online retailers, and airplay is monitored with BDS (Broadcast Data Systems) www.bdsonline.com.

So, what can you learn from all that?

First of all, you can get an idea about trends, providing that you're also listening to a lot of radio and are familiar with the songs on the charts. If you have Internet access, you can also play short clips of the songs on CDNow and other online sales sites. You'll see what artists and songs are most popular in their respective styles and which artists and songs cross over between two or more charts. There are also editorial sections relating to those styles, providing analysis and news about artists, labels, and trends. There is more information today on the music industry, music genres, and artists only a click away than at any other time in history.

Veteran record company executive Russ Regan says he studies the charts for the "gaps." If he sees there are a lot of up-tempo dance tunes crowding the charts, he knows it's time for a great ballad, or vice versa. Also, once the public has bought and feels at home with a "sound," when the group who created it drops out for a while, it may be a good time to release a similar sound. Though the time lapse between your writing a song and its being recorded and released probably wouldn't allow you to take advantage of the chart information the way Russ Regan could, it gives you some idea of the way it's used in the business.

There are some other practical applications of that information. The listing of the writers' names can tell you if the writer is also the producer or artist. If that's the case, the percentages are against your being able to place a song with him. That, of course, isn't cut and dried. Many writer/artists are open to outside tunes, but your songs would have to be better than those written by the artist or artist/producer. You're also likely to be asked to give up your publishing interest in the song.

The best bets for song placement are, obviously, with artists who consistently show up on the charts with "outside" material. You can locate the numbers or e-mail addresses of the artist's producers or managers by calling the A&R or artist relations department of the listed record company. Then you can pitch your songs to the artist's producers and managers. Though those people may not be open to unsolicited material, your knowledge of their work and ability to discuss it intelligently may get you through otherwise closed doors. It shows them that you're paying attention and you're serious enough to do the research. Consequently, they may guess that you're in that 5 percent that's worth listening to. (See "Casting," chapter eleven.)

The international music market is so important now that it's always enlightening to check out the international charts for the types of English language songs that are popular in other countries. If you're publishing your own songs and write in a style that is popular in certain countries, you'll know to concentrate on those countries when you look for a foreign subpublisher. (See "Foreign Subpublishing," chapter eleven.)

If you are an artist or group looking for a producer, you can look at the charts for a group that is produced the way you would like to hear yourself and find the listed producer. Since he/she has an artist on the charts, it is reasonable to assume that they have pretty good leverage with a label or labels. It's good to hit these producers when they're hot, though you have to realize the record companies are also trying to get them to produce their acts and producing an unknown act (like yours) may not be a priority. (But if there's enough money behind you, it changes everything.)

If you're actively trying to get something going, either as a writer or a recording artist, it's important to know the names and meet the people in the business. If you're on the outside looking in and you're not hanging out at any of the industry watering holes, it gets very difficult to keep track of who's who, who's what, and where these people are. It's complicated by a musical chairs game unequaled in any other business, except maybe advertising. In some cases, people didn't know they'd been fired until they read it in the trades. So, *Billboard* calls its column "Executive Turntable," *Music Connection*'s column is called "Signing and Assignments," where you can see where your favorite A&R person, publisher, etc., is working this month. Another great resource is the *Music Business Registry*. (See "Other Sources," in this chapter.) Another way to track industry pros is to just go to the search engine, Google.com (my personal favorite), and search under the person's name. If there's been an article written about them somewhere online, it'll show up.

You may have run into an A&R person who liked your act or your songs but couldn't get anything going for you at her previous label. You see in the "Executive Turntable" that she's at a new company now, so it's worth another shot. In a new company she may have more respect, more power, and a renewed motivation to prove herself. Yours might be the act she'll sign or your songs might be better suited to the artists on her new label. It may also be worthwhile to contact the executive who took her place at the old company.

Most of the same considerations also apply to executives and professional managers at publishing companies. Again, do a search on www.google.com for the name of the company and you'll get the info, even if you missed *Billboard* the week it was announced.

In the case of publishers, keep in mind that if you've already signed a publishing contract on a song and you see that the person responsible for signing your song to that company has made an exit, you should call the company and make an appointment with his replacement. If you don't bring your song to his attention, it may get lost in the shuffle of thousands of others the new person has to represent. It also gives you a chance to make a new contact and expose some of your newer songs. Also call your old contact at his new job, congratulate him, and go to see him at the new company.

Occasionally, a whole company will be restructured by a new president who wants to put together his or her own "team." This is also valuable info for anyone looking for a job in the business. That kind of news will be carried in the trades' news columns and is also likely to be found in a more detailed feature article. You'll learn about new companies forming or branch offices being set up locally, and you'll have a situation where people are eager to prove themselves by finding some great new local artists or songs. Call right away to make an appointment.

Billboard's "Pro Audio" and *Music Connection*'s "Studio Mix" are other valuable columns for writers. If you're the aggressive, creative type, you can find out, as publishers do, who's recording, at what studio, and the names of the producer and engineer. If you're

A GOOD GAME TO PLAY WITH THE TRADES

Listen to a station that's not afraid to take a chance to add a new song by a new artist now and then. When you hear one you think is a hit, look at the *Billboard* Hot 100 chart or other trade charts to see if it's there. Buy the CD or go the cheap route and check it out on the listening stations at your local record store or online retail site. Analyze the song stylistically and predict what charts it'll show up on. Is it a "crossover" that will show up on both AC and R&B/hip-hop, country and AC? Pretend it's your song and follow it up (or down) the charts over a few weeks. Check out the Single and Album Radio action charts (*Gavin* and *Radio & Records* are great for that.) and see who's adding it to their play lists. What kinds of stations are playing it? What other songs are those stations playing? This is a useful exercise for you because it's a game that record companies and publishers play for real and it gets you into the excitement of second-guessing. By comparing these songs to your own, you can second-guess your songs before even taking them to a publisher. It gives you the opportunity to critique your own song in the context of the real music world. Too many songwriters are totally out of touch with what is going on. To be ignorant of contemporary artists and styles is inexcusable when you claim to be trying to write commercial songs.

very sure that your songs are appropriate for the artist, you'll know how to get to them.

It's important to develop your critical abilities, and you have an opportunity to do that by reading record and live performance reviews, not only in the standard and other consumer music periodicals trades, but search the Internet under "CD reviews" and "concert reviews." Listen to the same records they do, go to the same concerts, and do your own reviews. Obviously, opinions differ among reviewers depending on their own personal taste and critical abilities. For your own learning process, though, it's as helpful to disagree as to agree, as long as you've paid careful attention to their critique and given some thought to your own.

The trades and consumer magazines contain interviews with music industry people that can be helpful on several levels. First of all, if you see an interview with your favorite artist (or a new artist you find on the charts) and want to write a song for her, you may gain some insight into her likes, dislikes, experiences, and fears that will help you write a song she'll identify with, a song that will "speak" for her.

If you're a performer or group looking for a manager, you can get an idea, through an interview, what a particular manager is like personally and professionally. What does he or she think is important? What kind of artists does he like? Why? What's the nature of his relationship with record companies? Is he feared, respected, loved, or all of the above?

Through interviews with record execs, you can find out what they look for, their company policies, their personal experiences, philosophies, and goals. All managers, record execs, and others share basic knowledge in their particular field of expertise, but everyone has a little different approach or a few "tricks of the trade" learned from their own experience and from their personal creativity and imagination.

There are many "right" ways to do almost anything in this business and it helps to know a number of them. Never be afraid to ask questions of industry people when you have the opportunity. In the interviews I've done through the years, with few exceptions, music industry people have spoken freely about how they do things and how they feel about what they do. Even as a struggling writer/artist, whenever I expressed a desire to learn about something, there was always someone who would take the time to explain.

Tip Sheets

Tip sheets are periodicals listing producers (primarily), publishers, or record companies who are in need of material for artists. Some are monthly, some biweekly, some weekly. Some are directed to all songwriters in general and some are restricted to publishers or pro writers with proven track records. The reason for the restriction is this. For its credibility, a tip sheet relies on listings by producers of major acts and other established producers with new acts. If the producers don't want to list themselves, publishers and others don't want to buy the tip sheet. If a tip sheet is sold indiscriminately to amateur songwriters who have no casting sense, don't know how to do their research on the artist, or don't know what the radio format terminology means, they may end up sending totally inappropriate songs. The producer then calls the tip sheet and says, "Who are you selling this to? I've been getting hundreds of terrible songs and if this keeps up, I'm never listing with you again."

There are many "right" ways to do almost anything in this business and it helps to know a number of them.

Are tip sheets worth the money?

Some tip sheets list producers willing to wade through amateur submissions and if you've got the right song, they'll hear it. Most of the heavy hitters, though, are going for the restricted lists or the lists that are so expensive that only the very serious can afford them, which is how some of them deal with the problem I just described. Others want proof of your previous recording activity. And others deal with it by canceling your subscription and refunding your money if they get complaints that your submissions are inappropriate or of poor quality.

With tip sheets, remember that you're rarely going to be among the first to know that someone is looking for songs. Any worthwhile publisher will know it before—or at least at the same time as—the tips, because they or their staffs are calling producers daily. The tip sheet takes some time to collect listings, print, and mail them. By the time you get it, the hot publishers will have their songs on the way to the listed producers. Publishers subscribe to them anyway because they can't afford to miss anything, and a new producer may come out of left field that they haven't yet made contact with.

The fact that you're not among the first, however, doesn't necessarily mean you don't have a chance. It's quite possible the producers won't find what they want in the first go-round and will keep looking. It's still important for you to be aggressive about responding to listings.

Every tip sheet will contain its own guidelines for the way you should submit songs. Additional information will also appear on the individual listings like "no ballads," "one song only," "SASE (Self-Addressed Stamped Envelope) required for tape return," etc. Following their instructions will help insure that your tape gets listened to. For further information, reread the sections on "Writing on Assignment" (see chapter five) and "Presenting Your Demo" (see chapter twelve).

Here are a few of the most popular tip sheets (subject to change):

TAXI

www.taxi.com

Tel.: (800) 458-2111

An innovative, very successful tip sheet/independent A&R service founded in 1992. Members receive over sixty-five listings every two weeks by major and independent labels, producers, managers, film and TV music supervisors, and publishers looking for writers, writer/artists, bands. All submissions prescreened and critiqued by industry pros, which is the reason it's respected by the industry. All styles including instrumentals. Monthly newsletter (past issues archived on Web site). Annual conference for members only.

One-year subscription for all of TAXI's benefits $299.95, 2-year membership is $499.95, 3-year membership is $599.95. There is also a $5 per song submission fee. (Highly recommended.)

SongLink International

www.songlink.com

23 Belsize Crescent

London NW3 5QY, UK

Tel.: +44 (0) 207 794 2540

Fax: +44 (0) 207 794 7393

E-mail: david@songlink.com

Great international tip sheet established in 1993 lists both new and established artists looking for material and pro writers looking for collaborators. Forty to fifty new leads each month. Also features industry news and extensive links to industry events, sites of classic songwriters, publications, songwriters resources, portals to European industry sites, organizations, and much more. A class act! One year (10 issues)—£185.00/US $285.00. Six and three month subscription available.

New On The Charts

www.notc.com

70 Laurel Place

New Rochelle, NY 10801

Founded in 1976, it provides current info on who's on the charts now in all genres with cross-referenced contact info on the artists, producers, managers, record labels, and booking agents, etc., of each hit. Also has Publishers Newsletter tip sheet listing artists who need songs, latest label, publisher and management signings, Soundtrack Newsletter for listings of film/TV music leads, Music Video Section, and International Deals. Different subscription rates for different segments of the services. To subscribe, songwriters must be able to verify at least one nationally released recording of their song. Full subscription (1 year—12 issues): $365 (plus $45 for international mailing).

Parade of Stars

www.beareware.com/paradeofstars

Chuck Chellman

P.O. Box 121355

Nashville, TN 37212-1355

Tel.: (615) 352-4848

E-mail: paradeofstars@home.com

Biweekly sheet for professionals and amateurs. The oldest tip sheet. Lots of country listings, but also lists gospel artists as well as R&B, pop, and rock artists. $129/year, $80/half year.

All Songwriters Network (ASN)

www.tiac.net/users/asn

Box 23912

Ft. Lauderdale, FL 33307, USA

Tel.: (954) 537-3463

E-mail: asn@tiac.net

Professional songwriters organization offering a monthly tip sheet. All styles. Web site has good songwriter-oriented links. Requires demo CD or cassette for audition. They don't accept amateur songwriters. U.S. $140. Outside United States, please add $10 per year.

Row Fax
www.musicrow.com
1231 17th Ave. S.
Nashville, TN 37212
Tel.: (615) 321-3617
Fax: (615) 329-0852

Best country tip sheet. Published forty-eight times a year by *Music Row Magazine* and sent to you every Friday. For professionals only. Entries include artist, record label, producer, recording date, and song description details. Address and contact information not given (If you're a professional, you'll already know that.) 1 year $185, 2 years $285, E-mail/Web 1 year $129, 2 years $240.

Pitchsheet.com
www.pitchsheetassociate.com

Though done online, this pitch service is more like traditional pitching in that it's active. Streaming audio files are sent to an industry user's password-protected A&R private listening room where he/she can hear songs or artists in response to listings that are e-mailed beforehand to subscribers. Credit card $14.95/month (on a month-to-month basis); check or money order, three months $43, six months $81, one year $150. Direct access ePitching to A&R representatives is available for an additional $1/transaction (billed separately).

| Online Pitch Services

These services provide opportunities for songwriters and publishers to make their music available for prequalified users (record companies, film/TV music supervisors, ad agencies, schools, etc.) via a searchable database. Some take a percentage of any uses generated by the site. Others charge based on the number of songs posted on the site. Still others involve active pitching via the Internet. Read their contracts carefully. The beauty of these services is that you can make a few songs or your entire catalogue of songs available, they're as valuable for publishers as for independent songwriters, they allow you the option of uploading audio file samples, lyrics, the song's (or instrumental composition's) recording history, contact information, and much more. They're presented in a searchable database in which a potential user can choose the parameters that fit his/her needs: style, tempo, male or female cast, length, and others. I believe this new category of services uses the technology in a way that's time-saving and practical for both writers, publishers, and users.

Here's a scenario. My friend, Steven McClintock, hit songwriter and former staff writer for several publishers, became discouraged when a publisher dropped the ball on a film song license that Steven had initiated, causing him to lose the use. He started thinking about all the songs he'd written that were sitting unused and unpitched in publishing companies as well as all his writer friends in the same situation. He found a financial partner and started SongCatalog.com. to do something about it. Here are a couple of ways his, and similar services, are used.

Publisher or writer phones user, says, "I've got a song I'd like you to check out," and e-mails user with a link to their own song database or to a specific song. User logs on, listens, and decides yes or no.

User needs song, goes to database, and searches under whatever parameters are needed for the pitch. Gets a list of songs that qualify, looks at lyrics to narrow it down, listens to what looks most promising, contacts the writer or publisher, and negotiates for the use.

Each of the services has its own combination of benefits and costs and are evolving new benefits, so visit their Web sites for up-to-date info.

PublishSongs.com	Songscope.com
www.publishsongs.com	www.songscope.com
SongCatalog.com	SongPitch.com
www.songcatalog.com	www.songpitch.com
Songnet	Pump Audio
www.songnet.com	www.pumpAudio.com

Pump Audio is a searchable online music library for sourcing and licensing pre-cleared original recordings for the Web, broadcast media and audio-visual production. (See "Production Music Libraries," chapter fifteen.)

Other Sources

Besides the trade magazines and tip sheets, other sources of information are:

Music Business Directory
www.musicregistry.com
7510 Sunset Boulevard, Suite #1041, Los Angeles, CA 90046-3418 USA
Tel.: (818) 769-2722   Fax: (818) 769-0990
This company, headed by former Arista Records A&R rep, Ritch Esra, publishes the A&R Registry, a comprehensive listing of record company A&R reps including their stylistic focus, direct phone and fax numbers, and the names of their assistants. The only directory updated every two months. They also publish an annual Music Publisher Registry and Film and TV Music Supervisors Directory.

Songwriter's Market
www.writersdigest.com/catalog
An annual directory that gives you listings of industry pros who are open to receiving unsolicited material, how they want the material submitted, and what types of music the

company specializes in. Includes an annual that gives you listings of industry pros who are open to receiving unsolicited material, how they want the material submitted, and what types of music the company specializes in. Includes Record Companies Category Index, Record Producers, Record Producers Category Index, Managers & Booking Agents, Managers & Booking Agents Category Index, Advertising, Audiovisual & Commercial Music Firms, Play Producers & Publishers, Play Producers, Play Publishers, Classical Performing Arts, Contests & Awards, along with informative articles on the craft and business of songwriting. In bookstores or order direct.

Billboard's Talent and Touring Directory and other directories (see Appendix), annually list hundreds of artists, their personal managers, booking agents, and other contacts.

Getting Ready to Face the Industry

Now that you've got some idea about how the business operates, you're ready to venture out into the real world and start making some contacts. Even when you feel physically prepared, like a soldier going into battle, you need to prepare yourself mentally. No matter which approach you take to get your songs heard and no matter who you decide to contact, knowing what to expect will give you a lot more confidence. There is a professional way to approach the industry, and the more professionally you present yourself, the more professionally you're treated.

Ethics in The Biz

Discussions about ethics in the music business frequently expose a great variety of feelings about it. A business like this that seems so blatant about its powers, pleasures, and extravagance draws many people to it who are greedy for those most visible things. It also draws very creative businesspeople. Most songwriters and musicians, though they're certainly enticed by the high stakes involved, are much more wrapped up in the music itself and seem to want to keep "The Biz" at a distance. Managers, attorneys, and others on the business end will say, "You shouldn't worry about anything but the music. Leave all the business stuff to us." It's exactly what a lot of musicians want to hear. They'll say, "I don't want to even know about that! Just go ahead and do it!" Both lines are candidates for "Famous Last Words."

I can't count the number of times I've heard musicians and writers say, after a sour business deal, "I should have checked him out before I signed" . . . "I should have seen an attorney" . . . "But the vibes really felt right! He told me we'd split the publishing; he'd record masters; he'd get me a record deal; we'd get paid right after the gig; we'd split the advance 50/50, etc., etc." (and a list of other famous music biz lies). But it wasn't *written* in the contracts.

In many of those cases, I'm sure the businesspeople were quite well intentioned and, at the time, really wanted to do what they promised. (I'm the kind of guy who'll give anybody the benefit of a doubt, once at least.) Others chronically take advantage of people and have bad reputations for it. Save yourself a lot of grief by doing some research and talking to others who have dealt with them. Don't feel obligated to work with the first people who show interest in you. Even when the voice of that poor, trampled part of you says, "Oh, thank you, thank you! I'm *so* glad you like me. Show me where to sign." Get a grip on yourself! This may indeed be someone you'll want to work with, but if you go into a deal with that frame of mind, you're begging to be victimized. Calm down, check him out, and don't sign anything without legal advice.

Don't feel obligated to work with the first people who show interest in you.

Also make sure that there's a "performance clause" in the contract, which states that if the terms of the contract are not fulfilled within X amount of time or in X manner, the contract becomes void. This can, quite literally, save you years of creative productivity. Without a performance clause, it's possible for someone to pick up one-year options for five or more years (whatever's in the contract) without doing anything he's supposed to do. Meanwhile, someone else may want to sign you but can't without paying some exorbitant amount of money to buy you out of the deal. According to you, you were ripped off. According to him, he made a good business deal. He recognized good talent, got you to sign, and made some bucks. That's his gig. You may not consider him to be ethical, but you did sign the contract.

Not everyone, of course, does business this way. There are lots of straightforward, honest, up-front people in the business who believe that, in the long run, a good reputation will make them more successful than a bad one. No rigid set of ethics governs practices in the music business short of what's actually illegal. Some industry people follow "situational ethics" or "It seemed like the right thing to do at the time." Some subscribe to the basic greed philosophy that "Anything goes if it gets me what I want." Others hold the "Everybody else is doing it" and "Do it unto others before they do it unto you" philosophies. You're likely to run into any of these anywhere, and the best protection you can have is to get to know enough about the business that you have some idea about whether you're hearing straight talk or jive. If you do turn your business over to someone, you should know enough about what they ought to be doing to know whether or not they are getting it done. Remember that *they* work for you. You don't work for *them*.

The type of people you associate with in the industry can have a great effect on your reputation, peace of mind, and your creative future. Take it very seriously and find good people to work with. Journalist Paul Lawrence once asked Ken Kravitz of Hit City West Recording Studio if he felt that "Nice guys finish last." "Maybe nice guys sometimes finish last in the rat race," Ken answered, "but that's not the only race there is."

| Ego

Also keep in mind, as you approach industry pros, that though your songs may be very personal and expose delicate parts of your being, people in the business must look at them as a *product.* They, in turn, must try to sell your product to someone else on the merits of its commercial potential alone. It's understandably difficult for a writer to keep from feeling that it's him or her who's being rejected rather than the song. Some of the most powerful songs written are very personal statements and confessional revelations that make the writer's ego quite vulnerable to destruction when rejected. So, don't stop writing those kinds of songs. Just get a grip on your ego and leave it at the door when you go in to show your wares.

Before you can successfully pitch your songs to the industry, you must become a good self-critic.

Before you can successfully pitch your songs to the industry, you must become a good self-critic. There's a point during or after the writing of a song where you must step away from it and try to look at it as though you were another person—a publisher, a recording artist, a radio program director, a J.Q. Public. Sometimes, in order to get that perspective, writers put a song away for a few days or even a few weeks so they can get a fresh look at it.

Ask yourself the same questions that, consciously or unconsciously, others will ask: Is this a song about an event or feeling that many people can relate to? Will the people most likely to relate to the lyric be in a certain age group? Will the music appeal to the same age group? Can the lyrics be understood by everyone? Is there a better, more powerful, more graphic way to say what I've said? Is every line of the song important? Is this a song that can compete with the best songs that I hear on the radio (not the worst songs)?

Doing this kind of self-critique will help you in important ways. It will help you write better songs. It will help you choose, from among your songs, those which are the most commercially viable and, consequently, the least subject to rejection. It will help you develop that professional detachment that will make it easier to look at your own work as a product, like someone who makes omelets or clothes or anything else. In accomplishing that, you'll find it much easier to approach buyers and to welcome their positive and negative comments. They, in turn, will find it easier to work with you.

Play your songs for friends before approaching the buyers. Even if they can't or won't give you honest criticism, it gives you some instant perspective. I've written songs I was perfectly happy with until I read the lyric or sang the song to someone else and it suddenly sounded trite or unclear. Back to the drawing board!

It helps in dealing with rejection if you can sympathize with what happens on the other side of the publisher's or producer's door. It does neither you nor them any good if they publish a song they're not genuinely enthusiastic about and in which they see little commercial potential. They'll have to invest in promoting it and they'll have to put up with your continued questions about what they've done with your song. They'll have to keep telling you nothing's happened or avoid taking your calls altogether. So if they can't really get excited about your song as a product, they *have* to reject it.

You shouldn't want someone to publish your song unless they're very enthusiastic about it. When they get rejections on your song, you want them to retain enough enthusiasm for the song to continue to pitch it. Several publishers have told me that they had songs in their catalogue that had been rejected over one hundred times! In spite of that, they continued pitching them because they totally believed in those songs.

Sometimes songs or styles are simply ahead of their time. In the late seventies, for instance, it was common for L.A. writers to get rejections because their "country" songs were "too country" for L.A. and "too pop" for Nashville (the Eagles, for example). There have also been black artists whose songs were too rock for R&B airplay (like Prince). Times and radio formats change but sometimes not until a previously unclassifiable artist becomes a major money-maker.

There are more reasons why you're more likely to be in the wrong place at the wrong time with the wrong song than vice versa. Probably 99 percent of those reasons have nothing to do with you personally, but with the marketplace, your product, and the buyer's ability and inclination to deal with it.

It's a certainty that no matter how good your songs are, they *will* be rejected. If you don't adopt some attitudes that help you to deal with that rejection, you can get too discouraged to persevere. And if you quit, nobody's hurt but you, and there will always be more writers out there to take your place.

J. Michael Dolan, cofounder of *Music Connection* magazine put it in perspective in his inspirational book *Mastering Show Biz . . . From the Heart*:

> It's common knowledge that rejection is a regular occurrence in Show Biz but that's the risk you take when you hang a "for sale" sign on your talent—you risk no one wanting to buy it. The payoff, however, is worth the risk. The payoff is the world benefiting from the actions of your Creative Spirit.

| Dealing With Rejection

It might comfort you to know that, at all levels, a substantial part of what happens in the music industry involves rejection. Rejection of songs, rejection of finished master recordings that people have sunk thousands of dollars into, rejection of record company product by radio stations, and, ultimately, rejection of individual records or styles by consumers.

Every day, for hundreds of different reasons, people in every different facet of the industry are facing rejections. They may accept it as an inevitability, an everyday occurrence, but it is never really easy for anyone to deal with. Egos are bent, reputations questioned, jobs are lost, and friendships are damaged or ended. There are hundreds of rejection stories of major songs and artists. Elton John was turned down by twenty-two record companies; the Beatles and Billy Joel were turned down by every major record company. The list goes on and on and continues today. I would venture to say that every major artist has been rejected numerous times before attaining any success. In fact, even after an artist is successful and subsequently goes through an unproductive period, he may again face those rejections. There's even an industry joke about being fortunate to be turned down by certain record execs because they've rejected so many successful artists that you should worry if they *like* you.

For songwriters it's particularly difficult, though, because you're usually creating in isolation, and it's difficult to find good critical feedback. Often your only artistic validation

It's a certainty that no matter how good your songs are, they *will* be rejected.

Every day, for hundreds of different reasons, people in every different facet of the industry are facing rejections.

comes from friends and family who are so knocked out that you're doing something they don't have the talent for that the last thing they'd do would be to criticize your efforts. They'll be supportive and keep you in that bubble until you smash up against the "real world" of the music business. Songs that your friends liked because they saw you reflected in them (and they like you), songs that audiences seemed to like ("They clapped, didn't they?") are meeting with "Sorry, not strong enough," "not appropriate," "no hook," and other standard lines.

When I ask a writer if he or she has been making the rounds of publishers, I often get the reply, "Yeah, but they passed on all my songs. I didn't have anything they wanted, so they told me to come back when I had some more stuff to show. I know they were just trying to be nice." Wrong!! Publishers seldom say stuff like that "just to be nice." They don't have time to keep making appointments with writers they feel have no talent. Believe that if they keep the door open to you after hearing your songs, it's because they think there's a good chance you'll have something later that they'll be interested in publishing. Don't let what you think is a rejection keep you from going back. Take them at their word. If you call back to make another appointment and it seems like they're putting you off, don't let yourself believe it. Keep trying! That's the place where it really gets tough psychologically. You're sticking your neck out again and your self-confidence is in danger. With every rejection it gets tougher to put yourself back on the line. But when publishers tell you that the door is open, believe them! It's hard enough anyway without *imagining* that you're being rejected.

The following are some ways that you can deal with rejection that will keep you from totally losing your self-esteem.

1. **Cultivate a support group.** Yes, there is life outside the music business. Sometimes you can get in a rut, take the whole thing far too seriously, and fail to take comfort in your families and friends who love you whether you write a hit or not. Cultivate friends outside the music business so you can tap into some other worlds and keep yourself from getting too isolated and from having tunnel vision. That cross-fertilization of experiences and ideas is also creatively stimulating. It also helps to hang out with other songwriters who understand what you're going through and can help you get back up when you're down. Stay away from those who will trivialize even your smallest successes or surround you with that "ain't the biz awful" vibe. You don't need negativity.

2. **Develop short-term payoffs.** It usually takes a very long time for anything to happen in the music business. So that big reward—the recording, the record deal, the hit, the royalty check, the film score, whatever, that's somewhere in the unseen future, isn't always enough to make you feel like a valuable human being today. Yes, you should be able to get that by just writing a good song and feeling good about it. But after you've done it, you're likely to set another goal for it that requires the validation of others and a dependence on a timetable and circumstances over which you don't have much control. So it helps to be actively involved in hobbies, sports, another job, volunteer involvement in a cause, or even something as mundane as cleaning the garage

Stay away from those who will trivialize even your smallest successes or surround you with that "ain't the biz awful" vibe.

or organizing your albums that gives you a sense of accomplishment and immediate positive payoff.

3. **Don't let rejection stop you from writing.** There's a particular song you keep pitching and it keeps getting turned down. You've already rewritten it twice. You're now so totally obsessed with getting it published or produced that you stop writing altogether. A little, self-destructive voice inside you says, "This is the best thing I've ever done. If I can't get anything happening with this one, I might as well hang it up because if they don't like this, they won't like anything." So you stop writing "just till I get this one cut." Meanwhile, you're forgetting several important things. The next song you write may be much better than this one or, at least, more interesting to publishers. You won't become a better writer or a more successful writer unless you continue writing. A song you haven't written yet may be just the song that gets everybody interested in everything else you've done. Just the process of writing can make you feel good about yourself.

4. **Stay healthy.** A depressed body begets a depressed mind. Nothing like a good physical workout to help you get rid of those pent-up frustrations.

5. **Only the "yes" is important.** There is an old line that salesmen use to keep themselves going in the face of rejection. "It's only another 'no' on the way to 'yes'." The "no"s aren't important.

6. **Honestly assess your strengths** and schedule time to discipline yourself to work on the areas you could improve. A schedule keeps you looking forward and gives you the feeling that you're actually accomplishing something, no matter how small, to keep you moving ahead.

7. **Have additional plans of attack.** If you strike out on one, you're ready to try something else right away so you don't have time to feel sorry for yourself. My wife, JoAnn, worked for several years in Creative Development at Walt Disney Imagineering, Disney's theme park think tank. A common problem among the designers there was a sort of depression after a big project was completed. The company helped to counteract this by giving them information about the next project so they had something to look forward to after the current project ended.

Query Letters or E-Mails

Now that you know what you're up against, you're ready to contact people and show them your stuff. One of the easiest ways to submit your material, especially if you live outside the major recording centers, is to mail your demo, but you still need to get past the "no unsolicited material" barrier. If you don't know whether or not they'll accept your submission, it makes sense to inquire ahead of time, preferably with a phone call. Otherwise, send a postcard or e-mail before going to the expense of sending a tape or CD. If you don't, they'll probably send your demo back unopened.

Here are some options:

Send a letter with a self-addressed return postcard enclosed. In the letter, list any credits you might have or anything that might interest them in your act or your material. Include live club or concert reviews. Not the whole thing, just a few high octane blurbs like "If this band doesn't get a deal, I'll run down Michigan Avenue naked!" "Could be the next biggest thing since the last biggest thing" obviously with the names of the paper or magazine; contest prizes (Don't mention "honorable mention.") or other awards you've won (State "Battle of the Bands Winner," is good.); music education and professional experience. Make it neat and professional or totally funny. Let it reflect your personality. Add a good photo of the band in action. Not head shots or group shots that look too posed ("OK guys, all look at the camera and smiiiile!"). Create a little intrigue, something that makes people think "Who ARE these people" (in a *good* way)? Forget the Polaroids ("Honey, we need a shot of the band looking stupid. Could you do a Polaroid so we can send it to the record company?") If you've sold over a thousand CDs of your band, let them know the sales figures, hopefully with SoundScan numbers to back it up. (There are probably acts on their label that haven't sold much more.) Don't lie to them. They can check. Don't ask what they're looking for. You should already know the styles of music they work with and be sending it to a specific A&R person who deals with your style of music. Describe your style as best you can. If you're primarily a writer, mention any film/TV or recording uses.

If you use snail-mail, your self-addressed stamped postcard makes it easy to reply. It can have a choice of replies as shown on the previous sample. Include the company return address on the front so you remember where you sent it—in case they don't write it in.

Yes, I'd like to hear your demo. I know it will make my day.

Address it to the attention of: _____

_____

Send: cassette, CD

E-mail an audio file in MP3, RealAudio or _____ format.

We're not listening to anything now. Try us: next month, next year. Or would never be too soon?

We only listen to unsolicited demos when your: attorney/manager/producer/Uncle Herman from the IRS sends them to us.
OTHER COMMENTS:

_____

_____

_____

Signed _____ Date _____

Company _____

(Know that the light nature of this letter is not unprofessional. They love it when you make 'em smile!)

If you use e-mail and don't have a Web site URL to send them to, send the same letter and send a photo as an "attachment," if possible.

For your own records, keep a notice like: *Card sent to Megahits Music 1/20/02.*

In-Person Interviews

We get our strongest impressions of people in person. It's helpful for you to be able to size up the people you do business with and for them to be able to put a face with a name and a song. That's assuming it's a good song and that you usually make a good impression when you meet people. I can assume you're already aware of that if you're old enough to read this.

Appointments for an in-person audition are usually rare without a referral by someone whose taste (or at least, power) an industry pro respects. But there still seem to be unknown writers who just come into town and are able to meet with several publishers in a day. Their success has a lot to do with self-confidence, personality, and timing. Obviously, your best shot is to be able to call ahead of time and say that you're in town for a short while and give them the name of someone who recommended that you see them. But you should call and try to set up an appointment even without a referral, especially if you have any notable credits. Let them know about your success on the initial call. Be nice to the receptionist, secretary, and/or assistant. If you don't get an appointment, ask if you can drop off a demo, and don't be discouraged. It's a long shot anyway. If you do get an appointment, find out approximately how much time the person can give you so you can prepare accordingly, and remember the following:

• Be there on time or ahead of time! If *they're* late, they'll likely be more accommodating out of guilt. If you're late, it puts a heavy psychological burden on you. If you're in a strange town, make sure you get good directions from someone and an idea about how long it'll take to get to your appointment. Allow extra time for emergencies.

• If something unexpected comes up and you can't be there on time, *call ahead to let them know.* They may have to cancel and reschedule. Personally, I'm extremely reluctant to reschedule if you've set up a meeting with me and didn't call or show up. It shows me that you don't respect my time.

• If possible, *bring each song on a separate cassette tape or know the numbers of the songs on your CD.* This will save time because it allows you to change the order of your presentation on the spot. If the person says, "Play me a ballad," and your ballad is at the end of your tape, you'll have to do a stop-and-start search for that song while you're saying, "No, that's not it. I think it's just a little further on," and on and on. Or "I think it's the next cut (on the CD)." When you have a limited amount of time available, you want him to spend his time listening to your songs, not waiting while you look for them.

• Before beginning to play your songs, *tell the person conducting the appointment that he's free to turn off your tape* (or your CD or live performance) *and go to the next song whenever he likes.* Be prepared to *give him lyric sheets* so he can scan your lyric as he listens. This maximizes the value of his time with you.

- Take extra copies of everything so that if he wants to keep something, you can leave it. Be sure that *your name, phone number, and address are on each cassette or CD and lyric sheet.*

- If you want criticism, ask for it. If not, don't. If they give it to you, thank them for it whether you agree or not. Don't argue! If they like something enough to ask for a rewrite and you like the person and are interested in forming a working relationship, tell them you'll try it. Do it and get back to them—the sooner the better. If you think there's a chance you won't or can't do it, don't make any rash promises. It's better to pleasantly surprise them than to let them remember you as a broken promise.

- When you leave, thank them and their assistant. Send a thank-you card or letter that same week. You'd be amazed at how rarely this happens.

Getting Heard in a "No Unsolicited Material" World

Once you've written that great song or completed your writer/artist masters or demos, you face the prospect of getting heard by the music industry. You take off your creative songwriter hat and put on your marketing hat. For some of you, this is an exciting challenge. For others, it runs a close second to major surgery. Like anything else, though, it gets much less daunting when you have some practical information. Let's start by understanding the barriers you may encounter when trying to get through the doors of the music industry.

| Why Is It So Hard to Get Through the Doors?

To deal with this problem effectively, look at it from the point of view of the publishers, producers, record company A&R representatives, or managers who are your most prominent targets. They have two major concerns: finding great talent/songs in the most time and cost-efficient way possible and protecting themselves from lawsuits.

In the first case, if they have an open-door policy, most companies are deluged with demo tapes and CDs. In fact, even with "no unsolicited material" policies, they're still deluged with solicited demos (those referred by other writers or industry people they respect). The biggest problem for those with open-door policies, particularly for producers and record companies looking for songs for specific projects, is that most of the songs they receive are totally inappropriate for their needs. Usually this is because writers who are sending in tapes haven't done their homework on the project. Consequently, those listening to demos already know that more than 90 percent of their time will be wasted. Pretty bad odds for someone who may have only one or two assistants who can screen demos.

Time is another barrier keeping industry professionals from listening to unsolicited demos. Music publishers who may just be looking for great songs or writer/artists for development will have a broader scope of material they're seeking. It may take more time to evaluate the songs they receive because they're listening for more than whether the song will work for a current project. They're also looking for writers who have potential for future success and who they can work with and develop.

The legal barrier is also a formidable door-closer, as most companies' legal departments advise them against accepting unsolicited material in fear of potential copyright infringement suits. A key factor in determining infringement is proof of "access." In other words, if a copyright infringement suit goes to court, the prosecution has to prove that the accused has had the opportunity to hear the material. Proving that someone at the company has opened the package containing your song is, of course, proof of access. You may wonder why an infringement lawsuit can't result from *solicited* material? Of course it can, but the odds are much lower because industry people already know that most infringement suits are brought by writers who are not seriously pursuing a career as a songwriter. These are referred to as "nuisance suits" in which, on scant evidence and understanding of copyright law, a writer says, "I wrote a song called 'I Love You' that contains the line 'I love you more than life itself' and that new hit by Joe Rock contained the same line and I can prove I sent it to his publisher/producer/A&R rep last year so I'm suing you." This is an oversimplification, but not by much. The hitch is that Joe Rock could have heard that line in a song while he was still in the womb and in many other songs thereafter. He didn't have to hear it from a demo in his publisher's office. Since a suit has to be dealt with by the company's legal department, it uses up valuable time and resources.

Is this fear of lawsuits why many companies ask you to have an attorney submit a demo for you? No. Certainly, your attorney could document very definitely the publisher's access to your demo. But most industry pros do not believe that submission of a demo by someone with a law degree guarantees its artistic and commercial quality. Not that there aren't entertainment attorneys whose musical tastes are respected, but it isn't the law degree that insures it. So why is it that they ask you to do it? After pursuing this question for years and asking a lot of questions of a lot of industry people, I've come to one conclusion: They want to know that you're serious. On countless occasions I've heard industry people say things like, "I don't accept unsolicited material, but if someone is really worth hearing, they'll find a way to get to me or I'll hear about them." This is sort of a "survival of the fittest" philosophy that, like it or not, has some merit. They figure that, if you're serious enough to pay a couple of hundred dollars an hour to have an attorney shop your tape/CD, you're serious enough for them to listen to.

| Getting Through the Doors

Showing the industry you're serious is the key. One of the most important things you need to do is research. Become aware of the industry people involved in your style of music. Read the credits on the recordings of your favorite artists—find out who produced them, who wrote and published the songs, the record label, and possibly even the record company A&R representative who works with that artist. If the A&R rep's name isn't on the package, call the record company's artist relations department or A&R coordinator and get his name. You can also get the phone and fax numbers of the artist's producer and manager. Also study the artist in order to cast the right song so you can be reasonably confident it will be appropriate. (See "Casting," chapter eleven.) Whenever possible, try to find out from the artist's producer, manager, or record company if there's a change in the artist's direction. If you're pitching for a new artist, get information from those same sources or find a tip sheet. (See "Tip Sheets," page 269.)

Research the names of companies, producers, managers, and A&R reps who know how to market the artists/groups in your musical style. You need to know their names and who they've worked with. By far, the best advice about doing your research is to read the trade magazines industry calls. Here's a hypothetical example: In *Billboard* you see Bonnie Newcomer's name on the charts with a new single. You don't have any of her CDs yet (you'll buy them today), but you've heard her on the radio and think you might have something for her. You've also read an article about her in which she talks about the songs on her new project, where she got them, who wrote them, and about working with her new producers. Though you've also seen their names listed as writers under the song title on the chart, you've also noticed other writers' names, so you know she's open to "outside" songs. You also learn she's on Hot Stuff Records. So you call Hot Stuff and ask for the A&R coordinator. "Hi! This is so-and-so at This and That Music. Will the same producers be working on Bonnie Newcomer's next album? Do you have a number for their companies? Who's doing A&R on the project?" Get those names down quick. If you ask them to spell it for you, you're already another step away from credibility with them. They figure that if you're the pro you seem to be, you'll already be familiar with the names. (Look to directories such as the Music Business Registry's A&R Registry to help you out.) (See "Other Sources" in this chapter.)

Once you have the name of the A&R person at Hot Stuff or someone in the producers' offices, call them directly and ask about the musical direction of Bonnie's next album and how to go about submitting songs for it. It's a good idea to ask if there's a code you should use on the package. They often use a personal code so their assistants or mail room personnel know that it's actually been "solicited."

All the trade magazines publish special-focus issues that contain a treasure of information on specialized areas of the industry. Among them are children's music, classical, heavy metal, alternative, folk, music publishing, Latin, Celtic, and film music. They may focus on cities and countries that are emerging as music centers such as Minneapolis, Seattle, Atlanta, Ireland, Germany, etc. You'll get information on the movers and shakers in those genres or places, the record labels, publishers, producers, managers, radio stations, booking agents and artists, along with stories about who signed whom and their career strategies.

The *Billboard* SoundScan technology revolutionized the industry by providing accurate retail sales and airplay information showing country music to be selling much more than was thought to be true. It's now showing several country artists on the Hot 100 pop chart. Webcasts over the Internet have opened a new avenue for exposing and selling music, and monitoring systems have been created to track them. The Internet now provides up-to-date research information from the performing rights organizations on their catalogs accessible to anyone with a modem. New standardized cue-sheet forms for music used in film and television are used by the performing rights organizations and can be filed via the Internet. There are now several Internet services available for exposing and selling independent recordings to the online audience. Among them are: Amazon.com (the biggest) and MP3 at www.MP3.com. Browsing the music-related Web sites on the Internet will turn up many more. These are all developments that you can stay abreast of by regularly reading the trades.

Think of your local record store as a research center. Record stores can be great sources of information. They usually have a list of current hits in your favorite style. Familiarize yourself with them and find the albums in the record bins. Many stores have listening posts where you can spend some time listening to new CDs. Some stores even have information kiosks where you can bring up artist information on a monitor and look up past albums, reviews, etc. If you have an Internet connection, see if the artist has a Web site you can contact. You can also look at an Internet directory under "record companies" and find Web sites for record companies, too. If you're an artist/band, check out the CDs of the artists who record your style of music and find out who the record labels are who distribute them. If you're selling your CDs yourself, ask to meet the buyer at the store to find out the requirements for stocking your CDs.

Think of your local record store as a research center.

There are obviously more advantages in *buying* the CDs. This is the best way to familiarize yourself with an atist's style, and the CD inserts usually contain all the info you need. Often the management company is listed with an address. You'll also find the name(s) of the producer(s) of that album or of individual songs on it. Of course, the next album may be produced by someone else. But at least you've done some homework and can call the record company, get the A&R or artist relations department, and ask if so-and-so will be working on the next album (if not, who is?) and how to get in touch. If you play it right, they may also give you the manager's office address and phone number. (Let's see Napster give you all that!)

Other good sources of information and contacts are local or national songwriters organizations and events. Most organizations have regularly scheduled events in which they invite music industry professionals to speak and listen to demos. Familiarize yourselves with those guests, their histories, and current needs. The personal contact has much more impact than a cold call. If you research the guests before the event, search their names online and read an article about them or an interview with them, listen to a song they placed or a record they produced, you're in a good position to start an intelligent conversation and you never know where it can lead you. "Behind the scenes" people always love it when you can talk about and ask questions about something they've done that you're familiar with or a fan of. "Hey I loved the guitar sound on that record (you produced).

How did you get that?" Don't b.s. them though. Be genuine. If you're not, they'll know it right away.

Support those organizations that produce the events with your membership and volunteer time and you'll often find yourself surrounded by opportunities. Organization newsletters also frequently provide valuable information about industry events of interest to songwriters.

| Making the Calls

If you know up front that industry people are deluged by calls from writers and artists who haven't done their homework, you have a distinct advantage if you put in the research time before you call. It lets you call with a certain amount of confidence in your voice. Don't be arrogant, but do project confidence. If you can let them know you're serious and have done your research, the "gatekeepers" will be afraid to shut you down too quickly because, for all they know, you may be someone important to their boss. The boss is also more likely to take you seriously. Don't beg for a chance to be heard! This is very unprofessional. Though you may not actually say it, the subtext of your conversation should be, "I have great songs that I know are appropriate for this artist. They deserve to be heard."

Regardless of the "we're not listening" policies and the reasons behind them, most publishers and A&R people still do listen to new songs and artists but very selectively. They want to weed out the writers who haven't learned anything about how the business works or the hobbyists with two or three songs taking a quick shot at it and then retreating. The pros size up a writer, his or her attitude and presentation, from the first contact and then decide whether to spend time listening or not. They know that even given all a writer or artist's positive attributes, the odds are still minimal that they'll find something they can publish or an artist they can sign with genius-level raw talent they'd like to develop. That's why it's important to them to set up a tough screening process.

On the front lines of that process are receptionists, secretaries, and assistants. Unless you have the name of a specific person at the company, your phone call won't get past that point. Even if you do have a name, you'll be referred to that person's secretary. She will say something like, "May I tell her what this is about?" or "He's not in right now. May I help you?" The worst thing you can say is, "Sorry, you can't help. I need to talk to the main man." That person's job is to save the main man's (or woman's) time. How you present yourself to a secretary or receptionist may determine whether or not your demo gets heard.

Here's a scenario:

Writer: Hi, I'm a songwriter and I've got a hit for Destiny's Child and another one that would be great for Shania Twain. Actually, I've written over twenty songs. Could somebody there listen to them?

Receptionist: Could you please drop off a demo? (You'd be very lucky to get this request.)

Writer: No, I won't leave a demo. How do I know you won't steal my songs?

Receptionist: Who referred you to us?

Writer: I got your name out of the phone book. Could you connect me to the man in charge?

This is not really that much of an exaggeration as any industry gatekeeper would tell you. What do you think are the odds that the caller will get through? An important part of a secretary's (and often a receptionist's) job is to screen out this type of call from songwriters. If they recognize your name or you've been referred by someone whose name they know and whose reputation they respect, your chances of getting through the door are much better. In other cases, it's pretty much up to their discretion who to accept demos from or whose call to put through to their bosses. Consequently, the first encounter you have with the front desk is vital. If you present yourself as a rank amateur, they'll assume your writing is just as amateur and that their chances of finding a great song from you are zilch.

Every secretary or receptionist has his own criteria for figuring the odds in favor of the boss. Let's look at the call again. Only an amateur who has done no research doesn't know that Destiny's Child and Shania Twain aren't likely to do outside songs. If you've written only twenty songs, you're obviously a beginner. You can't be on the scene long and not know you're going to have to leave demos. Get them protected first so you won't have to worry about songs being stolen. You also haven't done your research if you don't have the name of a person at the company and have to resort to the phone book for the company name. If you don't know the name of "the man in charge," you just might be insulting the *woman* in charge. Do your homework. (See "Researching the Music Industry" in this chapter.)

I asked the receptionist at a major publishing company how she screens unsolicited calls. She said she tells writers that the company is not listening to demos now. If they ask when the company will be listening (and they seldom ask), she tells them to call back in a month. If she *does* get a call back from that writer, she accepts his or her demo. It shows her that writer is persistent, professional, and organized enough to follow up the call. She figures you're serious!

I've gained a lot of insight into this process by going from being a struggling songwriter to being on the other side of the desk as a screener. I learned some important lessons that have been corroborated by my "other side of the desk" peers.

We always respect persistence, even though we may at times find it annoying and guilt-provoking. We know that no matter how talented you are, you need persistence to succeed. The hardest part of being persistent is continuing to be pleasant about it and not allowing yourself to become bitter or desperate from the rejection you'll experience. It turns people off when they sense that desperation in you.

A secretary I talked with said, "It's a real turnoff to have someone spill their guts out to me that this is their last chance or they need to pay their doctor bills or whatever. I don't want to subject my boss to that either. It's very unprofessional."

There's also a thin line between confidence and arrogance. We like to feel that you believe in yourself and are confident about your talent and abilities even though you're open to criticism and direction. If you come off arrogantly with the attitude, "I'm God's gift to the music world and if you can't recognize it, you're a Neanderthal," it will be difficult for you to find people to work with you.

(I highly recommend Dan Kimpel's book, *Networking in the Music Business*. [See Bibliography.] I mention it here because he has a chapter on phone etiquette with several typical phone scripts. There's somewhat more than is necessary to include here.)

No matter who you're trying to get to, be nice to assistants and secretaries. Treat them with respect. There's a better than average chance that they are the ones who will initially be listening to your demo.

No matter who you're trying to get to, be nice to assistants and secretaries. Treat them with respect. There's a better than average chance that they are the ones who will initially be listening to your demo. In fact, you may acknowledge that possibility ahead of time by asking for *their* opinion on your songs. Also, by the next time you call, they may be the boss, and the relationship you developed on the phone gets you into their office. If you're serious enough to want a career as a writer or artist, you need to think years ahead and build bridges now.

Always request permission to submit tapes or CDs. For the reasons I described earlier, you must get permission to submit your demo. It's always preferable do this by phone, but you may not have much time to "sell" yourself. A short fax or e-mail can be more efficient. (See "Query Letters or E-Mails" in this chapter, on page 279.)

Follow Up!

If you do get through the door, consider it a great accomplishment but only the first of a series. Don't figure that all you have to do now is just wait around for them to call you back and tell you how great your song is. Know that they're very busy and you may have to remind them that they have your demo. Two weeks is an adequate amount of time to follow up once you know someone has your demo. That doesn't necessarily mean he should have listened to it in that time. He may have hundreds of tapes to hear, and listening to them is not a major part of his job in most cases. Don't get upset and demand your tape back. He'll be only too glad to get rid of it. Leaving a tape somewhere indefinitely means, at worst, you lose the cost of the tape/CD. At best, a producer or publisher goes through a box of demos in a couple of years, finds yours, and calls you. Don't think it hasn't happened.

After calling to make sure they've received it, always ask them to give you a date or time frame to check back. You might say, "Look, I know you are busy and I don't want to make a pest of myself, so I'd appreciate it if you could give me some guideline about when to check back." Make sure you get a name so that when you call back you can say, "_____ suggested I call back in a couple of weeks." Call back several times. No one in the music business will ever fault you for persistence. Though it will be frustrating, don't let it affect your professional attitude on the phone.

Stay in touch. "The squeaky wheel gets the grease," is a cliché that remains true. If someone calls me looking for a singer for a project "right now," and I have no time to research and get to my lists, and you're a good singer I know who I just talked to a couple days ago, your name will jump out of my mouth. If I haven't heard from you in a year, it won't happen. The lesson here is that no matter how positively someone has responded to you and your music, never assume that people will remember you and what you're doing if you don't remind them periodically.

Say "thank you." If someone (a boss or gatekeeper) has given you her time, advice, or help in any way, drop her a "thank-you" card. It's another positive way to make contact, to acknowledge the value of her contribution, and to let her know that you're appreciative, organized, and taking care of business. If you knew how seldom this was done, you'd realize what an impact it has.

Other Avenues

If you plan to pitch your songs directly to record companies, managers, producers, and artists, you're being a publisher. You'll get through their doors easier if you have your own company, logo, and letterhead. Don't choose a name for your company that reflects your own (JoJac for Joe Jackson). This makes it obvious that you're a "hip-pocket" publisher (a writer only representing your own material) rather than a company who has invested in a writer it believes in. Yes, I know you believe in yourself, but it doesn't give you that business edge here. If you decide to pitch your songs to publishers, don't send it on your publishing company letterhead. They'll wonder why another publisher is sending them a song. (See "Self-Publishing," chapter eleven.)

You *can* send your letterhead packages to record companies, producers, and managers. Managers should not be overlooked because they are usually very close to the decision process on selection of songs, direction of the artist, choice of producers, etc., and may not be deluged as are record company A&R and producers.

Keep a demo and lyric sheets with you at all times. You never know when you'll get an unexpected opportunity to give it to someone such as the artist's hairdresser, limo driver, recording engineer, road manager, touring musician, friend, or anyone else with access to the artist or the artist's official "team." Offer them a sales incentive of a percentage of the income on whatever song they are responsible for helping you place. (See "Negotiating," chapter eleven.)

Always remember that this is a "people" business.

Always remember that this is a "people" business. As in most other business, maintaining your personal relationships, networking for new contacts, taking advantage of your memberships in organizations that can put you in touch with the industry, doing favors for your colleagues, researching the trade magazines, and being ready to immediately take advantage of opportunities are all things that will contribute to your success.

| Survival

Getting through the door involves continuously and consistently making contacts and being able to support yourself while you're doing it. If you're a writer who isn't working as a performer, don't assume you'll be making it "any day now" and borrow from friends and family to survive till your big break comes.

Get a day job so you can spend your evenings writing with others who have day jobs, attending industry events, workshops, and clubs, and be able to afford it. You'll also need money for demos, postage, and other songwriting expenses.

Try to get a job in some aspect of the industry. It's tough because everyone else wants those jobs, too. Don't be afraid or too proud to start on the bottom rung. If you have good typing or other office skills, get work with temporary employment agencies that specialize in the entertainment industry.

In Dan Kimpel's insightful book, *Networking in the Music Business*, he offers:

SIX WAYS TO GET A JOB IN THE MUSIC BUSINESS

1. Be an intern for a label.
2. Develop computer skills; you'll find your employee potential is greatly enhanced.
3. Apply for a mailroom position.
4. Meet promotional representatives from the labels on the local and regional level who can provide a bridge to their companies.
5. Write articles about bands for magazines and newspapers in your area. You'll meet the publicity department and they'll soon have clips of your writing.
6. Promotional jobs at record labels have a high turnover rate. If you're optimistic, energetic, and great on the phone, apply to this department.

I'll add another one. If you're what I call "cyber-savy," there's a lot of work for you. Beyond basic computer skills, companies are paying well for people who can contribute to their online marketing plans.

Volunteer! Do volunteer work for songwriter or other industry organizations that put you in action centers where you can keep in touch with what's going on. Volunteer to work in recording studios in exchange for studio time. If you're a dedicated, hardworking volunteer for a music company or songwriter organization, when a paid position comes up, you just might be considered first because the boss already knows you and likes your work. Whether you get a job in the industry or not, the security of a regular paycheck will preserve you from desperation and taking the first deal that comes along. There's definitely an advantage to negotiating a deal knowing that you don't have to have the money.

The Options of an Out-of-Towner

The best advice if you're serious about a career as a songwriter is to move to a major music center: New York, Nashville, or Los Angeles. The next best advice is to move to a not-so-major but active music center. Periodically, places like Austin, Seattle, Minneapolis/ St. Paul, Boston, Chicago, and San Francisco get a burst of heat when a local act or two breaks nationally. Even when they're not hot, these cities seem to support a thriving live music community. The recording scenes there tend to evolve around local producers and studios that have spawned successful acts. The area may also have a characteristic music style based on what those particular producers have had success with. Find out who those producers are and get their attention if you migrate to or live in one of those areas.

I have a philosophy about what takes place to bring music industry attention to a city. Networking and mutual support between local bands will always bring more industry attention to a scene than competition between bands. I've noticed through the years that the scenes that always seem to explode are ones whose musicians share their contacts and resources and help to promote each other. What's at work there from an industry stand-point is record companies seeing a cluster of activity. Somebody makes an industry contact and maybe that A&R rep, for example, is interested in a band, comes out from L.A. to check the band out, and the band he came to see says, "You've gotta see my friend's band. They're great! What begins to happen (assuming the other band is good, too) is that the A&R rep starts to feel the "buzz," the energy in the place, saying to himself and his company, "Hey, there's a real scene here and we'd better get on it because this place is going to explode. There's a bunch of great bands here and if we don't sign somebody here, everybody else is going to hear about it too and start signing them." Seattle in the late eighties and early nineties was a scene like that in great part due to the wisdom and community building of Sub Pop Records in Seattle, who nurtured Nirvana, Soundgarden, and other bands. When bands have a "small town" mentality of competition, it signals that there's not enough success to spread around to everybody and they need to keep information to themselves or they'll lose an advantage. It's deadly! Anyway, back to business.

If you stay in your own town, find out if there are any local recording studios, producers, publishers, booking agents, or radio programmers and DJs. Meet them and let them know what you're doing. Aside from specific programs that feature local talent, the radio people won't give you airplay unless you have a record deal. But they may refer you to local record promoters who will, in turn, refer you to the record companies they represent. This is a good way to network from your local scene to industry people in the major recording centers. If you're not a performer, have a hot local act record your demos and pitch them to the above. If your musical style is at odds with the local focus, give it a shot anyway. You may be the breath of fresh air they've been looking for. If not, start packing your bags for a reconnaissance trip to greener pastures.

"But," you say, "I have a good day job, a wife (or husband), and five kids, so relocating is not exactly a practical solution. What's the next best thing?"

Try a vacation trip first. Do some online research, use the resources provided here, or get some info from your local songwriters association if you have one. Write, call, or e-mail some publishers at your destination. Try to get an appointment set up for when you'll be in town. (See "In-Person Interviews," page 281.) If you can't accomplish that, at least get their permission to send them some songs. Maybe they don't want to meet you till they know they like your material. The point in trying to meet with them is that they'll remember you better when you contact them from home later. Those solid, in-person contacts will make it much easier to continue your long-distance relationship.

When you're far away from recording centers, it becomes more important that you establish an identity by way of your correspondence, packaging, and graphics. Then, when they get your package, they know (from across the room) whose it is. (See "Successful Pitching Strategies," chapter eleven.)

If you're sending in tapes, send one or two songs at a time but send them more frequently so people don't have time to forget you. Better to send a couple songs a month than to send several every six months.

Another thing that works for you as an out-of-towner is that industry people seem to be more accommodating if you call ahead and say you'll only be in town for a few days and would like to schedule an appointment. I used to tell writers how tough it was to get appointments until a couple of them told me they'd had four or five appointments in a day in L.A. by doing just that. There's a mystique about anyone from somewhere else. It's the flip side of the "No matter how good you are, you can't get any respect in your own town" syndrome.

Over the years, I've seen many writers set up long-term business relationships with industry people in this way. On the other hand, I've also seen in-towners get complacent and not nurture those relationships because they feel as though they can do it any time. Hit country writer Steve Seskin ("Daddy's Money," "Don't Laugh at Me") lives in the San Francisco area. I asked him once how he managed to get success in Nashville when everybody says you have to live there to make it work. He said he went there often enough and made sure he saw lots of people when he was there, and he figured people actually thought he lived there. Let's face it, no matter where you are, it all gets down to how much you want success and how persistent you are about working for it.

Marketing Your Lyrics

The situation for lyricists in the marketplace has its positives and negatives. On the plus side, it's necessary for you to collaborate to have a suitable melody for your words. I know that doesn't really sound like a plus, but if you're a prolific lyricist, finding several collaborators represents an opportunity to produce a great number of finished songs. Those who insist on writing both lyrics and music, in my experience, are rarely so prolific. As a lyricist, you can develop your lyric skills in a variety of styles without needing to restrict yourself for marketing purposes, as do many writer/performers.

When you're far away from recording centers, it becomes more important that you establish an identity by way of your correspondence, packaging, and graphics.

On the minus side, it's very difficult for you to get a staff-writing deal. You really have to be an extraordinary lyricist with some commercial success under your belt to get an exclusive staff-writing situation. And it's virtually impossible to make a single-song deal on a lyric with no melody. There are audiovisual firms that commission lyricists to write material for them. Check with local firms to see what their needs are, and find additional contacts listed in *Songwriter's Market*.

So, outside of that, what can a lyricist do? Find collaborators. Along with the methods listed in chapter seven, "Collaboration," pay particular attention to political strategy. Find cowriters who are further ahead in their careers than you and still moving forward. Among collaborators to consider are new bands that are getting some industry attention or at least drawing great audiences locally. Good lead singers and keyboard players are usually worth considering because they're more likely to write exciting melodies that may need equally exciting lyrics. Find other writers who are starting to get their songs recorded or those who are already on staff at a publishing company. Find writers in strong positions to make contacts with artists, such as studio musicians and recording engineers. With all the above you have the advantage of writing with people who could get good demos made at a reasonable cost, a big plus for you.

If those situations are just not available to you, look for skilled musicians in bands, college music departments, churches, theaters, and so on.

If you speak another language fluently, gather samples of your song translations from and into the language. Contact publishers both here and in the countries where the language is spoken. They can be found in directories like *Songwriter's Market* and *Billboard's International Buyers Guide*. The Spanish-speaking market, for example, is enormous.

Make contact with as many potential cowriters as possible; enter lyric-writing contests; put notices in music stores, schools, and magazines. Let everyone know what you're looking for, and you'll find that your opportunities will grow quickly.

Caution: Do not send your lyrics to companies who advertise in magazines for "song poems" and ask you to pay a fee to have them write melodies to your lyrics. (See "Avoiding the Songsharks," chapter eight.)

Organize Your Song Shopping

If you plan to actively "plug" your own songs, it's important to keep track of what's going on. You'll want to act as professionally as the successful music publishers who are out there pitching their writers' songs to some of your same contacts. (See "Successful Pitching Strategies" and "Casting.") Develop a list of producers and recording artists for whom your songs may be appropriate. Keep a card file (5″x7″ or larger index cards) or a computer database file on each of them so that every time you make contact, you can note who they're producing, what type of material they need for the upcoming LP, where they're recording, what kind of demos they prefer, whether they usually ask for a percentage of publishing, and so on. If you're also shopping for publishers, keep a similar card file for them.

Here are good computer programs available for keeping track of songs, writers, contacts, casting, contracts, forms, and more. Go to their sites and check them out in detail. The inefficiency of file card systems doesn't quite make sense anymore when computers can run software that gives you the kind of comprehensive control over your business that these programs do.

Songtracker.com
www.songtracker.com
Box 976, Simi Valley, CA 93062-0976
The original, started in 1975. SongTracker 3.0 is designed for songwriters, musicians, studio owners, DJs, radio music directors, artists, and film composers ($349 list); and SongTracker PRO 3.0 is designed especially for music publishers, copyright administrators, independent production companies, management, legal departments, and record labels (about $2000 list.).

Yeah Solutions
www.yeahsolutions.com
P.O. Box 163507, Austin, TX 78716 USA
Tel.: (512) 347-9324   Fax: (512) 347-9325
Offers a high-end Music Publisher software suite for Windows only. Featuring A&R, Business Affairs, Copyright, Licensing, Royalties, and Subpublishing for approximately $1,800 (2000 price).

Network Marketing
www.musreview.com/musicdata.html
P.O. Box 41635, Nashville, TN 37204-1635   Tel.: (615) 599-5793
If you want to promote your CD project, here's a series of databases that you can download to your system. They say they update daily. Radio Station Data Base—$139.95 over 13,700 stations; Distributors—$79.95 1500 plus distributors; Retailers, Book Stores—$89.95; 2000 plus Booking Agents—$79.95; 1600 plus All Data Bases—$269.95.

Visit www.johnbraheny.com for updates on prices and any new software packages and prices.

The information you need to gather regardless of your system:

1. Information on the artist should include vocal range, what style he or she prefers, and information about personal idiosyncrasies like "hates sexist songs" or "positive lyrics only." This information can be obtained from the producer, consumer and trade magazines, tip sheets, radio and TV interviews, or, if you're one of the more fortunate ones, from the artist personally.

2. It's also smart to keep a record of personal items about the producer such as "plays golf," "anti-nuke activist," "just had a baby," "going to England in August," and so forth. This type of information is useful in all businesses where personal contact

is important. It allows you an instant recap and reminder when you call someone or set up a meeting, gives you an idea for opening a conversation to break the ice, and lets them know that you're concerned about them as people. It doesn't take the place of having good songs, though, since many producers have little time for small talk and are best served by a brief presentation of your material. It can, however, create a better climate for you to get feedback on your songs and help you develop as both writer and publisher.

3. After every meeting or phone call, make notes regarding the outcome, such as "loved 'Don't Take That Away,' doesn't feel it's right for (artist's name) but wants to keep demo for future reference—remind him," "didn't like 'Do It Again' but maybe if the hook was stronger, rewrite," "will be producing (artist's name) in September—start writing."

4. Set up file folders with the name of each song you're working on. (Yes, it is a good idea to keep hard copies, even if you have a database you back up frequently.) Use one folder for each song (alphabetical by title, if you have several songs). Each folder will contain:

• Lyric sheet and/or lead sheets for that song. If you keep your rough drafts and rewrites, mark them accordingly, so you don't send out the unfinished versions by mistake!

• The names, phone numbers, and addresses of each cowriter on that song AND their performing rights affiliation (BMI, ASCAP, or SESAC).

• If there are any copublishers on that song, include their names, addresses, and phone numbers on a page for reference.

• Photocopies or printouts of any correspondence pertaining to that song. (If a letter you receive mentions more than one of your songs, make a photocopy for each respective file.)

• Photocopies or printouts of any contracts that pertain to that song (for example, a cowriter's agreement, a copublisher's agreement, an assignment of copyright agreement) or any legal documents that pertain to that song, so you don't have any unpleasant surprises looming over your future about anyone who has ties to your song without your knowledge.

• The copyright registration certificate (or the letter saying you've sent for it) or any forms from other song protection services.

• The performing rights clearance forms (BMI, ASCAP, or SESAC) and any correspondence to or from them.

• Any correspondence or forms from the Harry Fox Agency or other agency collecting your mechanical royalties (or reports from the record company about these).

The value of these files and cards will become apparent after you've called about thirty producers and are preparing for another call or visit when you discover you can't remember whether it was producer X or Y who already passed on the song you want to present.

Aside from the obvious value in being able to keep track of what you have or haven't done with a song, this organizational process is psychologically valuable in helping you view your songs as product in the marketplace. It takes a little of the edge off rejection by keeping you constantly involved in pitching your songs on an ongoing basis to many industry people.

Keep your tape/CD copies well labeled with the song titles on each. Once more, don't forget to put your name, address, and phone number on the tape/CD, the insert, the box, and your lyric sheets. Have everything ready so you don't need to delay if someone asks you for a copy.

It's also a good idea to keep some 3″ × 5″ cards or a small notebook with you or PDA (Personal Digital Assistant like Palm Pilot, Handspring, etc.) at all times so you can jot down any info you pick up "on the street." The cards are better than little scraps of paper or matchbook covers because they don't get lost and are easier to file. The street information you pick up is usually about who's recording now, a new producer with an unknown act who might give you the opportunity to get in on the ground floor, or a valuable Web site or service.

Showcasing

Performing your own songs on live showcases, either alone or in the context of a band, is yet another way to expose them for various purposes:

1. For feedback from an audience.
2. For other songwriters as a way to network and find collaborators.
3. To audition for record companies or other industry people (producers, managers, publishers).
4. To audition for booking agents and club owners to get live performing gigs.

Most cities, regardless of how small, have a club where you can play a few original songs. Though most professional club gigs require that you play predominantly contemporary hits or standards, depending on the audience, you can usually get by with throwing in a few of your own over the course of an evening. This is a good way to gauge audience reaction to your songs. You don't always get it right away, but after they hear them a few times, you'll see which ones start to get requests.

In most big cities there are "writers' nights" somewhere that are fairly loose. They are informal gatherings where you just show up and play or prescheduled, organized events that you may have to audition for in advance. Talk to whoever's in charge of organizing the talent and get the real story so you don't sign up late and end up showcasing for two drunks and a bartender at 3 A.M.

If money is tight for you, you may have to weigh the value of taking part in these showcases. You will rarely, if ever, be paid for writers' night showcases. Occasionally a club owner might split part of the admissions collected at the door with the performers, but don't count on it. If you're a working band and you have to give up a paying gig somewhere to showcase without pay, you're going to want some assurance that someone worthwhile will be listening. If you do it just for fun and performing experience, that may be enough. The deciding factor is the degree of benefit you get out of it.

Established, well-publicized showcases in major music centers that regularly draw industry people are always worth playing at (and attending regularly, even if you don't play). Networking is the most important benefit of these showcases. You not only have a chance to meet and be heard by industry pros, but meeting, hearing, and being heard by other writers and artists can lead to an amazing number of career opportunities. For example:

- Someone likes the way you sing and wants you to play on a demo or master session— or you want them to play on yours.

- Someone likes your songs, lyrics, or music and wants you to collaborate with them— or vice versa.

- You make new friends and become part of a mutual support group.

- You find out about resources, organizations, and services that can further your career.

- You get the gossip about local artists' recording sessions and other projects needing material.

- You are inspired and motivated by being around other creative people who are being inspired and motivated.

The more people you meet, the more possibilities open up for you. One person introduces you to a few more who, in turn, introduce you to others. All these contacts increase your odds of finding whatever you're looking for.

If you're auditioning for record companies, it's imperative that you perform primarily original material. A&R people are not interested in the way you play the hits unless you do them in a totally unique way. If you're working a "cover" gig, check with the owner to see if you can throw in a set of predominantly originals to play when you know the company reps will be there. Make sure the companies know what time you'll be doing your original set. Hopefully, by now, you've developed a snail-mail or e-mail list of appropriate music industry people who should be invited.

Print handbills. If you're working a regular gig at the club, try to get the owner to help pay for them (Good luck!). Tell him you'll distribute them. Hopefully, you're working at a club that has a mailing list of its own. If not, try to get the club owner to put one together by having his patrons sign a list. If they like you, they'll receive a notice when you're playing there again.

Consultant/author Tim Sweeney suggests that you have a rubber stamp made with your Web site address on it. Give it to the doorperson at the club to use (instead of the one they usually use) to stamp people's hands as they enter. It reminds people to check out your Web site once they get home.

If you're doing a one-shot, one-night showcase at a club you haven't played before:

1. Make sure your appearance is listed on their mailer if the club has one. If it's a regularly scheduled "showcase night" that promotes itself generically, it may not mention specific acts.

2. Check with the people who run the showcase for any tips that will help you come off well in their club. Remember, they've seen lots of acts win or lose in their place, and that perspective can be very valuable to you.

3. If you have a band, make sure the stage is big enough to accommodate your instruments, amps, etc., with enough room for whatever stage movement you need to show yourself to best advantage. If there isn't enough room, look for another club.

4. If there is a house P.A. system, talk to whoever runs it. Generally, if you have a sound person you work with regularly and the house system is adequate, it's better for your person to work with the club's sound person to get the best sound out of the room. If the club's sound system isn't adequate and you bring in your own, the procedure is riskier. Your sound person should be someone who can tailor the sound output to the acoustic properties of the room with the right E.Q. (treble/bass adjustments) and speaker placement and who is willing to accept advice from the club's sound person. I've seen some good groups empty the house because they wouldn't listen to advice and played too loudly for the room. Volume must be tailored according to the size and shape of the room and whether the walls are reflective or absorbent. If you're doing a record company showcase, being able to hear clean vocals is important, so start there and mix around it.

5. Make sure you have a sound check to work out all the problems and to set your instrument levels.

6. Show up on time for sound checks and performances.

7. Make sure the lighting is adequate. Will someone be running the lights? Make sure they're aware of any lighting cues you might need. Write them down.

8. See if they have a place to display your photos.

9. Know ahead of time exactly how much time you can have for your set and stick to it.

10. If you need a piano, make sure it's in tune.

11. Be cooperative with everyone at the club, including the waitresses. It's the difference between your coming back to the club or not, between having the employees tell everyone to come and see you or telling everyone you're losers.

12. Talk with the owner about guest lists and guest policies beforehand so you'll know what arrangements to make for them. This will avoid a bad scene at the door involving guests whom you want to be in a receptive state of mind toward your group.

13. Dress with some conscious thought about how you look individually or as a group on stage. No matter what you decide to wear, make it a calculated choice rather than looking like you just got off work as a mechanic and didn't have time to change.

14. Plan your sets carefully, considering the length of the set, pacing, and where you should place your strongest material. Generally, if you have a potential hit single or other very commercial material, begin and end with it. If you're going to be the last set, put strong material at the beginning of your performance. Record people frequently have other places to go and are in a hurry to leave. If you play less commercial tunes to open

and think you'll finish strong, you'll find when you hit the heavy ones that your guests have already gone.

15. Make sure all information concerning the showcase is conveyed to the whole group.

If you're auditioning for a club gig, most of the above list will also apply; but here are some additional questions to ask that will help you tailor your performance to the needs of the club. What does the club owner want? Classic rock and R&B, all Top 40 stuff, Top 40 with some originals? Who will be in the club's audience? Under eighteen? A singles' bar drinking crowd?

Pick a club that wants the kind of music you enjoy playing or you're wasting your time. The audience won't like you and the gig will get old very fast. The attitude "We'll make them dig what we do" is admirably ambitious, but chances are the owner knows the audience better than you do.

Contests

Contests provide songwriters, singers, and bands with an opportunity for validation/acknowledgment of their talent as well as an opportunity to win prizes.

Contests are created for many different reasons and it's important to be able to assess whether or not you're wasting your money to submit material at all. Most contests are created to make money, though there are always contests that spring up for other reasons, for example, to find a theme song for an organization or a city. There have been several competitions for a new national anthem, for instance. Many nonprofit songwriting and music organizations use competitions to raise operating funds. These contests are usually open to writers from all over the world.

The loftier reason, aside from making money, is to find and expose new talent. Seldom do contests translate *directly* into commercially successful record deals, hit songs, etc. There are, however, a wide range of potential benefits, depending on the scope of the contest.

The long-defunct American Song Festival and Music City Song Festivals offered, by virtue of their judging procedures, the benefit of being heard by many judges and of each song being heard by several judges who could turn in the code numbers of songs they particularly liked. After the contest was over, the judge would be provided with a list of the writers he/she requested and their addresses and phone numbers so the judges could, on their own, request additional material. This benefit was a valuable door opener for many writers to establish ongoing relationships with the music publisher and producer judges.

Beyond prizes and validation, one of the valuable prizes was that winners were provided with more door-opening tools via the publicity they received as contest winners. This could, in turn, be used for inclusion in query letters or e-mails to industry professionals requesting permission to send tapes.

Submission Procedures

Each competition will give you its own submission requirements on the entry blank, but the following are common to all.

An *entry form* is submitted with each song submitted in each category (if there is more than one category). Fill out each form completely as though it was the only one submitted. In nearly all cases, it is acceptable to make photocopies of the original form. To save yourself some work, fill out the basic name/address/phone information on the original before making the copies so all you have to add is song titles, writer(s), if different, and categories.

A *fee* is required for each tape submitted in each category. Fees can range up to $15 or more per song per category. Entry fees are certainly justifiable. It is not cheap to promote and organize a contest of any kind. Advertising is expensive and, as the now-defunct American Song Festival discovered, it's not enough to just announce that the deadlines are rolling around and assume that those songwriters who entered last year will automatically enter again. Each year they have to go after a whole new group of writers because last year's entrants who didn't at least receive an honorable mention are likely to believe that, if someone didn't recognize their hit, the contest is a rip-off and the judges don't know anything. The last thing they'll allow themselves to believe is that their song just wasn't good enough.

In addition to advertising, contests must hire people to process entries, book, coordinate, and supervise judges and judging sessions; keep financial records; answer phone inquiries; and many other tasks. In some cases, judges are also paid.

Some critics have actually advised writers not to pay a fee for submission to contests, particularly if they get a critique because "you should never pay for a critique." Nonsense! That philosophy originated as a way to protect writers from songsharks who would ask a writer to pay a small fee for a critique and then give their song a rave review as a way to set them up for a publishing contract for which they would unscrupulously ask for an additional fee.

Songwriting competitions usually require one song per cassette to facilitate easy coding and tracking of a song, eliminate confusion among judges regarding which song is to be heard, and make it easier to re-que for the next judge.

A lyric sheet is usually requested to speed the judging process. A judge can listen to and judge a song by listening to a verse and chorus of the song while scanning the remainder of the lyric. Lyric sheets should always look as professional as possible, be neatly typed with sections (verse/chorus/bridge) separated.

Rules and Regulations

Many competitions request that your name not appear on the tape or lyric sheet to avoid the possibility of favoritism should the judge recognize the writer's name. It is especially important, in those cases, for the writer or performer to completely fill out the submission form so that the person initially processing the tape can code the submission form, the lyric sheet, and tape. Don't be too concerned about it, though. If you don't eliminate your name, the contest will black it out themselves. In fact, it's always a good idea to have a proper copyright notice (© year, copyright owner) on each lyric sheet no matter where you send it or for what purpose.

| Categories

There are great variations between contests in the areas of categories. The major groupings are amateur and professional. Some contests will rightfully place great importance on the division between amateur and professional songwriters with a variety of methods of making the distinction. One method is to disqualify you in the amateur category if you are a member of BMI, ASCAP, or SESAC with the erroneous assumption being that, to be a member of a performing rights organization, you must have a song released on record. In reality, though it is impractical to belong if you don't have a record released, the organizations may sign a writer if they feel he/she is talented enough that it is likely to happen in the future.

Another method is that used by the *Billboard* Song Contest in which you can only enter if you have not averaged more than $5000 per year in songwriting royalties since 1992. This method gives great latitude because one can still be an excellent professional songwriter and not attain that goal.

Yet another method is that one may not enter the amateur category if they've had a song released on a recording before a certain date, usually the deadline date. This method has caused great problems, at times requiring notarized affidavits as proof and delaying the final disposition of prizes based on objections of amateur entrants. However, this is still, probably, the fairest way to divide categories.

Your best strategy, if you feel you are an exceptional writer, is not to allow your ego to take you into the professional category, but without breaking any rules, to stay in the amateur group.

Stylistic categories, though more fair for obvious reasons, are problematic mostly because amateur songwriters in particular often have difficulty distinguishing pop from R&B or rock, country from folk, etc. They either enter the same songs in several categories just to be safe or risk entering one song in an inappropriate category and having it eliminated, not because it's not a quality song but because of a poor category choice. The best approach is to play it safe by entering more than one category, if you can afford it, after getting as much feedback as you can from fellow writers and friends on the most appropriate category.

Some of the criteria to consider in making the choice of songs to enter involves a process of elimination, which, in fact, is involved in the judging as well. So it may be instructive to come from the viewpoint of a judge who knows that certain factors will preclude a song being a winner even though it may receive an honorable mention. Here are a few:

1. A song without a chorus
2. The title doesn't appear in the chorus or first or last line of the verse.
3. Clichéd lyrics
4. Little or no melodic contrast between verses, chorus, and bridge

Along with those factors that will immediately eliminate a song from competition, another factor that will enhance its chances of staying in the race is a well-produced demo. This doesn't mean spending $500 to $1000 in a state-of-the-art studio. It does mean that your singer should be convincing. (Don't sing it yourself if you're not the best singer for it.). The sound should be clean, and the tape copy clean.

| Prizes

You will partially base your decision whether or not to enter a competition on the lure of the money or hardware offered to winners. Customarily, a grand prize is awarded to an overall winner and first, second, third, and more prizes awarded in each stylistic category. In addition, honorable mention certificates may be awarded to songs that judges felt deserved special consideration but didn't make the finals.

| Cautions

A history of take-the-money-and-run contests makes it important to be on the lookout for some distinguishing factors that help you recognize legitimate contests. Here are some things to look for:

1. If a contest has been in operation for more than a year, they should be willing to provide you with a list of previous winners.

2. If they offer you merchandise prizes, they should be able to prove to you that they have either purchased them or with an affidavit from the manufacturer that the merchandise has been donated. *Note:* Most manufacturers no longer directly donate equipment, but may work in conjunction with a local music store to make it available to the contest in consideration of publicity.

3. If the contest offers a cash prize, they should be able to offer proof that the money is in an escrow account that may only be distributed to winners. A common downfall of contests is to promise prize money with the honest hope that money received from entries will exceed the prize amount by enough to cover all expenses and profit. A very risky gamble because it is expensive to get enough publicity to insure *that* many entries, and once a contest fails to provide prizes on time, its reputation has been destroyed.

4. The individuals responsible for the contest should be listed in the advertising or on a Web site and there should be an address (street number) and phone number where they can be reached.

5. The contest officers, owners, representatives, judges, and their families should be ineligible to enter the contest.

6. Prize schedules and amounts as well as entry deadlines, deadlines for notification

of winners and awarding of prizes should be clearly listed on the application and the contest's Web site. If a deadline becomes impossible to meet, a predetermined process for notifying contestants should be implemented. New deadlines must be clearly stated.

7. Judges of the contest should be music industry professionals with proven experience in judging and critiquing songs and, hopefully, in a position to further your career.

8. Don't enter contests in which your entry becomes the property of the contest. In fact, look for a phrase that specifically says that it doesn't. However, the contest should have the right to play the song, print it, or use your name and photo for promotional purposes. Your career benefits directly from that publicity and is one of the unstated "prizes" for a winner.

Don't enter contests in which your entry becomes the property of the contest.

There is another caution related to ownership of your entry or winning song. Every year there are at least two or three individuals who want to get into the music publishing business and think that a great new way to find songs and finance their businesses is to have a contest and offer the winner a publishing contract. Sometimes they'll form a record company and their first recording artist will sing your song. Savvy writers don't enter these contests for two main reasons:

1. If you believe in the commercial potential of your songs, the worst "prize" you can imagine is that your song will be owned by an inexperienced and unconnected new publisher whose only means of financing a company and finding songs is to hold a contest.

2. Legitimate publishers never charge you to screen your songs. It is part of the business of a music publisher to find material and convince the writer that he can represent your song better than anyone else. So to set themselves up as someone who you "automatically" would want to publish your songs, without a track record or connections, is arrogant, to say the least. Frankly, under certain circumstances there may be writers who should not even sign with well-established major publishers because, in their individual circumstances, it may not be in their best interest.

Finding Contests

There are some well-established sources for info about contests:

- Jeff Mallett's Songwriter Site www.lyricist.com
  One of the best sources, which always has a fairly comprehensive list of contests.

Among the established and reputable contests are:

- The Unisong International Song Contest
  www.unisong.com
- The *Billboard* Song Contest
  www.billboard.com/songcontest
- The John Lennon Song Contest
  www.jlsc.com

- The Mid Atlantic Songwriters Contest
  www.saw.org/sawa.htm
- USA Songwriting Competition
  www.songwriting.net

Web Sites

If you're a songwriter and *not* an artist/band, having a Web site may not be worth the trouble. If you check the Net, you'll find relatively few. Here are some pros and cons to weigh.

Pros

1. If you want a place for people to listen to your songs, it can work fine. It's nice to be able to give someone a card with your Web address on it where they can get your personal information.

2. If you have great singers doing your demos, they're featured on your site, and you link to their sites, their fans might like to know more about the writer.

3. If you have collaborators, those writers can send people to your site, too.

4. If you're looking for collaborators, it's convenient to be able to send potential collaborators to your site to hear what you do. It saves time and the emotional stress of someone telling you they're not into what you're doing and could bring people to you who do like your music (or lyrics), even though you may never have met.

5. A Web site can create an incentive to write, particularly if you need deadlines to give you a push. Promise to have a new song posted on your site every week or every other week. Failure will produce incredible pangs of guilt, which, depending on your upbringing, can be a great motivator.

Cons

1. It'll cost about $70 per year to register your URL (Web address). If you're good at graphic design, want to invest in the software, and want to take the time to build it yourself, go for it. Otherwise, you'll need to hire someone to build and maintain the site. If you're good at learning from manuals, you can, without a lot of difficulty, learn to write html (hyper-text markup language) and maintain your own site. This involves periodically updating your site, uploading samples of your songs and lyrics and any personal info you want to add, and to the extent it's important to you, to promote it by actively linking to other compatible sites and making sure it's searchable by all the search engines.

2. Just because you build it doesn't mean anyone will automatically want to visit. It just doesn't work that way. Most of the people who will visit are those you'll send personally unless you have the time to invest in a promotional campaign. This might make sense if you're a writer who's very successful, like Diane Warren (www.realsongs.com), and everybody already knows about you and wants to know what you're up to. If you're an unknown songwriter just trying to get people to notice you, there are probably better options. (See "Online Pitch Services," in this chapter.)

If you do decide to create a Web site, you're a prolific songwriter, and you can upload audio files of great demos of your songs on a fairly regular basis, you can keep people coming back, assuming your songs are good enough to make people *want* to come back.

To make it more interesting, whenever you post a new song, write a piece to go with it explaining why and how you wrote it. Make it a kind of songwriter's diary, where you talk about what's going on in your life, what you do to promote your songs, what songs of other writers you like. My favorite sites of songwriters contain this kind of diary information.

If you're a writer/artist or band, there are more benefits:

1. Fans can keep track of when and where you're performing.

2. You can post:

- samples of your recordings
- interviews, both text and audio
- video clips
- photos of the band in action
- bios of band members

3. You can communicate with your fans via e-mail via your Web site. This communication could be one of your biggest assets in building your fan base.

4. Sales of your records and merchandise (T-shirts, hats, etc.)

5. Promote contests, events, and offer free recordings for special fans.

The con side for artists includes all those mentioned above for songwriters. It takes time and money to make it work for you and take advantage of all the benefits it provides. Regardless of all that, I feel that those benefits to your career can more than make up for the work.

I feel it's beyond the scope of this book to get into how to build and promote your Web site. There are a lot of great books and other Web sites out there that can do the topic much more justice than I could. The technology advances so quickly that the Internet itself becomes the most expedient way to research the latest books and sites about the topic. The changing technology also makes possible new and efficient services to help you market your music, like some of those mentioned in this chapter. Visit my Web site, www.johnbraheny.com to keep up to date.

(See the Appendix for a list of great songwriters' information Web sites.)

chapter fourteen

Additional Markets

Good songs have many different markets. Though most writers seem to think in terms of commercial radio, your skills can be used in a variety of ways.

With a little imagination, you can market even your most "off-the-wall" efforts. A friend of mine once wrote a song about his dog that expressed the sentiments of a lot of dog lovers. He sent the lyric to a magazine devoted to dogs; they printed it and paid him. He also sells a version suitable for framing via an ad in the magazine. He still makes money from it. It was a song a publisher would never have been interested in and he knew it, so he took that extra step and asked himself, "Who would be?"

The following are some additional markets to be aware of. For more of an in-depth look at each, check the Bibliography for recommended books and visit my Web site, www.johnbraheny.com, for up-to-date articles and resources in all these areas.

Film and Television

Film and television, though always important users of music, have become even more important in recent years. The success of TV shows featuring popular contemporary music and youth-market films that spawn million-seller soundtrack albums have combined to leave no doubt among film and television producers of the commercial power of contemporary music. That awareness has prompted them to hire, or contract on a project basis, music coordinators and music supervisors with record company and music publishing experience to make sure they get the best contemporary composers and songwriters for their projects.

The two major areas of music usage in film and TV are:

1. the background music score (also called underscore)
2. the song written for a film

Songs will either be pre-existing songs/and recordings or a song written and recorded specifically for the film. They are either "featured" (used prominently in strategic places) or used as "source music" you hear coming from a radio, stereo, jukebox, or other source on the screen.

Skills

If your goal is to do instrumental scoring and themes, you're ahead of the game if you know how to arrange and orchestrate. It also pays to have a good working knowledge of current synthesizer, MIDI, music composing and sequencing software, and recording technology. Keyboard players have an advantage in this area because the technology that allows a composer to create and record a substantial amount of the music simultaneously is keyboard-oriented. The best opportunities are available to those who have the greatest variety of skills because film and TV producers want a finished product (composed, performed, produced) for as little money as possible. Those who can do it with the least manpower in the fastest time can quote them the best prices. The best-paying, but most demanding of all the jobs in this area are the weekly TV series, which require technical skill, discipline, and speed.

Richard "Koz" Kosinski is a successful scorer and songwriter for both film and TV. He describes the pressure of film scoring.

> Typically, a film starts out allowing about six weeks to do the music for, say, an hour-long film. Then it takes a week to choose a composer from maybe six who are up for the job, then another week to work on the contracts. So you might have three to four weeks at the most to write, arrange, produce, record, mix, and transfer (to the film). Then the music, dialogue, and sound effects are mixed to the film at a soundstage studio that has been booked six months ahead of time. There are a lot of projects booked in there afterwards, so if you don't make it, you're in deep trouble.
>
> With TV, especially cartoons where it's almost all music, it's a rough situation, too. Sometimes I'll work thirty-six hours at a stretch. This is a crazy job.

Koz and a partner usually do the complete score digitally. The other method of scoring is for a composer, arranger, and copyist to write out the complete score and record it "live" in the studio. This is sometimes a faster method, but the pressure is still great.

Learning

Colleges and universities with film and TV departments offer the best opportunities to learn the craft of scoring. In the major film and TV centers (Los Angeles, in particular), there are excellent classes taught by professional film and TV composers. To gain experience with a minimum of pressure, there are also opportunities to score industrial, educational, student films, and cable shows if you're competent and aggressive. Find out about *student films* by finding your closest college or university film department and posting your credits, skills, and availability on the department bulletin board. For *cable shows,* visit your local cable TV station and find out if there are any local programs that use different music on each show or new shows being produced that may need theme music.

Cable "public access" shows are low-budget shows created by local entrepreneurs using

The best opportunities are available to those who have the greatest variety of skills because film and TV producers want a finished product for as little money as possible.

production interns. They satisfy the cable companies' agreements to provide community access. You won't make much money on these projects, but by the time you've done a few of these, you should have an impressive demo reel or reels (a tape or CD containing samples of your work).

Whenever you finish a job, transfer the highlights to a videotape that you can use as an audition for your next project. Since, in scoring, it's as important to know where *not* to have music, you'll best demonstrate your taste by presenting a video demo that can demonstrate your ability to "spot" (determine the appropriate music for the appropriate spots in the film).

| Finding Work

You may also win friends and admirers along the way who will turn you on to yet more lucrative jobs. Those who become successful enough to score several series often hire assistants who are orchestrators, arrangers, copyists, and engineers. If you have those skills, working for a pro is a great way to get hands-on experience. Most professionals work in their own studios and can be found through the TV network on which the show is broadcast. Each show has its own office, so always ask for that specific show.

As soon as you've acquired enough credits to interest a film and TV music agent, you move into another strata where it gets easier to gain access to the big opportunities.

Songwriters have several ways to make contact. Each of the major film and TV studios has a music director or music supervisor who is the liaison with songwriters and film composers. Most prefer to deal with established writers, agents, music publishers, or record companies, but "open door" policies exist at some companies. Independent music coordinators and supervisors who deal with film projects are generally more accessible, but you can't afford not to try them all.

Reading *Variety* and *Hollywood Reporter* will give you leads on what films are casting, in preproduction, and currently shooting.

A backdoor approach is to present your songs to the music editors, producers, and directors of specific films so they can use them as "temp tracks" (i.e., songs used in scenes temporarily to establish a mood or set a dance tempo before making a final decision on songs). If they use one of your songs that has the right tempo and groove, they may ultimately want to replace it with a current hit. However, they may not be able to negotiate the rights to use the hit in the film and may end up using yours.

One of the most common strategies of film producers in obtaining soundtrack songs is to find a major recording artist to sing at least the title song. A hit song in a film can be a major marketing tool for both the record and the film, so they'll look first for hit artists and hit songwriters. But several things can go wrong. The artist or record company may reject the offer because they may not feel that the film will help the artist's career, the release schedule of the film may conflict with the release of other product from the artist, or, in the end, the film company may not be able to afford the artist. The film company can be running out of time (and money) without finding that major song and major artist to sing it. With your "temp track" approach, after hearing your song used repeatedly (even if "temporarily"), the editor and director may begin to feel as though it belongs there. If other strategies fall through, you're already in position. The above scenario happens predominantly in mid- to low-budget films. Major big-budget film producers don't leave anything to chance. There are so few great film vehicles compared to TV that publishers will even split the copyright to a song as an investment in what a successful film could generate in royalties.

It's important to be aware that the decision-making politics in filmmaking are, in most cases, extremely erratic. Financial backers, producers, directors, stars, agents, and others vie for decision power. These are most often people with no musical background who "know what they like" or "I have a nephew who's a songwriter," a situation that can be both a blessing and a curse. One day you've got a song in a film, the next day it's out. Or vice versa. If your song is good and is perceived that day to be appropriate (or you *are* the "nephew"), you've got a shot.

On the subject of appropriateness, writers often feel that it's desirable for their song to tell the story of the film. Wrong. It's much better to express the emotion of the scene. The music shouldn't compete with the visuals, but complement and support them.

If you want to write for TV, look for TV series that use lots of new, unknown songs. You have the luxury of "researching" while you watch TV since the credits list the production company and music supervisor. Film and TV representatives at BMI, ASCAP, and SESAC can also help, but I suggest going to their Web sites to get as much information as possible first.

Writers often feel that it's desirable for their song to tell the story of the film. Wrong. It's much better to express the emotion of the scene.

How You Get Paid and What You Can Earn

The pay in film and TV ranges from ridiculously bad to incredibly good based, as usual, on your bargaining power and the budgets of the projects. Your bargaining power comes from your talent, skill, speed, and your past credits. For already existing songs, synchronization licenses are granted to the film or TV production company by the copyright owner (publisher) and are totally negotiable. But film and TV producers usually want to own the publishing rights to your song. In cases where they pay you to write a song or score specifically for the project, they want it to be a "work for hire" so they'll own it outright. Either way, you'll probably get an advance, retain 50 percent of the performance royalties from airplay, 50 percent of the mechanicals if it gets into a soundtrack album, and hopefully writer credit on screen. For TV, the biggest income comes from themes and scores for series that play every week or, even better, every night. You'll receive performance royalties from BMI or ASCAP every time they're shown. You'll hope the shows go into syndication so you'll continue to get paid. Check with your performing rights organization regarding proper reporting procedures. The performing rights organizations do not pay royalties on American theatrical performances for films, but will collect from their foreign counterparts for theatrical performances in those countries. In the United States, performance royalties are paid if the film is shown on television.

If you're offered a contract to have a song in a film or to score a film, get the advice of an entertainment attorney who specializes in film and TV, as this is a complex area. If you have a publisher, they'll negotiate with the production company, and if you self-publish, you'll hopefully have an administrator who will do it.

In "Motion Picture Soundtrack Songwriting and Performing" from *The Musician's Business and Legal Guide* (see Bibliography), Mark Halloran (a founding partner at Erickson & Halloran law firm and former vice president of Feature Business Affairs at Universal Pictures) and Thomas A. White (a business affairs advisor in the record and music publishing industries) give the following picture of writer royalties for a chart-oriented single from a film by a writer/artist/producer. The information was gathered in 2001.

Let's assume you make a deal at Paramount. You are a writer/performer/producer who writes a title song and records a title song master. You are paid $25,000 for the song and $25,000 to record. You retain the writer's share, but Paramount retains the publisher's share. You receive a royalty of 12% retail U.S., prorated, on CDs, and 9% on singles. Your master is three minutes long. The picture is a blockbuster. Your single sells 1,000,000 copies in the United States, 750,000 foreign, and hits number one on *Billboard*'s Hot 100 Pop Chart. The soundtrack CD, on which you have one of the ten cuts, sells 500,000 copies in the United States and 375,000 copies overseas. Exhibit 3 gives you an idea of what your earnings might be.

Exhibit 3

ROUGH INCOME SUMMARY

The following rough income summary is designed to alert you to sources of income rather than to provide exact figures (although we have done our best to be accurate).

A. Writer

1. Writing Fee (nonrecoupable)	$25,000
2. Song Synchronization License for Film	0
3. Performance Income (worldwide)	
(a) From Film in Theaters	
(i) United States	0
(ii) Foreign	$20,000
(b) Radio Performances	$100,000
(c) Home Video	0
(d) Pay TV	*
(e) Free TV	
(i) U.S. Network TV (two runs)	$3,000
(ii) U.S. Syndicated TV (two runs 150 stations)	$600
(iii) Foreign	$5,000

4. Sheet Music (40,000 copies @ 10 cents/copy)			$4,000
5. Mechanicals			
(a) United States (¾ statutory)			
(i) Single (A-side only) (1,000,000 × 2.831 cents)			$28,310
(ii) CD (500,000 × 2.831 cents)			$14,155
(b) Foreign			
(i) Single (750,000 × 3.00 cents)			$22,500
(ii) CD (375,000 × 3.00 cents)			$11,250
		Total	$233,815
B. Recording Artist			
1. Recording Fee (nonrecoupable)			$25,000
2. Master License for Film			0
3. United States Record Sales			
(a) Singles (one song) (1,000,000 copies)			$76,500
(b) CDs (500,000 copies)			$49,401
4. Foreign Record Sales			
(a) Singles (750,000 copies)			$47,812
(b) CDs (375,000 copies)			$27,225
Less Soundtrack Conversion Costs			($3,000)
		Total	$222,938

* Figures presently unavailable.

I highly recommend reading *The Musician's Business and Legal Guide*. For additional in-depth information, there is an excellent excerpt online regarding the business of film and TV from Todd Brabec and Jeffrey Brabec's book, *Music, Money & Success* at www.asca p.com/filmtv/filmtv.html. I also highly recommend reading their book.

Commercial Jingles

Here's some background on the making of commercial jingles and the qualities, beyond creativity and composing and production skills, needed by a jingle music producer to be successful.

To air a single thirty-second commercial on a prime-time network TV hit show may cost a client (sponsor) over $500,000. That's just to pay for the airtime alloted to it, not for the time and effort to create it. This explains the tremendous responsibility ad agencies have to deliver commercials that bring results to the clients who make that kind of investment. There are advertising agencies with multimillion-dollar-a-year clients without whom those agencies would not exist. This explains the legendary paranoia of ulcer-ridden advertising executives. It also explains why it's so difficult for beginners to get into the business of making music for commercials. Like the old Catch-22, "If you're not already successful, how do we know you can do the job?"

With the stakes so high, ad agencies can't afford to gamble. If they choose music that sounds less than professional and appropriate, they risk losing an account and their jobs. So a composer must not only understand the advertising medium and be thoroughly professional, but must be a kind of psychologist, instilling confidence in his abilities and making agency personnel feel secure in their musical choices.

As a composer, your problems may be compounded by the fact that few ad agency people really understand music and may not have the language to convey their needs to you.

So you need to become adept at translating lines like, "I want something like Metallica, only softer." (Translation: He wants high energy but low volume.) He may request a musical style in terms of a particular artist or song ("I want something that sounds sort of like Madonna's last single"). It's important that you keep current. Avoid using technical or musical terminology. You don't have to impress them—they already accept that you know your business. You must also learn to mix demographics into your music. In other words, you must target the audience. How old are they? What do they like? What do they already buy? Where do they live? How much disposable income do they have? In general, what are their needs as a group? What style of music appeals to them? Those are some of the questions agency personnel will be able to answer. They'll usually have a storyboard already worked out—a series of drawings (like a comic book)—or an animated computer script depicting the way they see the commercial from beginning to end. Each section is timed.

They may also be able to give you a script so you can get a feel for the emotional content of the scene and perhaps a lyric or slogan to work from. (If you're lucky, the lyric is actually singable.) You'll seldom have the opportunity to create the lyric yourself, but will be creating an "underscore" (instrumental background), music for the lyric, or some of each.

You and several other producers will usually be asked to come up with demos to play for the client. Usually you'll be given a minimal budget to cover demo costs, but occasionally you'll be asked to do the demos on spec (your money). Synth demos are usually not hard to put together for a maximum sixty-second spot and not hard to adapt and change quickly. It's a good idea to come up with more than one to give them a choice. If you get something they like, you can just embellish the tracks you have for the final recording.

Ad agencies prefer to do business with music people with whom they have good rapport, who are professional, who understand their needs, and who deliver the goods at an equal or better price than anyone else. They also like to deal with people who are personable and even charismatic, because they can depend on them to impress the multimillion-dollar clients. It won't do to have the client come to your session and have the ad executive who hired you have to apologize for your bad attitude. That's not the way business is done at that level. He wants the client to love you and compliment him on his good taste. A great personality will never substitute for competence in this business, but in this case, at least, it can provide a competitive edge.

The Audition Demo

Because the competition in commercials is heavy, having a first-rate demo that shows your skill and versatility is essential. Collect not more than ten pieces of music on not more than five minutes of tape or CD. If you've already got legitimate credits, include them. If not, don't be intimidated. The agencies are always looking for new talent because some composers, after a few years, get too expensive and their style gets old. Agencies look for fresh ideas and very contemporary styles, particularly for youth-market products. Put a sample of whatever you do best first on the demo. Do a piece of atmospheric background on it, create some jingles for imaginary products, show them some different moods in both vocal jingles and instrumentals, and some different styles. Many commercials only identify the product on screen and not in the jingle. Create a couple of evocative jingles with lyrics that express some emotional comment on life in general. Print a label and CD insert with your logo so you'll look like a pro. Print some credits or other self-promotion on the insert, and don't forget your address, phone number, e-mail address, and Web site. If you have a site devoted to your business, with samples of other commercials you've done, you're ahead of the game; but you also want them to have an actual CD (or CD-Rom or videotape) with the actual commercial and resumé that they can keep on file and put their hands on quickly.

Making Contact

Everyone I talk to in the jingle business seems to have entered it in a different way. Some started out as singers on jingle sessions, some were musicians and arrangers. Personally, I got started when an advertising executive in Montreal heard an electronic music cut on my album and called me in L.A. to see if I'd do something like it for a Toyota commercial. After doing that and a couple more for that agency, I systematically started pursuing jingle jobs. I secured a copy of *The Standard Directory of Advertising Agencies* (available at most libraries). It's also called the "Red Book" (http://library.dialog.com/bluesheets/html/b10178.html) and it lists all the ad agencies, their clients, and who to contact at the local offices.

These people, called "creative directors," are the ones who screen and choose the creative talent for the "spots," including actors and actresses, locations, film production companies, and jingle music composers and producers. I called every agency in Los Angeles that produced commercials for radio and TV. (Some were print only.) The first question I asked was whether they ever used or were open to using original music in their spots. Some replied that they only used "library" music (see "Production Music Libraries," in this chapter) that they bought inexpensively by the minute.

After locating the ones who at least used original music occasionally, I made appointments to meet the creative directors or their assistants, who were in most cases quite open and eager to hear something new. My presentation included the info that I was a recording artist, coproduced my own album, and had already composed and produced music for national network spots. (I brought copies to play.) I'd never been good at promoting myself, but, in advertising, it is absolutely necessary to go in with all your credits blazing. The competition is fierce! I don't know how eager they would have been if I hadn't had any credits.

When you get a meeting, take copies of your audiovisuals. After the meeting, send a card to thank them for their time. On a file card or database, keep track of:

1. their contact information
2. their clients (always subject to change)
3. who you met there
4. their comments on your presentation
5. the names of their secretaries and assistants
6. a date and time to call back (Ask them before you leave the meeting.)

You'll probably make several calls before you talk to your main contact, but you'll make friends with the secretary or assistants, who also will be able to give you valuable information on upcoming projects. Continue to update your data file every time you call, noting the date. All this is important because after your first twenty appointments (or sooner), you'll start to lose track of who's where.

You're known to the agencies as a "music producer," and they count on you to deliver them a finished product. If you can do all or most of it yourself, fine. It's important not to kid yourself about your own abilities, though. This is serious business. Hire pros to do whatever you can't do *extremely well.* Depending on what they're looking for, you may be hiring an arranger, singers and musicians (including filling out union contracts), and booking and paying the studio.

Most major jingle activity is in New York, Chicago, Dallas, and Los Angeles, so if you don't live near those cities, you need to pursue some other options. Among those options is to establish an Internet presence with a great-looking Web site. Make that your online office. Since audio files can be sent anywhere and since any ad agency worth approaching these days has a high-speed Internet connection, you can do a lot of business that way.

Here are some other suggestions for finding work as an independent jingle producer:

• Place ads in advertising and production trade magazines such as *Adweek* (www.adweek.com), *Advertising Age* (www.adage.com), and *Millimeter* (www.millimeter.com).

• Contact your state film commission and try to get listed as a music resource in the catalogue they send to companies to solicit film projects in your state. These catalogues are also sent to companies within the state. Search the Internet under "film commission."

• Most major cities have an ad club whose members include ad agencies, media professionals, clients, and music producers in that region. They also have newsletters in which you can advertise. The American Advertising Federation is a national organization for advertising professionals. They have periodic conventions in various cities that provide valuable opportunities to show your wares and make contacts. Get information on membership and schedules from:

American Advertising Federation

Web site: www.aaf.org
1101 Vermont Avenue, NW Suite 500
Washington, DC 20005-6306
Tel.: (202) 898-0089
Fax: (202) 898-0159

Western Region Office
251 Post Street, Suite 302
San Francisco, CA 94108
Tel.: (415) 421-6867
Fax: (415) 421-0512

Start a Local Agency

Yet another possibility is to form your own small-scale ad agency and music producer combination dealing with small local accounts. It requires some research, but check out local restaurants, clubs, hotels, tourist attractions, and similar businesses to see if they do or will do radio ads. If you have a home studio, put together a catchy jingle for some of them. Write a sample script, get a voiceover actor to read it, and present your potential "clients" with a thirty-second version of the whole thing. If it sounds professional, you'll be surprised at how positively people react to hearing their very own commercial jingle. If you lay down several different kinds of tracks, you can just put new vocals and lyrics on them for each different prospect you approach.

Your competition for local radio ads are the radio stations themselves, whose salesmen sell businesses package deals that include their staff announcer's writing and reading the ad copy. A good plan is to form alliances with the ad sales people at the stations and help them put together those packages. Your advantage is that you can provide the client with an original jingle and likely can do it cheaper than a jingle house, which has more overhead. You would sell the jingle to the client and have the station's announcer write and read additional copy.

A drawback to this approach is that, in order to give the client an inexpensive deal, you'd pretty much have to do it without union help. When you do non-union spots and play on them yourself, you do not receive residuals. You'll charge a one-time "buyout" fee that includes your creative fee and covers your production cost. You'll hope to create a lasting relationship with the client and periodically create new jingles for him.

Go to http://musicoffice.com to see a good example of a commercial jingle agreement and how to negotiate it. There are also some other resources there to help you get started. Also check out www.jinglebiz.com. They have a great list of resources and offer a reasonably priced course in starting your own jingle business. If you're not interested in being in business for yourself, another alternative is to hook up with a jingle music production company or "jingle house." These are established businesses that usually represent several composers. You may not have the potential to make as much money if you choose this route, but you wouldn't have as many expenses and headaches, either. Find them in the Yellow Pages and on the Internet, usually under "music arrangers and composers," "music producers," "jingle production," or "commercial music production." Also, check out the local recording studios and find out if any jingle production is done there and who is doing it. Compile a demo of your best work and play it for them.

What If You Have a Jingle Idea for a Major Product?

If you think up an outstanding jingle or concept for a particular product, can you sell it to an agency? Your odds are not good. Remember, ad agencies who represent those products pay a lot of money to copy writers in their company to come up with those ideas. There's a good chance they don't want to hear yours. If they do, you risk that they'll borrow your idea or some important aspects of it without paying you. Ideas are not copyrightable. What you *can* copyright is an actual slogan or jingle (song), but unless it's compatible with the product image already planned by the agency, the odds are against the company using it no matter how clever the idea. Having said that, if you believe enough in your idea, you should give it a shot anyway. The best shot is to present them a finished product.

The Money

Today's commercials use a lot of recent or oldies hits (depending on the age of the target consumer), either in their original versions or rewritten for a specific product. In those cases, the ad agencies will negotiate a "synch fee" with the song's publisher, assuming that the writer doesn't have a clause in the writer/publisher contract preventing the song from being used that way. The writer and publisher split the synch fees, which, for use of a hit, can be $150,000 to over a million dollars for a year. In addition, if the agency wants to use the original recording instead of a new version, an additional "master use" fee must be negotiated with the record company, which can, in some cases, exceed the cost of the synch license. In either case, the writer and publisher will also receive performance royalties for airplay of the song (see the next page).

Let's assume now that we're not dealing with a previous hit but with the writer of a commercial jingle with lyrics or just instrumental tracks ("underscores"). These have three sources of income, depending on how you work it: creative fees, union session payments and residuals, and possibly performing rights royalties.

You can negotiate a "creative fee" over and above the cost of production because you're creating the music. Creative fees usually range from $5,000 on the low end to $50,000 on the high end, depending on whether it's a local or national spot. Just as it is in any other business, the amount of that fee also depends on clout and chutzpah (nerve). It takes a lot of chutzpah to ask for twice what you think you can get and negotiate from there. At any rate, figuring out what to ask for is one of the most difficult parts of the business. You don't want to downgrade yourself by asking too little or price yourself out of business by asking too much.

I once bid against two competitors on a job that was to be a series of thirty-second spots, variations on a basic theme. My bid was based on my figuring out a low-cost way to do the variations. I lost the bid, and it wasn't till two years later that the agency representative would tell me why. The spots had gone for nearly twice my figure, because the other two bids were in the same neighborhood and the client decided that if my competitors, both well-known pros, were charging that much, he didn't see how I could possibly deliver for half that amount. The ad man tried to convince the client, but the psychology of "If it costs more, it must be better" worked against me, and it has since changed my negotiating tactics.

Bid high, and let them tell you it's too steep. You can then say, "Well, let me see if I can figure out some shortcuts without compromising the quality." You get back to them with something like, "I made a good deal with a new studio so I can knock off a couple hundred," or "I can use three singers instead of six," etc. If you have a solid relationship with the ad agency, they may hint at what sort of ballpark figure they're thinking about, but they'd rather not. Obviously, if you're talking about Coca-Cola, you're dealing with a company that annually spends billions on advertising, as opposed to a local jewelry store that spends thousands. Creative fees, those over and above production costs for a national commercial jingle, can range from $1,500 to $15,000 per spot, depending on your clout, the budget, and how big and time-consuming the job is. It's all negotiable.

If you play on commercials, other money is available to you from union scale payments, from the American Federation of Musicians (AF of M), or, if you sing, even higher payments from the American Federation of Television and Radio Artists (AFTRA) or the Screen Actors Guild (SAG). At the end of every thirteen-week period in which a spot is run, you'll receive a residual check for the same union scale you made on the original session.

The rate schedules are available from your local AF of M and AFTRA offices. They're comprehensive and complex, but anyone involved in producing or playing on commercials should be familiar with them for their own protection.

The performing rights societies (ASCAP and BMI) have instituted performance royalties for music used in commercials. Since those organizations are continually updating their rates and conditions of payment, you should check with them for current payment schedules.

Except for pre-existing music licensed by the copyright owner to be used in a commercial, nearly all music written for commercials is considered "work-for-hire," in which the client (sponsor) retains all rights to the composition. In that case, performance rights may only be paid if the writer obtains a licensing provision from the agency/client that *excludes* the performance rights from the rights granted the client. Contact your performing rights organizations for a license that protects your right to receive these royalties.

In the above-mentioned income sources for jingles, the amounts paid are based on the ways the music is used in the jingle, whether it's broadcast locally or on network, whether it's used regionally or nationally, whether it's played on radio or television, and how often and in what time period it is played.

Production Music Libraries

Songwriters and composers don't always realize that income isn't just generated by their own performances of their songs or other artists recording their songs. There's a world of opportunities beyond having radio hits. Production music libraries can pay your rent if you get enough uses of your music going at once. Here's how it works.

• Problem for video, TV, film producers: They need music for their small-budget productions and find that hiring a composer to create an original score is too expensive. If they need songs, it's also too expensive to use songs and recordings that have already been successful. They also don't have time to deal with calls from hundreds of composers and songwriters who'd like to submit material. Others who use music are producers of multimedia projects, video games, commercials, and radio "bumpers" between programs.

• Problem for unknown writers: They don't have the clout to get their songs into big-budget productions and don't have the time to constantly research all the new low-budget shows that may be in production and in need of underscore music or songs. It would involve contacting hundreds of little production companies and establishing relationships with their busy music staffers, only to find that they frequently change jobs. (Though if you can keep up with them, they usually end up in similar jobs because *their* relationships with writers are extremely valuable to the visual producers who hire them.)

• Solution: Production music libraries. These companies secure the rights (more about that later) to songs and instrumental underscore compositions submitted to them that they feel they can place in audiovisual productions. They then assemble and reproduce "libraries" of these collections on CDs and send them to all the production companies. They're indexed by musical style; mood; instrumentation; length; tempo; male, female, or group vocal; and any other attributes that allow an audiovisual producer to target the type of music they need. They find the piece, use it, and fill out a cue sheet for the appropriate performing rights organization (ASCAP, BMI, SESAC), which includes information on how the song is used, how long, name of the piece, composer(s), and owner of the copyright.

• Some of the bigger libraries hire their own in-house composers to create music for them but will occasionally look outside for songs. They will also have lists of independent composers they've worked with in the past to fill in if their staff composers get overworked or if they can't provide a unique style their clients are looking for. That's where you have your best opportunity.

How good does it have to be?

Since they can only use "master quality" recordings for film and television, they have to be excellent. If you're submitting instrumental pieces, they should be well arranged.

Stay away from using stock sounds that come packaged with your keyboard. Try to create fresh sounds. Generating a mood is important. They'll use pieces with strong melodic themes but will also use underscoring that just enhances a mood. It's also a good idea to produce mixes with and without lead instruments.

Songs are used in many different ways. Sometimes the lyric is important. Sometimes it's irrelevant, and your song will be barely audible in a bar scene behind a conversation. It may be more important that the *style* is authentic.

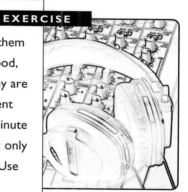

EXERCISE

Tape TV shows (try a drama and a comedy) with just an audio recorder. Play them back and make lists of all the "cues" (pieces of music used) with info about mood, number of instruments, style, length, use of songs vs. underscore, and how many are under the dialogue. Are they using different mixes of the same track for different cues? There are actually cases of entire shows being scored using a single five-minute piece of music that's dissected and used in different configurations for each cue: only drums and bass in one, just the string pad of part of the piece in another, etc. Use this information as a guide to the cues you'll submit as demos.

If you're used to creating songs and you want to compose underscore, your knowledge of conventional pop song structure won't help you as much as an understanding of harmony and grooves.

Never lose sight of the fact that you and your music aren't the stars here. The film is. So think of how your music would sound with dialogue and sound effects over it and how appropriately you can serve the needs of the visual producer.

How do you get paid?

Royalties for use of songs and instrumental music in audiovisual media come in two different ways. There may be a "synch fee" (synchronization fee for music that is used in "timed relationship" to a visual medium) that is negotiated by the library company up front. The other income is received on "the back end" through your performing rights organization based on the information in the cue sheet and how many times your music appears in the production and how many times the production is aired. If your music is used in a television show that later goes into syndication, you get paid again. If your music is used in a film that is shown on television anywhere in the world or in motion picture theaters outside the United States, you'll get paid. Royalties aren't paid for music used in theaters in the United States. (No, it's not fair, but that's another story.)

In addition to royalties paid for the composition, there is also an up-front fee paid for use of the master recording you submit. It's called a "master use" fee. For the master recording, a license must be granted to the audiovisual producer that states that you control all the rights to the performances on the recording. Each musician or singer who contributes a performance to your recording has a copyright interest in performance. You must make some kind of arrangement with them so that, if the recording is used for something (beyond demo purposes) for which you get paid, *it is clear how* (or even if) they will be compensated. Cover yourself with a release agreement with your musicians spelling out what they'll get, even if you get a buyout from them. You won't have to show these releases to the production music library or the audiovisual producer, but you'll have to "warrant" in the contract that you've done it so your singer doesn't sue them when she hears herself on that TV show.

Frequently, the license with the audiovisual producer will combine both the "synch fee" for the use of the composition and the "master use fee," and for the purpose of compensating musicians, you'd consider the "master use fee" to be half the total.

What's the deal?

Though each production music library has its own contract, the general points are:

1. They'll want to own all the publishing on the pieces they choose to represent. They ask for this because it's very expensive for them to produce, distribute, and update their libraries and they want to be able to use your music forever. They also defend this position by saying that a song often gets popularized by its appearance in a production and other uses may result for which they should be compensated. Some companies restrict their involvement to audiovisual uses only, so you can also use the song on your own CD or pitch it to recording artists without their benefiting from uses that they did not generate. One way to accomplish this, according to music attorney Steven Winogradsky, is for the library to retitle your music and re-register the compositions under their publishing company. This allows you to continue to market your music and collect any royalties earned from your own efforts and allows the library to collect only on any uses generated directly by them. By having the songs listed under separate titles with different publishers, the performing rights societies can pay whoever is listed on the music cue sheet. Obviously, this is a better deal for you.

2. Advances. Some companies will offer you an advance of $100 to $1,000 depending, as always, on how badly they want your music. This, in turn, is determined by how much they project that they'll earn for its use. Other companies resist giving advances at all.

3. Royalty percentages vary with each company. Some libraries pay a portion of the synch and master fees to the composer in addition to the performance royalties generated. Some offer their music "royalty free," which means that the client never pays a synch fee and the "back end" performance royalties are all the composer and library receive. In some cases, the library does an outright buyout of all the rights to the music and that's the last money the composer sees. In this situation, the library pays an up-front fee to the composer for the music and has all rights thereafter without having to make any further payments to the composer. Ordinarily, the composer will continue to share in the "back end" performance royalties. However, some companies have been known to substitute their own name for the composers on the cue sheet and collect those royalties themselves. Or they may allow the client to buy out the performance right as part of the deal. Make sure your contract allows *you* to collect those performance royalties.

Try the following site for lists of production music libraries:
www.cftech.com/BrainBank/COMMUNICATIONS/MusLibSrc.html
Or, just search under the Google search engine, "Production Music Libraries."

Children's Music

One of the many good things about writing and recording music for children is that it's a stable market. Unlike the pop record business, where, if the planets or cards (or whatever you believe in) are aligned right, you can make a lot of money in a relatively short time, the children's market is slow but sure and doesn't burn out overnight. Walt Disney Productions, for instance, will consistently sell well (many times over a million copies) on just about every record it releases because everyone trusts Disney to have consistently good products. In many cases, parents are buying the same records for their kids that they themselves grew up with.

If you establish yourself with a body of work in this market, you can sell a million records over several years. You'll never make the *Billboard* charts, but chances are that if you're genuinely interested in this market, it won't matter to you.

Styles of children's music range from the same contemporary rock, R&B, and country that kids hear on the radio to more traditional folk music, classical, show, and novelty tunes. Lyrics, however, are directed toward kids. There is a strong push for nonsexist, nonviolent, nonracially-stereotyped messages that promote positive self-images. There's also the feeling that children should not be "talked down to" but should be treated as intelligent individuals.

Children's music is roughly divided into two main categories: the home entertainment market and the educational music market.

The *home entertainment market* is made up of the major companies involved in children's music for entertainment purposes, though some (such as Sesame Street) cross over into the educational market to some degree. These include Disney; Henson Associates (the Muppets); Children's Television Workshop (Sesame Street); HannaBarbera (Flintstones, Yogi Bear, Jetsons, Scooby Doo); Warner Bros. (Bugs Bunny, Road Runner, Porky Pig, Daffy Duck); Parker Bros. (who also manufacture many children's games); and Music For Little People.

These companies frequently produce albums based on their characters. Individual songs submitted for these characters have little chance of being used, since the companies usually have staff writers who supply the songs for specific stories. It's best to make your presentation through an agent or attorney.

Also included in this category would be live performers who specialize in original songs and stage shows. These performers include Parachute Express, Raffi, Tom Chapin, John Lithgow, etc. Usually, these performers write their own material, but check their CD liner notes for information on where to submit your songs.

Go to a local record store featuring children's records and tapes (some large toy stores will have a good selection), copy the addresses from the record sleeves, and send for information about submitting material. Your local library may also have a children's record department.

Educational record companies specialize in records that have a direct educational value for developing children's language, motor, and social skills even though they're likely to have entertainment value as well. The greatest share of business in this category is done by mail order. The records are sold through ads in parents' and teachers' magazines and education conventions and are used in workshops, day care centers, parks and recreation departments, public and private schools, and preschools.

Writers such as Hap Palmer, Ella Jenkins, Pete Seeger, Shel Silverstein, Raffi, Greg and Steve, Joni Bartels, and Peter Alsop have contributed much to this field, but there are many others breaking in. Educational music, though it may sound deceptively simple, is not easier to write than other kinds of music. You must have some experience and understanding of current teaching trends, child psychology, and learning processes to be an effective writer in this genre. Often, these recordings include activity suggestions. A good sense of humor is also valuable, since, after all, nothing communicates quite as powerfully to a child as a good laugh.

You could do your research by going to the periodical section of the library and researching magazines such as *Early Years* and *Instructor* for ads of companies that supply these records. Buy a few and study them.

The educational music market. This category deals primarily with printed music and includes easy choral pieces (two or three part) for grade school and junior high, children's musicals or vaudeville/variety shows, and computer-related products such as CD-ROMs, DVD-ROMs, and Internet Web sites. Internet sites are easily accessible for research.

Writing for children's theater is of particular interest to community and professional theaters. Often, touring shows come to schools and provide children with their first exposure to live music and theater. Packages for the latter usually come with suggestions for costumes, props, staging, background music, and the like. Educational touring shows come with study guides to stimulate class discussion and theater appreciation. Experience in teaching music to children is very important in this category so that you understand their capabilities at various ages.

Resources:

The Childrens Music Web Guide

www.childrensmusic.org

The Children's Music Network

www.cmnonline.org

Children's Entertainment Association

www.kidsentertainment.com

National Association for the Entertainment of Young Children

www.naeyc.org

MENC: The National Association for Music Education

www.menc.org

Musical Theater

Musical theater is a wonderful collaborative art form combining music, drama, dance, design, and who knows what else in the future?

For a musical to succeed, it requires the collaborative efforts of a composer and lyricist working closely with a *librettist* (book-story-script writer) to spot songs within text and maintain emotional clarity as to what is required in each musical moment. Once the musical is written and moves into presentations or a production, the collaborative team expands to include the director, choreographer, and music director, all of whom will point out problems, discrepancies, and needs from their particular perspective. For songwriters, it demands great discipline, craftsmanship, and patience, since it will inevitably require constant rewrites to accommodate running time, pacing, choreography, and the personalities of the characters and the actors who portray them. Even the best writers discover that songs and musical scenes they'd visualized won't work on stage quite the way they were envisioned and require quick rewrites.

Though some of the most memorable recorded hits to come from musicals have been ballads, stage musicals depend heavily on fast pacing and choreographed up-tempo numbers to generate the visual and auditory excitement that reaches to the last rows of the theater. The vast majority of the music written for shows is specific to characters and plot points and usually cannot "step out" of the show, though within context they can provide thrilling theatrical moments.

Launching a major musical theater production is a tremendous undertaking. The weight of selling the show is on the shoulders of you and your partners. Once the show is written—a process that can take several years—a key step is interesting a producing theater or independent producer in your project. Until they come in to support and promote the show, the financial burden of launching the show is yours. This includes all expenses of recording and copying the demo recording, sending out script and tape/CD to potential producers, and putting together a presentation/backers audition of your material. For this, you will need to hire a director, singers, and possibly a musical director/accompanist; lease a hall; negotiate contracts; and invite potential financial backers.

I've attended many backers' auditions (theatrical sales presentations of a shortened version of the show for potential producers, directors, and financial backers). In the most common means of putting one together, a narrator tells the story and describes the action while actor/singers read the dialogue leading into the major musical numbers. Sometimes the music for those numbers is pretaped and sometimes musicians are hired, depending on your budget. Contract permitting, these presentations are videotaped so the material can be shown again to anyone who couldn't attend. Be aware, however, that theater on video carries only a fraction of the impact of a live performance. Be prepared to edit the video to highlight its strong points and eliminate whatever doesn't sparkle. As an alternative to sending a video, it is standard practice to submit a synopsis and audio sampler from the show.

Training

Most writers I know who write for musical theater are those who have always loved it and know all the musical scores. They've been "going to school" in musical theater for a long time, though they may have no formal training. It's definitely an asset to be a fan. The public library, as always, is a great place to do research. The Samuel French bookstores in New York and Los Angeles have many libretti for sale. Read every libretto you can find and see as many new musicals as possible: readings; workshops; small theater, community or high school productions; dinner theater, and major touring productions. Don't just attend shows that you think you'll like or that are well reviewed. There is often more to learn from an unproduced or undeveloped musical than from a hit.

The key to writing a successful musical lies in the strength, emotional complexity, and clarity of the libretto.

The key to writing a successful musical lies in the strength, emotional complexity, and clarity of the libretto. You can be the best songwriter in the world, but if the book (i.e., script) of your show doesn't work, the show will inevitably fail. Without a strong book, you might as well be writing a musical revue, a collection of songs with perhaps a connective theme, but without a coherent story line. While revues may contain marvelous songs, theatrically they do not pack the emotional punch of a full book show. In addition, they tend to be a harder sell to producing theaters and do not have long runs and years of viability that book shows do.

The theater world is filled with stories of shows that had wonderful scores but died because the book tanked. Book writing for a musical is a highly underappreciated talent, one that is practiced by few scriptwriters in these cinema-obsessed days. If you find a librettist who understands your musical vision and whose dramatic vision matches your own, nurture the working relationship and consider yourself very fortunate. Traditionally, the book writer supplies songwriters with structure, script, dialogue, and descriptions of what is needed within an emotional moment before the song is written. That way, the music and script fit with each other to embellish character and plot—one of the goals of a fully integrated book musical.

While New York has been the home of musical theater, an increasing amount of development is happening in Los Angeles, much of which is centered around the organization, Broadway on Sunset. ASCAP sponsors a musical theater workshop in L.A. and New York. BMI currently sponsors the Lehman Engel Workshop in New York. Other organizations involved in new musicals and/or helping new musical theater writers include New Tuners in Chicago; Musical Theater Works in New York; and the Association of Canadian Librettists, Composers, and Lyricists in Toronto. Contact information on these organizations follows.

For more information on workshops, contact BMI and ASCAP in New York and Broadway on Sunset in L.A. Workshops not only teach specific crafts, they are good places to find out how to market your ideas and projects. They also may lead you to collaborators. The Annual Songwriter's Market publishes a list of play producers and publishers looking for original musicals.

Take part in any aspect of university, dinner theater, community theater, and summer stock musical theater productions and write for as many original projects as possible. These are great places to try out your ideas. There's no better way to learn.

| The Money

Those interested in writing for musical theater will be pleased to know there's a potential to make very big money. The Dramatists Guild, the world's strongest protective organization for writers, provides model contracts for musical theater writers at every level of production.

On Broadway, writers of most musicals now share in a royalty pool. The composer, lyricist, and librettist share equally in between 15.6 percent and 17.8 percent of the weekly profits. (Profits = gross minus running costs.) About 10 percent of Broadway musicals still follow the Dramatists Guild minimum contract, which provides the writing team with 4.5 percent of the weekly gross of any first-class production until investors recoup their costs, then moves to 6 percent of gross after that. If the show is a hit, the royalty pool can actually provide a greater return for the writers.

Off-Broadway, writers generally receive 20 to 25 percent of the weekly profits. Road companies usually work on a guarantee plus an overage. For local, regional, and college productions, licensed under a play publisher such as Samuel French, Music Theatre International, or Dramatists Play Service, the pay is on a less grandiose scale, generally a negotiated percentage of box office receipts or a per performance fee.

This may not sound like much, but when you consider the ticket prices charged for stage musicals and the fact that a successful show may have several road companies performing in several cities simultaneously, with additional productions performed in countless high schools and colleges, plus cast albums on top of that, you're looking at a formidable financial return for your efforts. Rodgers and Hammerstein's "Oklahoma," after almost sixty years, still makes several million dollars a year in subsidiary markets, which include touring productions, colleges, high schools, and community theaters.

For up-to-date contract information, contact:

Dramatists Guild

234 W. 44 Street

New York, NY 10036

Tel.: (212) 398-9366

Consult the Appendix and Bibliography for several excellent books and Web sites on the subject.

ORGANIZATIONS

ASCAP—Michael Kerker, 1 Lincoln Plaza, New York, NY 10023
    Tel.: (212) 621-6000   www.ascap.com
BMI—Lehman Engel Musical Theatre Workshop, Jean Banks, 320 West 57th Street,

New York, NY 10019-3790

Tel.: (212) 586-2000   www.bmi.com

Broadway on Sunset—Kevin Kaufman, Executive Director, 10800 Hesby Street,
North Hollywood, CA 91601

Tel.: (818) 508-9270   www.broadwayonsunset.org

E-mail: Broadwayonsunset@cs.com

Lehman Engel Musical Theatre Workshop—John Sparks, 335 N. Brand Blvd.,
Glendale, CA 91203

Tel.: (818) 502-3309

New Tuners—c/o The Theatre Building, 1225 West Belmont Avenue,
Chicago, IL 60657-3205

Tel.: (773) 327-5252   www.adamczyk.com/newtuners/

Association of Canadian Librettists, Composers, and Lyricists—Robert Asselstine,
Vice President ACLCL

Tel.: (519) 572-3575   Fax: (519) 884-8452

www.geocities.com/canadiamusicaltheatre/aclcl.html

E-mail: innisfun@nonline.net

Valuable Web Sites

www.Playbill.com

www.Broadway.com

Music for Games

Recent technological innovations have given rise to many other uses for expertise in scoring, including video games, computer games, arcade games, location-based entertainment, and interactive gallery installations. Software-based entertainment has become a major component in the spectrum of global media. Pay a visit to any game arcade and you'll find games that have originated from comic books, feature films, television series, and rock artists. Games for both home use and arcades in a great variety of hardware and software platforms are becoming increasingly sophisticated, and music plays an integral part in generating the excitement needed for their success. There is a cult following for music featured in games, particularly in Japan. Popular pieces can end up on compilations marketed both online and offline that earn money for the writers, though there is also plenty of unauthorized trading of favorite titles over the Internet.

I don't feel it's within my scope here to go very deeply into this area, but I want you to know it's a growing industry (in case you hadn't noticed) with opportunities available.

If you're interested in this field, chances are you already have high-speed Internet access. Search under "video game music" or "multimedia music." Another great resource is the DMOZ Open Directory Project, www.dmoz.org. Go to "music," then "video games," and you'll get a good idea of the scope of this area.

Corporate Events

An area that gets little attention but is nonetheless an ongoing opportunity is writing theme songs and other special material for corporate events. They include: in-house corporate events, e.g., regional, national, or international meetings of, say, Toyota dealers, IBM salespeople, etc. There are also trade shows in which various manufacturers display their products for retailers. These involve every conceivable product area, including musical instruments, health food products, automobiles, baby products, hospital and health care products, furniture and appliances, building materials, electronics for entertainment and industry. The list is endless.

Making the Contacts

These events usually take place in major hotels with convention facilities or independent convention centers. They'll have either in-house coordinators or a list of outside independent contractors who supply or arrange a variety of services including catering, comedians, dancers, singers, sound, music, staging, and decorating for these events. Call the facilities, find out who the coordinators and contractors are, and contact them. Tell them what your special skills are and, if they're receptive, send them a CD and résumé.

If they need original material, it will usually be for a company that wants a theme written around a slogan for a new product, not unlike a commercial jingle. In fact, I know writers who have done that so successfully that the corporation actually asked them to create the jingle for broadcast. You'll be required to write, arrange, produce, and record the piece or to write, arrange, and deliver sheet music for a band or small orchestra to play. These are first-class productions and require a high degree of professionalism.

Coordinating these events is a major international business with its own trade organizations and magazines. If you want to pursue this area further, you should connect with one of these resources to get a better picture of the opportunities:

> *Meeting Planners International*—4455 LBJ Freeway, Suite 1200
>   Dallas, TX 75244-5903   Tel.: (972) 702-3000
>   Fax: (972) 702-3070   www.mpiweb.org
> *Special Events Magazine*—23815 Stuart Ranch Rd., Malibu, CA 90265
>   Fax: (310) 317-9533
>   www.specialevents.com (When you get there, search under "music.")

Local Events

You really can't look at this as a big money-maker unless you're in a major convention city, have good writing and arranging skills, feel comfortable dealing with corporate types, and plan to pursue it nearly full-time. Otherwise, outside those major centers, you can make a few hundred dollars here and there writing special material for company anniversaries and retirement parties, more if you're booking, playing in the band, and singing. The more skills you have, the more valuable you become, since the planners usually would rather have to hire only one person, not several, to get the job done. So if you can subcontract decorators, florists, printers for invitations and programs, comedians, clowns, etc., you can make a good business out of it. If you don't want to do all that yourself, just get your résumé, videos, and CDs out to those who do provide event planning services and give them a follow-up call every couple of months so they remember you. It's one of those "You never know where it'll come from" situations where networking can pay off when you least expect it.

chapter fifteen

Getting a Record Deal

For the performer or songwriter/performer, obtaining a recording contract is a major step toward mass public exposure. Remember, however, that the real goal is not the record deal. It's only the *means* of manufacturing and marketing your artistry. The recording contract is, at the least, just a piece of paper. It is far from a guarantee of fame and fortune, At its best, it represents the legal basis for a cooperative marketing effort in which a team of experts exposes a product (you) to an audience who will translate their appreciation of your music into purchase of your records. The record deal is only part of a larger effort by your own personal team to promote your career in as many ways as they can and to earn you (and them) as much income as possible.

When approaching this or any other career decision, it's important to get as much information as possible about the circumstances, needs, and responsibilities of the other parties involved. In this chapter I'll explore the information you need from the point of view of the record company. You'll learn how a record company looks at you as an artist, at your songs, and at your professional team. And since a deal with an established record company is not something every artist can count on (there was a time when even the Beatles couldn't get a deal), we'll also look at the very viable and sometimes preferable "do it yourself" option.

The Artist vs. the Writer/Artist

Exceptional writer/artists have always been around. Until the fifties and sixties, however, with the increasing exposure of country music, black music, and the birth of rock and roll, most popular songs on the radio were not performed by their writers. With the phenomenal success of the Beatles, record companies began to discover that they could get publishing rights to the songs the artists were writing and thus be able to keep the potentially enormous publishing income along with the recording profits. The self-contained act was an attractive package because, though they would (in most cases) pay writers one of the two cents (the old rate) per side per unit sold, by also owning the publishing rights, they could keep that other penny "in house." They could also participate in the performance royalties collected from BMI and ASCAP.

Today, virtually every record company has a publishing affiliate. But though the business affairs departments of the major record companies and their publishing companies will aggressively pursue the publishing rights of new artists signed by the company, if they want the artist badly enough, refusal is rarely a deal-breaker. Also, the publishing affiliates operate on their own and have lots of income from other projects, so they don't depend on deals their affiliated labels give them.

Small, independent record companies, however, don't sell as many records. The royalties they receive from the ownership of the publishing rights, along with record sales, can help to offset their overhead, making the publishing a very important consideration in the deal. In that situation, being a self-contained act with publishing rights to offer is an asset.

For both the major labels and independents, an even bigger advantage of the self-contained artist or group is that it eliminates the need to come up with outside material. That's because, even though the record company A&R staff is constantly on the lookout for songs for their artists who are not self-contained, they don't always have enough time to screen songs as well as to deal with the responsibilities to the many other acts on their rosters. So the trend has been to give that responsibility to the producers or writer/producers (sometimes several for the same album) to write (or find) and produce songs for the project. Though that's generally a better gamble, I know of many projects that have been doomed by writer/producers who have insisted on writing all the material themselves and ended up with no hits. Having said that, major labels would still rather bet on the skills and promotability of attaching a well-known producer to the project, particularly for a new artist.

One of the most exciting attributes of the self-contained artist is the potential to create a consistent fusion of style and material that is quite unique.

One of the most exciting attributes of the self-contained artist is the potential to create a consistent fusion of style and material that is quite unique and that offers fans the opportunity to get to know the writer/artist in a personal way. With a nonwriting artist, though he or she may have a consistent vocal identity and style, it's much more difficult to achieve a consistency with the material. The most common way has been in the long-term relationships between writer/producers and artists.

One drawback nonwriting artists face is the never-ending search for hit material that they and their record companies can agree on. The flip side of that problem is that those artists have access to the best writers in the world. Certain companies, such as Clive Davis's Arista Records made a specialty of signing nonwriting artists. (Davis formed a new label, J Records, in 2000.) His roster at Arista included Whitney Houston, Aretha Franklin, and Dionne Warwick and continues at J Records with O-Town and Luther Vandross, among others. Davis has always subscribed to "the song comes first" philosophy and has delayed many recording projects until he had what he felt were the right songs for the artist.

So though the self-contained artist will most likely be the first choice of a record company, each situation is unique, and many different factors will be weighed in the decision to sign an act. The following sections will delineate those factors. Remember, while you read them, that these are all presented as ideal situations and the likelihood of a record company finding an act that "has it all" is almost nonexistent. The reality is that they take the best combination of ingredients they can find, try to compensate somehow for what's missing, and roll the dice.

The Demo

One of the most important elements in a successful campaign for a recording contract is your demo. By way of explaining how the demo and the act are judged, I'm going to play the part of a record company, with a few asides thrown in to explain what's happening or why.

I'm assuming that you're looking for your first record deal, so I'll ask about things I need to know to make a decision about signing you to my label. I know I'll need to spend anywhere over a million dollars to record, promote, and market your record. If I don't recoup, I'll have to eat that expense. It might take that much again on a follow-up album, but I'll spend it if I'm still as excited about the music as I was when I signed you and the numbers on the first album are promising enough. I know the odds are against me because less than 10 percent of the albums released recoup their costs.

Also, I want to see that you're not sitting around waiting for me to make you a star. I want to know that you're writing and I want to hear new songs on a regular basis.

Are you working on your act? The visuals? Arrangements? Concepts? I want to know that you're working to improve your vocal and instrumental chops. I want to know that if I do invest in you, both you and your manager know what to do to make the most of my investment and that if you're not already a road veteran you'll be ready to go soon and start getting fans of your live shows to buy your CD. We'll get reviewers out to see you and my ulcer dictates that I be confident that you have your act together.

Let's say, typically, that I received your demo through your attorney, manager, someone in my company, your producer, your publisher, or someone else whose taste I respect. Before I listen to that demo, I know what I want to hear:

• I'm looking for songs that I think are hits or that will appeal to a large number of people because of your point-of-view, style, etc. Artists like Phish, Dave Matthews, and Metallica have an appeal based on their live performances rather than hit singles. (See "Singles, Albums, Live Performances, and Video," chapter three.) They're known as album artists, and it takes more time and money to market them successfully because hit singles and videos are proven to be the fastest and most cost-effective way to promote an artist.

• I'm looking for craftsmanship that tells me that those songs I liked were not just an accident and that you know exactly what you're doing and can do it again. Otherwise, I risk spending my money on a "one-hit wonder" with little chance of recouping my investment.

- I'm looking for identity. I want that audience to be able to recognize you after hearing your record once or twice. If your voice doesn't have a distinctive character, what you do with it stylistically should be unique. If that isn't happening, I should be hearing an instrumental sound and production concept that are unique. I should know that you and/or your producer can continue to re-create that sound once the public has grown to love it.

- I'm looking for something that has an emotional impact. I want to be moved by the way you sing your song. I want to know that you are totally involved with what you're saying in your song. If you don't believe it, why should I? If it's not the kind of music that's lyrically oriented, I want it to move my body. If you've been playing your songs at your lounge gig every night for the last three years, there's a danger that they'll sound tired and unenthusiastic. I want to know that you can get into those songs *every time* you perform them.

I will assume that what I'm about to hear on this demo is the very best that you can do. I have no evidence to believe you'll ever perform it any better than on the demo, so don't tell me "That was a bad day for me" or "It's just a demo. I'll do it better on the master."

When I'm spending this company's money, I'm not taking your word for it; I need to know. I'll have control over the technical quality of the final record, so if it's a convincing *performance*, it won't bother me that the technical quality of your demo isn't up to par unless you're also trying to convince me that you're a producer. (See "Who Gets What and How Elaborate Does It Need to Be?" chapter ten.)

If you show me a record you produced and distributed yourself and can show you've developed a marketing strategy for it as well, it tells me you're very serious about your career, you have a realistic view of the process, and you're proceeding with your career whether I sign you or not, so I'd better pay attention. Obviously I'll be more impressed if you've sold a few thousand records. I'd like to see a good, well-maintained Web site and that you're staying in touch with the fan base you've developed with frequent e-mails, updated performance schedules, and personal messages (not necessarily one-to-one) to help your audience get to know you better.

The Live Performance

As a record company executive, my bottom-line question has to be, "Can my company make money on this artist?" Other related questions are, "Will this artist enhance the prestige and contribute to the image of the company?" and "Will I be a hero or lose my gig on the success or failure of this act?" (I should say here that there are A&R reps who have kept their great jobs by not risking signing artists at all.) For those reasons, I need to hear the right sounds, ask the right questions, and get the right answers. Let's assume that I liked what I heard on the demo. I thought the songs had commercial potential and the performance was excellent. Those are really the basics. Now I also have to ask another series of questions, not necessarily in order of importance, but all, nonetheless, very significant:

- **How is your live performance?** It would impress me to know that you had spent a few years as a live performer. I'd like to see some great reviews of your performances, preferably by recognized critics (your high school or college newspaper won't quite do). But most of all, I want you to excite a tough audience—not one where all your friends are stacking the house. So I'd prefer to see you perform in a club or in concert, but if you could pull off a powerful performance in my office for me and my critical staff, I'd also be impressed.

- **Are you visually interesting?** If you look great or at least have an interesting and memorable look, it's a major plus because this is a time when TV is a major component in exposing you to potential fans.

- **Do you move and speak confidently?** Remember that we retain more information with our eyes than our ears, which is one reason we can sell a lot of records to people who attend your concerts and see your videos. Do you have a good sense of your personal identity? I want the audience to go away from your performance with a feeling that they know who you are and like you or that you've given them enough pieces of yourself in your musical visual presentation to create an intriguing mystery that makes them want to know who you are.

- **If you're a band or vocal group, I want to see you all involved and interacting with each other**, not standing there like robots, each in your own little world. That doesn't mean you have to do the splits, moonwalk, and choreograph dance steps if that's not your style. But I do want to sense that there's a real, honest chemistry between the group members that inspires your music. I want to know you're giving me something and enjoying it. I'll also be looking at your stage movement, your choice of songs and their placement in the set, your arrangements, and the way you dress.

- **Can you reproduce your demo sound in person?** I'll want to know that the things I liked on your demo can be reproduced live. I don't expect to see an orchestra, but the basics have to be there. For example, if a significant degree of your appeal to me is based on your group vocal sound, I'd better hear it in your live performance. Though it's technically possible to pull off lip-synched vocals and to get a technically perfect vocal through the magic of ProTools and other studio technology, I'd like to know that some reviewer won't trash you for lip-synching vocals in concert or from seeing you try it without the technical aid and not be able to sing on pitch.

- **Do you love to perform?** I want to know that, ideally, I'll be working with an experienced professional who knows and understands (and accepts) the hardships of the road and loves to perform. I know that in spite of TV exposure and hit records, there's no substitute, in the eyes of fans (and potential fans), for the magic of a great live performance.

Live performance sells a lot of records and is a great marketing tool for us. It gives us reviews in the press, it helps us to keep your name in front of the public, and gives local DJs and fans something to talk about. It gives you contact with your audience so you'll know what they like about you. It gives you a kind of high that can't be duplicated.

- **Are you willing to sacrifice?** Though it may take a couple of years of money-losing opening-act status, touring can eventually provide a major source of income (as can concert merchandising of T-shirts and other items), particularly for group members who don't receive songwriter's royalties.

Marketability

Now I have to assess how, if I sign you, I'm going to make people aware of you. One of my best tools is the "story" that I use to get the press interested in you. Maybe you're the brother or sister, son or daughter of somebody famous (Eagle Eye Cherry, Jakob Dylan), though after the curiosity of the first album wears off, you'd better be able to deliver something substantial and very much your own. It also helps if you have famous friends who would like to sing or play on your record. That in itself doesn't get you signed, but it does give me something of an incentive.

That's what I need: PR (public relations/publicity) potential! "He/she has been in the background as a musician, a backup singer, or a writer and is now coming up front to make his/her own music." That's a good hook for us because there may be quite a few people out there who remember you when you were doing whatever you were doing in the background. If not, then maybe we can arouse their curiosity by association. "Oh, yeah, if he played with that artist, who I really like, he must be something like him. I'd probably love his stuff." Did you write a well-known hit?

What's interesting about your life? Jewel grew up in Alaska and lived in her car in San Diego while trying to get gigs in clubs. Christina Aguilera and Britney Spears both got their start on the *Mickey Mouse Club*. Did you make a living playing in the New York subways? Did you live in the park while you played for tips in Santa Monica? Did you get your start driving a cab/collecting trash/waiting tables/writing songs in jail? Do you have an interesting and flamboyant personality or hang out in social circles that automatically attract attention from the press?

What were the turning points in your music, in your personal outlook on life, your philosophy, your inspired decisions? What incidents, experiences, changed your whole life?

I want to know things about you personally that enhance the mystique; that reveal you as a human being of substance, strangeness, virtue, or character; or ideally, all of the above.

Can you speak well and confidently and do you have something interesting or funny to say? If not, I'll make sure Letterman and Leno don't invite you to talk to them after you sing and that you don't do interviews. If you have strong and well-articulated opinions, on the other hand, I might want you to be on a show like *Politically Incorrect* with Bill Maher. Are you willing to do radio and TV interviews and in-store appearances?

Those things are important in that they give us "hooks" that we can use to let people know about you, and the press needs that kind of story to work with.

More important, though, is the marketability of your music itself. It's important that the music has a unity of style so that, when we do find the audience, you're the same artist from album to album and still show artistic growth and change within your general style.

Writer/artists frequently ask if record companies like to hear stylistic variety. "I can write country, hip-hop, pop, rock, anything! Why don't I give them a little of each and see what they pick up on?" That's commendable if you want to be a staff songwriter, but a record company will no doubt ask, "But who are you, really?" If country music is what you write and perform best and enjoy most, what's the point in trying to market you as an R&B artist and release an R&B single on you? If it takes off, are we going to be trying to sell half an album of country tunes to a rock or R&B audience, or vice versa? So it's a marketing problem. Of course, we don't want all your music to sound the same and we do want you to grow; we just need for you to have developed your style to the point where you're the same, identifiable artist from one album to the next. Ideally, you know who you are and how you want to be presented to the public. Maybe you've found a way to blend your stylistic influences into something totally unique and identifiable.

| Personal Factors

Considering the tremendous investment the company will make in your career, it's important for us to know that we're not going to be flushing it down the drain due to your lack of commitment or other personal factors beyond our control. These are important factors that I have to weigh.

I (and everyone else on your team) don't want to worry that you're a heavy drug user and that you'll die of an overdose or you'll spend all your advance on drugs or that the drugs will ruin your health or your relationships with your group. I'd like to know you're responsible enough to show up for gigs and interviews.

I'd be glad to know that you have a reasonably stable domestic situation, that your wife/husband/live-in can deal with your being on the road or that family problems won't interfere in any other way with your career.

Are you a networker? Do you like to meet new people? Do you enjoy hanging out with other artists and musicians. Do you systematically network, making and keeping industry contacts?

Ideally, I want to like you since we'll probably be spending a lot of time together. I like to enjoy my work and don't look forward to putting my neck on the line for someone I don't like and respect. Life's too short!

If you're a band, I want to see that you've established a strong bond between band members and that each knows and accepts his function within the group. I expect that there may be strong egos involved, but I also know that if they're out of hand, they can ruin the band. Money changes everything, and if you're successful and doing heavy touring, the pressures of both can do more to break up the group (and lose our investment) than anything else. So, I need to get a sense of who you are as individuals and how you interact with each other.

It's important that the music has a unity of style so that you're the same artist from album to album and still show artistic growth and change within your general style.

As I said earlier, this is the ideal situation. I know I won't necessarily be able to get all these elements in an artist, and if I love the music, I'll take some trade-offs, but I will always look for them.

The Professional Team

Now we get to a subject that, in my assumed role as a record company executive, is very important for me to consider—the people on your team.

I'm likely to be impressed if you have a team of professional people who believe in you, particularly if they are people whose work I respect. If you come to my attention through the efforts of your manager, producer, and attorney, who have been generating energy and momentum on your behalf, it will tell me important things: (1) that if I sign you, my company will have lots of competent aid from your team, to insure your success, and (2) that if I don't sign you, someone else probably will.

First of all, let's assume that all my questions until now have been answered to my satisfaction and I'm very excited about you as a writer and an artist. Another thing that will impress me and tip the scales in your favor is knowing that you have a competent manager and producer. Let's talk about the best situation for me as the record company and, consequently, what's best for you.

| Your Manager

A manager, among other things, should be able to initiate publishing, record company, and production deals; know what clubs or concerts you should play and what radio and TV shows you should do and when. She should oversee or coordinate the activities of your booking agent, road manager, publicist, accountant, attorney, business manager, publisher, and producer and be your official contact with the record company. She is the buffer between you and the business, your advisor and alter ego and the captain of your team. Ideally, your manager is also excited about you and your talent and is dedicated to helping you become a successful artist. I'd be more impressed if she is a manager with a record of successes, one who has managed other successful acts, one who knows the record business and understands the functions of all the component parts of the talent machine and the need for coordination and teamwork. I'll want to know that your manager knows your strengths and limitations and has a plan for the development of your career.

What if your manager does not have a stellar track record and is not knowledgeable about the record business?

Unless she is willing to learn and take direction, I know I'm going to have lots of problems. Enough arguments erupt between record companies and managers who do know the business. It's particularly crazy to try to deal with someone who has no way of knowing when I'm making important concessions to her or suggesting a course of action that from our experience is advisable, but one that the manager does not understand.

Inexperienced managers may assume adversary roles to cover their ignorance, rather than finding ways to work with the company. I would rather you had a manager with whom I already have a good working relationship because our problems may have already been worked out or at least we've learned how to argue with each other. I might even sign an artist that I'm not totally sold on if I believe in the abilities of the manager.

So, if you have an inexperienced manager, I'd try to hook her up in a comanagement situation with a successful manager so that she could learn and you wouldn't have to suffer from her inexperience. Otherwise, I'd rather you didn't have one so I could help you find a good one. Another option is a fresh, young manager who already works for a superstar management company. Often they acquired that job because they already brought a new artist to the company.

GENERAL INFORMATION

Managers get paid between 15 percent and 20 percent of your gross income, sometimes, of your net, and sometimes, a combination. That includes songwriting, publishing, record royalties, touring, everything. Management deals can be complex, and I recommend you do your homework on it. Don Passman's *All You Need to Know About the Music Business* is a good source. And, at the risk of being redundant, *never* sign a management agreement without an experienced entertainment attorney to negotiate for your interests! It's difficult but not impossible to get a good, experienced manager unless you already have a record deal. The best managers don't have to take on the burden of building a career totally from scratch, since they can afford to be choosy. But it's not an impossible situation. There's no accounting for human chemistry and a manager's basic gambler's instinct. If she thinks you've got star quality, she just knows she can get you a deal!

Some artists need a manager they can relate to on a very personal basis. Others just need a manager to take care of their business and stay out of their personal life. You should know which one you need before you start looking and let him or her know what you're looking for right away.

One of the things a manager will ask you to do is give them "power of attorney" so they can make deals and sign contracts, cash your checks, hire and fire your crew on your behalf. There will be occasions in which it's physically impossible for you to sign every live performance contract and power of attorney might be valuable. You should, however, be sure about the scope of this power. It's a good idea to limit that power to certain types of contracts and specific dollar amounts and only if you're not there to do it yourself. Anything beyond those limits, you have to approve in writing. This is easy to do with e-mail. This is one of those areas that can ruin you if it gets out of your control.

You find an established manager by looking at the credits on CDs of artists who are in your genre of music (though some managers like to diversify). *Billboard* annually publishes a list of artists, their managers, and booking agents. Your local songwriters organization or music association may also have a list. If possible, try to contact an artist who the company manages (though they might see you as competition) or who the company *used to* manage. (You'll hear the worst, but you'll be forewarned.)

| Your Producer

If the demo I first listened to was a finished master recording, ready for the radio, and produced by someone with a successful track record, it gives me another way to hype you to radio and the press, as well as ensures that the rest of the product will be competently produced. With a successful producer as part of the package, it isn't even necessary to bring me finished masters, just demos of exceptional songs and performances.

If you bring demos produced by yourself or an unproven producer, even if I like them, I have no way of knowing that I'll get a well-produced finished product. It's a judgment call that depends on the strength of the various ingredients in that particular situation. It's possible that I'll want to hear a finished master before I decide or I'll want us both to find you a producer who *I know* can deliver a great record. Another option is to find a great remixer, who can take what you have and tweak it to be airworthy. One of the problems is that a producer (whether it's you or someone else) can sometimes lose objectivity and can benefit from a fresh set of ears to mix the record.

If you've produced masters I love, I'm happy because I truly have a self-contained package and don't have to worry about your having problems with your producer (though the potential for you to be less objective in your choice of material will make me keep a close eye on it).

If you're already signed to producer "A," who I believe to be incompetent or inappropriate, then I know I'll either have to buy out your contract with that producer, convince him to allow another producer ("B") to work on the project through "A's" company, or not sign you at all.

Your producer should know your strengths and weaknesses and have a plan for how he will produce you to make you as commercially viable as possible.

GENERAL INFORMATION

Producers have a dual responsibility: to deliver the record company a record it can sell and get the best performance from the artist or group. Part of this includes choosing the best components needed for that particular project, which may mean songs, studio(s), musicians, arranger, engineers, and recording equipment. The producer bears the responsibility for both the technical and artistic quality of the record.

The worst way to find a producer is to send your demos randomly to producers whose work you don't know. The best way is to buy records of artists in your general style of music and listen to the sound of the record. If you like it, try to find out what other records that producer has worked on and listen to them. Often the production company's address is listed on the record. If not, call the record company A&R or artist relations department and ask for it. Also, *Billboard* lists the producers of hit records on its charts in all styles of music, and *New on the Charts* (see Appendix) gives you their contact info.

If you read *Billboard* on a regular basis you'll get to know who's producing your favorite records. (You can read much of it for free at www.billboard.com.) Some producers have their own characteristic style no matter who they produce. If you need a stylistic direction, look for one whose style feels right for you. Others work to enhance the unique qualities of the artist or group, and a producer with that philosophy may suit you better. So beyond the question of liking their work is the question of compatibility.

Producers come from a variety of backgrounds. Some are engineer/producers who went to "producer school" by engineering hundreds or thousands of sessions in which they've observed and participated in the work styles of many different producers. If you're a writer/artist/arranger with a unique sound based on your arrangement ideas, your vision may be enhanced more by an engineer/producer than by an arranger/producer.

Arranger/producers with experience as studio musicians go to that same producer school and benefit from the same exposure but from the other side of the glass. They'll excel in creating the musical dynamics and hooks that may have already helped launch some hits. If you're a singer or singer/songwriter who needs the most assistance in creating an instrumental sound, check out the musician/arranger/producer. Many of them are also writers who like to cowrite with the artist. This could also be advantageous if you need material and like to collaborate. That producer will also be attracted by the additional royalties he'd receive for his writing contributions.

Regardless of his background, a producer needs to be able to choose the best songs for a project whether choosing from among your own or finding appropriate songs from other writers. Some are better than others at this; and if finding or writing strong commercial songs is a problem area for you, it'll be necessary to have an expert working with you. As you can see, an assessment of your own strengths and weaknesses is essential in finding a producer who can make up for your weaknesses and enhance your strengths.

As an artist without a record deal, your chances of getting a major, established producer to work with you are slim. They usually have projects booked far into the future. Though you shouldn't abandon that approach, you should also check the charts for new producers who have recently had their first hit(s). It's more likely that they're not booked so far ahead and may be looking for their next project.

Producers get paid a royalty as percentage points based on record sales, a flat fee per song, or, most commonly, a combination of the two.

| Attorneys

As a record company executive, I will frequently be approached by attorneys representing artists with demos or masters. This is happening more and more frequently. Since attorneys are negotiating many contracts with record companies, they have made good contacts at the labels and find themselves in a position to know if and when a company is looking for a certain type of artist. Since they have an inside track, it's easier for them to "shop the product" than, for instance, an out-of-town manager or a new one who doesn't know his way around yet. From the record company point-of-view, I want to deal with an

An assessment of your own strengths and weaknesses is essential in finding a producer who can make up for your weaknesses and enhance your strengths.

entertainment attorney and, in particular, a record business attorney. When he comes to me or my company attorney to negotiate a deal, he must speak the language and have up-to-date knowledge of current record industry practices. If not, we will end up engaged in needless hours of fruitless negotiations and we'll end up having to educate your attorney at your expense.

For instance, you're presented with a production or record contract and you call your uncle, whose specialty is suing auto manufacturers. He *should* refer you to an entertainment specialist. But suppose business is slow this month, he knows there are lots of bucks in the music business, he has visions of his nephew being a big rock star, he thinks it would be great to get involved in a more glamorous business, and he figures, "What the hell, how hard could it be to negotiate a record contract?" He gets the contract and the first thing he objects to is the fact that this big record company wants all recording costs recouped off the top from your royalties. He thinks it's terrible (it actually is terrible, but he may be unaware that it's a firmly established practice in the industry) and decides he should try to negotiate that point, thereby exposing his ignorance. The record company attorneys will either not want to negotiate with him at all or eat him alive for breakfast.

Needless to say, none of this helps you at all. Entertainment law is very complex, and just knowing law academically is not enough to make one a good attorney in that field. Personal experience, good contacts (politics), and a knowledge of current industry practices as well as a knowledge of the policies and contracts of specific record companies are equally important. As a record company, I want to deal with an attorney whose philosophy is that the best deal is one that comes closest to being fair for both parties. Obviously, I'll negotiate for my own advantage, but if that means it's unfair to you, I know I'm going to have problems with you later and you won't be happy with the deal. (Though if you're successful, I know we'll be renegotiating.) So, as you can see, it's very important to choose this team member well.

GENERAL INFORMATION

In relationships with attorneys, fees are always a major concern. Attorneys in this field are expensive, and fees range from $125 (not many) to $500 per hour. They'll log all the time spent on your behalf on the telephone, in meetings with you, with the record company, or whatever, and bill you for that time. Some attorneys, in lieu of an hourly rate, will offer to shop your demos or masters and negotiate your deal for 5 percent of your income from that contract for the life of the deal. Make sure you're very clear about the parameters of this. Some may also want to include other types of income in the deal including touring and merchandising and, in a sense, operate as if it were a management commission. On the surface, this may seem like a good deal, particularly if you're broke, but you should consider that maybe in a couple of months you'll become disenchanted with your relationship and want to get another attorney. You'll then be paying two attorneys, and that original 5 percent is part of your income that you might find a better use for.

An attorney working on a percentage may also be tempted to "front load" a deal.

Here's a simplified scenario for the sake of illustration: In negotiations, the attorney has an opportunity to obtain maybe a $500,000 advance from the record company for you, the artist, by trading it off for a 7 percent artist royalty instead of 10 percent. Let's say that for 10 percent there would only have been a $350,000 advance. If the attorney is getting 5 percent of that advance (because he gets 5 percent of all your income from the deal he negotiated for you), he may have a quick fantasy about $7,500 with wings on it, flying out of his pocket if he gets you the higher royalty and lower advance. If he decides to act on that fantasy, he can go back to you and say, "Great news! I got you a $350,000 advance," and never tell you about the extra 3 percent artist royalty he gave up for it, which down the road could mean a substantial amount of money. If he's ethical, he'll give you the pros and cons and let you make that decision. This is the kind of thing that could happen. You should ask and they should inform you about the pros and cons of their negotiations.

Attorneys will sometimes work on "spec" or "deferment," which means that they'll keep track of their time spent on your project but defer payment until they've made a deal for you and then collect their accumulated fees from the front money. They're most likely to do this if a producer or record company has shown enough interest in you to present you with a contract or if they have good ears and feel you've got a favorable shot at a deal. It is a very high risk for them, though, because they could conceivably spend a lot of time, the deal wouldn't happen, and they'd risk not getting paid. You're more likely to find a new attorney who'll do this.

Another way they can work is an hourly fee against a monthly retainer covering everything they do. That may be part of an overall fee for the project depending on what they'll be required to do, then deduct what you've already paid from the final overall project fee. They'll give you an estimate up front and, hopefully, let you know when it looks like they'll have to go past it.

Here are some additional tips on dealing with attorneys:

1. Never sign a contract without some legal advice. I'm sure you've heard this before, but I'm still appalled by the number of unfortunate situations I come across in which people who knew better ignored the advice. They say something like, "The people were so nice . . . ," "They said they would . . . ," but, unfortunately, what they said they would do wasn't written into their contract and, consequently, they don't have to do what they merely said.

2. If you or your manager are discussing your deal with a company, take notes on the verbal points they're offering you. Relay this information to your attorney so he can incorporate it into the contract in case the company selectively forgets. (Your attorney will clarify this immediately, though, since A&R reps will often talk about deals in broad strokes that they're pretty sure you don't quite understand.) Most companies already have their own contracts that they've worked out over the years from their own legal battles, and those of associates, reflecting industry practices as well as innovating their own terms. A good reason for hiring an experienced music industry attorney is that he's had to

negotiate with a great variety of companies and is familiar with the negotiating practices and contract terms of most of them. If your attorney has already negotiated deals with a particular company, that experience could save a lot of the attorney's time and your money.

3. Don't ask the company with whom you're negotiating to recommend an attorney. Never go to an attorney for advice who also represents those who are offering you a contract. To avoid conflict of interest, your attorney should have no connection with your manager, producer, record company, or anyone else with whom you are doing business. An ethical attorney will always let you know that, but ask anyway.

4. Always ask an attorney what his/her fees are and try to get some sort of estimate of how much the service you need could cost. It will sometimes be hard to tell you exactly, but you should at least have a ballpark figure. That way you can determine whether it's out of your league.

5. Your conversation and business with your attorney is confidential unless you consent to "leak" information as a business tactic (such as the amount of money another company is offering you).

6. If you "discharge" your attorney and decide to get a new one, the new attorney has the right, with your authorization, to copy your files from the previous attorney. They're your files.

7. Communicate in writing whenever you can. It documents and dates your requests and comments and avoids communication breakdown due to lapses of memory and human error.

8. Keep a photocopy of all correspondence with anyone you do business with, including a copy of every contract presented to and signed by you, *before* you return it. You do this because it is possible to add a clause to a contract after you sign it and you'd otherwise not be able to prove that you didn't consent to the added clause.

9. Ask an attorney what he's done lately. If you're looking for an attorney to represent you in negotiating a record deal, you'll want to find one who has had *recent* experience in negotiating that kind of contract and uses up-to-date contracts.

10. Shop for an attorney with expertise in the area in which you need help. There are many specialists among entertainment attorneys as well as veterans who've done it all. You may want different attorneys to negotiate management, publishing, production, film music, or recording contracts. Ask them what they specialize in.

Booking Agents

Back to my role as a record company exec. Even though it's essentially your manager's job to find the right booking agency for you, I may be able to help, since here at the record company we have ongoing relationships with many of them. Sometimes they help me "discover" new artists. I'll get demos of hot new artists from them because they're constantly being approached by artists and bands looking for work. They may also be booking artists in parts of the country that I don't have much regular access to for scouting talent. If you already have a good agency and you're working regularly, it's a plus for me because you may already have a strong following of potential record buyers.

If you're an artist who loves to perform, the booking agent is an important part of the team. The decisions you and your manager make with her about where and when you play could be very important to the success of an album. In the coordination of album releases and touring schedules, timing is critical.

GENERAL INFORMATION

Booking agents (also referred to as talent managers, as opposed to personal managers) are those who secure work, negotiate contracts, and collect your money for live performance gigs, film work, and so on. Though major agencies occasionally work with unknown artists without record deals, it's rare. If you're a new act, you're better off finding a small or medium-sized agency that deals with unsigned or newly signed acts because they regularly deal with clubs and small concert venues that feature talent at your level of development.

Booking agents, with a career development plan in mind, can do a lot to advance your career. Major agents can assist by bringing you to the attention of record companies who they deal with on behalf of other major clients. Their approach, if they can get you close to a record deal, is to try to get the label to agree to let them represent you as an agent; however, it's ultimately your call since you sign the contract.

Booking agents, with a career development plan in mind, can do a lot to advance your career.

It's also to the advantage of smaller agencies that you get a record deal even with a small independent label, because they can then charge more for your appearances. However, acts who are on the road constantly and making $5,000 or $6,000 or more a week may find that their agents balk at the time off the act may need to produce an album. For every week you don't work, your agent doesn't make (at 10 percent) $500 or $600 or more. Those agents truly concerned with your growth will not obstruct your career. In the long run, the additional fees the agent will be able to charge once you have a record out will more than make up the temporary loss.

One of the best ways to locate a reputable agent is through your local AF of M (American Federation of Musicians), AFTRA (American Federation of Television and Radio Artists—www.aftra.org), AGVA (American Guild of Variety Artists—http://home.earthli nk.net/~agvala/agva1.html), or SAG (Screen Actors Guild—www.sag.org), who keep an up-to-date list of those agents who they've licensed and who comply with their regulations. Another way to find them is through other musicians who seem to work regularly. Finding an agent who deals with college concerts is a good way to go if you just want to play primarily original material. (Club gigs, in general, discourage a predominance of originals in favor of a cover tunes or "standards" repertoire.) You can find such agents by calling some college student activities directors and asking which agents they like to deal with.

Agents charge 10 percent of the gross receipts from the jobs they secure for you. If you sign exclusively with an agent, they'll want that percentage on all the gigs you get, regardless of whether you or they secure the job for a period of one to more than three years. If you already have formed your own relationships with clubs or colleges where you've performed in the past, you may want to exclude them from the clubs where the agent can collect a percentage. If you can get them to agree to this, you'll need to put it in your contract with a specific list of excluded clubs. On the other hand, the more you limit the situations they can get their percentage from, the less enthusiastic they'll be and may never book you into those clubs. All contracts sanctioned by the unions have clauses that get you out of the contract if the agent doesn't get you work within specified time periods.

Booking agents obviously look for a combination of musical talent and the desire and ability to entertain in the acts they consider representing. Some agents specialize in specific musical styles. Some are "full service" agencies for those who also have the talent to expand their careers into acting, modeling, writing, and other directions. Some also represent composers for film and TV music. This is an area that, ideally, is dealt with by your manager, who will have the most contact with the agent.

Songwriters frequently ask if there are agents just for songwriters. Except for those who specialize in film and TV and represent *very* successful writers (and composers) whose songs or songwriting ability they promote for film and TV themes, the answer is no. Independent songpluggers come closest to filling that bill though. (See "Independent Songpluggers," chapter eleven.)

The Campaign

If you want a record deal, you can't afford to wait for it to find you. You and/or your representatives need to plan an effective campaign to make sure you get heard by those companies in which you're interested.

A&R people at record companies seldom go to clubs at random to see artists they've never heard before. They'll respond to a "buzz" (talk on the street or in the industry about a hot, new band). They'll also go to see a band whose songs and sound they liked on a demo they've heard. Except for the most aggressive A&R reps (and those without a personal life), they have little time to see an artist otherwise. They'll always try to improve their odds of finding a great band and waste as little time as possible in the process. So, if there's such a thing as a standard campaign (and there isn't) that makes the most efficient use of your time and theirs, it's close to this:

1. Put together your package with masters or high-quality demos, press kit, photos, reviews, and bios.

2. Send or deliver your demos, preferably via an attorney, manager, or agent, to whomever that person knows in the record company A&R department who is appropriate for your style of music. It's not necessary to see the vice president of A&R unless you know him. Staff A&R representatives may be much more accessible.

3. Schedule a showcase about three or four weeks after delivery of the demos. Announce the showcase, if possible, in the package you present and e-mail reminders.

4. About two weeks before your showcase, send out a special invitation to the people

who have your package, the press, booking agents, producers, or anyone else you'd like to be there. Again, an e-mail will do.

5. Follow up a few days later with phone calls to find out: (a) if they have heard the demo, (b) if they liked it, (c) if they got the invitation, (d) if they're coming to the showcase. If so, tell them you will put their name(s) on the guest list. If not, ask if they'd like to be notified of future appearances. (Keep your mailing list current with their present job and e-mail addresses and phone numbers.)

6. If they attend the showcase, follow up immediately with a thank-you card and a phone call to find out what they thought.

7. If all that fails, cut some new demos and try it all again. Persist!

You can either do this project yourself or have a friend, manager, spouse, or a combination represent you. Know that rarely does this work the first time. You will have to continue, so don't be discouraged. There is value in just getting your name in front of them periodically. Generally speaking, in the case of rock groups, most A&R reps would rather hear about your great performance and the buzz you created and pursue you themselves. Concentrate on getting reviewers there.

| Your Web Site Is a Critical Factor

Also, sometimes it's more effective to bring them to your Web site with e-mail, where you can let them hear your music, see where you're playing next, and read the reviews. Keep them on your e-mail list. And keep your Web site updated. Make sure you attach a link to your site in every e-mail.

Why a Major-Label Deal May Not Be Best for You

Though it's been possible for writer/artists to release independent recordings for many years, the more recent availability and affordability of great digital recording equipment and the marketing potential of the Internet have done a lot to level the playing field for indie artists. Though the five major labels still control most of the expertise and capital to market, influence airplay, and fill shelf space at record retailers, they're no longer the only game in town. It's possible, with a lot of work, for an artist or band to develop and expand their own audience without airplay. Many artists are gaining the attention of the majors *because* they have already accomplished it. At that point, they may be making a good enough living to hire their own team, control their own careers, and keep the profits themselves, rather than risking the following problems of signing with a major.

1. Your odds of being successful are about one in ten.

2. The allegiances of major labels are primarily to their shareholders and only to artists to the extent that they contribute to the bottom line. That is not to say that there aren't employees of those labels who are passionate about the music and the artists they sign. It's just that they're forced to perform a kind of triage on a regular basis that makes them

prioritize in favor of the most likely to succeed at the moment and take their attention from those who aren't, despite what may be their best efforts. It's just the nature of the beast. A friend of mine who was a major-label tour publicist quit his job in frustration at having too many artists to deal with and having a limited window of time to deal with each. It seemed that with just a bit more work with an artist, he'd be able to see a breakthrough, but was required to turn his full attention to another before he could make it happen. He ended up working for artists on his own time because he believed in them. He finally couldn't handle it anymore. This is not an unusual story.

The music industry is full of horror stories from that 90 percent of artists who placed all their dreams in the hands of major labels and felt betrayed by them. To be fair, some of them weren't prepared for those deals to begin with.

3. In "standard" label deals, the company recoups, *from your artist royalties*, the costs of your advance and producing the records (in "all-in" deals, production costs are covered in the advance), partially recoups video costs and costs of tour support, and anything they can list in the contract that's not negotiated away. (They don't ordinarily recoup promotion, manufacturing, advertising, marketing, shipping.)

You understand, though, that if you market yourself, *you'll* be paying those costs, though you won't be spending as much and you'll be getting all the profits after recouping your own costs of recording, marketing, and distribution.

4. Though maximum contract terms are seven years, many contracts also contain clauses that require a specific number of albums delivered, and rarely are artists allowed to deliver the required number of albums within the time period, nor can they record for anyone else until those requirements are met regardless of the time period.

5. Also, until the requirements are met, the artist's contract can be assigned to any other company regardless of the wishes of the artist. So the artist may end up on a different label than the one she wanted to sign with, often without anyone at the new label who has an interest in her career. This can effectively keep the artist out of the marketplace for many years.

Should You Do It Yourself?

For many years, as it's been increasingly difficult for acts to get signed to major record labels, a grassroots movement of independent artist-owned labels have emerged. You're a good candidate for this approach if you fall into these categories:

• In the process of pitching yourself to major labels, you constantly hear, "I really like it personally, but the company doesn't see it as something they can sell," (meaning that they don't see you as a "mass market" artist) or, "This is really good, but I don't know what radio stations would play it."

• You find yourself difficult to categorize stylistically and so do others. You sort of "fall into the cracks" now, though what you do might be very hip in two or three years. Innovative artists are usually ahead of the marketplace.

- You're an excellent live performer with a strong, enthusiastic following. This is very important if you're going to make your own record because, if you don't get radio or video play or create a style of music with an established marketing network, you must rely on live performances for people to sample your wares. People don't just walk into a record store and buy an album by someone they've never heard. The press is very important, but if you're not playing somewhere, they can't review you.

- You're an ambitious artist with a good business head who's not afraid of hard work, is good at delegating, and has good people skills.

It's my firm belief that there is an audience out there for anything that's done well. The problem of the major labels is that the cost of their star-making machinery, including their offices, personnel, and studios, dictate that it takes half a million to a million dollars to record and market a new artist's album to the public. They have to sell a lot of records to recoup that investment, and only about 10 percent of the albums released ever do recoup. That fact makes major labels very cautious, so they sign only artists that appear to have a clearly defined market and fit an existing radio format.

However, a sort of "farm team" approach has developed within the record industry, and many small independent labels that have managed to find their own markets successfully have made distribution agreements with major labels.

Apart from that development, new networks and avenues of exposure and distribution have developed, particularly for focused genres such as women's music, children's music, new age music, blues, reggae, and other non-mainstream genres that are already served by a network of fans, clubs, magazines, Web sites, and underground and college radio stations and shows. Through these networks, independent labels have become increasingly sophisticated in finding their audiences.

Mail-order forms shipped with CDs, astute ad placement, exposure at conventions and music festivals, Web site links, Internet and street distribution of free samples of their artists' work, building fan e-mail lists, and promotional "street teams" of fans all contribute to marketing plans for independent labels. When you consider that, unlike the major labels, you may be able to recoup your investment after sales of as few as one thousand records (depending on how low you keep your recording costs), the prospects look very good. In fact, it's quite likely that your odds are better to make money doing your own record than making money with a major label contract simply because the odds at a major label are against you.

(For some excellent books on marketing your own recordings, see the Bibliography.)

Internet Record Companies

Today, the recording industry is in a state of rapid change. Mergers of traditional record companies with Internet services as well as new Internet marketing divisions within the international entertainment conglomerates themselves, threaten their longstanding symbiotic relationships with traditional "brick and mortar" retail stores. The capability of delivering music via the Internet directly to computers and MP3 players can cut retail record

It's quite likely that your odds are better to make money doing your own record than making money with a major-label contract simply because the odds at a major label are against you.

stores completely out of the picture. This is expected to be a gradual process, but the retailers are already feeling the heat and are looking for new ways to preserve those old relationships. For some time, retailers will still provide a valuable function, since people will always like to actually see the merchandise and shop, though a new generation of fans will be increasingly comfortable searching for and learning about new artists online. And independent recording artists will feel increasingly comfortable making new and nontraditional deals that offer them options they'd not be able to get at traditional labels.

For writer/artists, this revolution offers new opportunities to take charge of their own careers. Online labels are proliferating to assist in the process, and while some of them still employ the same draconian contracts as traditional record companies, others are offering considerably better options. In *Music, Money & Success*, Jeffrey Brabec and Todd Brabec list the following:

1. sharing of all income from sales 50/50
2. a sharing of a defined net (a company's operating and other costs taken out first and then a 50/50 split)
3. a pay for play scenario where the company provides a specific amount in lieu of mechanical and performance royalties
4. an exclusive deal where a portion of the advertising revenue is shared
5. a fee covering the creation of an artist's URL and Web pages with all sales going to the artist
6. a percentage of the sales revenue taken by the company with content and pricing all controlled by the artist
7. a weekly fee to have a band's material available for download
8. a sharing of monies from subscription fees based on the number of downloads
9. an offer to owners of masters of a higher percentage for downloads than would be made under a normal record company contract, etc.

Many of the arrangements are nonexclusive or are exclusive only for a short period of time. Practically none of these arrangements transfer ownership in the master recording or the song away from the artist or writer. Because of this, if an artist or writer becomes successful from one of these types of situations, they will definitely own many more rights than they would have under a normal record company contract.

Appendix: Songwriters' Resources

The following resources will be updated continually at: www.johnbraheny.com

For Industry Contacts

RECORDING INDUSTRY SOURCEBOOK

(800) 233-9604

www.artistpro.com/Sourcebase.cfm

More than 10,000 listings in 55 categories. Listings include names, titles, phone, fax, styles of music and whether unsolicited material is accepted. Producer listings include rates, credits, and specialties. Registered users can search the book online.

BILLBOARD DIRECTORIES

(800) 344-7119

www.billboard.com/store/directories/

The comprehensive Billboard directories of business-to-business listings include Billboard International Buyer's Guide, Billboard International Talent & Touring Directory, Billboard Record Retailing Directory, Billboard Tape/Disc Directory, The Radio PowerBook, Billboard International Latin Music Buyer's Guide, The Nashville 615/Country Music Sourcebook, Music & Media/Billboard EUROFILE, Musicians Guide to Touring & Promotion. For many of these, specialized mailing labels and data extracts are also available.

MUSIC BUSINESS REGISTRY

(818) 769-2722

www.musicregistry.com

This company, headed by former Arista Records A&R rep Ritch Esra, publishes the A&R Registry, a comprehensive listing of record company A&R reps including their stylistic focus, direct phone, and fax numbers and the names of their assistants. The only directory updated every two months. They also publish an annual Music Publisher Registry and Film Television Music Guide.

THE MUSICIAN'S ATLAS

www.musiciansatlas.com

A comprehensive guide to clubs, studios, showcases, tape/disc manufacturers, record stores, record distributors, major and indie label A&R reps, producers, film/TV music supervisors, publishers, music journalists, managers, agents, attorneys, commercial and college radio, national and regional press, conferences, creative services, promotion companies, publicists, Web sites, and schools.

POLLSTAR

(559) 271-7900

www.pollstar.com

For nearly twenty years, Pollstar has provided music business professionals with a reliable and accurate source of worldwide concert tour schedules, ticket sales results, music industry contact directories, trade news, and unique specialized data services. In addition to publishing the concert industry's leading weekly trade publication, Pollstar also maintains the world's largest database of international concert tour information. Its contact directories include a biannual Agency Roster for ten thousand artists and their booking agencies; biannual Record Company Rosters, including a list of major label executives, biannual Talent Buyer Directory listing concert promoters, clubs, fairs, colleges, festivals, and theme parks; Concert Venue Directory, Concert Support Services Directory, and ConneXions, an annual directory of ten thousand music industry company listings. Though its Web site doesn't list it, Pollstar also publishes a semiannual Manager Directory of artists and their managers.

For Getting Your Demos Directly to Music Industry Pros No Matter Where You Live

TAXI

(800) 458-2111

www.taxi.com

An innovative tip-sheet/independent A&R service. Members receive listings every two weeks by major and independent labels, producers, managers, film/TV music supervisors, and publishers looking for writers, writer/artists and bands. All submissions are prescreened and critiqued by industry pros. Covers all styles including instrumentals. Highly recommended.

ONLINE PITCH SERVICES

These services provide opportunities for songwriters and publishers to make their music available for users (record companies, film/TV music supervisors, ad agencies, schools, etc.)